The Backpacker's Field Manual

The Backpacker's Field Manual

A Comprehensive Guide
to Mastering Backcountry Skills

Rick Curtis, Director,
Princeton University Outdoor Action Program

THREE RIVERS PRESS

New York

This manual would never have been possible without the contributions of thousands of students at Princeton University; the Outdoor Action Leaders. These wonderful people, students and alumni(ae) of Princeton, have shared their joy of living in the wilderness and working together as a group with thousands of others students. This book is dedicated to all of those people, who have made Outdoor Action the successful program it has become.

The publisher gratefully acknowledges permission to reprint excerpts from Recovery Engineering's instructions for the PUR Hiker and PUR Voyager water filters; from American Whitewater Affiliation's AWA River Safety Cards; from the Coleman Company's operating instructions, repair instructions, and graphics from Peak 1 product literature; from Mountain Safety Research, Inc.'s instructions for the MSR Whisperlite and Whisperlite Internationale 600 stoves and the MSR Waterworks II and Miniworks water filters; and from *Weathering the Wilderness,* by William E. Reifsnyder, copyright © 1980 by William E. Reifsnyder, reprinted with permission of Sierra Club Books.

Published by Three Rivers Press, a division of Crown Publishers, Inc., 201 East 50th Street, New York, NY 10022. Member of the Crown Publishing Group.

Random House, Inc. New York, Toronto, London, Sydney, Auckland
www.randomhouse.com
THREE RIVERS PRESS and colophon are trademarks of Crown Publishers, Inc.

Printed in the United States of America

Design by 2^b Group, Inc., NY

Library of Congress Cataloging-in-Publication Data
Curtis, Rick.
    The backpacker's field manual : a comprehensive guide to mastering backcountry skills / Rick Curtis. — 1st ed.
    Includes bibliographical references (p.   ) and index.
    1. Backpacking—Handbooks, manuals, etc.   2. Camping—Handbooks, manuals, etc.   3. Low-impact camping—Handbooks, manuals, etc.
    I. Title
GV199.6.C87   1998
796.51—dc21   97-38922
                                                         CIP

ISBN 0-517-88783-5

10   9   8   7   6   5   4

Acknowledgments

A lot of people have been extremely helpful in reviewing the content of this book and I am greatly indebted to all of them for their time and patience, especially Marit Sawyer at NOLS for her helpful assistance on Chapter 5 and Todd Schimelpfenig at NOLS for his review of Chapter 9.

I also want to thank many close friends with whom I have traveled the trails, peaks, and rivers over the years: Liz Cutler and Tom Kreutz; Ed Seliga; John Gager; Warren Elmer; and all the folks from Princeton, OA, and other places who have enriched my outdoor experiences. Thanks also to all of the members of the Friends of Outdoor Action for their support, especially the many people who have served as board members, my brother Ben, who took me on my first backpacking trip at age sixteen and who later introduced me to Outdoor Action during my freshman year at Princeton while he was a senior; and to my mom, Ann Curtis, for all her support and encouragement throughout my career in outdoor education.

In addition, I want to thank the following people and groups, who granted permission to use some of their material in the earlier editions: The North Carolina Outward Bound School for material from the *NCOBS Instructor's Field Manual* and the *NCOBS Instructor's Handbook;* Peter Simer and John Sullivan, for material from the *NOLS Wilderness Guide;* James A. Wilkerson and the staff of The Mountaineers for material from *Medicine for Mountaineering;* and The National Outdoor Leadership School for material from the NOLS Minimal Impact Camping Practices, and *The NOLS Cookery* by Sukey Richard, Donna Orr, and Claudia Lindholm and *NOLS Wilderness First Aid* by Todd Schimelpfenig and Linda Livesey.

Finally, I want to thank the many Princeton students who have helped to develop and implement our principles of outdoor education: Dan Ronel '86 and Doug Weinberg '86, the founders of HEART (Health Education and Rescue Training), which has provided quality wilderness first aid training to Princeton students since 1985; Barbara Cestero '88, Katherine Deuel '89, Larry Friedl '90, Susan Lynch '90, Josh Yamamoto '90, Pat Farrell '92, Spence Reynolds '92, Lise Edleberg '93, Dede O'Mara '93, Peter Reese '93, Jenna Beart '94, Jean Drouin '94, Rebecca Greene '96; and to

Nick Weinreb '94, Shane Woolf '94, Jud Brewer '96, Taylor Kimberly '96, Pete Schwartz '95, Chris Sibley '96, Robin Hibbert '97, Pei-lin Hsiung '97, Andrew Levin '99, Tasha Reddy '99, Ben Urquhart '99 for their recipes, and to Chris Marrison for the Marrison Bear Bag System. Special thanks go to Erik Bue '96 and Chris Sibley '96 for their excellent work on Chapter 9 and to Saumyen Guha for his work on the forest fire section and his patient editing of the map and compass section. I also want to express my thanks to the folks at Three Rivers Press, especially Eliza Scott, whose excitement made this book happen.

Contents

Introduction

The Outdoor Action Program at Princeton University began in 1973 as a pilot program organized by the Dean of Student Life Office for incoming college students experiencing an adjustment period. The first program took a group of Princeton University students, faculty, and staff up to the Delaware Water Gap on the Appalachian trail in New Jersey for a weekend wilderness experience. In September 1974, ten groups of ten students headed off for six days of backpacking and canoeing, to develop self-confidence and new friendships with which to start their first year of college. Since then, the OA Frosh Trip program has grown to more than 600 students each year.

As the program expanded, it became clear that we needed a training program for trip leaders, and the Outdoor Action Leader Training Program began. It continues to this day, having evolved through the work of generations of Princeton students to become one of the best college wilderness training programs in the country. Outdoor programs nationwide have turned to Outdoor Action for help in developing their programs and training leaders. The OA Web site continues the tradition of sharing our information (www.princeton.edu/~oal).

The Backpacker's Field Manual evolved from a project created in 1985, when it became clear that the students leading our wilderness trips needed a manual to take with them that provided basic backpacking information. That first edition, *The Outdoor Action Leader's Manual,* was twenty pages, produced on a DOS word processor in a Courier font. The manual, although extremely limited, was a big success. Over the next three years it became apparent that a more substantial manual should be developed as the base text for our student leaders. The goal was to provide leaders with a field manual that would help them plan all aspects of their trip, and be portable, so they could take it with them on the trail for reference. After hours of collecting, writing, editing, and formatting, the second edition of *The Outdoor Action Leader's Manual* was born in 1988—180 pages longer and more complete than the last. In 1992, it was time for a revision. I spent a year working with students, adding new chapters and material, some from outside sources and some written at Princeton. I expanded the graphics and made extensive design changes. The third edition was completed and handed to the leaders the day before our Frosh Wilderness Orientation Program began in September 1993.

In 1995 I decided it was time to do a major rewrite of the manual to add the latest information that we were teaching in our Leader Training Program and to create a book that other backpackers and outdoor programs could use as a field guide—*The Backpacker's Field Manual* was born. When it's time to cut back the weight in your pack, I hope you leave that extra dessert at home and bring this book along instead. Happy hiking.

A WORD ABOUT LEAVE NO TRACE HIKING AND CAMPING

Throughout the manual, we refer to the techniques and practices of a program called Leave No Trace. This is a national awareness program, originally developed by the Bureau of Land Management, National Park Service, U.S. Fish and Wildlife Service, and the National Outdoor Leadership School. Out of this cooperative effort have come a number of excellent publications and Leave No Trace, Inc., a nonprofit educational organization. Since 1995, numerous private companies and organizations from the outdoor industry have joined as sponsors. The goal of the program is to provide wilderness users with the most up-to-date information about Leave No Trace practices in different ecosystems. I think learning the skills of Leave No Trace camping is as important as taking a wilderness first-aid course. I want to thank all of the organizations who developed the program for permission to use the Leave No Trace materials in this book. Chapter 5 provides complete information about this program.

DISCLAIMER

Backpacking can be hazardous. You need the necessary knowledge and experience and proper equipment to travel in the backcountry. This book is designed to be a resource, but it is not a replacement for professional training and personal experience, especially regarding first aid and emergency response. The author, Random House, and Princeton University assume no liability for any personal injury, illness, property damage or loss that may arise out of use of this material.

Specific equipment, such as stoves and water filters, is discussed in this book. There are many other products that could have been included but were not due to space considerations. The inclusion of *these* items does not imply any endorsement of these products.

CHAPTER 1
Trip Planning

BASIC TRIP PLANNING

Planning a trip requires more than simply deciding where to go and when. Whether it's a weekend trip with friends, a formal outdoor program, or a major expedition, you need to evaluate your trip across a number of categories and develop a solid plan. One or two people may take on the role of planner, or the process of planning can be spread out among the entire group. Here are the elements I consider when planning any trip.

GROUP SIZE AND ABILITY

Whenever you're planning a trip, you need to determine if the route should fit the group or the group fit the route. The group may have a range of experience levels, physical conditions, and goals, in which case, your goal should be to plan a trip that is appropriate for everyone. Other times, you may have a specific trip you want to do that may be very challenging. For this kind of trip, you need to select a group that has the right qualifications to participate. Here's a checklist of questions to ask when planning a group trip:

- How big is the group?
- What is the age range of group members?
- What is the experience level of each member? What is the average experience level?
- What is the physical condition of each member?
- What is the medical condition of each member?
- What kind of group are you working with? Are these friends, students, volunteers, paying customers, people required to attend? (This factor can have a significant impact on how committed [or not] the group is to the wilderness experience.)
- What are the goals of each group member? Does the group have collective goals?

Determine the level of experience, physical ability, etc. as much as possible *before* you set out. This will enable you to plan a smoother and more successful trip. More important, it will diminish the potential for dangerous situations. Keep the groups' parameters in mind as you evaluate the other categories, thinking in terms of both optimal challenge and safety. Be aware that you will often have a great range of experience levels and physical abilities, so plan the trip at a level that will be fun, educational, challenging, and safe for everyone. Be particularly aware of the high end and the low end of the experience level and physical condition, and err in the direction of the low end. Participant information forms will help you determine different abilities and experience levels (for a sample, see page 337).

ACTIVITIES

When planning the activities for a particular trip, you need to consider the following:

- What activity(ies) do you want to do on your trip (backpacking, peak climbing, or glacier travel, for example)?
- What are the goals for the trip?
- What skills will people need?
- How do you integrate time for teaching skills with time for traveling?

Once you've evaluated the group members' abilities, you can adapt your goals to an appropriate level. Plan activities that will be both appropriately challenging and safe. Be aware of how mileage, elevation change, and time for teaching and learning skills will affect your route (see Estimating Travel Times, page 9). Work toward starting easy and increasing the level of difficulty gradually so that participants can be progressively challenged at appropriate levels, rather than placing them in a situation that is beyond their abilities.

LOCATION AND WEATHER

Research Your Destination

- Investigate the availability of guidebooks and maps.
- Contact area rangers or park managers to get more information.
- Talk with other people who have been to the area before. If possible, check their trip logs, which may have important information not found in guidebooks.

Trip Planning Questions

- How long is the trip? Can the trip be self-supporting in terms of equipment and food, or will you need to resupply? How will you do the resupply—cache items ahead of time, hike out, or have someone hike in?
- How remote is the trip from "civilization" and help in case there is a problem?
- What are the trail conditions?
- Are there special places you want to see?

- Are permits needed, and how do you obtain them?
- Are there limitations to group size?
- Where is camping allowed and not allowed?
- Are there shelters available on a daily basis, or do you need to bring your own?
- Where is parking and trailhead access?
- Are fires allowed?
- What is the water availability and water quality on a daily basis?
- Are there any restricted areas, hazardous zones, protected areas for endangered species, and such?
- Are there any special natural hazards (for example, flash floods in desert canyons)? (See How Accidents Happen, page 193.)
- What Leave No Trace practices will you need to implement to safeguard the environment? (See Chapter 5.)

Weather

- How many hours of daylight will there be?
- How will the season determine the weather? Are storms or particular weather patterns likely? (See Chapter 7.)
- How will weather affect trip activities? How may it affect the safety of the group?
- Will altitude changes during the trip have an impact on weather or temperature?

FLEXIBILITY

When planning a trip, remember that the ultimate goal is for people to have fun. Here are some tips to planning a trip that everyone can enjoy:

- Make a plan that can be modified during the trip. All sorts of factors—bad weather, broken equipment, ill-prepared participants, an injury—may require you to change your itinerary.
- Don't plan long or difficult hikes on every day of the trip. Vary the mileage so that you have some days when you can get a later start or get in to camp early.
- On longer trips, schedule a rest day every five to seven days.
- Make sure that people have some time during each day to kick back—to read, watch the sunset, or write in their journals.
- When hiking at high altitudes, people acclimatize at different rates. You may have to adjust your trip to give people time to properly acclimatize before going higher. (See Altitude Illnesses, page 323.)

EQUIPMENT

Once you have determined your trip activities and location, you will be able to put together an equipment list. Sample equipment lists are included in this guide, but remember that they should be used only as guidelines (see pages 343–353). Each trip and each person may have special requirements.

FOOD

It is important to have food that is both nourishing *and* edible. On longer trips, with specialized activities, or in different seasons (e.g., cold-weather trips), it may be necessary to plan a menu that supplies a specific number of calories per day and includes certain food groups more than others. On any trip, it is essential to be aware of any special dietary requirements for some trip members—those with food allergies, vegetarians, and kosher eaters—and plan a menu accordingly. Check this information on the Health History Form (page 337). For food, nutrition, and menu planning guidelines, see Chapter 3, "Cooking and Nutrition."

TEACHING PLAN

Depending on the type of group you're traveling with, people may have varying levels of experience. There may be specific skills that need to be taught on the trip, such as how to set up camp or how to use a backpacking stove. There are so many different skills I use on a backcountry trip that I find it hard to remember them all—many I just do automatically. Take the time to make a list of skills to know so you don't overlook anything (a sample Teaching Plan is included in the Appendix). If you are in the role of trip leader, or if you're just traveling with friends who are less experienced, plan time to cover the important subjects.

TRIP PREPARATION CHECKLIST

Use this checklist to help organize all the tasks that need to be accomplished *before* you start your trip. If you are going on an extended expedition, expand the list and establish specific timelines for each task. For example, trips to remote areas might require you to apply months or even years in advance for a permit.

PRETRIP

- Contact participants and arrange meetings to talk about the trip (activities, experience level, individual and group goals, etc.).

- Make lists of necessary personal equipment and group equipment, based on trip activities, location, and weather.
- Identify potential environmental hazards and develop an environmental briefing (see How Accidents Happen, page 193).
- Have all participants fill out a Health History form (page 337).
- Evaluate the physical ability of each participant and develop a route appropriate for all members of the group. In planning the route, include driving time, daylight time needed to set up camp, changes in elevation, and other factors.
- Make arrangements for any permits needed.
- Develop a menu based on personal preferences and special dietary needs.
- Assemble the group equipment and first aid kit.
- Purchase and repack the food.
- Meet to distribute the group equipment and food for final packing.
- Put together a trip packet with cash, credit cards, vehicle keys, maps, emergency numbers, travel directions, and the like.
- Contact area rangers for last-minute weather and trail information.
- Designate a person to be "on call," someone who is not going on the trip, and give her or him your Trip Logistics and Safety Plan (page 339), establishing your planned starting and ending points, daily route, campsites, emergency phone numbers, and return time.

DURING THE TRIP

- Keep track of all expenses on a Trip Expenses Form (page 354).
- Fill out your Trip Log (page 355) as you hike so you have detailed information on hiking times, campsite locations, and water availability for future trips.
- Document any accidents or first aid treatments. These should be reviewed after the trip.

ON RETURN

- Contact your "on call" person and let him or her know you have returned safely.
- Have all participants return any borrowed personal or group equipment.
- Clean all cooking gear and tarps or tents, if necessary. Water bottles and water containers should be treated with iodine or chlorine bleach solution (see Water Purification, page 83).
- Dispose of any medical waste properly (see Universal Precautions for Working with Blood and Body Fluids, page 244).

DETERMINING PARTICIPANTS' PHYSICAL CONDITION

Whoever decides to plan the trip should first determine the physical condition of the people going, which can be difficult. It's best to rely on some form of objective measurement rather than counting on the "yeah, I'm in great shape" reply. Assessing physical condition ranges from asking some basic questions about health and exercise activities to administering a required physical exam. Base your degree of assessment on the level of difficulty for the trip: If the trip is of low to moderate difficulty, staying relatively close to civilization, then you'll have greater resources to fall back on in case of a problem. If the trip is more difficult or ventures into a remote location with limited access for evacuation or medical care, you need to do a much more thorough screening. In some cases, you may even require a specific conditioning regimen. Part of making sure that a person is going on the right trip is giving the individual as detailed information as possible about what the trip will entail.

For average trips, a few basic questions on the Health History Form (page 337) will give you a general sense of an individual's physical fitness. Keep in mind that some people underestimate and others overestimate their condition. Depending on how much time has elapsed between when the assessment was done and when the trip takes place, the person may be in better or worse shape. Remember that assessing the individual is only half the process; you need to evaluate the difficulty level of the trip as well. For a more rigorous trip, you might want to use systems such as the Body Mass Index and the Harvard Step Test to evaluate participants' fitness levels.

TRIP DIFFICULTY RATING

Rating the difficulty of a trip is extremely subjective. I look at the following factors and rely on my own hiking experience as a gauge. On a scale of 1 to 4 (1 being easy and 4 being difficult), here are the factors I use to establish trip difficulty:

- Daily mileage
- Daily elevation changes and steepness of ascent or descent
- Trail conditions (smooth, rocky, switchbacks, etc.)
- Amount of weight the person is carrying, as a percentage of their body weight (see The Backpack, page 23)
- Altitude, and the effect of reduced oxygen and acclimatization (see page 324)

PLANNING A ROUTE

- Use the Trip Logistics and Safety Plan (page 339) to help document your route and to give to your "on call" person.
- See Estimating Travel Times (page 9) to determine how long each day's hiking will take. For each day, establish a time control plan that includes hiking time and other factors to calculate your total travel time for the day.
- As you plan your route, develop a daily evacuation plan and document it on your Trip Logistics and Safety Plan (see page 339). For each day of the trip, know, in general, where you would go to get help in case of an emergency. Obviously this information will change all the time, but you should know the area well enough to find nearby roads or towns.

TRAVEL LOGISTICS

- Where is your starting point? What type of road or other access is there to the trail?
- Where is your ending point? What type of road or other access is there to the trail?
- Is everyone traveling together to get to the trailhead or going separately?
- Is this a loop route or in and out back to your original starting point (A to A) or a one-way route (A to B)? If A to B, do you need to get back to A to get to your car? Do you need to be picked up at B?

Once you are out on your trip, keep an accurate daily trip log about where you went, what you saw, how long it took, and so on. This will be a great help in planning your next trip.

CAMPSITES

Trip planning is often done from campsite to campsite. You need to make sure that at the end of the day, you will have a place to set up your tent or tarp that is not in the middle of a bog or perched on a steep rockslide. A lot of campsite selection can be done using guidebooks and maps (see the Bibliography). Select a site that allows your group to set up a good Leave No Trace campsite (see Chapter 5, "Leave No Trace Hiking and Camping"). Unfortunately, sometimes you don't have the information you need to determine a good campsite in advance, and you'll have to locate a spot as you hike. More than once, I've looked at the map contours and thought, "That looks flat; there must be a good campsite there," only to discover thick underbrush with no open spaces. Here are some general guidelines for campsite selection:

- **Water Availability** Preferably you want a site near a water source; otherwise you may need to carry in enough water for dinner, breakfast the next day, and possibly the next day's hike.
- **Campsite Space** You want a site that provides enough open space for sleeping, cooking, and washing. (These areas do not have to be right next to each other.)
- **Campsite Location** If you don't know of a specific campsite, start looking for campsites early in the day. It's better to stop at a good campsite earlier on and make up the mileage the next day, rather than to continue hiking, only to find nothing there—which means either backtracking or continuing to hike on, potentially difficult if it's getting dark.
- **Private Land** Be sensitive about hiking on private land. In some cases hiking through is permitted but overnight camping is not. If conditions (bad weather, an injured group member) require it, you may decide you need to. If so, recognize that you may be breaking the law and must live with the consequences.
- **Restricted Areas** Don't camp in a restricted area (unless a group member's safety is at stake). The area is restricted for a reason. If you choose to camp in a restricted area, recognize that you may have to live with the consequences (tickets, fines, even arrest). Explain your situation to rangers or other officials and ask for their assistance. Get them involved as allies helping you in a difficult situation rather than as law-enforcement officials prosecuting you for an offense. In most cases involving safety, rangers and wilderness managers are understanding. They may still require you to move, but may be helpful in finding another location.

ESTIMATING TRAVEL TIMES

Here is a general formula for calculating travel time for backpacking trips. Use this only as an estimate; on a day hike with less gear, you will move faster than on a difficult trail with a heavy pack. Also, groups of people with different physical abilities or of different ages may move faster or slower.

General Guidelines

- Average hiking speed on generally flat terrain is 30 minutes per mile (1.6 kilometers), so 1 hour equals 2 miles (3.2 kilometers)

- Add 1 hour for each 1,000 feet (305 meters) of ascent
- Plan about 5 minutes of rest for each hour of hiking

Calculating Miles per Hour Divide the number of miles to be hiked by 2. Calculate the total feet of ascent, divide it by 1,000, and multiply that number by 1 hour. Add up all the hours to find the total hiking hours for the day.

Example: A group hikes 8 miles in Rocky Mountain National Park. The day includes a total ascent of 2,000 feet (610 meters). The estimated time to hike this route would be:

8 miles ÷ 2 miles per hour = 4 hours + (2,000 ÷ 1,000) × 1 hour [ascent]
4 hours + 2 hours = 6 hours + (6 × 5 minutes) = 6 hours 30 minutes

Calculating Kilometers per Hour Divide the number of kilometers to be hiked by 1.6. Calculate the total meters of ascent, divide it by 305, and multiply that number by 1 hour. Add up all the hours to find the total hiking hours for the day. Using the same example from above, the estimated time to hike this route would be:

12.8 kilometers ÷ 1.6 kilometers per hour = 4 hours + (610 ÷ 305) × 1 hour [ascent]
4 hours + 2 hours = 6 hours + (6 × 5 minutes) = 6 hours 30 minutes

Once you are hiking, check your actual time against the time you calculated for your route. By keeping a daily Trip Log with information on hiking times, trail conditions, rest breaks, etc., you can refine your estimates. Use your actual travel time to revise your time control plan estimates for the next day of your trip. If there is a significant discrepancy, you may need to revise your route plan.

PLANNING YOUR DAY

The following table will help you plan each day. Start with what time you will get up and then fill in times for each of the day's activities. Remember all of the factors discussed earlier to help determine your route, such as participant age, experience, and physical condition, as well as trail conditions, pack weight, and weather. Add up all the times and then subtract that from the hours of daylight.

If your result is a negative number, you're in trouble. Go back to the drawing board and make some changes—cut down the mileage or get up earlier.

Time Required

+	How long will it take you to break camp?
+	Are there any special places you want to explore?
+	Based on your estimated travel time, how long will your group take to hike the distance?
+	Are there any hindrances to travel, such as river crossings or bushwhacks, that will add additional time?
+	How much time is needed for rest breaks and meals?
+	How long it will to take to set up a proper Leave No Trace camp?
=	Add all of the above for your total time.
−	Subtract the number of hours of daylight.

CHAPTER 2
Equipment

EQUIPMENT ASSESSMENT

Whether for a one-day hike on a local trail or a month-long expedition to a remote area, you need to thoroughly plan what equipment to bring. The equipment assessment for your trip should cover the following areas:

PERSONAL EQUIPMENT

- **Clothing** Shirts, pants, boots, hats, and so on
- **Travel Equipment** What is needed for travel—just your feet or a canoe, a bike, cross-country skis, etc.
- **Storage Equipment** What you use to carry personal and group equipment—a backpack, panniers, waterproof bags, etc.
- **Sleeping Equipment** Sleeping bag, foam pad
- **Miscellaneous** Water bottles, toiletries, personal items

GROUP EQUIPMENT

- **Shelter** Evaluate the type of shelter required for the size of the group and anticipated weather conditions—tarp, tent, lean-to, etc.
- **Cooking Equipment** Stoves, cooking gear (also depends on your menu)
- **Hygiene Equipment** Items for water purification, handwashing, bathroom
- **First-aid Equipment** First aid items needed
- **Repair Equipment** Anticipate what might break and have the necessary replacement parts and tools.

When deciding what equipment to bring, review your planned route and answer the following questions:

- How long is the trip?
- How many people are going? How does that affect the amount of group equipment needed?
- Are people providing their own personal equipment?
- Who is providing group equipment?
- What season is it? What are the typical maximum and minimum temperatures during the day? What is typical weather (foggy morning, afternoon thunderstorms, etc.)? What is atypical weather (can it snow in July)? (See Chapter 7.)
- What is the altitude? What effect will the altitude have on temperature? (See Temperature Ranges, page 178).
- What are the trip activities?
- Where is the trip? Is it remote or accessible?

- Is equipment resupply a possibility or will you have to carry everything?
- Do you need any special equipment for Leave No Trace camping?
- How will you deal with equipment repair if things break? What equipment items are more likely to break? What equipment items, if broken, would create serious problems for the trip (e.g. stoves)?

THE 12 ESSENTIALS

No matter where you are going, and whether you are out for a day or a month, there are a few things that each member of the group should always carry. These items are considered essential for safe backcountry travel. There are countless tales of hikers who have gotten into trouble, even on short day hikes, because they neglected these essentials.

1. Map
2. Compass (and knowledge of how to use it)
3. Flashlight with extra batteries and bulb
4. Extra food
5. Extra clothing (wool, pile, or other insulating clothing and rain gear)
6. Pocketknife
7. Matches
8. Candle or firestarter
9. First-aid kit
10. Sunglasses and sunscreen
11. Water bottle (full, 1–2 quarts)
12. Water purification system (chemical or filter)

Other recommended items include:

13. Watch
14. Tube shelter or small tarp
15. Ground insulation (sleeping pad)

CLOTHING

REGULATING YOUR BODY TEMPERATURE

In order to plan the right equipment for a trip, you need to understand how your body reacts to the temperature and weather conditions you are likely to experience. Balancing the heat you are losing to the environment with the heat you generate from exercise and absorb from the environment is called *thermoregulation.* According to *The Outward Bound Wilderness First Aid Handbook,* if you gain more heat than you lose, you experience a *heat chal-*

14

lenge (see Thermoregulation, page 286). If you lose more heat than you gain, you experience a *cold challenge*. The ability to regulate body temperature is critical for preventing hyperthermia and hypothermia (see Heat Challenge, page 289, and Hypothermia, page 293).

One way to regulate body temperature is to wear the right clothing and layer your clothing properly. Clothing items should be versatile enough to meet the various seasonal and weather conditions you may encounter. Since each person's body is different, experiment to determine your individual requirements. A clothing log is a good way to keep track of what types and layers of clothing work well for you in different conditions.

How Your Body Loses Heat

Heat leaves your body in the following ways:

- **Conductive Heat Loss** occurs when contact is made between your body and a cooler surface. It can be minimized by not sitting on the cold ground, especially on snow or rock. Conduction occurs 25 times faster with wet clothing than with dry.
- **Convective Heat Loss** occurs when body heat warms the air (or water, if submerged) adjacent to the body; that air then rises and moves away from the body and fresh colder air replaces it. Wind increases the speed of heat loss through convection. The impact of heat loss from convection is measured by the windchill factor (see Windchill Index, page 288). An important element in dressing for the backcountry is trapping the air around the body.
- **Radiant Heat Loss** is caused by the escape of infrared radiation from the body. It is minimized by wearing insulative fabrics or with reflective fabric that reflects the heat back to the body.
- **Evaporative Heat Loss** occurs when perspiration (water) on the skin evaporates, drawing heat from the body. Minimizing the amount of sweating is important in reducing evaporative heat loss. In hot weather, on the other hand, evaporation is essential in cooling the body to prevent heat illnesses (see Heat Challenge, page 289).

Trapping Your Body Heat

In most cases, you want clothing to insulate you from the environment by trapping body heat. The best insulation is a layer of static, unmoving air close to your body, known as "dead air." This air is warmed by heat given off by your body (through radiation, conduction, and convection) and maintains a warm microclimate around your body. Clothing insulates by creating pockets of such dead air. All clothing does this, but some materials do it more efficiently than others. (In hot desert environments, clothing is worn primarily to provide shade from the sun to minimize overheating rather than to insulate.)

THE LAYERING PRINCIPLE

If you combine different fabrics in multiple layers, you can maintain a comfortable body temperature without excessive sweating (which can lead to heat loss). Throughout the day you will need to "layer up" and "layer down" as temperature conditions and activity levels change. Through experimentation, you can determine which of the inner, middle, outer, and shell layers you require in various situations. Also, different parts of your body may require different layering combinations. The layers should not restrict your movement and the outer layer, especially, should not be too tight, since tight layers can compress the dead air space in layers below, thereby reducing their insulation value.

You can modify one or all of the following factors, to properly thermoregulate.

- **Activity Level** Increasing or decreasing your activity level increases or decreases the heat you generate.
- **Clothing Layers** The number and type of layers you wear allow you to create sufficient dead air space for insulation and protection from external conditions (wind, rain, etc.).
- **Staying Dry** An important factor in retaining heat is to minimize wetness, since you can lose heat 25 times faster in wet clothing than in dry. Moisture comes internally from perspiration generated by exercise or externally from rain or snow. You want clothing layers that minimize the buildup of moisture close to your skin and also protect you from external moisture.
- **Ventilation** Opening up or closing the layers of your clothing allows you to decrease or increase heat loss as needed, without having to actually remove or add a layer. As you move, a bellows action occurs in clothing that pumps your accumulated warm air out through openings and pulls the cooler air in. In some conditions, this bellows action can reduce your body's insulation by 50 percent or more. Thus, it is important that all layers have effective methods of being sealed or opened (i.e., buttons, zippers). Opening and closing the zipper on a jacket will allow you to either ventilate if you are getting too hot or seal up if you are getting cold. Ventilating also prevents moisture buildup from perspiration. Look for clothing that allows for easy ventilation, such as full-zip outer shell jackets, armpit zippers, zip-front turtlenecks, and button-down shirts.

THE CLOTHING LAYERS

The Inner Layer keeps the skin dry and comfortable. It is best to wear a hydrophobic ("water-hating") inner layer to transport the moisture from body perspiration away from the skin. In cool weather, close-fitting layers provide insulation. In warm weather, loose-fitting absorbent clothing offers ample ventilation and absorption for the skin to remain cool and dry.

- **Polypropylene and Polyester** are synthetic fibers that do not absorb water. They are extremely effective worn directly against the skin to keep it dry and reduce evaporative heat loss. Some fabrics are hydrophobic on the inside, so they actually push the water vapor from the area of highest concentration (next to your skin) to the outside of the fabric. Some fabrics are hydrophilic ("water-loving") on the outside and pull the water outward. Others use both a hydrophobic inner layer and a hydrophilic outer layer. *Pro*: Minimizes moisture next to the body, where high conductive heat loss can occur. *Con*: Not windproof, so best used as an inner layer.

❧ TRICKS OF THE TRAIL

Vapor Barriers (Second-Level Inner Layer) A vapor barrier is a clothing item that is waterproof, serving as a barrier to the transportation of water vapor. When worn near the skin, it keeps water vapor near the skin. Eventually the humidity level rises to the point where the body senses a high humidity level and shuts off perspiration. This prevents evaporative heat loss and slows dehydration. It is best not to use vapor barriers directly against the skin because any evaporation of moisture directly at the skin surface leads to greater heat loss. Wearing polypropylene or some other hydrophobic layer between the skin and the vapor barrier allows the moisture to be transported away from the skin. There is no doubt that a vapor barrier system is effective *for some people in some conditions.* Before using a vapor barrier, consider your activity level, the amount you naturally sweat, and your "moisture comfort."

The Middle Layer provides some insulation and protection from the elements. Shirts, turtlenecks, pants, sweaters, and jackets keep you warm and absorb the inner layer's moisture. Zip-front turtlenecks and button-down shirts allow for ventilation during periods of high heat–producing activity. Middle-weight to expedition-weight polypropylene or lightweight pile or wool tops and bottoms work well for this layer. Extra layers may be added in the cooler hours of the morning or evening, or when your activity level drops, such as when you take a lunch break.

- **Fleece** is a synthetic fabric often made of a plastic (polyester, polyolefin, polypropylene). It remains warm when wet, does not absorb moisture, and dries very quickly. This material has an insulative capacity similar to that of wool. Fleece is manufactured in a variety of thicknesses, offering different amounts of loft and insulation and numerous layering possibilities. Some fleece garments are now made from recycled plastics or with a middle windproof layer. *Pro*: Fleece is able to provide the equivalent warmth of wool at half the weight. *Con*: Fleece has poor wind resistance and almost always requires an additional wind-resistant layer.
- **Wool** derives its insulating quality from the elastic, three-dimensional wavy crimp in the fiber that traps air. Depending on the texture and thickness of the fabric, as much as 80 percent of wool cloth can be air. Wool can absorb a fair amount of moisture without imparting a damp feeling because the water "disappears" into the fiber spaces. Even with water in the fabric, wool retains some dead air space and will still insulate you. The disadvantage to wool is that it can absorb a lot of water, making it very heavy when wet. Maximum absorption can be as much as one-third the garment weight. Wool releases moisture slowly, with minimum chilling effect. *Pro*: Tightly woven wool is quite wind resistant. Wool clothing can often be purchased cheaply. *Con*: Wool garments tend to be heavy, take a long time to dry, and can be itchy against the skin. Some people are allergic.

The Outer Layer provides insulation. A heavy wool sweater or fleece jacket is an excellent insulator. In cold conditions, fleece or wool pants may be added. These layers are often worn at the beginning and end of the day in camp, when activity levels are low. Vests provide insulation where you need it most, around the torso. Vests and light jackets made of fleece, down, or synthetic polyester fibers like Polarguard or Primaloft offer additional warmth in colder temperatures.

The Shell Layer is an outer jacket and pants layer that protects from wind, rain, snow, and sun. It is essential to have an outer layer that is windproof and at least water resistant, if not waterproof. Acting as a windbreaker, the shell layer minimizes convective heat loss, containing the warmth trapped by layers beneath. If your shell layer is waterproof but not breathable, moisture buildup from perspiration is possible, so look for garments that provide ample ventilation options, such as full-front zips and armpit zippers. Waterproof, breathable fabrics provide both wind and rain protection. In a driving rain there is almost nothing you can do to stay totally dry when you are being active. You will either zip up and get moist from sweat or ventilate and get wet from rain.

- **Breathable Shell** Typically made from nylon or nylon blends, windproof garments are lightweight and tightly woven, so there are no open spaces for the wind to penetrate. They dry quickly and make excellent outer shells. *Pro*: Windproof. Allows body moisture to escape. Lightweight. Inexpensive. *Con*: Not waterproof.
- **Waterproof Shell** These are fabrics that use some type of impermeable waterproof coating (i.e., coated nylon). These will keep you dry from rain but allow water vapor from perspiration to build up in layers underneath. *Pro*: Very waterproof. Windproof. Inexpensive. *Con*: Allows for significant body moisture buildup.
- **Waterproof and Breathable Shell** There are a number of ways to make a waterproof and breathable outer shell. All rely on the principle that water droplets from rain are more than 20,000 times larger than water vapor. With a fabric that has a layer with very small pores, water vapor can pass through from the inside to the outside while the outside remains impenetrable to water droplets. Nevertheless, there is always a trade-off between the degree of waterproofness of a fabric and its breathability. Some fabrics use a microporous membrane (Gore-Tex); others have an added microporous coating (Ultrex). *Pro*: Degrees of waterproofness. Degrees of breathability. Windproof. *Con*: Degrees of waterproofness. Degrees of breathability. Some body moisture buildup. Expensive.

🍁 TRICKS OF THE TRAIL

Bringing Your Gore-Tex Back to Life After frequent use, all waterproof and breathable fabrics start to lose their edge. You can revitalize them by washing with a mild nondetergent soap, machine drying, and then lightly ironing the outer fabric on a medium temperature setting. The washing helps restore the membrane or coating's effectiveness, and the heat of the iron helps bring back the ability to resist water (water will bead up rather than penetrate the fabric).

Since many fabrics have a water-repellent coating on the outside to help water bead up, this same trick works with other types of waterproof or water-resistant garments. Check the manufacturer's label or instructions before you try it out. Finally, if your garment has really had it, look for a spray-on coating such as 3M Scotchguard or, better yet, wash it back in with a liquid treatment, like NikWax TX-Direct.

The Head Layer is for sun and rain protection, and to reduce heat loss. In cold weather the head is most important in heat conservation, since up to 70 percent of the body's heat can be lost through radiation and convection at the head. Wearing a hat (preferably wool or synthetic) will conserve heat, allowing the body to send more blood to cold peripheral areas (hands, toes, feet). Other items like wide-brimmed hats can help in a downpour, keep sun off your face, and help prevent overheating.

The Hand Layers insulate your hands in cold conditions. Gloves and mittens should fit snugly, not tightly. Gloves provide greater flexibility for your hands, but they are colder than mittens since they have greater surface area at the fingers for radiating heat. A combination of polypropylene glove liners and wool mittens is excellent for cold weather. Also good are mitten shells, which add a windproof/waterproof layer. Fingerless gloves are great for cooking or other activities that require dexterity (like trying to untangle the loop of parachute cord for your cook tarp).

The Feet Layers serve as insulation and cushioning on your feet and help prevent blisters. You should wear a lightweight, synthetic liner sock, which helps pass moisture away from your foot. On top of the liner, wear a medium to heavy wool, wool-nylon blend, or synthetic hiking sock. Having two sock layers means that your socks will slide against each other, so the friction from your boots is taken up between the sock layers rather than against your skin (friction against the skin leads to blisters). The outer sock provides cushioning and passes the moisture from your foot outward, keeping your foot dryer. If your feet stay damp, they get wrinkled and are more prone to blisters. *Don't* wear cotton socks. The cotton absorbs and retains the sweat from your feet, keeping your feet wet throughout the day and increasing the potential for blisters or trenchfoot (see page 302). Before putting your boots on, smooth the socks of all wrinkles to prevent blisters. You should always carry extra socks, with a recommended rotation of one set to wear, one to dry, and one always dry.

CLOTHING TECHNIQUES

- When you first get up in the morning, your activity level will be low, as will the air temperature. You will need to have many, if not all, of your layers on until breakfast is over and you become active.
- When you get ready to be active, you will need to shed some layers, since you will start generating heat. A good rule of thumb is, just before you get ready to hike, strip down until you feel just cool, not

chilled. Then start hiking. If you begin with too many layers on, you will only start overheating and sweating; you will have to stop 10 minutes down the trail to take layers off anyway. Opening or closing a zipper, rolling sleeves up or down, taking a hat off or putting one on all help with temperature regulation.

- If you stop for more than a few minutes, you may need to add a layer to keep from getting chilled, so keep an extra layer close at hand.
- If your clothing gets wet—especially if it's cotton—take it off and change into something dry. You won't be able to warm up if you are in wet clothing. Remember, wetness can lead to hypothermia (see Hypothermia, page 293).
- At the end of the day, as activity decreases and temperature drops, you will need to add layers. Once you start to cool down, it takes a lot of the body's resources (calories) to heat up again, so layer up immediately, before you get chilled. It may be good to put on more than you think you need; it will only get colder. If you are too warm, you can open up the layers and ventilate to reach the proper temperature.

🌿 TRICKS OF THE TRAIL

Cotton What's the worst thing to bring on a backpacking trip? Blue jeans. In most climates and environments, you should minimize your use of cotton clothing. Although cotton is comfortable to wear, cotton fibers absorb and retain water (hydrophilic). Once wet, cotton loses heat 25 times faster than dry clothing. Wet cotton clothing can be a significant factor in hypothermia (see Hypothermia, page 293). In warm weather, some cotton-synthetic blends can be used, since they dry more quickly than 100 percent cotton and do not absorb as much water. Never wear cotton in cold conditions as a form of insulation. *Pro*: Comfortable when dry. *Con*: Absorbs water, causing increased heat loss. Loses all insulating value when wet. Difficult to dry.

BOOTS

Your boots are among the most important pieces of equipment that you bring into the backcountry. They should be selected according to your needs—trail conditions, terrain, pack weight, and personal requirements. Boots are an investment. Selecting, fitting, breaking in, and caring for your boots will help them last a long time and will maximize your own comfort. For Leave No Trace camping, you should also bring a pair of tennis shoes or sandals to wear around camp.

FITTING

Proper fitting of boots is essential. You should try new boots on in the afternoon, since your feet swell during the day. Select a sock combination of a liner sock and outer sock, and try the boots on. The boots should fit comfortably with moderate tension on the laces so you can tighten or loosen the boots as needed. With your foot flat on the ground, try to lift your heel inside the boot. There should be only ¼ to ½ inch (6 to 12 millimeters) of heel lift.

BREAKING IN

Break in a pair of boots *before* your trip. Begin with short walks and gradually increase the time you wear them to allow the boots to soften and adjust to your feet. Easy day hikes are a good way to break in boots. Each time you lace your boots, take the time to align the tongue and lace them properly; otherwise the tongue will set into a bad position. If you haven't worn your boots for a while, it is a good idea to wear them for several days before a trip to rebreak them in.

BOOT CARE

Boot care varies with the type of material—leather, synthetic leather, nylon, and combinations of these. If you have leather hiking boots, find out what type of leather it is. Oil-tanned leather is usually treated with wax or oil, chrome-tanned leather with silicone wax (a beeswax-silicone mixture is recommended). The primary reason for treating boots is not to completely waterproof them, but to make them water repellent and to nourish the leather to prevent it from drying and cracking. Boots should be treated when they are new and on a regular basis to keep the leather supple.

Wet boots should be air-dried slowly or with low heat (put them in the sun). Don't try to dry boots quickly (for example, near a fire or a radiator)—different thicknesses of leather dry at different rates, which leads to cracking and curling. I've seen boots peel apart from drying too fast, and a boot that was too close to some hot coals actually caught on fire. While walking on the trail, the heat from your foot will help dry the boot. At the end of the day, when you take off your boots, open them up as much as possible to help them dry out. (This will also make them easier to put on in the morning.) You may want to leave your boots upside down at night to prevent dew from forming inside.

When you return from a trip, always clean your boots before you store them, or the dirt will corrode the stitching at the seams. Use a stiff, nonwire brush to remove caked-on dirt. For leather boots, rub them with moistened saddle soap. Wipe off the residue, air dry them thoroughly, then apply a generous coating of wax or sealer. Store your boots in a cool, dry place to prevent mildew. Boot trees can help maintain the shape of your boot and cedar boot trees can absorb moisture from the inside of the boot, helping it dry slowly.

THE BACKPACK

There are two basic types of frame packs: external and internal. The purpose of the frame is to transfer most of the weight of your gear onto your hips, so the strong muscles in your legs carry the load, rather than your shoulders. If you remember trying to carry loads of books home from school in a day pack, you know what I mean. The ideal distribution is about 80 percent of the weight on your hips and 20 percent on your shoulders. This split in weight also lowers your center of gravity, making you more stable. Recent advances in pack design offer an incredible range of sizes and options.

External Frame   Internal Frame

- **External Frame** The external frame pack helped revolutionize back-packing. Suddenly, much larger amounts of weight could be easily and safely carried, allowing for longer trips. External frame packs typically use a ladderlike frame of aluminum or plastic. The hip belt and shoulder straps are attached to the frame (see diagram, page 23). A separate pack bag attaches to the frame, usually with clevis pins and split rings. Some external frame packs come in specific sizes based on the length of your spine; others are adjustable to fit a range of sizes. Look for good lumbar padding, a conical hip belt, recurved shoulder straps with good padding, and a chest compression strap. *Pro*: Good for carrying weight. The external frame allows for some air space between your back and the pack bag so you don't sweat as much. The weight is carried higher in the pack, allowing for a more upright posture. Frame extension bars and space for a sleeping bag outside of the pack allow you to strap on lots of gear when you need to, making the carrying capacity of the pack more versatile. Less expensive than many internal frame packs. *Con*: Most external frame packs have little if any flexibility, so the pack tends to wobble from side to side as you walk. This is usually not a problem on a regular backpacking trip, but can throw you off balance if skiing or snowshoeing. Don't take it on an airplane unless you have boxed it up—that is, if you want to be able to use it again. Pack volumes range from 3,000 to 4,500 cubic inches (49 to 73 liters).

- **Internal Frame** Internal frame packs use a wide variety of materials—aluminum stays, carbon fiber, plastic sheets, and foam—to create a rigid spine to which the hip belt and shoulder straps are attached (see diagram, page 23). The pack bag runs the full height of the pack, although it may be divided into several compartments. Some internal frame packs come in specific sizes based on the length of your spine; others are adjustable to fit a range of sizes. As with an external frame pack, you should look for good lumbar padding, a conical hip belt, recurved shoulder straps with good padding, and a chest compression strap. A removable top pocket and a bivy extension (a fabric layer sewn around the top opening of the pack bag that, when pulled up, adds to the overall pack volume) on the pack bag will let you lift the top pocket and store more gear. Also, make sure that the pack has side compression straps to squeeze the pack down if you are carrying a smaller load. *Pro*: Good for carrying lots of weight. Conforms to the body for better balance. Generally more comfortable to wear for long periods. *Con*: Since the pack bag and frame are directly against your entire back, back perspiration can be a problem. Since the weight is carried lower in the pack, you may have to bend over more. You can't cram as much on the outside, so the overall carrying capacity of the pack is somewhat fixed by its internal volume. Tends to be more expensive than external frame packs. Pack volumes range from 3,000 to 7,500 cubic inches (49 to 122 liters).

- **Day Packs** Day packs typically forgo a frame and use a foam sheet for the back panel. This provides some rigidity and helps distribute weight to the hips (up to a point). Look for well-padded shoulder straps, a foam hip belt rather than just a webbing strap, and a chest compression strap. Day pack volumes range up to 3,000 cubic inches (49 liters).

Size is an important factor when selecting a pack. You need to make sure that you can adequately carry all the equipment and food you will need for the length of your trip. Keep in mind that the pack bags of internal frame packs are smaller than external frame packs. This is because there are spaces on the external frame pack to strap large items directly to the frame. For example, a sleeping bag in a stuff sack may be 1,000 to 1,500 cubic inches (16 to 25 liters). Here are some rough guidelines on pack size and trip length.

Length of Trip	External Frame Pack Volume	Internal Frame Pack Volume
2–4 days	1,500+ cubic inches (25+ liters)	3,500+ cubic inches (57+ liters)
5–7 Days	2,000+ cubic inches (33+ liters)	4,500+ cubic inches (73+ liters)
8–10 days	3,000+ cubic inches (39+ liters)	5,500+ cubic inches (90+ liters)

🍁 TRICKS OF THE TRAIL

Buying a Pack When you go to the store and try on a pack, the salesperson will help you adjust it, and it will feel great. Then she will give you a few sand bags (25–30 pounds or 11–13 kilos) to add some weight. Chances are it will still feel good. The real test is when you get home and try to carry 50 to 70 pounds (22–31 kilos). Make sure that the store will take the pack back if it doesn't feel right. I bought a pack once without doing this test *until* I hit the trail. With 60 pounds in the pack, the hip belt slipped off my butt and I ended up carrying much of the weight on my shoulders. I hiked in discomfort for days.

EXTERNAL FRAME PACKS

Sizing an External Frame Pack

It is essential to have a pack that fits properly. Packs vary from company to company, so check the manufacturer's instructions for both fitting and loading. The idea behind an external frame pack is to have the frame transfer most of the weight to your legs through the hip belt. Therefore, when fitting a pack, the place to start is with the hip belt. Here are some general fitting guidelines:

- Put on the pack and adjust the hip belt to fit your hips; the top of the belt should be at or just slightly below the top of your pelvis, which you should be able to feel with your fingertips.
- With the hip belt on and properly positioned, tighten the shoulder straps and note their position. The straps should come off the frame about even with the top of your shoulders. If the straps drop down, the pack is too small, and too much weight will be pulled onto your shoulders. If the straps go up, the pack is too large, and too little weight will go onto your shoulders. Some packs will allow you to adjust the point at which the shoulder straps attach to the frame to fine-tune your fit for height and/or width. Be sure the width of the straps is positioned so that they neither pinch your neck nor slip off your shoulders.

Loading an External Frame Pack

The major consideration in packing a pack is how best to distribute the weight. There are two basic principles: for trail hiking over generally flat ground, the weight of the pack should be high and relatively close to the body. The heavier items should sit between your shoulder blades; for consistently steep or rough terrain, carry the weight lower to give you better balance and avoid falls from having a high center of gravity. In this case, heavier things should be placed more toward the middle of your back. To achieve either arrangement, load the heavier, bulky items into the large top

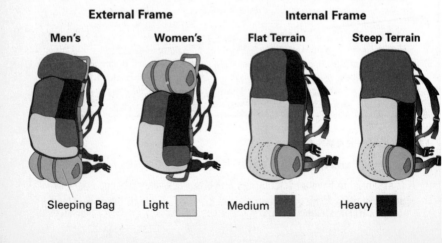

External Frame — Men's — Women's
Internal Frame — Flat Terrain — Steep Terrain

Sleeping Bag   Light   Medium   Heavy

compartment in the position where you want most of the weight. Then fill this and the remaining compartments with lighter items (see diagrams, facing page). Tents and tarps can be lashed to the extender bars at the top of the pack and sleeping bags can usually be lashed to the frame at the bottom of the pack. In either case, the horizontal weight distribution should be balanced so that the left side of the pack is in balance with the right. A woman's center of gravity is generally lower than a man's. So, for women, the heavier items should be placed close to the body but lower in the pack, as in the case for rough terrain above. Packs designed especially for women take this into account by lowering the pack bag on the frame. Load these packs as described above and then lash sleeping bags and tents or tarps to the extender bars at the top of the packs.

INTERNAL FRAME PACKS

Sizing an Internal Frame Pack

Internal frame pack systems vary, so check the manufacturer's instructions for both fitting and loading. Here are some general fitting guidelines:

- Put on the pack and adjust the hip belt to fit your hips: the top of the belt should be at or slightly below the level of the top of your pelvis, which you should be able to feel with your fingertips.
- The frame stays or frame structure should extend 2 to 4 inches above your shoulders.
- The shoulder straps should follow the contour of your shoulders and join the pack approximately 2 inches below the top of your shoulders. The position of the shoulder harness can usually be adjusted. The lower ends of the straps should run about 5 inches below your armpits. On the shoulder straps you may find load lifters that connect to the pack at about ear level and meet the shoulder straps in front of your collarbone. These help pull the top of the pack into your shoulders.
- The sternum strap should cross your chest below your collarbone. If the frame stays are shaped correctly and the pack is properly fitted, you can adjust the load lifters and other fine-tuning straps to make the pack hug your back. Adjustments can also be made while hiking to divert weight to other muscle groups, thus making hiking less tiring.

Loading an Internal Frame Pack

Your gear will help form the structure of support for an internal frame pack. For easy, level hiking, a high center of gravity is best. To achieve this, load bulky, light gear (e.g., sleeping bag) low in the pack and stack heavier gear on top of it. For steeper terrain, a lower center of gravity is best because it lessens the chance of falls from a top-heavy pack. In this case, place heavier items a little lower in the pack and closer to your back than normal. Women may prefer this arrangement under all circumstances (see page 26).

SUGGESTIONS FOR EITHER PACK TYPE

- Stuff your clothes into the pack or pack items in stuff sacks rather than fold them. This serves to fill all the available space of the pack better so that things don't shift around and allows you to get more into the pack.
- The more common weight distribution (general trail hiking) has the lighter, bulkier items on the bottom: the sleeping bag below the pack bag and clothes stuffed into the bottom of the pack. The heavier items such as food, stoves, and fuel go into the upper section or on top of the pack, with the heaviest items closest to the pack frame. A general rule is that 50 percent of the weight should be in the upper third of the pack.
- For consistently steep or rough terrain, carry the weight lower to give you better balance.
- The horizontal weight distribution should be balanced so that the left side of the pack is in balance with the right.
- Your hip belt should have enough room to allow you to loosen or tighten it for different layers of clothing beneath. If the belt is too loose, socks or shirts can be inserted between the belt and your body. This adds an extra layer of padding to the belt as well, which may increase the comfort of the fit.
- Avoid hanging things all over the outside of your pack—no one wants to listen to you clank and clang your way down the trail; also, all that junk can snag branches. If you find yourself having to tie things on all the time, your pack may be too small.
- Think about the things you will need during the day and have them relatively accessible so that it doesn't take a complete emptying of your pack to find lunch, the first-aid kit, or your rain gear. Also, group and store items according to function. For example, keep toiletries together. Small stuff sacks help organize your gear.
- For protection from rain, line your sleeping bag stuff sack and main pack compartments with plastic garbage bags. These can be reused on subsequent trips and recycled when you are through with them. Pack rain covers are also useful.
- An old duffel bag serves as a great food compartment. It allows you to quickly find the food you are carrying and can be used as a bear bag, too (see Traveling in Bear Country, page 155).

- Fuel bottles should be placed in a leakproof bag and kept separate from any food items.

How Much Weight?

How much weight to carry depends on your size, weight, and physical condition. The general rule for a multiday backpacking trip is to carry up to 25 percent of your body weight. On longer trips, trips with more gear (like winter camping), this figure may go up. The bottom line is, don't carry more than you can handle. Here are some things to do to make your trip as comfortable as possible.

- Try on your loaded pack at home before you leave.
- Fiddle with the pack and adjust it to the best fit (you probably won't take the time to do this at the trail head while your friends are waiting).
- Weigh your pack and compare that to your body weight.
- Take a good look at what you are bringing along. Prune out the nonessentials (that second book you won't have time to get to anyway, the watermelon for Day 4).
- Look and see what other people are carrying and how the whole group can share the load in a way that makes sense for each member, given size, weight, physical condition, and experience.

Checking Your Pack Before a Trip

- Take a look at the shoulder straps, hip belt, and other compression and load-carrying straps.
- Check all pack buckles.
- Check all zippers.
- Check the pack bag itself for rips or tears.
- If the pack is an external frame pack with a pack bag mounted onto the frame, check the attachment pins (typically clevis pins and split rings).

Putting on a Heavy Pack

There are a number of methods for putting on a heavy pack.

- With the pack on the ground and the shoulder straps facing you, lift the pack up and rest it on one extended knee. Slide one arm through a shoulder strap. At this point, your shoulders will be slightly tilted, so that the shoulder strap is sliding onto your shoulder toward your neck. Lean forward slightly and rotate your body to swing the pack onto the rest of your back. Slide your other arm through the other shoulder strap. Adjust the hip belt first. The easiest way to do this is to bend over at the waist so the weight is being carried on your back rather than your hips and the hip belt is free to be snugged up tightly. Then you can straighten up and adjust the shoulder straps. Aim for 70 to 80 percent of the weight on your hips.

- Follow the same technique with a friend to help stabilize your pack. This is especially helpful if you are carrying a large or very heavy pack.
- Lift the pack up onto an object that is about waist high (rock, log). Stabilize the pack and slip your arms through both shoulder straps. Pull on the pack and tighten the hip belt.

I *don't* recommend putting your pack on while sitting down and then trying to stand up. This puts too much strain on your lower back. This method should be used only if you have two friends who can pull you up.

SLEEPING EQUIPMENT

SLEEPING BAGS

When selecting a sleeping bag, you need to consider a number of factors. Unlike clothing layers, a sleeping bag doesn't offer much in the way of ventilation to control your body temperature. As a result, you might have more than one bag: a summer-rated bag for hot summer conditions, a three-season bag for spring and fall, and a winter bag for serious cold-weather conditions.

Sleeping Bag Temperature Ratings

Sleeping bags come with temperature ratings to give you a general idea of how cold it can get and if the bag will still provide adequate insulation to keep you warm. Remember, some people sleep "colder" than others, so you may need a bag with more or less insulation to be comfortable at a particular temperature. Also, ratings differ from manufacturer to manufacturer. To calculate the temperature rating you will need, look at the lowest normal temperature for the trip location and season you are going, and then subtract 10° or 15°F (9° or 12°C) from that temperature. This gives you a margin of safety in case the temperature is colder than expected. Here are some general guidelines for sleeping bag ratings:

Season	Temperature Rating
Summer	40 to 60°F (4 to 16°C)
Three season	20 to 40°F (−6 to 4°C)
Cold weather	0 to 20°F (−17 to −6°C)
Winter	−30 to 0°F (−34 to −17°C)

For example, if the usual nighttime temperature is 50°F (10°C), bring a bag that goes to 35°F (2°C).

Sleeping Bag Styles

The following are three general styles for sleeping bags:
- **Rectangular** Simple rectangular bag typically without a hood.
- **Mummy** A form-fitting bag with a hood. The bag tapers in width from the shoulders to the legs, with little room. This tight fit means that there is less convective heat loss in the bag, making for a warmer bag.
- **Modified Mummy** A form-fitting bag with a hood. The bag tapers in width from the shoulders to the legs, but is wider in the torso region to provide more room.

Sleeping Bag Fit

Fit is as important in a sleeping bag as it is in clothing. In sleeping bags, you want the bag to snugly conform to your body. If the bag is too big, you will have large spaces for convection currents and you will be cold. You might need to wear clothing layers to help fill up the space. If the bag is too tight, the insulation may actually be compressed, decreasing its effectiveness. How comfortable you feel in the bag can also affect your night's sleep—some people feel confined in a snug sleeping bag and need more "wiggle room" than others.

Specific Features to Look for

- A hood allows you to insulate your head to prevent heat loss.
- The draft tube is an insulated tube that runs along the zipper line and prevents cold spots at the zipper.
- A draft collar provides a closure at the neck area to reduce the bellows action of heat leaving the bag.
- Well-designed zippers allow you to open and close your bag easily from the inside.

🍁 **TRICKS OF THE TRAIL**

Drying Things Off You can dry out damp (but not soaking wet) items by placing them in your sleeping bag alongside your body. My feet always get cold, so I change into dry socks just before I get into my bag. This makes my toes much happier. I take the damp socks from the day's hike and lay them in the bag along my thighs. The next morning they are dry and I stow them in my pack for the following day.

Insulation Types

When we talk about sleeping bag insulation, we mean the loft of the bag. Loft is the amount of dead air space created by the fill used in the sleeping bag. There are a variety of different fills for sleeping bags, but they basically break down into two categories: synthetic fibers and down. There are a multitude of synthetic fibers, such as Polarguard and Quallofill and "super-thin" fibers such as Primaloft and Microloft. Some fibers are produced in sheets, while others are loose fills. Loose fill fibers (synthetic or down) require the bag to have sewn compartments, or baffles, to keep the fibers from shifting. This typically increases the manufacturing cost of the bag.

- **Synthetic Fibers: Polarguard, Quallofil, and Others** These are primarily used in sleeping bags and heavy outer garments, like parkas. The fibers are fairly efficient at providing dead air space (though not nearly as efficient as down). Polarguard is made in large sheets. Quallofil uses seven "holes" running through the fiber to increase dead air space for greater thermal efficiency. *Pro*: They do not absorb water and dry fairly quickly. Some fibers are produced in sheets that do not require baffling. *Con*: Heavy. Not as efficient an insulator as down. Hard to compress to a small size. Some are loose fibers that require baffling. Fibers produced in sheets tend to break down over time, losing their loft more quickly.

- **"Superthin" Fibers: Primaloft, Microloft, Lite Loft, and Others** These synthetic fibers are based on the principle that by making the fiber thinner you can increase the amount of dead air space around the fiber. Some superthin fibers are close to the weight of down for an equivalent fiber volume. They stuff down to a small size and have similar warmth-to-weight ratios as down without the worries about getting wet. *Pro*: Lightweight and thermally efficient. They do not absorb water and dry fairly quickly. Some fibers are produced in sheets that do not require baffling. Can be stuffed down to a small size. *Con*: Some are loose fibers that require baffling.

- **Down** The very soft underbody feathers of geese or ducks provide excellent insulation and dead air space for very little weight. Down is useful in sleeping bags since it tends to conform to the shape of the occupant and prevents convection areas. It is also very compressible, which is an advantage when packing. But be aware that your body weight compresses the feathers beneath you so you need good insulation (e.g., a foam pad) underneath you, more so than with a synthetic bag. The one problem with down (and it can be a *major* problem) is that it absorbs water. Once the feathers get wet they tend to clump together and lose dead air space. A wet down bag has almost no insulating value and is very difficult to dry in the field. When using a down bag, take special care to prevent it from getting wet. For example, a vapor barrier sleeping bag liner in a down bag will help the bag stay dry from the inside and a Gore-Tex bivy sack will help the outside keep dry. The effectiveness of a down bag is directly related to the quality of the feathers used. Down is rated by its fill-power—a 700-fill bag lofts better and is more thermally efficient than a 550-fill bag. Check to make sure that your down bag is made of 100 percent down; otherwise you may be getting a percentage of regular feathers, which is less thermally efficient. Since down is a loose fill, sleeping bags must have baffles sewn in to prevent the down from shifting in the bag. *Pro*: Very lightweight and thermally efficient. Can be stuffed down to an extremely small size. *Con*: Absorbs water, so if the bag gets weight it can loose all its insulating value. Expensive. Requires baffling. Significant compression of fibers occurs underneath the body. Down may not be appropriate for trips where there is a high probability of getting wet (like river trips). Some people are allergic to feathers.

Sleeping Bag Care

Keep in mind that sleeping bags age. Over years of use, the fibers that create the loft in the bag break down and no longer create as much dead air space. This means that the bag is no longer capable of keeping you warm at its original temperature rating. Keep the age of your bag in mind if you are counting on it to keep you warm. Here are a few things you can do to prolong the life of your bag:

- Stuff your sleeping bag into its stuff sack rather than rolling it. Rolling compresses and ultimately breaks the fibers in the same direction, decreasing loft faster. Stuffing is a random pattern of compression that helps your loft last longer.
- Don't keep your sleeping bag in its stuff sack between trips. Keep the bag unstuffed in a large breathable bag like a laundry bag.
- Follow the manufacturer's instructions for washing your bag.

Sleeping Bag Extras

Here are a number of sleeping bag extras that can be useful on your trip:

- **Sleeping Bag Liner** A cotton-nylon liner can help keep the inside of your bag clean, reducing the number of times the bag needs to be washed (repeated washings tend to reduce the loft of the bag).

- **Vapor Barrier Liner** A vapor barrier liner (VBL) can add about 10°F (9°C) to the rating of your bag by reducing evaporative heat loss. You may feel a little moist inside, so wear polypropylene or other hydrophobic long underwear.
- **Bivouac (Bivy) Sack** This waterproof outer shell can add about 10°F (9°C) to the rating of your bag.

🍁 TRICKS OF THE TRAIL

Sleeping Warm Your sleeping bag will be whatever the ambient air temperature is. (For some unknown reason, nylon always feels colder than it really is when you first slip into your bag.) Here are some tricks for warming things up:

- After dinner, fill a water bottle with hot water. Put the hot bottle inside your bag before you get in to preheat the bag. The water should stay warm all night.
- Get in your bag and do a bunch of sit-ups. The surge of body heat will warm you and the bag.
- Change into dry clothing (like polypropylene) before getting into your bag.
- Wear extra clothing. How much clothing to wear in your bag depends on how much extra space there is around your body in the bag, whether you are adequately hydrated, and whether you sleep "warm" or "cold." If there is space, wear extra layers to increase the dead air space around your body. Remember, you will need to warm up all your layers as well as the bag. Wearing an insulating hat will make a big difference.

SLEEPING PADS

Sleeping pads are used to insulate and cushion your body from the cold or rocky ground. In cold conditions, a sleeping pad is essential in maintaining your body heat by preventing conductive heat loss to the colder ground. Sleeping pads come in two basic types: closed-cell foam such as Ensolite or inflatable pads such as Therm-A-Rest Pads. Closed-cell foam pads are lightweight and roll up to a small diameter. They tend to get a little stiff in cold weather. Inflatable pads are typically open-cell foam covered with coated nylon, and have an inflation valve at one end. Both types work extremely well. With inflatable pads you should carry repair items to patch any holes that develop in the nylon outer layer.

For three-season camping, a pad that is $\frac{3}{8}$ inch thick (10 millimeters) is adequate. In colder conditions, you should have $\frac{1}{2}$ inch (12 millimeters) of insulation between you and the ground. Pads are available in either full length or partial length (three-fourths or two-thirds). You can save weight by not using a full-length pad. Full-length pads are recommended in very cold environments, so that no part of your sleeping bag is in contact with the cold ground.

SHELTER

When planning your trip, you need to know whether to bring your own shelter or whether there will be shelter options available on a daily basis along the trail. If you need to bring your own shelter, there are two basic options:

- **Tarps** *Pro*: Lightweight. Inexpensive. *Con*: Not as weatherproof as a tent. Does not provide bug protection. May require trees to set up.
- **Tents** *Pro*: Good weather protection. Good bug protection. *Con*: Heavier. Expensive.

Other options include shelters such as the Black Diamond Megamid. This is a single, center-pole pyramid tent with no floor, somewhat of a cross between a tarp and a tent. It requires some staking but is reasonably roomy for two or three people.

GENERAL SHELTER TIPS

- Whenever you use a tent or tarp, think carefully about site placement so that you leave no trace. A tent on grass for more than a day will crush and yellow the grass beneath, leaving a direct sign of your presence. Stakes can damage fragile soils and guylines and tarp lines can damage trees.
- Find a resilient or already highly impacted location. Try to find a relatively flat location; hollowed-out areas pool water in a storm.
- If possible, identify the prevailing wind direction and set up your tarp or tent accordingly. If rain is a possibility, set up so that the openings don't face the oncoming wind.

TARPS

Tarp setup can be an art. You typically use a ground sheet underneath to provide a floor and protect your sleeping bag and gear from wet ground. You need trees located an appropriate distance apart in order to set up a tarp, although you can also rig a tarp from overhead branches or tent poles. There are many variations, but the most weatherproof shape is the basic A-frame.

A-Frame Tarp Setup

- Select an appropriate location in your campsite to set up your tarp (see Chapter 5). Have a tarp line of sufficient diameter (¼ inch or 6 millimeter braided nylon) to prevent knots from slipping.
- Secure one end of the tarp line to a tree using a bowline knot (see Bowline, page 161) at an appropriate height for the size of your tarp, and stretch the running end to the other tree. You can set your tarp height so that the bottom edges lie above the ground sheet, allowing for ventilation, or wrap the edges of the tarp under the ground sheet for better weather protection.
- Wrap the running end of the tarp line around the second tree and tie it off using an adjustable knot such as a tautline hitch or a truckers hitch (see Tautline Hitch, page 162; Truckers Hitch, page 163). This will allow you to set and later reset the tension of your tarp line. To tighten the tarp line, simply slide the tautline hitch or pull on the truckers hitch and tie it off. The tautline hitch is preferred since it can be easily retensioned. If you need more friction from the tautline hitch, add a few extra wraps.
- Place your ground sheet beneath the tarp line.
- Place the tarp over the tarp line and stake out the corners of the tarp. This can be done using stakes or by tying the guylines to rocks or other trees. Make sure the tarp is adequately guyed out so that strong winds won't tear it down. Or you can fold the edge of the tarp underneath the

ground sheet and weigh it down with rocks on the inside to create a very rainproof shelter.

Tarp Tips

- To prevent rainwater from running down the tarpline into the tarp, tie a bandanna on the line just outside the tarp. It will redirect the water drips to the ground.
- You can create your own grommets for guylines by placing a small stone on the inside of the tarp and tieing parachute cord around it from the outside. The free end of the parachute cord can then be staked out. This is useful if grommets are broken or if more support is needed for the tarp.
- Rain ponchos can be used as makeshift doors to prevent wind and rain from blowing in through the ends of the tarp.
- If there aren't trees around, try boulders, rock outcroppings, or other objects to string up your tarp. If you know you are going to a place without trees, take along two extendable tent poles—the type used on big family tents. You can use one at each end of the tarp as vertical supports. It's best to have a grommet in the center along each edge to insert the pole.

TENTS

A multitude of tents are available—everything from simple A-frames to complex geodesic domes. When selecting a tent, consider the following:

- The size of your group and how many people each tent sleeps.
- Freestanding tents are generally preferred over nonfreestanding tents. A freestanding tent has a pole arrangement that maintains the tent's functional shape without the need for guylines.
- Examine the floor space of the tent and the usable internal volume. Dome-style or arch-style tents typically have greater usable overhead space than A-frame tents.
- Tents are typically rated as three-season or four-season. A four-season tent is rated to withstand some level of snow loading.
- Most tents use a rain fly—an outer waterproof layer that is separated from a breathable layer beneath. A breathable inner tent wall with a waterproof fly outside helps reduce condensation in the tent. It also helps provide better insulation by increasing the layers of still air.

Tent Tips

- Each tent comes with its own set of instructions. Practice how to set up your tent before your trip so you can do it in the dark, in bad weather, or in bad weather in the dark.
- Make sure you bring extra poles with you or pole splints in case a pole breaks.
- Make sure that you have the right tent stakes for your environment. Ever try to hammer one of those narrow wire tent stakes into rocky soil and watch it bend at a right angle? In soft surfaces like sand or snow, you will need a stake with a much greater surface area (especially for sand). In snow, you can create a "dead man" by tying your guyline to a branch and then burying the branch in the snow and packing the snow down on top. When the snow sets, the dead man will be solidly fixed. (You may have to chop it out when it's time to go.) In sand, fill a stuff sack with light bulky items, tie your guyline to it, and bury it.
- Use a ground sheet, a space blanket, or a tarp to help protect your tent floor from rips and tears (better the cheap tarp than your expensive tent).
- Always stake your tent down if you are going to be in windy areas or will be leaving your tent during day excursions.
- Avoid cooking in a tent. The nylon most tents are made of is flammable, and the water vapor from cooking leads to extensive condensation inside the tent. Carbon monoxide gas released from a burning stove can lead to suffocation (see Carbon Monoxide, page 305).

COOKING EQUIPMENT

GENERAL COOKING EQUIPMENT

Basic cooking gear is listed in the general equipment list on page 350, but here are a few necessary items:

- **Pots** It's best to bring at least two pots. A pot set that nests is easiest to carry. The pot size depends on the size of your group: for 1 to 3 people use a 1.5-liter and a 2.5-liter pot. For groups of 6 try a 2-liter and a 3-liter pot, and for 8 or more go with at least a 2-liter and a 4-liter. Pots should have lids that seal well. Flat lids allow you to build a small fire on top of the lid for baking. Having a rim on the outside of the pot is essential for picking it up with a pot-gripper. Stainless steel pots weigh a little more than aluminum, but will last longer. There is a great debate about pots with non-stick coatings. The non-stick coating makes it easier to clean the pot, but you can't use harsh abrasives to clean them, which eliminates some of the best natural cleaning materials, such as sand. My favorite pot is actually produced as a food container and is sold by Liberty Mountain Sports. Because the pots are narrower at the bottom than at the top, two pots of the same size can be stacked to form a double boiler, increasing your cooking options (fondue!). (*Note:* If you use these pots, make sure you remove the rubber gasket on the lid before cooking.)

- **Frying Pan** One is usually plenty per trip. Choose your size based on the size of your group (or how big you like your pancakes). Frying pans are generally available in 8-, 10-, and 12-inch models. Using a frying pan with a cover will reduce your cooking times.
- **Utensils** Lexan plastic utensils are basically indestructible. Be careful cleaning them. Harsh abrasives can create scratches that will hold dirt and bacteria.

TRICKS OF THE TRAIL

Baking Soda—the wonder product is a great thing to have in your cook kit. It does a wonderful job of cleaning pots, and even removes burned-on soot. It also can be used to create a rehydration formula for someone who is dehydrated (see Fluid Balance, page 285).

OUTDOOR BAKING EQUIPMENT

Baking in the backcountry requires a system that spreads heat to both the top and the bottom of your pan. There are a number of cooking pans and devices that let you do this. One basic technique is to build a small twig fire on top of your pot lid. Some pots have special lids designed with a rim to contain the fire. There are also several commercial products, such as the Outback Oven and the BakePacker, that spread the heat from your stove around the pot (see also Chapter 3, "Cooking and Nutrition").

- **Outback Oven** The Outback Oven works on the convection oven principle. A grate lifts the pot off the stove so that it is not directly on the flame. A heat reflector around the stove burner deflects heat up and underneath an insulated pot cover. This heated air heats the pot and does the baking. The insulated pot cover can also be used by itself to help your pot retain heat, making your stove more efficient.

- **BakePacker** The BakePacker uses steam heat to bake. The food is placed in a plastic bag and is supported above the water in the pot by a grate. Premixed recipe bags are available.

BACKPACKING STOVES

There are two basic types of backpacking stoves: those that use liquid fuel and those that use some form of compressed gas in a cannister. Most backpackers rely on liquid fuel stoves.

- **Liquid Fuel Stoves** burn Coleman Fuel (a.k.a. white gas), kerosene, or alcohol. *Pro*: Fuel readily available (alcohol and kerosene available worldwide). *Con*: Require more maintenance. Some stoves don't simmer well. Alcohol doesn't burn well at high altitude (over 7,000 feet or 2,133 meters).
- **Compressed Gas Stoves** burn butane, isobutane, or propane. *Pros*: Easy on and off. Low maintenance. Easy to control temperature. *Cons*: Difficult to tell amount of fuel left. Cannister disposal. Butane doesn't burn well at high altitude (over 7,000 feet or 2,133 meters).

How Liquid-Fuel Stoves Work

Fuel is stored in a separate tank. In most cases, this tank uses a pump to help pressurize the stove. The tank should be filled only to the ¾ point, leaving some air in the tank. The pump forces air through a one-way valve into the tank, increasing the pressure inside. Opening the fuel flow valve allows the pressurized liquid fuel to flow from the tank through the generator tube, out a small opening called the jet, and into the priming cup. Initially, vent only a small amount of fuel into the priming cup, then shut off the fuel flow valve. When you light this small amount of fuel, it will heat up the generator tube. This process is known as "priming the stove." It can also be accomplished by using a separate priming source such as alcohol or priming paste. Once the generator tube is hot, the fuel flow valve can be opened and the stove burner lit. The pressurized fuel from the tank flows through the heated generator tube, where it is vaporized. The fuel that now flows through the jet is gasoline vapor. It strikes the flame spreader and ignites. The flame spreader redirects the flame from a single, vertical "candle" flame to a wider flame for more efficient heating. When the stove is properly primed, you should see a blue flame similar to that on a gas range. If the flame is yellow or orange, it means that the fuel is not being completely vaporized in the generator. As the generator heats up further, it may begin to run properly, or you may have to turn off the stove and reprime it.

Prime Your Stove Properly The biggest problem with lighting backpacking stoves comes from not priming sufficiently to preheat the generator tube. White gas tends to ignite with a poof and a burst of yellow flame that can be a foot or more high and then burns out quickly. Instead of priming with white gas, bring along a small bottle of alcohol or use priming paste. These ignite much less violently and burn for a long time. Also, you won't have to worry about singeing your eyebrows when you get too much white gas in the priming cup. Prime the stove for several minutes, then light it; you should be rewarded with a nice blue flame.

Stove Safety Guidelines

- Know how to operate a stove properly *before* you light it.
- Make sure your stove has enough fuel *before* you light it.
- When cooking on a stove, always work from the side. Never put your face or body directly over the burner.
- Do not overfill a stove.
- If using a stove with a separate fuel bottle, make sure that the fuel bottle is designed to hold pressure (such as MSR bottles). Also make sure that the bottle is in good shape. I've seen plenty of banged and dented fuel bottles that I just don't trust to hold pressure. These may be used to carry fuel, but should not be connected to a stove.
- Be careful if a hot stove goes out. Do not relight it until it has cooled down for at least 15 minutes. Priming a hot stove with fuel can result in *instantaneous and violent ignition.*
- *Never* use a white gas stove inside a tent, snow cave, or other enclosed or poorly ventilated space. Stoves give off carbon monoxide, which could lead to asphyxiation in a poorly ventilated area (see Carbon Monoxide, page 305). Also, tents are often made of flammable materials.
- Fuels should always be stored a safe distance from the stove when it is being used. Care should be taken to note the wind direction in relation to the fuel storage area so that fuel fumes cannot reach the flame source or sparks reach the fuel source. Always refill stoves far from any source of flame or heat.

What to Do if Your Stove Catches on Fire

I've seen a number of different models of stoves leak and catch fire. The first thing to do is to back away quickly. The best methods for putting out a stove fire are dousing with liberal amounts of water (a 4-liter pot works great), dumping sand on the stove, or if water or sand are not readily available, tossing an empty pot over the stove. The hope is that lack of oxygen will put out the fire; however, the pot also concentrates the heat, which could cause a more violent ignition before the fire is extinguished.

How Much Fuel to Bring

The amount of fuel you need depends on the size of your group and the type of items on your menu. Cooking at Altitude (page 68), boiling water for purification, or melting snow for water will increase your fuel requirement.

Liquid Fuel Guidelines	
Season	**Fuel/Person/Day**
Summer	⅛ quart (157 milliliters)
Spring and Fall	¼ quart (236 milliliters)
Winter or at high altitude	½ quart (473 milliliters) If you need to melt snow for water

COLEMAN PEAK 1 FEATHER 400 AND 442 OPERATION

The Peak 1 Feather 400 and Feather 442 operate in the same manner. The Feather 400 burns only Coleman fuel. The Feather 442 stove can burn unleaded automotive fuel or Coleman fuel. *Never* use kerosene, gasohol, regular or premium leaded automotive fuel. You should read the product literature that comes with your Peak 1 stove carefully for the latest instructions and information on how to assemble the stove properly. The following instructions are reprinted with permission from Coleman product literature (with author's additions in brackets).

The stove consists of four main components: the Tank, Pump, Fuel Valve, and Generator. The Tank is designed to hold both the fuel and air. To avoid a fuel leak during lighting, an adequate air space *must* exist above the fuel level in the tank. Never overfill the tank, as this will decrease the needed air space. To avoid overfilling, *always* fill the stove on a level surface. Never tip the stove on its side in an attempt to pour extra fuel into the tank.

The Pump pressurizes the fuel tank. Opening the pump knob one turn allows air to be pumped past a check valve and into the air space above the fuel.

The Fuel Valve controls the flow of fuel and air from the tank to the generator. The OFF position closes the Fuel Valve and prevents fuel flow. In the HI/LIGHT position, fuel flows through the valve to the Generator, where it is heated and vaporized before reaching the burner. When the stove is first lighted, both fuel and air from the tank pass through the Fuel Valve. As soon as the stove lights, it is important that additional air be pumped into the tank to replace the air that is passing through the Fuel Valve. Pump for at least

30 seconds. Time your pumping so that you pump one stroke per second.

The function of the Generator is to absorb heat from the burner and vaporize the liquid fuel passing through the Generator. Moving the Red Fuel Lever from LOW to HI/LIGHT moves a needle in and out of a small orifice in the end of the Generator. The needle both cleans the orifice and regulates the flow of fuel. Always light the stove with the flame adjustment lever in the HI/LIGHT position so that the stove is delivering full heat output to the generator.

If you notice an intermittent yellow flame when operating at a low heat setting, move the Red Fuel Lever to a slightly higher setting. This will increase the heat on the generator and eliminate the yellow flame.

To Fill Tank

1. Extend feet and place stove on a smooth level surface.
2. Move the Red Fuel Lever to the OFF position.
3. Close Pump Knob firmly. Turn in the direction of the arrow on Pump Knob.
4. Remove Fuel Cap. Use a funnel and fill with clean, fresh fuel. *Do not tip stove.*
5. Replace Fuel Cap on stove and on fuel container. Tighten firmly. Move fuel container away from stove. Wipe up any spilled fuel and dispose of in a safe place.

To Pump

1. Make sure Red Fuel Lever is in the OFF position.
2. Open Pump Knob one turn.
3. With thumb over the hole in Pump Knob, pump approximately 25 full strokes.
4. Close Pump Knob firmly.

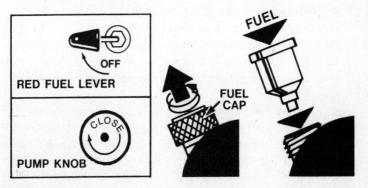

RED FUEL LEVER

OFF

CLOSE

PUMP KNOB

FUEL

FUEL CAP

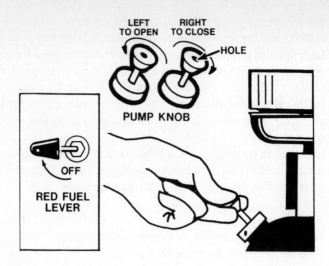

To Light

1. Place stove on a smooth, level surface.
2. Hold lighted match at burner and then turn Red Fuel Lever to HI/LIGHT.
3. As soon as burner lights, open Pump Knob one turn and pump for 30 seconds (30 pumps). Close Pump Knob. CAUTION: If fuel or flames appear below burner, immediately turn the Red Fuel Lever OFF. Allow stove to cool. Turn stove upside down to empty any fuel that accumulated in the burner. Wipe dry. Carefully review instructions before relighting stove.

RED FUEL LEVER

4. Adjust flame to desired heat with the Red Fuel Lever. If the stove is hard to light or does not produce full heat output on HI, quickly move the Red Fuel Lever from OFF to HI several times to clean the Generator gas tip. Some unleaded fuels may require gas tip cleaning every 30 to 60 minutes of use. Additional pumping may be required for full heat output.

Note: In temperatures below freezing, preheating may be required. Place generous amounts of preheating paste on the burner cap beneath the Generator. Light the paste. After the paste is almost consumed, follow the above lighting instructions.

To Turn Off

1. Move Red Fuel Lever from OFF to HI several times.
2. Latch Red Fuel Lever in OFF position. Flame will linger on burner for 1 to 2 minutes after the fuel lever is OFF.

Things You Should Know

- During operation for an extended period at a low heat setting, you may notice an intermittent yellow flame. This can be corrected by adjusting the flame to a slightly higher level with the Red Fuel Lever.
- The generator gas tip can be cleaned by moving the Red Fuel Lever quickly from OFF to HI several times. If the stove is hard to light or burns with reduced heat output on HI, clean the tip.
- Periodically check the tightness of the packings and, if necessary, tighten the Packing Nut on the Red Fuel Lever just enough to prevent leaks (about ½ turn). Behind the nut is a packing or gasket material. The purpose of the packing is to put tension on the levers so they don't move too easily and also to prevent fuel from leaking around the lever. If the levers loosen up from use or if a fuel leak should occur, tighten the packing nut.
- Periodically squirt a few drops of oil into the hole in the Pump Cap. This will keep the pump functioning properly.
- Rinse tank twice a year with fresh fuel to remove sediment, gum formations, and moisture accumulations.

Peak 1 Maintenance

- **If the stove leaks at the lever** Tighten the packing nut that holds the lever in place.
- **If the flame is erratic or unbalanced** Clean the orifice and/or pump more air into tank.
- **If you see yellow tongues of flame or voids mixed with blue flame** Match heads or other foreign objects are in or around the burner ring outlets. [Turn off the stove and] thoroughly clean the burner section. **Make sure the stove has cooled down.**
- **If there is a flame at the generator tip** Tighten the tip protector.
- **If the stove loses air pressure in operation** This may be caused by several things, including a poor gasket on the filler cap (replace cap), a leak in the pump assembly (new parts needed), or a leak in the upper port on the tank (new parts needed).

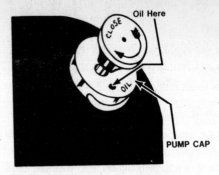

Oil Here

CLOSE

OIL

PUMP CAP

- **If there is a yellow flame or loss of pressure** This may be caused by insufficient preheating (start over); low pressure (pump more); carbon or other food on burner (clean when cool).
- **If the pump does not work** Rotate the pump cap counterclockwise so that the flanges line up with the slot. Some stoves have a clip that holds the pump cap on. Remove the clip from the pump cap. Turn the pump counterclockwise several times to disengage the air stem, then pull out the whole pump assembly. Work several drops of oil or Vaseline into the pump leather. Replace the pump assembly and reattach the pump cap.
- **If you see flames blowing away from burner** There is too much air pressure. Turn [off the stove, let it cool] and reduce pressure through the filler cap.

MSR WHISPERLITE STOVE

MSR Fuel Bottle

Control Valve

Catch Arm

Windscreen

Generator Tube

Flame Reflector

Pump Plunger

Fuel Line

Priming Wick

Priming Cup

Heat Reflector

Operation

The MSR Whisperlite Shaker Jet and the
MSR Whisperlite Internationale 600 are
similar in both operation and repair—the
only difference is the fuel. The Whisperlite
Shaker Jet runs only on white gas; the
Internationale 600 operates on white gas
and automobile gas with the standard jet

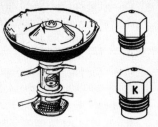

and kerosene or jet fuel with the jet marked K. Both models have
a built-in shaker needle for cleaning the jet orifice. Older Whisperlite stoves
do not have a shaker jet for cleaning the jet orifice and use a separate needle
tool instead.

You should read the product literature that comes with your Whisperlite
carefully for the latest instructions and information on how to assemble your
stove properly. The following instructions are reprinted from MSR product literature, with permission of MSR (with author's additions in brackets).

Assembling the Stove

1. Fill an MSR Fuel Bottle to the 2 inch Fill Line. Use only MSR fuel bottles. Non-MSR fuel bottles may result in fuel leakage and/or separation
   from the Pump. Fuel may ignite, possibly resulting in injury or death.
   [Make sure the bottle is not dented. Small holes can cause pressure
   loss or fuel leaks.]
2. Screw the Pump snugly into the Fuel Bottle.

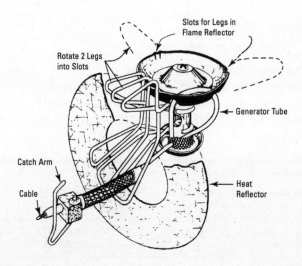

Slots for Legs in
Flame Reflector

Rotate 2 Legs
into Slots

Generator Tube

Catch Arm

Cable

Heat
Reflector

3. Pump the Plunger 15 to 20 strokes. If the Fuel Bottle is half full, pump the Plunger 40 to 55 pump strokes or until firm resistance is felt when you push down on the Plunger. *The less fuel in the Fuel Bottle, the more Pump strokes needed to pressurize it for proper stove operation.*
4. Insert the Fuel Line through the hole in the Heat Reflector.
5. Rotate two legs into the slots in the Flame Reflector.
6. Lubricate the end of the Fuel Line lightly with MSR Pump Cup Oil, saliva, or other mineral-based lubricant, then insert it into the Fuel Tube Bushing on the Pump.
7. Snap the Catch Arm securely into the slot on the Pump Body. [If the catch arm doesn't lock into place, you may need to bend it so that it does. *Failure to lock the catch arm can result in the fuel line and fuel tank detaching from the stove during operation, an extremely hazardous condition.*]

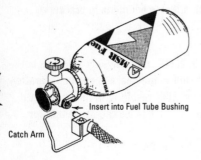

Catch Arm

Insert into Fuel Tube Bushing

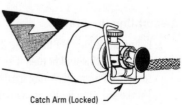

Catch Arm (Locked)

Operating the Stove

Before lighting the stove make sure that:

- The Stove assembly has no fuel leaks.
- The Catch Arm is locked and stove is properly assembled.
- The area is clear of flammable material and spilled fuel.
- The correct Jet is installed (for the MSR Whisperlite Internationale 600 only).

🍁 TRICKS OF THE TRAIL

Be Careful with Stove Fuel and Plastic Pumps: Make sure that you don't spill fuel on stoves with plastic pumps. If there is fuel on the outside of the pump while the stove is lit, it can catch fire. A fire on a plastic pump can melt the pump, allowing more fuel to flow out, a potentially hazardous situation.

Priming

To preheat the stove, the priming flame must contact the Generator Tube. Insufficient priming may result in flare-up.

1. Open the Control Valve until fuel flows through the Jet and fills the Priming Cup ½ full. [Alcohol may be used as an alternate priming fuel to reduce soot buildup from the preheat process.]

Note: Do not over-prime. Do not fill the priming cup with fuel. Only a small amount of fuel is needed. Excess fuel can result in a dangerous flare-up.

2. Turn the Control Valve off.

3. Check for leaks at the Control Valve, Pump, Jet, and Fuel Line. If leaks are found, do not use the stove.

4. Light the Priming Fuel. [On the International 600, light the Priming Wick.]

5. Place the Windscreen around the stove, then fold the ends together to keep it securely in place.

[Note: The burner assembly will get extremely hot during operation, so place the stove on a suitable flat, insulated surface before lighting.]

Turning the Stove On

1. As the priming flame gets smaller, slowly open the Control Valve. Do not force the Control Valve past the Stop Nut, since this can strip the threads of the Pump.

2. If the stove:
   - Goes out, turn the Control Valve off. After the stove cools return to "Priming."
   - Burns with erratic yellow flames, but the Priming Cup flame is still burning, turn the Control Valve off and preheat longer.
   - Burns with a blue flame, wait 1 minute then adjust to the desired setting. There is a delay between turning the Control Valve and changes in the amount of flame.

3. To maintain stove performance, pump the Plunger 3 to 5 strokes as needed to keep enough pressure in the Fuel Bottle. You should feel firm resistance when you pump down on the Plunger. The less fuel in the Fuel Bottle, the more Pump strokes needed to pressurize it for proper stove operation. Do not overpressurize. Fuel Bottle pressure that is too high causes erratic flames. Fuel Bottle pressure that is too low causes low flames and very slow burn times.

4. To simmer: Operate the stove at low Fuel Bottle pressure. Turn the Control Valve down until the flame becomes unsteady, then open Control Valve until the flame stabilizes.

Turning the Stove Off

1. Turn the Control Valve off. The flame will take a few seconds to die out. Wait for the stove to cool before disassembling.
2. **To Depressurize the Fuel Bottle** [Making sure that you are away from heat, sparks, or flame] unlock the Catch Arm, and pull the Fuel Line out of the Pump/Fuel Bottle assembly. Hold the Fuel Bottle upright, turn the Pump/Fuel Bottle away from you, and unscrew the Pump to release pressure.
3. **For Transporting or Storing** Keep the Pump assembled in the Fuel Bottle or, to be sure the Control Valve does not open by mistake, remove the Pump and replace it with the Fuel Bottle Cap.

Operating Suggestions

- [The wind screen and heat reflector provide up to a 20% improvement in performance. Do not use the wind screen without the heat reflector.
- Climatic conditions affect the performance of all liquid fuel stoves. At temperatures below $-10°F$ $(-24°C)$ impurities that can clog the stove will begin to freeze in the fuel.
- At temperatures below $-10°F$ $(-24°C)$ the O-rings in the pump may become stiff and can leak or break, causing a fire. Keep the pump warm at night by placing the pump in a plastic bag at the foot of your sleeping bag (remove the pump from the fuel bottle).]

Burner Maintenance

- [If you notice a reduction in stove performance, the burner assembly should be cleaned thoroughly to remove any carbon deposits that may have accumulated inside the Fuel Generator Tube assemblies.]
- Cleaning the Jet Orifice [Fuel flow will be restricted if the orifice in the jet assembly becomes clogged.]
  - Turn the Control Valve off. Wait for the stove to cool.
  - Shake to clear the jet. [Whisperlite Shaker Jet and the Internationale 600. For older stove models: use the jet-cleaning wire to clear carbon deposits from the jet.]

Cleaning the Jet and Fuel Line

1. If the Shaker Jet Needle does not move freely inside the Jet, clean the Jet. Unscrew the Priming Cup. Pull the Generator Tube out of the Mixer Tube. Unscrew the Shaker Jet using the Jet and Cable Tool. Remove the Needle and clean inside the Jet. If the stove is still clogged, go to step 2.

2. Scour the Fuel Line. Pull the Cable out of the Fuel Line using the Jet and Cable Tool. Wipe the Cable [with clean stove fuel]. Push the Cable in and out of the Fuel Line to scour the Generator Tube. Repeat scouring and wiping until clean. Reinstall Cable.

3. Flush the Fuel Line. With the Jet and Needle out, insert the Fuel Line into the Fuel Tube Bushing. Pump Plunger 15 to 20 strokes. Open the Control Valve and run a ½ cup of fuel through the Fuel Line. Warning: When flushing keep away from heat, sparks, and flame. Do not spill fuel. Reassemble. [Here's the trick to reassembly. The fuel line goes into the fixed leg of the stove. Turn the open end of the Elbow upside-down (so the Needle would fall out if it were in). Lower the Elbow through the leg opening from the top. Now, rotate the Elbow 180°. To do this you will have to follow the curve of the Generator Tube. When the Elbow is facing right-side up, slide the top bend of the Generator Tube into the slot in the Flame Reflector.]

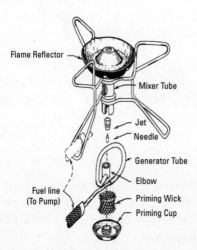

Flame Reflector

Mixer Tube

Jet

Needle

Generator Tube

Elbow

Fuel line
(To Pump)

Priming Wick

Priming Cup

Pump Maintenance

- **Leather Pump Cup (on Pump Plunger)** [If the leather pump cup becomes dry, the pump will not properly pressurize the fuel bottle. To check pump performance hold one finger over the air hose and pump the plunger. Air should blow through the hose and resistance to pumping should be felt.] If the Pump will not pressurize the Fuel Bottle, stretch out the Leather Pump Cup slightly and lubricate it with MSR Pump Cup Oil, saliva, or other mineral-based oil [like 3-in-1 Oil]. Remove the Pump Plunger by turning the shaft of the Plunger (below the swiveling head) and pulling the Plunger out. Rub oil into the Leather Pump Cup until it becomes soft and pliable. If pumping still does not pressurize the Fuel Bottle, replace the Leather Pump Cup. [It's good preventive maintenance to oil the pump cup occasionally.]

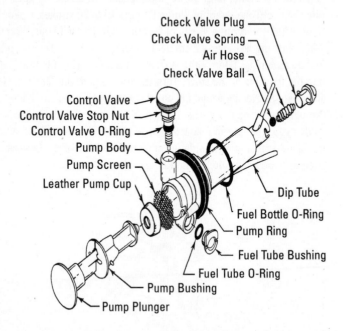

- **Check Valve Assembly** If the Pump does not hold pressure in the Fuel Bottle, clean the Check Valve Assembly. Turn the Check Valve Plug counterclockwise. Remove the Check Valve Ball and Spring and wipe with a cloth. Reassemble.

- **O-Rings** To prevent fuel leaks, inspect the Pump O-Rings regularly for cracks or damage. [If the O-Ring is cracked, pitted, or damaged, replace it before using the stove.]
  - [**Fuel Tube O-Ring** Leaks at the Fuel Tube are the result of a torn Fuel Tube O-Ring. To replace, insert a coin into the slot on the Fuel Tube Bushing and twist counterclockwise. Replace the old O-Ring, reinsert the Bushing, and tighten by twisting clockwise.
  - **Control Valve O-Ring** The Control Valve O-Ring should not be changed unless leaks occur. To do so, turn the Control Valve counterclockwise and pull gently until it comes completely out of the pump body. The worn O-Ring can then be snipped off. To prevent damaging the new O-Ring, wrap tape around the needle end of the Control Valve, then gently move the new O-Ring into place. Remove the tape and carefully reinstall the Control Valve into the pump. Do not overtighten.
  - **Fuel Bottle O-Ring** Check the O-Ring for damage and replace if needed.]

CHAPTER 3

Cooking and Nutrition

Food can be one of the most important and complicated elements to plan for a trip. You have to be aware of nutritional requirements, individual dietary needs, and amounts needed to feed the entire group. Plus, the food has to be appetizing—there is nothing better than a delicious hot meal to bolster morale after a long, hard day of hiking, and nothing worse than trying to keep your strength up while staring into a cup of disgusting mush. It can be difficult to get people, particularly inexperienced backpackers, to eat a meal that doesn't look or taste appetizing.

ENERGY AND NUTRITIONAL REQUIREMENTS

Good nutrition is just as important in the backcountry as it is at home. Food supplies energy to your body to fuel your physical activity and keep you warm. Food also provides essential nutrients that your body cannot produce: vitamins, minerals, certain amino acids, and certain fatty acids. The amount of energy the body takes in from food is measured in units of heat energy called *calories*. When planning a menu for a trip, it is important that the foods be high in calories in order to meet these requirements.

CALORIC REQUIREMENTS

We all know that people have different body metabolisms and that some eat like mice while others eat like horses. Below are the general ranges for calories required to maintain good health, and what you will typically need to carry. Keep in mind that the food weights are averages, since carrying only dehydrated foods, for example, would mean carrying less weight. Also, at higher altitudes the caloric requirements per day increase.

Activity	Caloric Requirement/day	Food Weight/day
Sedentary occupation (couch potato)	1,500–2,000	Varies
Three-season backpacking or normal exercise output	2,500–3,000	1.75–2 pounds (0.8–0.9 kilograms)
Cold weather backpacking or strenuous exercise output	3,500–4,000	2–2.25 pounds (0.9–1 kilograms)
Winter backpacking or very strenuous exercise output	4,500–6,000	+2.5 pounds (+1.1 kilograms)

FOOD SOURCES

Carbohydrates (four calories/gram, energy released quickly) regularly make up about 50 percent of a person's daily caloric intake. For hiking trips you may need to increase this up to 70 percent of the daily caloric intake. Starches and sugars provide both quick energy and longer-term fuel. Processing and refining can reduce the nutritional value of carbohydrates, so it is best to use whole grains, raw sugar, and other unprocessed foods in your menu. Simple carbohydrates (sugars such as trail snacks or candy) are broken down very quickly by the body for quick energy release, and complex carbohydrates (such as pasta) release energy more slowly.

Fats (nine calories/gram, energy released slowly) are another important source of energy in the backcountry. It is recommended that about 25 percent of your daily intake be fats (during the winter this should increase to about 40 percent). Fats take longer to break down than carbohydrates, and thus are a better source of long-term energy. For example, adding a spoonful of butter or margarine to a cup of hot chocolate will increase the caloric rating and the length of time the energy is released.

Proteins (four calories/gram, energy released slowly) are an essential part of any diet. Proteins are the essential building blocks of all tissue. Each protein in the body is made up of 22 amino acids. Fourteen of these amino acids are produced in the body, and the other eight, known as the "essential amino acids," are not. Both types are essential to a complete diet. Foods such as meat, poultry, fish, eggs, and milk products are called "complete proteins" since they contain all 8 essential amino acids. However, it is often not possible to carry such products on a backpacking trip owing to weight or spoilage. Foods such as beans, lentils, peanuts, cereals, vegetables, and fruit are incomplete proteins since they do not contain all eight amino acids. However, a backcountry menu can be planned using proper combinations of these incomplete proteins in order to get all eight amino acids daily. An easy way to plan meals that include all eight amino acids is through using the "Nutritional N" to create food combinations. The N contains four elements: Dairy, Grains, Legumes, and Seeds. The N shape provides lines that connect two food groups that, when combined, provide complete protein.

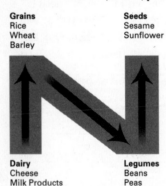

Grains
Rice
Wheat
Barley

Seeds
Sesame
Sunflower

Dairy
Cheese
Milk Products

Legumes
Beans
Peas
Lentils
Peanuts

- **Dairy** Cheese, milk, yogurt
- **Grains** Breads, crackers, pasta, granola and other cereals, rice, couscous, bulgur, bran, potatoes, corn, oats

- **Legumes** Beans, peas, lentils, peanuts, tofu
- **Seeds** Sunflower, sesame

The phrase "Don't Get Love Sick" may help you remember the four different groups and the *order* in which they form the nutritional *N*. A combination of any two consecutive initial letters of the phrase will provide complete proteins. Dairy and grains, for instance, will form a complete protein together, whereas dairy and legumes will not. The other two complete protein combinations are grains and legumes or legumes and seeds.

Sample Complete Protein Combinations

Dairy (or Eggs) and Grains Macaroni and cheese; cheese and crackers; pasta with Parmesan cheese; milk and cereal.

Grains and Legumes Rice and beans; refried beans and flour tortillas; peanut butter and bread; rice or bread and tofu.

Legumes and Seeds Peanuts and sunflower seeds in GORP.

FOOD GUIDE PYRAMID

The Food Guide Pyramid was developed by the U.S. Department of Agriculture to provide guidelines for a healthy diet. These recommendations specify a number of servings of each food type you should eat on a daily basis. The

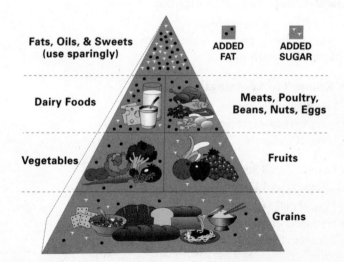

SOURCE: *Nutrition and Your Health: Dietary Guidelines for Americans,* Fourth Edition (Washington, D.C.: U.S. Department of Agriculture, U.S. Department of Health and Human Services, 1995).

majority of daily foods should come from the bottom levels of the pyramid. Foods higher up on the pyramid should make up less of your daily food intake. The average American diet is about 45 percent carbohydrates. Owing to the increased energy demands of hiking, you should plan your menu to get closer to 70 percent of your daily calories from carbohydrates. This means increasing the number of daily servings in the grains group and decreasing daily servings in other groups.

SERVING SIZES

Below are examples of what constitutes a single serving. Remember that a particular meal can provide multiple servings of different food groups and that many normal meals add up to multiple servings of a food group. For example, a cheese sandwich with lettuce and tomato provides two grain servings, two vegetable servings, and one milk serving. Remember to adjust the number of servings per day to increase your carbohydrate load.

Grain Products Group: 11+ Servings/Day
(Bread, Cereal, Rice, and Pasta)

- 1 slice of bread
- 1 ounce of ready-to-eat cereal
- ½ cup of cooked cereal, rice, or pasta

Vegetable Group: 3 to 5 Servings/Day

- 1 cup of raw leafy vegetables
- ½ cup of other vegetables, cooked or chopped raw
- ¾ cup of vegetable juice

Fruit Group: 2 to 4 Servings/Day

- 1 medium apple, banana, or orange
- ½ cup of chopped, cooked, or canned fruit
- ¾ cup of fruit juice

Milk Group: 2 to 3 Servings/Day
(Milk, Yogurt, and Cheese)

- 1 cup of milk or yogurt
- 1½ ounces of natural cheese
- 2 ounces of processed cheese

Meat and Beans Group: 2 to 3 Servings/Day
(Meat, Poultry, Fish, Dried Beans, Eggs, and Nuts)

- 2 to 3 ounces of cooked lean meat, poultry, or fish
- ½ cup of cooked beans
- 2 tablespoons of peanut butter
- 1 egg
- 2 tablespoons seeds and nuts

Sweets Group (Fats, Oils, Sugars)

- Use sparingly

High-sugar foods like candy and GORP provide quick energy along the trail and are burned off fairly quickly, so you can indulge more than your normal diet. Fats and oils from cheese or nuts are also excellent energy sources. In cold weather or winter conditions, increasing the oil and fat content in your diet helps maintain body heat.

> **❧ TRICKS OF THE TRAIL**
>
> **GORP:** Everyone has their own favorite recipes for "GORP," which stands for Good Old Raisins and Peanuts. I start with equal parts raisins and peanuts and then add a quick sugar source. You can increase the variety of the mix by adding smaller amounts of different sugar sources. Some ideas for additions include M&M's, coconut, walnuts, carob chips, malt balls, dates, dried apples, dried pineapples, banana chips, and sunflower seeds. When using chocolate, consider the melting factor. Also, if you use items that are smaller than most of the other things in your mix, like sunflower seeds, they will eventually filter down to the bottom of the bag, so be prepared on the last day to find a bag full of sunflower seeds.

BASIC FLUID RECOMMENDATIONS

Water is an essential part of personal nutrition on the trail. It aids digestion, regulates body temperature, keeps cells healthy, and carries waste from the body. Dehydration leads to headaches, fatigue, and irritability. Mild dehydration is often easily relieved by drinking half a quart (½ liter) or more of water. Remember that these general recommendations are for backpacking in temperate forest conditions. You may need to increase your fluid intake based on your own metabolic needs, physical condition, medical condition, age, sex, or different weather conditions (such as high temperature and humidity), or in specific ecosystems (such as desert climates).

Water is always being lost by the body through the "–tions"—respiration, perspiration, urination, and defecation. Strenuous activities like backpacking result in increased water loss. Dehydration is one of the most preventable backcountry problems but also one of the most ignored. I've seen people avoid drinking for all sorts of reasons: it was too much trouble to get the water bottle out of their pack or they didn't want to have to urinate. The bottom line is, *stay hydrated*. Failure to stay adequately hydrated can lead to serious and even life-threatening conditions (see Fluid Balance, page 285; Heat Challenge, page 289; Hypothermia, page 293).

Keep your water bottles handy and keep drinking all day long. Drink 16+ ounces (500 milliliters) before starting to hike and then 10 to 12 ounces (200 to 300 milliliters) every 20 to 30 minutes while hiking. It is easier on your body to handle small amounts of water spread out rather than sucking down a whole quart at once. The sensation of thirst comes *after* the body is already low on fluid, so don't wait until you are thirsty to drink. The best way to tell if you are adequately hydrated is to check your urine output. It should be "copious and clear."

❧ TRICKS OF THE TRAIL

There are a number of water carriers such as the Camelback and the Platypus that use a collapsible plastic bag in a fabric liner. You can place the carrier in your pack and, using a plastic tube on the carrier, drink as you hike.

Keep your daily route and the availability of water in mind when you are planning your menu. If water will be scarce, you need to plan meals that do not require lots of water for cooking or rehydrating.

Season/Weather	Amount/day	Explanation
Fall and spring backpacking*	2 to 3 quarts 1.8 to 2.8 liters	This is what an average person will need on a daily basis in a general temperate climate.
Hot-weather backpacking*	3 to 4 quarts 2.8 to 3.7 liters	In hot and humid weather, you lose additional fluid through sweating, which must be replaced.
Winter backpacking*	4+ quarts 3.7+ liters	In the winter, you lose moisture through evaporation to the dry air and especially through respiration. Dry air entering the lungs heats up and is exhaled saturated with moisture.
*High altitude, all seasons	Add 1 quart 1.8 liters	At high altitudes the body loses more fluid. Increase your fluid intake if you are traveling at high altitudes (over 8,000 feet/2,438 meters)

Remember that these are general recommendations only. You may have different fluid requirements based on your own metabolic needs, physical condition, medical condition, age, sex (e.g., during her menstrual period, a woman will need more fluid), or different weather conditions.

MENU PLANNING

When planning food for a backpacking trip, there are two approaches that can be taken. The first is a menu planned meal-by-meal; the second is a ration system of many different ingredients, enabling the group to create its own menu (see pages 341–42). On short trips (2 to 6 days), a meal-by-meal menu often works best. The ration approach is useful on longer trips (7 to 10+ days), as it provides room for greater flexibility and creativity. Below are some important things to think about when planning your menu.

HOW LONG ARE YOU GOING TO BE OUT?

The length of your trip is essential when planning a menu. You need to bring enough food to feed everyone, but you don't want to carry too much heavy food. For any trip, you can start with a variety of fresh fruits and vegetables, which will typically last several days.

- Less than a week: carry any types of food that won't spoil.
- 7 to 10 days: add some dehydrated or freeze-dried foods to cut down on weight.
- Greater than 10 days: increase the proportion of dehydrated or freeze-dried foods, or arrange for food resupply.

On longer expeditions, the types of foods you can carry become more limited. You may need to supplement your diet with vitamins and minerals to make up for nutrients that you may not be getting.

EASE OF PREPARATION

It is important to consider what the activities will be during the trip. This will determine whether you will want quick, one-pot meals, or will have the time to be more elaborate (e.g., on a winter camping trip, one-pot meals may be best because they are quick and require less stove fuel). Also, think about how your meals will be affected by the number of stoves and pots you will have.

WEIGHT

You understand what a good diet is and how many calories each person is going to need. But how are you going to carry all that? For three-season backpacking, assume that each person needs about 2 pounds (0.9 kilograms) of food per day (this increases in winter). You need to plan your menu with the weight of the food in mind. Here are a few things to keep in mind:

- Some foods are lighter than others and packaging, especially cans, adds weight.

- Freeze-dried or dehydrated foods are lighter, but more expensive.
- Fresh foods, such as fruit or vegetables, are heavy because they contain water, but they provide a welcome treat on the trail.
- You can save weight by eliminating the water carried in foods. For example, carry dried beans instead of canned beans, which contain water. You can rehydrate the beans on the trail by placing them in a full water bottle. After soaking for a few hours, they will be rehydrated and ready to cook. (This also decreases the cooking time and saves stove fuel.)
- Plan your meals to use the heaviest items first and then move to lighter-weight items at the end. This way you will quickly reduce the amount of weight you will be carrying.

TRICKS OF THE TRAIL

Freeze-dried Foods Cooked or fresh food is frozen and then the water is allowed to sublimate off. This removes about 99 percent of the water and leaves most of the nutritional value.

Dehydrated Foods Dehydration is a process using heat to evaporate water slowly. About 90 percent of the water is removed during the dehydration process. Some nutrients are also lost. Dehydrated foods can take longer to cook, which adds weight back into your pack in terms of extra stove fuel.

Both freeze-dried and dehydrated foods save on weight but require significant amounts of water to rehydrate. In situations where water is limited, these foods may be a problem. Whenever you are thinking of packing prepared freeze-dried or dehydrated foods, try them out at home first. You want to know that you will like the taste and the quantities. It may say it feeds four, but after a long day of hiking, it will only feed three.

PACKAGING/REPACKAGING

This is important in terms of weight and minimal impact (see Chapter 5, "Leave No Trace Hiking and Camping"). Glass, cans, and foils should be avoided as much as possible since they add weight and must be packed out. Glass containers are obviously unwise to carry in a backpack, unless you want to scrape the honey, for example, off the inside of your pack. A simple way to repackage any food is using sealable plastic bags such as Ziploc or plastic bags tied with loose knots at the top. Double bagging is important with powders and grains to prevent leakage if one bag tears. Spices often can be purchased in small plastic containers. Whenever possible, bag all the contents of a meal together and label it lunch Day 2, dinner Day 3, etc. Another approach is to put food items in separate stuff sacks—breakfast, lunch, and dinner.

Leave No Trace camping begins at the store. The idea is to be environmentally conscious when buying items by evaluating the packaging of different foods and brands.

- **Reduce** the amount of packaging you buy by buying in bulk. Choose items that are bulk packaged rather than individually wrapped. This can also reduce your costs.
- **Recycle** all cardboard, glass, and other original packaging when you repack your food. Look for food brands with recylable packaging.
- **Reuse** After a trip, plastic bags that have no holes can be washed out and reused. Other containers are reusable, too (a plastic peanut butter jar can be reused on future trips). Tupperware or other plastic containers can be reused.

🍁 TRICKS OF THE TRAIL

BEWARE: Do not use discarded film canisters to store food or spices. They contain chemical residues that can be harmful if swallowed.

SPOILAGE

On longer trips, and even short trips in hot weather, it is usually not possible to carry fresh foods or meats for very long because of spoilage. Here are some guidelines for how long different foods will keep:

Fruits

- Fruits stay fresh for different lengths of time. Harder fruits like apples, oranges, and tangerines are best. If you buy softer fruits like pears, peaches, or nectarines, buy them before they ripen and let them ripen on the trail. Avoid putting easily smushed fruits like bananas in your pack unless you are very brave.
- Dried fruits last for months.

Cheeses and Dairy

Note: The ability of cheese to keep unrefrigerated for extended periods of time is primarily based on the moisture content of the cheese. Any cheese can be out for a few hours, but only some cheeses are appropriate for multi-day trips.

- **Grated and Grating Cheeses** (Moisture content 34% or less.) Parmesan and Romano do not need refrigeration.
- **Hard Cheeses** (Moisture content 36% to 43%.) Cheddar, Colby, and Swiss can go without refrigeration for up to a week. Over time, high

temperatures result in oiling off of liquefied milk fat. Though unsightly, this is not a spoilage problem. Waxed bricks or wheels hold up best.

- **Semisoft Cheeses** (Moisture content 44% to 52%.) Brie, Camembert, blue cheese, Monterey Jack, and Muenster should be refrigerated.
- **Soft Cheeses** (Moisture content greater than 50%.) Cream cheese, ricotta, and cottage cheese require refrigeration for long-term storage.
- **Milk** Most people take powdered milk to conserve weight. UHT (ultra-high-temperature pasteurized) milk such as Parmalat can be carried for months unopened without refrigeration. Once opened, the milk should be refrigerated, but if you can use it up at a meal it should be fine.

Meats

- Hard salami, pepperoni, smoked meats, and jerky all last for weeks without refrigeration.
- Canned meats and fish last almost forever. (Make sure your tuna is dolphin-safe.)

Other Foods

- Eggs can be carried unrefrigerated for 2 to 3 days if they are cracked into a wide-mouthed water bottle that is topped off with water to remove all air. Eggs can also be carried uncracked in plastic egg containers or in other containers with sufficient padding.

🍁 TRICKS OF THE TRAIL

Cook Before You Go A number of delicious meals or add-ons can be made ahead of time and packed with you. Fresh breads, biscuits, muffins, and deserts can add a lot to a trip. Cold salads such as bean salad, hummus, and tabouli can also be made ahead (or on the trail).

Precook and Freeze For special meals early in the trip you can pre-cook meals and freeze them in a plastic container. Seal the container well with tape. The food will slowly melt, but should be fine for the first 24 hours. Reheat on the stove for a quick dinner.

COST

Cost is also a factor in planning your menu. Buying in bulk can help. Keep in mind that freeze-dried and dehydrated foods, while lighter, can be significantly more expensive. Balance your weight requirements against the cost.

EATING ON THE TRAIL

Everyone has different preferences for mealtimes. When hiking, you are expending energy all the time, so you constantly need to replenish that energy. This typically means eating three meals a day. Some people prefer to get up, have a light breakfast, get an early start, and then stop for a bigger meal at midday. Whatever your preference, you should have an ample supply of water and snacks during the day to keep your energy level up. Remember that more falls and injuries take place on hiking trips around 11:00 A.M. and again at 3:00 P.M. than at any other time, because blood sugar is low and people are dehydrated.

SPECIAL DIETARY CONSIDERATIONS

It is important to take into consideration the different eating habits of the group members. There may be people with food allergies, vegetarians, and those who keep kosher. It is also important to plan a variety of foods, especially for longer trips. Asking trip members about specific dietary needs before shopping will help make everyone on the trip feel included. Finally, a tip for cooking for people with particular dietary restrictions: cook whatever food cannot be eaten by everyone *separately*. Put it aside in a separate dish for people to add to their own plates.

VEGETARIANISM

Not all vegetarians exclude the same foods. It is important to discuss with people what foods they can and cannot eat. The most common forms of vegetarians are:

- **Ovo-Lacto Vegetarians** These people will eat eggs and milk products but no red meat, poultry, fish, or animal by-products (lard, etc.).
- **Vegans** These individuals eat only foods of plant origin. They must plan a careful diet to make sure that they are getting adequate nutrients.
- **Almost Vegetarians** Technically not vegetarians, these people will eat fish and/or poultry, but avoid eating red meat.

Refer back to the nutritional *N* for guidelines on food combinations that offer the essential amino acids. One alternative for vegans is to bring vacuum-packed containers of tofu (soybean curd), which is an excellent source of protein. When you shop for vegetarians, you need to look closely at the label. Animal products are often hidden in foods. Gelatin, for instance, is almost always made with animal products, unless it is specifically labeled otherwise. Refried beans are often made with lard, an animal fat. For vegans, milk is disguised as "whey" in many baked goods and some cereals. It is also important to remember that the daily demands of wilderness travel require high caloric intake, which may be difficult for some vegetarians since fats are often obtained through meat and dairy products. Nuts and peanuts contain oils that are good sources of both fats and calories.

FOOD ALLERGIES

This is a critical safety consideration to know before you go out on the trail. Someone who is extremely allergic to a food can have an anaphylactic reaction (see Anaphylaxis, page 312). In many cases, you can find substitute foods for the offending item. I once had someone on a winter camping trip who was allergic to wheat. At first I was stymied about what to do—no pasta, no bread, crackers, and so on. We ended up buying rice cakes and corn-based pasta from a health food store. You may need to do some real detective work for people who have serious allergies. For example, even *regular* M&M candies (not peanut) have small amounts of peanuts in them (unused regular and peanut M&Ms are reprocessed together into new candy) and should not be eaten by someone with a severe peanut allergy.

KOSHER MEAL PLANNING

If you have someone on your trip who indicates that they keep kosher, you should learn about how they choose to observe this practice. In some cases, keeping kosher involves avoiding certain foods, for some it will mean using only kosher versions of foods, and in other cases it may mean using cookware (pots, utensils, etc.) that have been kept kosher.

- **Kosher and Non-kosher Products** Foods items that are kosher are manufactured under strict standards supervised by a rabbi. These items typically are labeled with a U symbol or a K symbol or the word *Parve*.
- **Unkosher Combinations** Mixing a meat (poultry, red meats) with a dairy product (milk, cream, cheeses, and butter) is not considered kosher. However, fish is not considered a meat, so fish and dairy can be mixed. But some fish and all shellfish are unkosher.
- **Solutions** The easiest way to keep food kosher on your trip is to avoid bringing any meat products (poultry and red meats). You can bring some fish products. If you do bring meat, make sure you don't mix meat and dairy.
- **Utensils** For those who need to have kosher utensils, make sure that all of your utensils (pots, pans, lids, spoons, spatulas, cups, etc.) are kosher and that you know which are for dairy (that is, they have only

been used to cook kosher, dairy products) and which for are meat. These items must be kept separate. Mixing nonkosher utensils with kosher utensils could make the kosher utensils nonkosher.

GENERAL COOKING GUIDELINES, INGREDIENTS, AND RECIPES

- **Hygiene** Before anyone handles food, make sure the person washes his or her hands thoroughly (see Keeping Yourself Clean, page 78).
- **Avoid Burning Your Meals** Cooking on a backpacking stove is a challenging affair, since some stoves don't simmer well and none offers the same control as a kitchen stove. Start with a clean pot to avoid burning last night's dinner. Turn the stove on full only when you are boiling water. Otherwise, turn it down to let the food cook slowly and evenly. It may take longer to cook, but once you burn food in the pot, you'll taste it the rest of the meal. Check periodically to see if food is sticking to the bottom. If so, turn down the heat or add water. If you are using large pots or frying pans over a small stove burner, you may need to move the pot around frequently to make sure the heat is distributed evenly.
- **Avoid Overcooking or Undercooking** The major cause of overcooking or undercooking is adding ingredients in the wrong order. Start with freeze-dried foods first in cold water and boil for 10 to 15 minutes to rehydrate. Next add rice or pasta. The last thing to add is thickeners like flour, potato pearls, milk, or cheese.
- **Spices** Spices bring your meal to life. Remember that many sauces, dehydrated soups, and other stocks are already salty. It is best to let people add their own salt when the food is done, rather than oversalt while you're cooking. Use only a little bit of spice at a time. It takes 5 to 10 minutes for spices to flavor food, so wait and taste before adding more.
- **Pots** If you have extra pots, put water on the stove to boil for hot drinks as soon as you take the dinner pot off. This will also give you hot water for washing.
- **Left-over Food** Any solid food left over should be placed in a plastic bag and packed out. Do *not* bury solid food waste; animals will only dig it up.
- **Don't Pack Fuel Near Food** Fuel vapors can penetrate plastic bags and contaminate food. Food contaminated with fuel is considered a toxic substance and can make you sick. Carry fuel in an outside pocket of your pack away from food or in the bottom of your pack with the food packed higher up.

- **Cooking at Altitude** At higher altitudes, the air pressure is lower. This allows water to boil (change from a liquid to a gas) at lower temperatures. You will need to plan longer cooking times. For foods that cook in 20 minutes or less at sea level, add 1 minute of cooking time for each 1,000 feet (310 meters) of elevation. For items that take more than 20 minutes at sea level, add 2 minutes of cooking time for each 1,000 feet (310 meters) of elevation. Something that takes 20 minutes to cook at sea level can take twice as long (40 minutes) to cook at 10,000 feet (3,048 meters). This also means that you may need significantly more stove fuel if your trip is at altitude.

Elevation	Boiling Point of Water	Cooking Time
Sea level	212°F (100°C)	10 minutes
5,000 feet (1,524 meters)	203°F (95°C)	15 minutes
7,500 feet (2,286 meters)	198°F (95°C)	18 minutes
10,000 feet (3,048 meters)	194°F (90°C)	20 minutes
15,000 feet (4,572 meters)	185°F (85°C)	25 minutes

TYPICAL MENU ITEMS

Breakfast

Granola
Grape-Nuts
Cracklin' Oat Bran
Grits
Oatmeal
Hash browns
Pancakes
Note: Consider packing cereals that won't be easily crushed.

Lunch and Trail Food

Dried fruit—provides bulk, fiber, and carbohydrates
Granola bars
Bagels, pita bread, tortillas, English muffins—travel better than bread
Nuts and seeds—provide protein and fat
Peanut butter, jelly, honey
Cheese
Tuna
Fruit
GORP
Energy bars (PowerBar, etc.)

Sweets: chocolate, hard candies, sesame/honey, caramels, jelly beans, yogurt malt balls, carob balls

Dinner

For simplicity on the trail, most dinners should be one-pot meals. Start with a starchy base for calories—pasta, rice, or other grains—and then add additional ingredients to build a full meal.

Lipton Cup-o-Soup

Risotto

Ramen noodles

Pasta

Rice (Minute Rice is easier and uses less fuel than brown rice, but it's also not as nutritious.)

Bulgur

Falafel

Couscous

Beans (dried beans take longer to cook; you can presoak them in a water bottle. Canned beans are *heavy.*)

Potato pearls or flakes

Dehydrated vegetables (peas, carrots, green and red bell peppers, mixed vegetables, dried onions)

Cheese

Pepperoni for pita pizzas (doesn't need refrigeration)

Dessert

Brownie mix

Instant gingerbread mix

Cheesecake Mix

Pudding/Jell-O

Miscellaneous

Brown, white, or raw sugar

Maple syrup, honey

Tea, coffee (herbal teas)

Cocoa

Powdered milk

Drink mix (lemonade, iced tea, fruit punch, Gatorade, Tang)

Margarine (Squeeze Parkay)

Spice kit: salt, pepper, garlic powder, chili powder, curry, cinnamon, oregano, basil, cumin, cayenne, dill, and personal favorites

Vegetable oil
Vinegar
Soy sauce
Vanilla
Tabasco sauce

SAMPLE RECIPES

To me, cooking is a lot like carpentry—the old adage, "measure twice, cut once" becomes "measure twice, cook once." Once when I was on a back-country skiing trip, I read a biscuit recipe too quickly and added too much water. In order to salvage the batter, I had to make enough biscuits to feed a small army for a week. In the sample recipes below, you should adjust the quantities to fit the size (and appetites) of your group. Don't be afraid to invent your own recipes, or check out some of the excellent backcountry cookbooks available (see the Bibliography).

Most meals will be "one pot" meals. These are often based on pasta, rice, or other grains. Below are the basic cooking directions for pasta and rice.

Pasta Use two parts water to one part pasta. Bring the water to a boil with salt (1 teaspoon per quart of water). Add the pasta and boil it gently for 10 to 15 minutes or until done. You can use the drained water for soups or carbo-loaded hot chocolate.

Instant Rice Use equal amounts of rice and water. Bring the water to a boil, add margarine (as desired) and salt (1 teaspoon per quart of water). Stir in the rice. Cover, and remove from heat. Let stand for 5 minutes, fluff with a fork and serve.

HUMMUS

This chickpea spread is the ultimate energy food! Full of protein and calories, it's great for lunch or snacks. You can make it before the trip or on the trail and pack it in a Ziploc or Tupperware, where it will easily last a week.

2 12-ounce cans of chickpeas	Juice of three lemons
2 tablespoons olive oil	4 garlic cloves, minced
6 tablespoons sesame tahini	

Mash the chickpeas with a fork. Add the olive oil, tahini, and lemon juice. If the mix is too thick, add a tablespoon or two of water. Add the garlic. Mix until smooth. Serve with slices of pita bread. If you want to carry less weight, bring dry hummus, which can be mixed with water on the trail. **Serves six.**

TUNA MELTS

This is a great hot lunch or appetizer for the days when you're feeling lazy and don't want to spend a lot of time cooking.

1 tablespoon margarine or oil   6 10-inch tortillas
2 8-ounce cans tuna fish,   1 cup diced cheddar cheese
   drained

Melt the margarine or heat the oil in a frying pan over medium heat. Place a tortilla in the pan and top with a thin layer of the tuna and cheese. Fold in half and cook over medium heat until the cheese is completely melted.

For a tasty variation, sauté the tuna with one chopped eggplant in the margarine or oil over medium heat. Add a few of your favorite spices and continue to cook until tender and hot, about 3 to 5 minutes. Slide the tortilla into the pan so that it's under the mixture. Add a layer of the cheese, fold the tortilla, and cook until the cheese is melted. **Serves six.**

Note: If you prefer, you can use pita pockets instead of tortillas. Slice the pocket open before placing in the frying pan, and follow the recipe, closing the pita when the recipe tells you to fold the tortilla.

🍁 TRICKS OF THE TRAIL

What to do with the remains:

Tuna Juice Buy tuna packed in water rather than oil. Depending on how you eat the tuna, you may be able to just pour the water into your pot. However, if you are eating tuna straight out of the can for lunch, you should properly dispose of the tuna juice. Pouring it over the tuna on sandwiches is best.

Noodle Water Anytime you cook pasta, you are left with noodle water. If possible, use this for something else later in the meal, such as hot chocolate. The chocolate will hide the pasta flavor, and you'll get the benefit of the extra carbos in the water. This is much better than putting the water in a sump hole (see Waste Water, page 112).

BURRITOS

Packed with protein and carbohydrates, burritos are another great energy meal. Repack the beans and salsa into water bottles before your trip, or use instant beans, so you aren't lugging cans around. The cumin makes a huge difference in flavor; don't forget to include it in your spice kit!

1 tablespoon margarine
½ onion, chopped
1 green pepper, chopped
3 4-ounce cans of chicken
2 12-ounce cans of refried
    black beans

2 12-ounce cans of salsa
1 teaspoon cumin
Tortillas
Cheddar cheese, sliced, for
    topping

In a large frying pan over medium heat, melt the margarine and sauté the onion for one to two minutes. Add the green pepper and chicken and continue to sauté, stirring frequently, until the onions are translucent, about 3–5 minutes. Add the beans, salsa, and cumin and cook over medium flame, stirring frequently, until hot. Divide the mixture among the six tortillas, sprinkle each with cheese, fold, and serve immediately. **Serves six.**

PITA PIZZAS

This meal takes a while if you have to cook one pizza at a time, but it's lots of fun to make. The recipe makes 18 small pizzas, a generous serving of three per person.

1 stick margarine
2 green peppers, chopped
1 onion, chopped
18 small whole wheat pitas

1 16-ounce can tomato sauce
1 pound Cheddar cheese,
    sliced

In a large frying pan over medium heat, melt one tablespoon of the margarine and sauté the green peppers and onion until the onions are translucent, about 3–5 minutes. Set aside in a bowl. Slice a four-inch-long opening along the edge of each pita. Fill each one with sauce, cheese, onions, and green pepper. Fry each pita individually in margarine (added to the pan as needed) over medium heat until the pita is browned and the insides are warmed. **Serves six.**

QUESADILLAS

Quesadillas are a wonderful excuse to use up any leftover cheese and tortillas you're carrying around. The longer your trip, the more you start fantasizing about fresh vegetables. Spinach is a good solution, because it's light and full of vitamins and fiber. Make sure it comes prewashed so you don't waste your water washing off sand and dirt.

1 stick margarine	2 onions, chopped
1 pound prewashed spinach	1 cup chopped cheddar
2 green peppers	6 tortillas

In a large frying pan over medium heat, melt one tablespoon of the margarine and sauté the spinach, green pepper, and onions until the spinach is wilted and the onions are browned, about 5–10 minutes. Set aside in a bowl. Fill a tortilla with one-sixth of the spinach/pepper/onion mixture, sprinkle with cheese, and fold in half. Reheat the frying pan and cook each quesadilla over medium heat until the cheese melts, adding margarine as needed. This can be a very sloppy procedure, but the meal's so delicious it's worth the mess. **Serves six.**

MACARONI AND CHEESE

Mac and cheese is a meal that I don't think to fix at home, but after a long day on the trail, even something this simple tastes good. Must be all those carbos.

2 pounds elbow macaroni or rigatoni noodles	4 tablespoons margarine
	1 garlic clove
1 pound cheddar cheese, chopped (mixing in other cheeses adds flavor)	Vegetables (optional)

Bring a large pot of water to a boil. Add the noodles, and cook over medium heat until tender, 5 to 10 minutes, depending on the type of noodle. When the noodles are tender, pour the water out (see Waste Water, page 112) or save it for hot drinks, leaving enough water in the pot to just barely cover the noodles. Add the cheese, margarine, garlic, and salt and pepper to taste, and stir until the cheese melts. Serve immediately. You can spice this meal up by stir-frying some veggies (broccoli, green peppers, etc.) in a separate pan with a little margarine until tender, and adding them in at the cheese melting stage. **Serves six.**

Pesto Pasta

Make a batch of pesto before your trip and you'll have a quick and easy meal for those long days when you're too tired to cook.

2 cups fresh basil
⅓ cup olive oil
1 teaspoon lemon rind
2 garlic cloves, minced

¼ cup pine nuts
2 teaspoon red wine or balsamic vinegar

Add all the ingredients to a blender or food processor and grind until smooth. Store pesto in a Tupperware container (tape it closed or you'll find oil and basil all over your pack). Serve over your favorite pasta. **Two and a half cups of pesto sauce serves 6 people.**

Chicken Fajitas

This is a fun meal to cook and to eat.

16 ounces refried beans
30 ounces canned chicken, drained
1 stick margarine
2 green peppers, sliced

2 onions, sliced
12 10-inch flour tortillas
16 ounces salsa
Grated cheese (optional)

74

In a large frying pay, heat the refried beans over medium heat until warm, then set aside in a separate bowl. Drain the chicken (save the juice to add to your frying pan as needed). Add one tablespoon margarine to the frying pan over high heat. When the pan is hot, lightly scorch the peppers, onions, and chicken until brown but still tender. For easier frying, cook only ¼ to ½ of the filling at a time, storing the finished filling in a separate covered pot. If desired, you can warm the tortillas—in a large frying pan, fry 2 tortillas at a time over medium-high heat, adding a small amount of margarine to the pan as needed. Fill tortillas with the beans and chicken/vegetable mixture. Cover with salsa and grated cheese, if desired. **Serves six.**

CORN, RICE AND BEANS

3 cups rice
1 tablespoon salt (optional)
2 chicken bouillon cubes
3 garlic cloves, minced
20 ounces kidney beans, drained

20 ounces yellow corn, drained
20 ounces chunky spaghetti sauce

In a large pot, bring the water to a boil. Add the rice and salt, if desired, and boil for 1 minute. Reduce heat to a simmer. Add the bouillon cubes and minced garlic and simmer, covered, until the rice is cooked. Drain any excess water. Add beans, corn, and spaghetti sauce. Stir over low heat until warm and ready to eat. Add spices as needed. **Serves six.**

FETTUCINI ALFREDO

Another pasta dish, the carbo lover's dream.

1½ pounds fettucini
½ cup powdered milk

2 tablespoons magarine
2 packages alfredo sauce mix

Bring a large pot of water to a boil. Add the noodles and cook until done, 12 to 15 minutes. While the pasta cooks, in a small pot combine the milk, margarine, and alfredo mix, and bring to a boil, stirring frequently. Reduce heat and simmer for 5 minutes. Cover and set aside until the noodles are ready. When the noodles are done, strain the noodles (reserving the water for hot chocolate, if desired), combine the noodles with the sauce, and serve. **Serves six.**

OUTDOOR BAKING

Baking in the backcountry is an art that requires patience. In order to bake, you need to be able to provide heat on both the top and the bottom of your pan. There are a number of cooking pans and devices, such as the Bake-Packer and the Outback Oven, that enable you to do this (see Chapter 2, "Equipment"). Another technique is to create a Dutch oven using a pot with a lid. You can do this on a fire if building a fire is appropriate or on a backpack stove: Place coals from the fire, or build a twig fire, on top of the lid. Lids designed with a rim to contain the fire make this much easier. Hold your hand about 6 inches above the coals. Your hand should feel hot but not burn. Once baking begins, periodically remove the lid and check your progress, and then quickly replace the lid. You will have to continue to feed the coals to maintain heat.

FOOD EQUIVALENTS

Here are some common menu items with information on how weight or volume converts to the number of servings:

Food Item	Weight/Amount	Volume	Servings
Instant rice	14 ounces	4 cups	12 servings
Macaroni noodles	1 pounds (6 cups)	8 cups cooked	8–12 servings
Oatmeal	1 ounce (⅓ cup)	1 cup cooked	1 serving
Flat noodles	6-ounce package	4 cups cooked	3 3-ounce servings
Drink mix	21 ounces	6 quarts	24 servings
Uncooked rice	1 cup	2½ cups cooked rice	3–5 servings
Potato buds	1⅓ ounces	⅓ cup buds	1 ½-cup serving
Parmesan cheese	8 ounces	2 cups	varies
Crackers (Stoned Wheat Thins)	10 ounces	56 crackers	varies
Pancake mix	1½ pounds (5 cups)	30 pancakes	10 servings
Tuna fish	12 ounces	2 cups	4 3-ounce servings
Hot chocolate	1 ounce (4 tablespoons)	1 cup	1 serving
Lipton Cup-o-Soup	1 envelope (14 grams)	2 cups	1 serving
Ramen noodles	3 ounces	2 cups	2 8-ounce servings
Peanut butter	40 ounces	5 cups	35 2-tablespoon servings

76

MEASUREMENT EQUIVALENTS

1 tablespoon	3 teaspoons				
1 fluid ounce	2 level tablespoons				
½ cup	8 level tablespoons				
1 cup	8 ounces	16 tablespoons	236 milliliters		
1 pint	2 cups	16 fluid ounces	473 milliliters		
1 quart	4 cups	2 pints	32 fluid ounces	946 milliliters	
1 gallon	16 cups	8 pints	4 quarts	128 fluid ounces	3.78 liters
1 pound	16 ounces	454 grams			

CHAPTER 4

Hygiene and Water Purification

Maintaining proper hygiene is a challenge in the wilderness. All too often, without the luxuries of hot and cold running water, toilets, showers, and dishwashers, we throw up our hands and surrender to the dirt that surrounds us, sometimes even wearing it like a badge of honor. Unfortunately, this attitude can lead to significant health problems. Bacterial infections can be spread through poor cleaning of cookware and poor personal hygiene. Get into the habit of using good cleaning practices for a safer and more enjoyable trip.

KEEPING YOURSELF CLEAN

One of the most common ways gastrointestinal illnesses are spread in the backcountry is through fecal-oral transmission. Fecal-borne pathogens get into your system through one of several routes:

- Direct contact with feces (even using toilet paper leaves germs on your hands)
- Indirect contact with hands that have contacted feces (shaking hands, for example)
- Contact with insects that have contacted feces
- Contact with contaminated drinking water

Imagine you stop for a rest along the trail. While the group snacks on GORP, Jim grabs the toilet kit and heads off the trail. He comes back to the group and unthinkingly reaches into the GORP bag to grab a handful. The next day, he and several others are showing signs of a gastrointestinal infection. The best way to reduce the risk of fecal-oral contamination is to utilize a strict handwashing protocol. Wash your hands before handling or cooking food and after each bowel movement (packed alcohol towelettes and unscented baby wipes are quick alternatives to handwashing—just remember to pack them out).

THE HAND-WASHING STATION

As soon as you get into camp (before you start cooking), set up a handwashing station (see Chapter 6, "Wilderness Travel"). You will need a collapsible water jug with a nozzle that can be easily opened or closed, a small bristle brush, and soap.

Orient the water jug with the nozzle facing down, perhaps hanging over the edge of a rock. Make sure that the area beneath the jug will be minimally impacted by the soap and water landing there (e.g., rock). Keep the soap and the hand brush next to the container. This station should be at least 200 feet (61 meters) from any water source. The cleaning procedure is as follows:

1. Wet your hands thoroughly.
2. Add a small amount of soap.
3. Lather up, especially your fingertips. Use a small hand brush to get out deep dirt and clean under fingernails (keeping your fingernails trimmed helps).
4. Rinse with water, then soap up a second time, brush, and rinse again.
5. Dry with a clean towel or bandanna.
6. Make sure you eliminate any signs of your handwashing station before you leave.

Another method is to hang a water jug from a tree. Just beneath the closable spout of the jug attach a small drinking cup with small holes in the bottom. Fill the cup with water and it will slowly trickle out the holes like a showerhead. One cupful of water will be enough to wet your hands. Then lather up. Filling of the cup again should give you enough water to rinse.

Using Soap

Soap poses a potential conflict between Leave No Trace camping and personal health. Most soaps contain phosphates, which, when released into water supplies, cause an increase in the growth of algae. These "algae blooms" quickly use up significant amounts of oxygen in the water. When the algae die off, the lowered oxygen content often kills other microorganisms, plants, and even fish. For this reason, *never* use soap directly in any water source (stream, river, or lake). If you are going to use soap, you should use only biodegradable soaps. The best soap to use is Klenz Gel Blue, which is both biodegradable and germicidal. Other biodegradable soaps (Campsuds or Dr. Bronner's Magic Soap) are good but don't kill germs, while other germicidal soaps like Betadine or Hibicleans are not biodegradable. Keep in mind that "biodegradable" means that the soap will *eventually* break down in the soil, not that it has zero impact. This is why all washing with soap should be done at least 200 feet (61 meters) from any water source. The soapy water filters through the ground slowly and breaks down before it reaches groundwater. Because biodegradable soap has some, albeit small, impact, whenever possible, it's good to avoid using soap. However, there are situations when soap or other cleaners are essential to maintaining good health.

PERSONAL BATHING

Getting the whole body clean is a bit more of a challenge in the backcountry. Collapsible water bags with shower attachments (shower bags), such as the MSR Dromedary Bag or a SunShower, make this process much easier. You can also use a large cooking pot. Make sure you have an adequate water supply available and ready at your washing site before you start (so you don't run screaming around camp with soap in your eyes, looking for water). Again, your washing site should be at least 200 feet (61 meters) from any water source and on a resilient spot that won't turn into a soapy mudpit as you wash. Here's the procedure:

- **Rinse** Rinse yourself off. If the only thing you have on you is dirt, you can rinse off in a stream. If you have "contaminants" on your skin (excessive body salt, sunscreen, insect repellent), do not rinse directly in a water source. Use the shower bag or cooking pot since *these chemicals can contaminate a water source* (see Tricks of the Trail, below). The rinse might be the end of your washing ritual if you don't plan to use soap.
- **Soap Up** Lather up, using the *least* amount of soap possible; you don't need a lot to get clean.
- **Final Rinse** Rinse yourself off with the shower bag or pots of water. The help of a friend always makes this easier. The soapy water will soak into the ground and be filtered by the soil.

🍁 TRICKS OF THE TRAIL

Body Salts and Toxic Chemicals After a day of hiking in hot weather, you may be covered with a variety of nasty things—loads of salt, sunscreen, and insect repellent. You know better than to wash with soap in a stream or lake, but people often forget about swimming. They see a cold pool and dive in. What you are leaving behind in that water is a load of body salts and possibly a toxic chemical slick. This can have a major impact on aquatic and other life, especially in small pools or potholes that, as they dry up, further concentrate this chemical pollution. In small pools in desert areas, even excess body salt can have an impact. If your body is carrying contaminants, rinse off on land before going in for a swim; otherwise don't dive in.

WASHING CLOTHES

Clothes usually can be adequately cleaned by thoroughly rinsing and wringing them out in the water. Don't rinse your clothes directly in a water source if they have been contaminated by chemicals (insect repellents, sunscreen).

Do not use soap on clothes, as it is difficult to rinse out all the soap, and residual soap on clothes can cause skin irritations and rashes.

WASHING DISHES, POTS, AND UTENSILS

Dishwashing is probably one of my least favorite chores on any camping trip. However, with the right equipment and a proper system, it can be done quickly and effectively. Depending on the environment, you may be able to avoid using soap by cleaning with natural materials (grasses, pinecones, sand, snow—see Chapter 5, "Leave No Trace Hiking and Camping"). Remember, natural materials can also contain germs. If you are using soap, make sure that you rinse dishes thoroughly, since soap residue can cause diarrhea (see Gastrointestinal Infections, page 316). Never wash dishes directly in a stream, lake, or river. If you are using soap and water is *not* in short supply, here is the recommended washing procedure:

CLEANING EQUIPMENT

- Pot
- Biodegradable soap
- Hard bristle scouring brush (easily rinsed out and does not collect food particles)

POT-CLEANING SYSTEM

1. Make sure people have gobbled up all the food from the pot before cleaning.
2. Boil a large pot of water; this can be the same water you use for hot drinks.
3. Pour some hot water into the pot as soon as people have finished eating.
4. Scour food residue from the pot using the brush or natural materials. Collect any large particles of food and pack them out with garbage. Depending on your ecosystem, pour any remaining liquid residue into a sump hole or scatter it (see Waste Water, page 112).
5. Add more hot water and a small amount of biodegradable soap to the pot. Wash using the brush.
6. Rinse thoroughly with hot water, and pour your water into a sump hole or scatter it. Then rinse again with hot water to make sure that all soap residue is gone. Once rinsed, the items can be air-dried.
7. Properly dispose of waste water after everything has been cleaned.

If the trip is for more than seven days, you should do a sterilization about once a week. Clean the items as described above, then prepare a rinse pot. Add a sterilization compound like chlorine bleach to a large pot of cool water (don't use hot water; it deactivates the sterilization chemical). Use the same proportion as you would for purifying water. Rinse all cups, spoons, pots, and utensils with this water and then air dry. Then rinse again with boiling water. Use a pot gripper to avoid scalding your hands.

🍁 TRICKS OF THE TRAIL

Cleaning Tips

- Having a hot drink at the end of the meal offers an opportunity for personal cups and spoons to be rinsed out with hot water.
- Oily foods will leave more of a residue that is difficult to clean out with natural materials. On a long trip, you may want to wash periodically with biodegradable soap to remove this oily layer, which could harbor bacteria.
- On coastal trips you can boil salt water for your first rinse. Then clean with lightly soapy water and follow with a chlorine or iodine rinse.
- Don't use scouring pads. They get gunked up with food particles and become a bacteria haven.

WOMEN'S HYGIENE ISSUES

Both women and men need to be comfortable talking about menstruation in the wilderness. For women who have not been in the backcountry before, the physical exertion of the trip can cause their period to start early or not to occur at all. Neither of these is uncommon or dangerous, but for a woman who is used to being very regular, it may be cause for concern.

Proper hygiene is important in minimizing the possibility of infections. Women should clean themselves daily, washing from front to back to keep fecal bacteria from entering the vagina or urethra. Wash your hands thoroughly after cleaning yourself. Premoistened, unscented cleaning towelettes can be a good way of preventing contamination from dirty hands. Keeping yourself odor-free is important when traveling in bear country.

TAMPONS VS. PADS

Some women have a definite preference for one form of protection. There are also some considerations for the backcountry. Tampons take up less space, may be more comfortable for strenuous hiking, and are preferable in bear country. To avoid infections, use tampons with applicators; tampons without applicators require scrupulously clean hands for insertion and are not recommended in the backcountry. Make sure you have sufficient supplies for the trip, even if you are not expecting your period. For some women, the increase in physical activity from daily hiking can bring on an early menstruation.

ON DISPOSAL OF TAMPONS, PADS, AND TOWELETTES

These should be packed out. Crush aspirin over soiled tampons and pads, then wrap them in tin foil. This will minimize the odor, which is particularly important in bear country, as bears may be attracted by the scent of blood. Hang in the bear bag (see Traveling in Bear Country, page 155).

WATER PURIFICATION

Dipping your head into a cold mountain stream and taking a long refreshing drink is an experience that has basically vanished from the wilderness areas of America. With the increased use of the wilderness there has also been an increase in the amount of bacteriological contamination of backcountry water supplies. The U.S. Environmental Protection Agency reports that 90 percent of the world's water is contaminated in some way. There are a variety of microscopic organisms that can contaminate water supplies and cause potentially serious, even fatal, illnesses among wilderness travelers. The major danger in the backcountry from these infections is fluid loss due to diarrhea and vomiting, which can lead to hypovolemic shock and possibly death (see Diarrhea or Vomiting, page 315; Fluid Electrolyte Replacement, page 286; Shock, page 238).

In order to drink the water, you should be prepared to treat it. There are numerous methods of water purification, described below in order of effectiveness. Remember, however, that infections can also be spread through poor personal hygiene, something that purifying your water won't prevent.

Biologically Contaminated vs. Toxic Water

Biologically contaminated water is water that contains microorganisms such as *Giardia* (a common microorganism that, if not killed, leads to intestinal disorders), bacteria, or viruses that can lead to infections (see Gastrointestinal Infections, page 316). *Toxic* water sources contain chemical contamination from pesticide runoffs, mine tailings, and so on. Boiling, filtering, or chemically treating water can remove or kill microorganisms, but it will *not* remove chemical toxins. This is also the case when using a solar still (see page 223).

BOILING

Boiling is the most certain way of killing all microorganisms. According to the Wilderness Medical Society, water temperatures above 160°F (70°C) kill all pathogens within 30 minutes and above 185°F (85°C) within a few minutes. So in the time it takes for the water to reach the boiling point (212°F or 100°C) from 160°F (70°C), all pathogens will be killed, even at high altitude. To be extra safe, let the water boil rapidly for one minute, especially at higher altitudes since water boils at a lower temperature (see page 68.)

CHEMICAL PURIFICATION

There are two types of chemical treatment: those using iodine and those using chlorine. There are a variety of products on the market, so follow the directions on the bottle. Be advised that many of the tablets have an expiration date and become ineffective after that point. Also, once the bottle has been opened, the tablets must be used within a certain period. When in doubt, buy a new bottle. Remember that chemical purification methods may only be partially effective, depending on the water temperature.

General Chemical Treatment Procedures

- The effectiveness of all chemical treatment of water is related to the temperature, pH level, and clarity of the water. Cloudy water often requires higher concentrations of chemical to disinfect.
- If the water is cloudy or filled with large particles, strain it, using a cloth, *before* treatment. Large particles, if swallowed, may be purified only "on the outside."
- Add the chemical to the water and swish it around to aid in dissolving. Splash some of the water with the chemical onto the lid and the threads of the water bottle so that all water areas are treated.
- The water should sit for *at least* 30 minutes after adding the chemical to allow purification to occur. If using tablets, let the water sit for 30 minutes *after* the tablet has dissolved.
- The colder the water, the less effective the chemical is as a purifying agent. Research has shown that at 50°F (10°C), only 90 percent of *Giardia* cysts were inactivated after 30 minutes of exposure. If the water temperature is below 40°F (4°C), double the treatment time before drinking. It is best if water is at least 60°F (16°C) before treating. You can place the water in the sun to warm it before treating.
- Chemically treated water can be made to taste better by pouring it back and forth between containers, after it has been adequately treated.

Other methods include adding a pinch of salt per quart or adding flavorings (e.g., lemonade mix, etc.) after the chemical treatment period.

Iodine Treatment

Iodine is light sensitive and must always be stored in a dark bottle. It works best if the water is over 68°F (21°C). Iodine has been shown to be more effect than chlorine-based treatments in inactivating *Giardia* cysts. *Be aware that some people are allergic to iodine and cannot use it as a form of water purification.* Persons with thyroid problems or on lithium, women over fifty, and pregnant women should consult their physician prior to using iodine for purification. Also, some people who are allergic to shellfish are also allergic to iodine. If someone cannot use iodine, use either a chlorine-based product or a non-iodine-based filter, such as the PUR Hiker Microfilter, MSR WaterWorks, or the Katadyn Water Filter.

Generally, the procedure is as follows:

- **Liquid 2% Tincture of Iodine** Add 5 drops per quart when the water is clear. Add 10 drops per quart when the water is cloudy.
- **Polar Pure Iodine Crystals** Fill the Polar Pure bottle with water and shake. The solution will be ready for use in one hour. Add the number of capfuls (per quart of water treated) listed on the bottle, based on the temperature of the iodine solution. The particle trap prevents crystals from getting into the water being treated. It is important to note that you are using the iodine *solution* to treat the water, not the iodine crystals. *The concentration of iodine in a crystal is poisonous and can burn tissue or eyes.* Let the treated water stand for 30 minutes before drinking. In order to destroy *Giardia* cysts, the drinking water must be at least 68°F (20°C). The water can be warmed in the sun before treating or hot water can be added. Refill the treatment bottle after use so that the solution will be ready one hour later. Crystals in the bottle make enough solution to treat about 2,000 quarts. Discard the bottle when empty.
- **Potable Aqua** This is an iodine tablet product. Follow the manufacturer's instructions for use.

Chlorine Treatment

Chlorine can be used for persons with iodine allergies or restrictions. Remember that water temperature, sediment level, and contact time are all elements in killing microorganisms in the water. Halazone is an example of a chlorine tablet product. To use, follow the manufacturer's instructions.

Backups Always have at least one backup method for water purification in case one fails. This can be any combination of methods. I'm the cautious type, so I always have two backup methods: water filter and 2% tincture of iodine or Polar Pure iodine crystals. And I can always boil the water. If boiling is your backup method, make sure you have enough fuel.

Fix the Taste Adding vitamin C (about 50 milligrams) to iodized water completely eliminates any taste or color of iodine. You must *wait until the iodine has purified* the water before adding the vitamin C. The vitamin C in drink mixes like Tang has the same effect.

FILTRATION

There are a number of devices on the market that filter out microorganisms. A water filter pumps water through a microscopic filter that is rated for a certain-size organism. The standard size rating is the micron (the period at the end of this sentence is about 600 microns). Depending on the micron rating of the filter, smaller organisms (like viruses) can pass through. Be cautious when selecting a filter. You should know what potential organisms you need to treat for. You don't want to go to an area where a virus like hepatitis A is present in the water (a problem in some developing countries) with a filter that will handle only a larger organism like *Giardia*.

Common microorganisms and the filter size needed:

Organism	Examples	General Size	Filter Type	Particle Size Rating
Protozoa	*Giardia, Cryptosporidium*	5 microns or larger	Water filter	1.0–4.0 microns
Bacteria	*Cholera, E. coli, Salmonella*	0.2–0.5 microns	Microfilter	0.2–1.0 microns
Viruses	Hepatitis A, rotavirus, Norwalk virus	0.004 microns	Water purifier	to 0.004 microns

There are two basic types of filters (descriptions of several popular models begin on the facing page).

- **Membrane Filters** use thin sheets with precisely sized pores that prevent objects larger than the pore size from passing through. *Pro*: Relatively easy to clean. *Con*: Clog more quickly than depth filters. **Example:** PŪR Hiker.
- **Depth Filters** use thick porous materials such as carbon or ceramic to trap particles as water flows through the material. *Pros*: Can be partially cleaned by backwashing. Activated carbon filters also remove a range of organic chemicals and heavy metals. *Con*: Rough treatment can crack the filter, rendering it useless. **Examples:** MSR WaterWorks II, Katadyn.

Note: There is a difference between a water *filter* and a water *purifier*. Filters do not filter out viruses, but there are water purifiers, like the PŪR Scout, that pass the water through both a filter and an iodine compound that kills any smaller organisms that have passed through the filter. These purifiers kill all microorganisms down to 0.004 microns; however, the filter should not be used by people who are allergic to iodine.

Common Practices for Using a Water Filter

- Filter the cleanest water you can find. Dirty water or water with large suspended particles will clog your filter more quickly.
- Prefilter the water either through a prefilter on the pump or strain it through a bandanna.
- If you must filter dirty water, let it stand overnight for particles to settle out.

❧ TRICKS OF THE TRAIL

Some water filters come as sealed cartridges, making it impossible to inspect the actual filter cartridge. If the filter takes a serious fall, it could crack internally. If the filter inside cracks, unfiltered water can flow through the crack. Treat your filter with care, and if it takes a significant impact, throw it away. Remember, any intake hose from a water filter has been submerged in unfiltered water. Treat this hose as "contaminated" and keep it in a separate plastic bag.

PŪR HIKER AND PŪR VOYAGER WATER FILTER

You should carefully read the product literature that comes with your PUR Hiker Filter for the latest instructions and information on how to assemble and

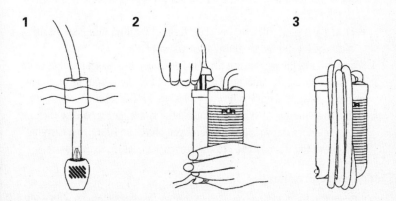

1 2 3

use your filter properly. The following instructions are reprinted with permission from PŪR product literature. (Author's additions are enclosed in brackets.)

The PŪR Hiker Microfilter produces drinking water free of protozoa (including *Giardia* and *Cryptosporidium*) and bacteria to 0.3 microns. It uses Anti-Clog technology to resist clogging and eliminate frequent cleaning. The Hiker is also available with an iodine cartridge which changes it from a water filter to a water purifier. When you first use a new microfilter or after the filter has been in storage, discard the first four cups of water (1 liter) to eliminate any stale taste.

1. **The First Time You Use the Hiker Microfilter** Attach the intake hose with the Acorn prefilter to the opening at the bottom of the Hiker. To flush the cartridge, place the Acorn prefilter in the water source, point the top of the cartridge toward the ground, and pump four cups of water. Then attach the output hose with the EasyFill Bottle Adapter to the top of the cartridge.

2. **For Normal Operation** Place the Acorn prefilter in the lake, stream, or other water source. Use the adjustable hose float to keep the prefilter off the bottom. Attach the EasyFill Bottle Adapter at the end of the output hose to a water bottle. Be careful not to let the Bottle Adapter fall into the dirt or unfiltered water.

3. Grasp the handle and pull the plunger up until it is fully extended. Push the handle down to expel the filtered water into your container. Repeat this pumping action until you have filtered the quantity of water you need. Pump at a comfortable rate, approximately 20 to 30 strokes per minute.
   - **Hint** Hold the Hiker with the intake hose pointing down toward water source while pumping. This will prevent accidentally constricting the hose.
   - **Hint** Each time you use the Hiker discard the first four cups [1 liter] of filtered water before filling your water bottle.

4. When you are finished using the Hiker, remove the Acorn prefilter from the water. Pump the unit until air comes out of the output hose, shake any excess water from the hoses, and wipe the Hiker with a clean dry cloth. Wrap the hoses vertically around the Hiker and secure by tucking the ends under the wrapped hoses. If you store the Hiker in a carrying case, leave the top unzipped to allow excess moisture to evaporate.

Cleaning the Prefilter

Occasionally the foam inside the Acorn prefilter becomes clogged with sediment. To clean this foam, pull the intake hose off the Acorn prefilter and remove the foam sponge. If the foam is difficult to grasp, use a small stick or the tine of a fork to pull it to the surface. Squeeze the foam several times under water to remove debris. Push the cleaned foam back into the Acorn prefilter until it is approximately flush with the top of the prefilter. Slip the hose over the barb on the prefilter until it fits snugly. (See figure below.)

Temporary Cartridge Restoration

The PŪR Hiker uses Anti-Clog Microfiltration Technology to produce a large volume of water without clogging. After repeated use, the microfilter in the cartridge will become clogged with sediment. When it becomes difficult to pump, it's time to change the cartridge. If you are in the field and do not have a replacement cartridge, you may temporarily restore some of the flow by cleaning the cartridge.

1. To begin the cleaning process, remove the Acorn prefilter from the lake, stream, or other water source. Pull the output hose off the top of the microfilter. Protect this hose from dirt and contamination. Grasp the top of the microfilter cartridge firmly with your fingertips and twist counterclockwise to unscrew the cartridge from the Hiker body. Pull the loose cartridge out. (See figure step 1.)

2. Hold the cartridge at the top and swish the cartridge in any relatively clear water to remove accumulated sediment. This rinsing water does not have to be purified. (See figure step 2.)
   Caution: Do not attempt to remove the protective screen and brush the microfilter surface. This may damage the cartridge and could result in unfiltered water.

3. Pour approximately ½ cup of water into the Hiker body. Swirl the water and rinse the inside of the body to remove any sand that has accumu-

lated. If you are filtering dirty water, it is normal for small amounts of sand to accumulate in the bottom of the filter body. (See figure step 3.)

4. Insert the cleaned cartridge into the Hiker and screw it into the body. Wash your hands to remove any microorganisms you may have come in contact with while cleaning the microfilter. (See figure step 4.)

5. Reattach the output hose to the top of the installed cartridge. Discard the first four cups of water you make.

6. Install a new cartridge when you get home.

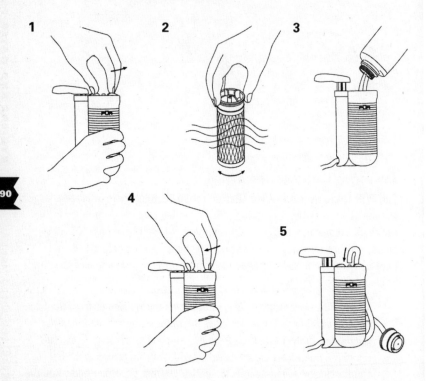

Storage

When you return from your trip, take a few minutes to properly prepare the Hiker for storage.

The Anti-Clog microfilter can be protected by pumping a very mild chlorine solution through it as described below.

1. Fill a quart container with water and add 2 teaspoons of ordinary household bleach.

2. Put the Acorn prefilter into the solution. Place the output hose in the container so the solution recycles back into the container.
3. Pump the filter for approximately 25 strokes or until you see the solution flowing freely back into the container.
4. Remove the prefilter from the container. Pump the Hiker for 5 to 10 strokes to remove any excess water.
5. With a soft cloth, dry the filter and the hoses.
6. Disconnect the input hose from the Hiker body. If you store the Hiker in a carrying case, leave the top unzipped to allow excess moisture to evaporate.

Note: Each time you use the Hiker after it has been in storage, discard the first four cups of water to get rid of any stale taste.

Tips for Improving Filter Performance

1. Filter the cleanest water available so less dirt is captured by the Anti-Clog cartridge and more water can be filtered before you need to replace the cartridge.
2. If you must filter dirty water, draw the water in advance and let it stand overnight or as long as possible before filtering. This will let the dirt settle out and extend the life of the cartridge.
3. Freezing will not damage the Hiker microfilter if the excess water has been pumped out of the filter. However, the microfilter must be completely thawed and free of ice to operate properly. Keep the microfilter in a plastic bag under your sleeping bag if you are in freezing conditions and need to operate it first thing in the morning.
4. You may notice a small amount of water in your new microfilter. This is a mild disinfecting solution used to test and protect your filter until you use it.

MSR WATERWORKS II AND MSR MINIWORKS WATER FILTERS

The MSR WaterWorks II and the MSR Miniworks water filters use the same cartridge. The WaterWorks II also contains a membrane which filters even smaller particles from the water. Other than the membrane, operation of the filters is essentially the same. You should carefully read the product literature that comes with your MSR Filter for the latest instructions and information on how to assemble and use your filter properly. The following instructions are reprinted with permission from MSR product literature. (Author's additions are enclosed in brackets.)

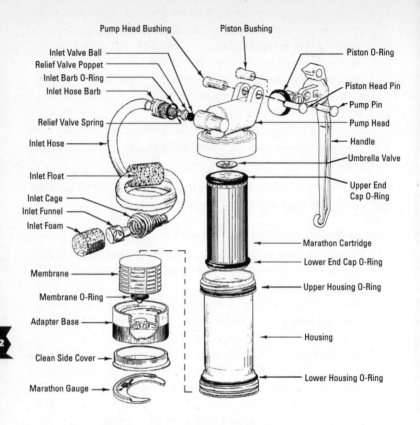

Pump Head Bushing   Piston Bushing

Inlet Valve Ball
Relief Valve Poppet
Inlet Barb O-Ring
Inlet Hose Barb

Relief Valve Spring

Inlet Hose

Inlet Float

Inlet Cage
Inlet Funnel
Inlet Foam

Membrane

Membrane O-Ring

Adapter Base

Clean Side Cover

Marathon Gauge

Piston O-Ring
Piston Head Pin
Pump Pin
Pump Head
Handle
Umbrella Valve
Upper End Cap O-Ring

Marathon Cartridge
Lower End Cap O-Ring
Upper Housing O-Ring

Housing

Lower Housing O-Ring

Using the WaterWorks II or Miniworks Filter

1. Unscrew the Clean Side Cover from the bottom of the filter.
2. Screw an MSR Dromedary Bag or wide-mouth Nalgene bottle onto the bottom of the filter for easy two-handed operation. Otherwise, place a clean container under the filter.
3. Put the Inlet Cage under water. Use the adjustable Float to keep the Hose above bottom sediments and below surface debris.
4. Pump the Handle no faster than 1 stroke per second. Although pumping faster does not alter effectiveness, it causes water to reverse through the Hose, increasing the number of pump strokes without increasing water flow. Pump at 1 stroke per second.
5. If the Pump Head has a trapped air bubble, this will slow the flow rate. To remove the air, turn the filter upside down while keeping the Hose under water. Pump the Handle 3 to 5 strokes until the air is purged, then return the filter upright for regular pumping.

6. After filtering, remove the Inlet Hose from water and pump the Handle to purge any remaining water. Screw the Clean Side Cover back onto the bottom of the filter.

Storing the Filter

When you return from your trip, air-dry the Marathon Cartridge and Membrane to keep the filter in good operating condition for your next use and to prevent organisms from growing:

- Unscrew the Pump Head. Unscrew the Adapter Base. Push the Marathon Cartridge up through the Housing.
- Air-dry the Marathon Cartridge and Membrane/Adapter Base assembly at room temperature. Wash and rinse other parts in clean water and dry thoroughly (3 to 5 days) before long-term storage.
- Another option is to sterilize the Marathon Cartridge by boiling. Do *not* boil the Membrane. Remove the End Cap O-Rings. Place the Marathon Cartridge in a pot deep enough to cover it. Bring the water to a rolling boil for 5 minutes. Remove the Cartridge when the water is cool. Do not handle the Marathon Cartridge when it is hot or the critical Lower End Cap seal may be lost. Air-dry the Cartridge before long-term storage.

Tips On Using Your MSR Filter

Always filter the clearest water available. Avoid filtering cloudy or muddy water (visibility less than 1 foot/30 cm), which can reduce the life of the Marathon Cartridge and Membrane.

- Let particles settle before filtering, especially when filtering poor-quality water. Fill a container with water and let it stand 1 to 2 minutes or as long as possible. Filter mid-container, then discard bottom sediments.
- Keep the Inlet Foam above bottom sediments by adjusting the Float at the end of the Hose.
- On longer trips, filter well or spring water when possible and bring along extra Marathon Cartridges, Membranes, and a Maintenance Kit.
- To keep the WaterWorks in good operating condition, air-dry the Marathon Cartridge and Membrane before long-term storage.
- After screwing the Pump Head onto the Housing, back it off slightly (about ⅛ of a turn) to make it easier to remove later.
- Lubricate the Piston O-Ring and Housing O-Rings regularly with a light film of food-grade lubricant (MSR Silicone Grease, lip balm, or petroleum jelly). Do not lubricate the Valves or plastic threads, since lubricant attracts dirt.

When Should I Clean the WaterWorks?

The MSR WaterWorks does not get harder to pump when it begins to clog. [Instead] you will notice that it takes longer and more pump strokes to filter a liter of water and that the flow rate has slowed. This is because the Relief Valve is reversing the dirty water back through the Inlet Hose. Clean the Marathon Cartridge when it takes more than $2\frac{1}{2}$ to $3\frac{1}{2}$ minutes or about 150 to 200 strokes to filter a liter of water (see "Marathon Cartridge," below).

Filter Element Maintenance

Marathon Cartridge If the Marathon Cartridge is clogged, unscrew the Pump Head and the Adapter Base/Membrane assembly. Push the cartridge up through the Housing. Brush the Marathon Cartridge with the Scrubbing Pad while rinsing it with water. Insert the Marathon Cartridge back into the Housing, making sure that both the Upper and Lower End Cap O-Rings are installed in the grooves on the Marathon Cartridge. Reassemble Adapter Base.

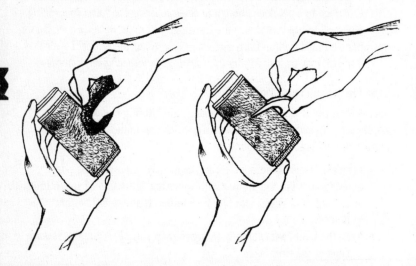

When Do I Replace the Marathon Cartridge? The Clean Side Cover has a Gauge attached to it. Slide this Gauge out from the Clean Side Cover. If the Gauge fits over the Marathon Cartridge, then it's time to replace it. You should get about 15 to 22 cleanings from the Marathon Cartridge. If you get significantly less than that, don't scrub the surface as hard or alternate cleanings using a less abrasive material, such as a soft cloth, to clean it. Note: Using a less abrasive method will give less recovery than the Scrubbing Pad.

Membrane Cartridge [WaterWorks II only] Although a clogged Membrane is not recoverable, you can use the WaterWorks II without the Membrane installed. The Marathon Cartridge removes bacteria, Protozoa (including *Giardia* and *Cryptosporidia*), as well as other particulate matter. The carbon core inside the Marathon Cartridge removes many dissolved chemicals, including iodine and chlorine, taste and odor compounds, and some pesticides and industrial pollutants.

Inlet Foam If the Handle is hard to pull or debris enters the Relief Valve or Umbrella Valve, clean the Inlet Foam. Slide the Inlet Cage up the Hose. Remove the Foam and rinse it like a sponge, then reinstall it through the center of the Funnel.

Troubleshooting

If water flows slowly, the filter seems clogged, or the pump stroke feels different than normal, here are some key areas to check:

Handle Is Hard to Push

- Clean the Marathon Cartridge with the Pad (see "Marathon Cartridge," opposite).
- Clogged Membrane (see "Membrane Cartridge," above). If the Membrane is clogged, you can still use the WaterWorks without the Membrane installed. [WaterWorks II only]
- Lubricate dry Piston O-Ring (see "Piston O-Ring," page 97).

Handle Feels Limp/No Resistance When Pumping

- Clean under the Umbrella Valve. If debris is entering the Valve, the Inlet Foam is not effectively installed. Clean and reinstall the Inlet Foam. Replace the Umbrella Valve if it is torn or damaged.
- Missing Inlet Valve Ball (in the Relief Valve Assembly). [Replacement parts are available from MSR.]
- Hole in the Inlet Hose. Remove damaged section or replace it.
- Damaged Inlet Barb O-Ring. Order a replacement O-Ring from MSR.

Handle Is Hard to Pull

- Clean the Inlet Foam (see "Inlet Foam," above). To prevent clogging, keep the Foam above bottom sediments using the Inlet Float.
- Make sure the Inlet Hose is not kinked or blocked.

Filter Squeaks When Pumping

- The Relief Valve is blowing due to filter clogging (see "Marathon Cartridge" and "Membrane Cartridge"). To determine which Cartridge is clogged, unscrew the Adapter Base/Membrane assembly. If the flow rate improves, the Membrane is clogged. If the flow rate is the same, clean the Marathon Cartridge.
- Pumping the Handle too fast. Pump no faster than 1 stroke per second.

Pump Stroke Is Normal but Water Flows Slowly

- Pumping Handle too fast. Pump the Handle no faster than 1 stroke per second for the most efficient filtering. Pumping too fast increases the number of pump strokes without increasing the flow rate because the Relief Valve reverses the water back out the Inlet Hose.
- Air bubble in the Pump Head. With the Inlet Cage under water, turn the WaterWorks upside down and pump the Handle to purge the air. To prevent air from entering, keep the Inlet Cage under water. Air in the Pump Head may also be caused by debris in the Valves (see "Umbrella Valve" and "Relief Valve Assembly," below).

Pump Head Maintenance

Umbrella Valve If the Handle feels limp on the pull stroke or air enters the Pump Head, debris may be caught under the Umbrella Valve. Unscrew the Pump Head and carefully rinse under the Umbrella Valve. Replace the Valve if it is torn or damaged.

Relief Valve Assembly If the Handle feels limp on the push stroke, debris may be caught in the Relief Valve or the Inlet Valve Ball is missing. Remove the Inlet Hose. Unscrew the Inlet Hose Barb from the Pump Head. Rinse the Relief Valve Poppet, Spring, and Ball. Reassemble.

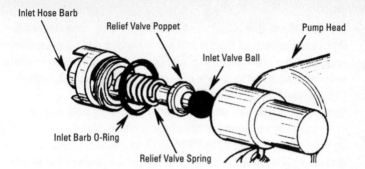

Inlet Hose Barb
Relief Valve Poppet
Inlet Valve Ball
Pump Head
Inlet Barb O-Ring
Relief Valve Spring

Piston O-Ring If the Handle drags when pumping, lubricate the Piston O-Ring. Pull out the Pump Head Pin and Bushing, then remove the Handle. Put a light film of food-grade lubricant (MSR Silicone Grease, lip balm, or petroleum jelly) on the Piston O-Ring. Reassemble. If water leaks from the Piston seal, replace the O-Ring.

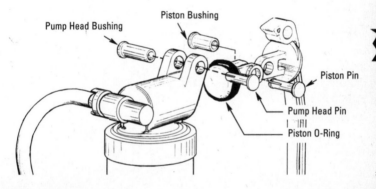

Pump Head Bushing
Piston Bushing
Piston Pin
Pump Head Pin
Piston O-Ring

Operating Suggestions

Killing Viruses Viruses need enough contact time with iodine to be effective. It is difficult to achieve this contact time with the fast flow rates that many portable water filters offer. To kill viruses, MSR recommends pretreating the water with iodine (follow manufacturer's instructions), then filtering the treated water through the WaterWorks. The carbon core of the Marathon Cartridge will remove the iodine taste and odor, leaving the water clear and good tasting.

Warnings

- The WaterWorks II or Miniworks Filters do not make salt water drinkable, do not remove all viruses (viruses not attached to 0.2 micron or larger particles) [0.3 microns or larger for the Miniworks], some chemicals and radioactive materials, or particles smaller than 0.2 microns [0.3 microns for the Miniworks].
- Keep the Inlet Hose and other dirty water parts away from filtered water containers to prevent contaminating filtered water.
- Do not expose any part of the Filters to chemicals other than as directed by MSR in these instructions. Do not use this product in any way other than one expressed in the instructions or specifically authorized in writing by MSR. Use only parts supplied by MSR.

CHAPTER 5

Leave No Trace Hiking and Camping

We all have different goals for traveling in the wilderness, but one thing that I think we all share is a desire to see it remain wild. Like any precious object, wilderness is fragile. The Leave No Trace Program, a national awareness campaign developed by the National Outdoor Leadership School and the U.S. Forest Service and other agencies, is designed to provide backcountry travelers with the most up-to-date information about how to travel in different wilderness ecosystems without disturbing the natural world. Look for the Leave No Trace logo on outdoor equipment and reading material, and use it as your source for the most up-to-date information about Leave No Trace practices. You can also call their hotline at 800-332-4100, or check out their Website at www.lnt.org. I want to thank all of the organizations who developed the program for granting permission to use the Leave No Trace materials in this chapter.

Leave No Trace camping is an attitude that should pervade every aspect of your trip, from your first look at the guidebook to assembling food and equipment, from where you hike to how you set up your campsite and clean up before you leave. Because each area is unique, consider the variables of each place—soil, vegetation, wildlife, moisture, the amount and type of use the area receives, and the overall effect of your presence. Only through such practices can we protect these wonderful places for ourselves and future backpackers.

GENERAL PRINCIPLES

The following apply to trips in any ecosystem.

- **Plan Ahead and Prepare** Good trip planning will properly prepare you for the environment you are entering.
- **Concentrate the Impact in High-Use Areas** When traveling in the wilderness, determine whether the area is already highly impacted. If so, you will have the least impact by continuing to use that highly impacted trail or campsite.
- **Spread the Use and Impact in Pristine Areas** You should avoid going to pristine areas unless you are committed to and can properly implement Leave No Trace techniques. If the area is pristine, showing little or no impact, then spread yourself out so that you don't create new worn trails, bald-spot campsites, and so on, that would encourage other people to also use the site and increase the impact to damaging levels.
- **Avoid Places Where Impact Is Just Beginning** If a site is show-

ing the beginning signs of impact, leave it alone and let it recover to its natural state.

- **Pack It In, Pack It Out** Whatever you bring in with you, you need to bring out. This means garbage, food waste, tampons, and so on. In some ecosystems, like the Colorado River in the Grand Canyon, this means *everything,* including feces and toilet paper. First, reduce litter at the source by buying in bulk, repackaging, and recycling packaging. *Trash* is all inorganic waste, mostly in the form of packaging. All trash should be brought out. Keep in mind that some trash items require special disposal (batteries are considered toxic waste and should not be thrown into municipal trash). Also, medical waste needs to be disposed of properly. *Garbage* is organic waste left over from cooking. The best solution is to plan your meals to avoid waste. Pack out whatever is left whenever possible.

- **Properly Dispose of What You Can't Pack Out** If you can't pack it out (waste water from washing or cooking, human waste), dispose of it properly for that ecosystem.

- **Don't Change the Environment** Don't alter the environment to suit you or bring back "souvenirs." You want the next person to see as much of the natural world as you did. For example, minimize any site alterations. Don't cut trenches around tents or tarps or build fire rings, shelters, or tables. Avoid damaging live trees and plants. Don't hammer nails into trees for hangers, cut wood from live trees, or tie tent or tarp guylines to branches, which can damage the tree. Be sensitive to picking flowers or foraging for wild edibles. Collect only a small amount over a broad area so as not to deplete local populations.

- **Leave What You Find** There is something incredibly exciting about finding an arrowhead or a deer skull in the wilderness. So why not leave it for the next person to be able to experience that same sense of excitement? Animal bones, petrified wood, and other natural objects should be left for others to appreciate. In many national parks, other federal lands, and hiking areas it is *illegal* to remove natural objects. The same is true for cultural artifacts such as pot shards, arrowheads, pots, and clothing items. The Archaeological Resources Protection Act makes it a crime to remove or disturb artifacts from any public lands.

- **Use Fire Responsibly** Fires, when used improperly, can create significant scarring of the land. Carefully evaluate both the need for a fire and your ability to create one that leaves no impact (see Campfires, page 112).

When you are planning your trip, think about a number of factors that can have an impact on the environment.

- **Group Size** The size of your group can have a significant impact on the area. Large groups (eight or more) may have less impact if they camp and travel in smaller units.
- **Ecosystem and Season** Learn all you can about the ecosystem to determine how best to deal with waste products (human waste and water waste). For example, the best way to dispose of human waste in the desert is very different from the best way in alpine and glacier areas. (See the Bibliography for resources about traveling in specific ecosystems.)
- **Camping Regulations** Know the specific camping regulations for the area. Some areas may not permit fires, may require you to camp only in certain locations, or may require you to pack out human waste.

GUIDELINES FOR TEMPERATE FOREST TRIPS

These guidelines are for subalpine, temperate forests in three-season (non-winter) conditions. High-altitude locations or winter conditions often require different techniques.

- **Respect Other Visitors' Need for Solitude** Travel quietly in the backcountry, whether hiking by trail or cross-country (the exception to this rule is when traveling in bear country; see Traveling in Bear Country, page 155). You will see more of your environment, wildlife will be less intimidated, and other hikers will appreciate the quiet. Avoid bright-colored clothing; wear earth colors to minimize your visual impact, especially if traveling with a group. (The exception is winter hiking or during hunting seasons when visibility becomes a safety concern.)
- **Litter** Pick up any litter that you can along your way. Consider it your gift to the next person who hikes down the trail.
- **Respect Wildlife** Remember that you are in their home and respect their needs for undisturbed territory. Disturbing animals can interfere with feeding or breeding behavior. When tracking wildlife for a photo or a closer look, stay downwind, avoid sudden motions, and don't chase or charge any animal. A good rule of thumb is, if you are close enough so that the animal is changing its behavior because of you, then you're too close. Resist the temptation to feed animals, even leaving bread crumbs and seeds for birds or squirrels. Feeding wildlife can upset the natural balance of their food chain, or make them dependent on human

food (bears are a major example). In addition, your leftovers may carry bacteria that are harmful to them.

BACKCOUNTRY TRAVEL

GENERAL TRAVEL GUIDELINES

When in the backcountry, hike on existing trails whenever possible. Existing trails have been designed to carry a high impact. Walk single file rather than abreast, so as not to widen trails. Walking side by side creates multiple lanes that make a trail look like an interstate highway. On wet or muddy stretches, slop right on through rather than skirt them, to avoid creating additional side trails and unnecessary erosion (good boots and gaiters will help). Never shortcut switchbacks. Switchbacks are designed to minimize erosion and ease ascent or descent on steep sections. Cutting off corners creates down-hill drainage patterns that can quickly erode a trail. If a trail is impassable, walk on as many hard surfaces as possible (rocks or sand) and notify area rangers of the difficulty.

When taking a rest break, move off the trail to a durable stopping place, such as a rock outcrop, sandy area, other nonvegetated place, or a location with durable vegetation, such as dry grassland.

TRAVEL GUIDELINES FOR PRISTINE OR HIGHLY FRAGILE AREAS

Hike in small groups. If you are hiking in pristine areas with no trails, it is usually best to spread out so as not to create a trail. If you are in a large group, break up into smaller groups of no more than six during the day. If this is not possible, try to find another route, even if it means hiking a longer distance.

Wherever possible, travel on durable surfaces such as rock, sand, snow, or stable nonvegetative surfaces. In extremely fragile areas, it may be best to walk single file so that only one path is created. This is especially true in desert areas where damage to fragile cryptogamic soil can have serious impact on the ecosystem. Avoid traveling in wet or boggy areas, on steep or unstable slopes, or where wildlife disturbance is likely. This may mean traveling "out of your way" in order to protect the environment.

If you choose a route without trails, do not blaze trees, build cairns, or leave messages in the dirt (except in an emergency situation). This can be extremely confusing and even dangerous for other backcountry travelers, who may become lost following your signs. Also, it can make their wilderness experience less enjoyable.

CAMPSITE SELECTION

According to the *Leave No Trace Skills and Ethics Series,* published by the National Outdoor Leadership School, selecting a campsite is probably the most difficult and critical aspect of Leave No Trace backcountry use. The choice requires the greatest use of judgment and information and involves trade-offs between environmental and social impacts. Before your trip, find out about local regulations for camping. For example, in the Catskills in New York, there is no camping above 3,500 feet (1,067 meters) and no camping within 150 feet (46 meters) of a trail. In some cases, a legal or required campsite may violate some of the general guidelines for a Leave No Trace camp; it may be right next to the trail or near water. This is especially true on corridor trails like the Appalachian Trail. Campsites in these areas are considered high-impact sacrifice areas and are selected by land managers as the best way of protecting the rest of the area.

HIGH-IMPACT CAMPSITES

- High-impact areas are frequently used campsites where most of the ground vegetation has been lost to trampling. Often these sites are equipped with fire rings and other signs of human activity. Whenever possible, choose an impacted site rather than risk creating a new site in a pristine area. If a site has already been highly impacted, it will show little or no additional impact, if you are careful. Continuing to use a high-impact campsite is the lesser of two evils—maintaining one high-impact site instead of creating a new site with new damage. On the other hand, by choosing to use a high-impact site you are in effect deciding to impact it further and not let it recover. Leave the high-impact site in good shape so that others will use it. A trashy camp might encourage the next group to create a new site nearby, further increasing impact.
- Low- or moderate-impact sites showing obvious signs of use may eventually recover if closed to human use. If you come to a campsite that is "just starting," don't camp there. Each time you camp on a site that is trying to recover, you interrupt or even reverse the recovery. It's best to look for a high-impact site. If you can't find one, it may be better to camp on an undisturbed site and carefully repair and camouflage the area to prevent other people from camping, thereby allowing the site to recover.

PRISTINE CAMPSITES

- A pristine campsite is one that shows no signs of previous camping. People often go looking for the "no one else has ever been here" campsite, not realizing how much damage they can do to the environment.

- When selecting a pristine campsite, your goal is to find a durable site that won't carry signs of your use. Select a site that has no vegetation (such as rock outcroppings, gravel bars, beaches, or snow) or durable vegetation cover (grassy areas, leaf-covered forest duff—with minimal plant seedlings). Avoid fragile areas.
- If you are with a group, be careful of overcamping. If you are staying in the same area for more than one night, it may be best to move your campsite (even if only a half a mile) before the impact becomes noticeable. Never spend more than a few days at a pristine backcountry campsite.
- When you leave, the pristine campsite should show *no* long-lasting signs of previous use. Cover up scuffed areas with duff or other natural materials to camouflage human activity and leave the area pristine for future visitors.

GENERAL CAMPSITE GUIDELINES

- Plan to arrive with enough daylight to set up a good Leave No Trace campsite. Arriving tired and in the dark makes this much more difficult.
- Choose a campsite *at least* 200 feet (61 meters) from water sources, trails, and scenic spots. The choicest camping spots are often prime areas for animal forage or for other hikers to stop and enjoy the view. Take the extra time to find a more camouflaged area. Be aware of animal runs that may be prime highways for the "local" inhabitants. This can be especially hazardous in bear country.
- Set up your camp thoughtfully in terms of traffic patterns. Think about where to situate the shelter, cooking area, handwashing area, bear-bag site, and where the water source is. Minimize the traffic patterns you create internally and how often you walk them to reduce your impact. Use the most durable part of the campsite as your kitchen area, and a place to store packs (large rocks are especially good).
- Lug-soled hiking boots can do considerable damage to soil and vegetation. Remove hiking boots and change to soft-soled shoes such as running shoes or sandals as soon as you get into camp to reduce damage to fragile vegetation and soil.
- A backcountry campsite should be reasonably organized. If you have laundry to dry or equipment to air out, make sure these items are not in sight of other campers or hikers.

- Avoid spending more than a few days at any one campsite unless it is an established campsite or sacrifice area.
- Leave the area as you found it or better. Do *not* trench around tents, cut live branches, or pull up plants to make a pleasant campsite. If you do clear the sleeping area of sticks, pinecones, and the like, be sure to scatter these items back over the area before you leave.

DEALING WITH HUMAN WASTE

Disposing of human waste in the wilderness must be done with good judgment and common sense. Newcomers to the wilderness are often embarrassed and unsure of how to cope without a bathroom. It's a subject that most of us don't spend a lot of time talking about. However, failure to learn the proper techniques can not only damage the environment but also lead to gastrointestinal illnesses from improper hygiene (see Gastrointestinal Infections, page 316; Keeping Yourself Clean, page 78). One of the sources for the spread of *Giardia* in backcountry water is the improper disposal of human feces.

Know your ecosystem and any camping regulations for the area. The techniques described here are the general recommendations for subalpine temperate forests in three-season conditions (spring, summer, and fall). In other ecosystems, such as glaciers, deserts, or seacoasts, the procedures may be very different. (For details on human waste disposal in other ecosystems, see the Bibliography.)

URINE

Urine is "relatively" free of microorganisms (unless the individual has a kidney or urinary tract infection). As a result, urine can be considered "clean," but not sterile. The major issues with urine are the smell it leaves and the concentration of salts left behind when the water evaporates, which can attract animals.

- **Location** Urinate wherever possible, but *at least 200 feet* (61 meters) —about 70 steps for an adult—away from the trail and any water sources. Urinate on rocks or in areas with thick humus layers and drainage (decaying leave piles, dirt piles). Try to avoid fragile vegetation, because the acidity of urine can affect plant growth. Avoid urinating on plants to prevent animals from defoliating or digging up the plants.
- **Techniques** Urinating outdoors is simpler for men than for women. In her book *How to Shit in the Woods,* Kathleen Meyer devotes a whole chapter to the subject. One technique for women is to sit on the edge

of a rock or log with your feet propped up on another rock or log in front. This prevents the dreaded problem of peeing in your boots. Another technique is to use a plastic funnel to direct the urine stream. Funnels such as the Sani-Fem are made specifically for women. These can also be used with a pee bottle in a tent (handy in bad storms or cold weather).

FECES

Human feces can create a *significant* impact on the environment. They can contaminate water sources, spread disease, and affect other wilderness travelers, both visually and by smell. Your goal should be to prevent contamination of the environment by limiting contact between your feces and insects, animals, people, and water sources. The other goal is to maximize the ability for the feces to decompose naturally.

Fecal decomposition is affected by a number of factors—sunlight (warmth), dryness, and soil bacteria—so different ecosystems require different methods of disposal. In three-season, subalpine temperate forests, the best answer is to bury feces or to pack it out. Burying slows down the decomposition, but it alleviates the problem of visual impact and reduces the chances for contaminating water sources. (For more information on human waste disposal in other ecosystems, see the Bibliography.)

Remember that bacteria is likely to be on your hands afterward, even when you've used toilet paper. Wash your hands after going to the bathroom to protect yourself and other members of your group from gastrointestinal infections.

Locations

Find a site far enough from the trail, away from water sources, perhaps with a good view, and with abundant natural toilet paper materials. In some cases, it can involve some pretty complicated acrobatics to keep your balance and do your business.

- **Outhouses** When available, you should always use existing outhouses. They concentrate use to minimize impact.
- **Catholes**—small pit toilets dug for individual use—are often the best solution. The cathole means smaller, less concentrated waste disposal, usually ensuring more rapid decomposition.
- **Latrines**—larger pit toilets dug for group use—are best if you're camping with a large group, or if you are remaining in the same camp over a number of days. This is not generally recommended, since this higher concentration of feces will decompose very slowly.

- **Smearing** Smearing is just what it sounds like. Deposit feces directly on the surface and smear it with a rock or stick. This spreads it out and maximizes contact with sun and wind to speed degradation. This presents a real Leave No Trace dilemma, however. Smearing should *only* be done in areas with very few visitors, where the chance of someone else discovering it is small. Otherwise, you risk not only visible and smell impact on another group, but also contamination if your bacteria are still living. This technique is best in ecosystems such as deserts or glaciers, where smearing will cause feces to degrade quickly (two weeks in some settings) and where burying significantly increases the time needed for decomposing.

🍁 TRICKS OF THE TRAIL

How Long Does It Last? You'd be surprised how long feces last in different environments. Research has also shown that buried feces can still contain live bacteria a year after burial. Feces left in glacial environments can remain there, unchanged, for years. This is one reason it is important to deposit feces well away from trails and campsites.

How to Dig a Cathole

- Catholes should be *at least 200 feet* (61 meters)—about 70 steps for an adult—away from streams, rivers, lakes, and marshy areas to allow human waste to decay and be filtered through the soil without polluting the water. You should be a significant distance from trails and campsites.
- Avoid digging a cathole in an obvious drainage area where water flow and erosion may unearth your deposit.
- Whenever possible, latrines or catholes should be dug in organic soil layers. Soil bacteria constitute major decomposing agents, so mix topsoil with feces before burial. In more sterile soils (sand or predominantly inorganic soil layers), subsurface moisture is often the critical factor, so feces should have a more shallow burial.
- Dig a hole 6 to 8 inches deep (15 to 20 centimeters) and 4 to 6 inches in diameter (10 to 15 centimeters). Bury the feces and cover the site with natural materials to disguise it.

Latrines are basically the same procedure, except you need to dig a deeper hole. Leave the pile of dirt next to the hole. After going to the bathroom, each person should cover the feces with a layer of dirt. Close up the latrine before it gets too full and scatter the extra dirt. Cover the site with natural materials to disguise it.

Packing Out Feces

In some locations (such as on canyon river trips) you may need to (or be required to) pack out feces. If you are backpacking, this means preparing a "poop station" each time you go to the bathroom. Here are a couple of standard procedures:

- A group approach is to go to the bathroom into a container that can be tightly sealed, like a surplus ammo box. Line the box with two paper or plastic bags. After each dump, toss in some kitty litter or chlorine bleach to help absorb odors. It's best if you don't urinate into the container. Close the lid after each use. When the bag gets full, use latex gloves to tie up both bags. Place them in another clean bag, seal it, and pack it out.
- The individual "pooper-scooper" approach is where each person collects their own. Turning a bag inside out and using it as a "glove" will allow you to pick up feces as long as it has a relatively solid consistency. You can help this process by going to the bathroom into a cathole, adding dirt or sand to help solidify the mass, and then picking it up with your bag.

After your trip, you need to properly dispose of feces. It's illegal to dump human waste in landfills, so you can't just toss it into the trash. Instead, dispose of feces in a sanitary waste disposal unit, either an RV collection site (found at many campgrounds), an outhouse, or a toilet. Paper bags are biodegradable and can be handled by waste disposal units, while plastic bags jam the suction units used to remove the waste. *Don't* put plastic bags in sanitary waste receptacles. If you prefer to use a plastic bag to store your poop, clean and disinfect the bag afterward (wearing plastic gloves) before disposing of it.

TOILET PAPER

The use of toilet paper is controversial in terms of Leave No Trace practice. You also need to consider hygiene practices (hand contamination may be more prevalent if you're using natural materials). It's not whether you use toilet paper, but what you do with it afterwards that has impact. If you use toilet paper, use biodegradable or recycled paper, avoid paper with dyes and perfumes, and never leave toilet paper out on the ground. Here are some disposal techniques:

- **Pack It Out** Place your toilet paper in a doubled plastic bag or doubled Ziploc bag that can be tightly sealed. Keep it in your pack away from food. Sprinkle some chlorine bleach in the bag to help kill bacteria and odor. When you get back to "civilization," dump the contents into an outhouse, portable toilet, R.V. receptacle, or other site. These sites cannot handle the plastic bag or container, so that must be disposed of separately. Take the container home, rinse it with water over your toilet, and rinse it with a bleach solution before disposing of it in regular trash.

- **Burying** If you bury your toilet paper, it will decompose more quickly if it is wet. Take along your water bottle and wet the paper down or urinate on it before you bury it.
- **Burning** Burning toilet paper is generally *not* recommended. Too many forest fires have been caused by sparks or smoldering paper. If you must burn toilet paper, burn it in a large metal can rather than on the ground. Always have a full water bottle with you to put out any flames.

🍁 TRICKS OF THE TRAIL

Use Care When Burning Toilet Paper! A number of years ago I was on a canoeing trip with friends on the Green River in Utah. As we approached the take-out at Spanish Bottom, the confluence of the Green and the Colorado River, we began to smell smoke. Soon clouds of thick gray smoke were pouring up the canyon. We were concerned about the fire flashing up-canyon toward us, so we paddled back upstream to camp. The next day we paddled down to find both sides of the canyon completely blackened by fire. A teenager from a camp had been burning his toilet paper when some hot ashes blew over into the dry grass and set it on fire. The fire spread quickly with the breeze, and sparks jumped across the river burning the other side of the canyon as well. Seeing the charred remains of cottonwood trees that had provided shade for over 100 years, and dead deer and other animals trapped by the fire, was a solemn reminder of the danger of burning toilet paper.

NATURAL MATERIALS

Some people prefer natural materials to toilet paper, because they can be used without damaging the environment. There are numerous choices, including leaves, pinecones, rocks, sticks, and snowballs. Natural materials should be disposed of with the feces (which in most cases means burying). If you are going to pack the feces out anyway, you might as well use toilet paper and pack it out as well. If you are going to use plants or other natural substances instead of toilet paper, you should observe these guidelines:

- Use smooth sticks, rounded rocks, or snow.
- Use dead plants or leaves before live ones.
- Know your plants and avoid using toxic plants like poison ivy, poison oak, stinging nettles, or other plants with toxins or barbs.

- Avoid plants with sharp edges, like reeds and bamboo, which can cause lacerations.
- Don't pick rare species or wildflowers.
- Gather plants or other materials from several locations *before* you start to go to the bathroom. That way you won't deplete a particular plant of too many leaves. Remove leaves only; don't uproot the entire plant.

🍁 **TRICKS OF THE TRAIL**

Life with Kids Hiking with young kids presents its own unique challenges. Diapers and baby wipes seem like they can take up your entire pack, both coming in and going out. Make sure that you bring as many as you will need and plan how you are going to pack them out.

OTHER TYPES OF WASTE

MEDICAL WASTE

Any medical equipment that has been contaminated with blood or body fluids is considered medical waste and must be disposed of properly. These items should be placed in a plastic bag marked "medical waste." Sprinkle some chlorine bleach into the bag to kill any microorganisms. Technically, this waste should *not* be disposed of with regular trash. If possible, place it in an appropriate medical waste container when you return from your trip. Be especially aware of any sharp objects (needles, scalpels) that might be in your medical waste, since getting a needle stick can transmit microorganisms. These should be placed in some rigid container or wrapped in cardboard and then taped to prevent injury to anyone handling the waste. (See also Women's Hygiene Issues, page 82.)

GARBAGE

Garbage is organic food waste from cooking, including such things as fruit and vegetable peelings, leftover food, and fish viscera. Here are some guidelines for dealing with garbage:

- Minimize garbage by repacking food before your trip.
- Avoid leftover food by carefully planning your meals.
- When leftovers do occur, they should be carried out in plastic bags.
- *Don't* try to burn food unless you have a hot fire and can completely incinerate the food. Partial burning leaves a charred food mess in the fire site.

- Food particles (like noodles) that inevitably occur in dish washing should be treated like bulk leftovers and carried out. Strain the dishwater through a bandanna to separate out these particles.
- Fish viscera are a natural part of the ecosystem. In high-use areas, your goal is to minimize other people seeing or smelling them, so consider burying them in a cathole. In remote areas with few visitors, you can scatter them widely, away from camp and trails, to reduce the chance that other people will come across them. In bear country, it is important to keep fish odors safely downwind and away from people, trails, and campsites. You can scatter or bury the entrails, but do so far away from human travel areas. Throwing fish viscera back into lakes and streams is controversial (except in places where bear danger is high and viscera can be thrown into deep water). Small mountain streams may be too cold to allow for rapid decomposition.
- If you are in bear country, garbage should be hung just like food.

WASTE WATER

There will always be some leftover water, either from cooking and pot cleaning or personal bathing. Strain any food particles out for garbage. Then dig a small sump hole at least 200 feet (61 meters) from any water source and pour the wastewater into the hole. Replace the dirt and disguise the area by covering it with natural materials. The other approach is to scatter the water over a wide area. (For details on wastewater disposal in other ecosystems, see the Bibliography.)

CAMPFIRES

Don't have a fire just to have a fire. Be aware of fire regulations in the area before you leave on your trip. In certain areas, or at certain times (like high forest-fire danger), fires may be illegal. Here are some guidelines for when it's appropriate to have a fire:

WHEN TO HAVE A FIRE

- When fire danger is low and you have abundant dead wood available, and . . .
- When there already is an established fire ring or conditions are such that you can create a Leave No Trace fire, or . . .
- When your stove is not working and hot food is important for the safety of the group, or . . .

- When there are first-aid considerations and you need a strong heat source for the safety of an individual or for the group.

WHEN NOT TO HAVE A FIRE

- When fire danger is moderate to high. If fire danger is *high,* you may even have to avoid using your stove.
- When there are restrictions against fires in certain locations or above certain altitudes.
- On windy days when sparks might be dangerous, especially when the woods are dry.
- When dead wood is scarce.
- When it's solely for group bonding. Although a fire can be a very enjoyable and useful part of group bonding, often sitting around a candle can achieve the same effect. Even building a fire with the best Leave No Trace techniques can result in serious impact on the land.

GENERAL GUIDELINES FOR FIRE BUILDING

Choose a resilient site for your fire or stove. Avoid lush meadows, fragile alpine tundra, and other areas that can be easily trampled. Try to disperse use throughout the campsite rather than concentrating activities in the cooking area. Good site selection and proper care of the cooking area and/or fire make effective camouflaging much easier.

Fires should be built far from tents, tarps, trees, branches, and underground root systems. They shouldn't be built in forest litter or duff. The organic layer of the soil is highly flammable and can actually smolder underground for weeks before erupting into a forest fire (see Forest Fires, page 214).

Fires should *not* be ringed with rocks (unless there already is an established fire ring). To avoid permanently blackening rocks, don't build fires against rock walls. Don't use river rocks for a fire ring. These rocks often contain minute amounts of water that, when heated, turn to steam and expand, causing the rocks to explode in the fire.

FIRES IN HIGHLY IMPACTED AREAS

Fire Rings

Often you may come upon one or more fire rings at a campsite. If you have decided to build a fire, use an existing ring. Pay careful attention to its location and avoid rings too close to water sources or other fragile areas. Make sure you burn your wood completely, scatter the coals and ashes, and clean all food waste and trash from the fire so that it will be attractive for the next visitors to use. If there is more than one ring at a highly impacted campsite, all but one should be dismantled.

If a fire ring is present in an area that otherwise appears to be pristine, the ring should be removed and not be used. When dismantling a fire ring, all stones should be widely dispersed and the ash should be scattered. The area should then be covered with duff and other natural materials to make it appear as natural as possible. If you can't have a safe fire without a fire ring, and there isn't one, don't have a fire.

FIRES IN PRISTINE AREAS

To create a safe fire you need to keep several factors in mind. First, never build a fire on the top layer of organic soil (the top layer of dirt full of decomposing organic material, usually 6 to 12 inches [15 to 30 centimeters] thick), as it is highly flammable and can smolder underground for weeks.

The heat from a fire can kill the microorganisms in organic soil responsible for breaking down organic matter, in effect sterilizing the soil. Instead, fires should be created on mineral soil, which contains no organic material, and is not flammable. Mineral soil is typically found below the top organic soil layer. It can also be found along riverbeds or under upturned trees or boulders. This is the reason it is less preferable to dig a fire pit. Even if you dig down to mineral soil for your fire, you are still going through the organic layer. The upper levels of the pit will be sterilized and roots and other organic material on the sides of the pit may smolder after your fire is out and buried.

114

METHODS OF FIRE BUILDING

The Mound Fire

Mound fires can be built virtually anywhere. All that is required is a trowel or shovel, a large stuff sack, and a ground cloth (optional). (See illustration.)

- Locate a good source of mineral soil. If possible, collect the mineral soil from an area that does not require excavation or is already disturbed (sandy areas, old streambeds, beneath the roots of a fallen tree).
- Turn the stuff sack inside out and fill it with mineral soil.
- Carry the soil to the fire site.
- Lay the ground cloth on the bare ground (optional) and create a circular, flat-topped mound of mineral soil 6 to 8 inches (15 to 20 centimeters) thick. The ground cloth is not essential but helps in the cleanup process after the fire is out. The mound insulates the ground below from the heat of the fire. The circumference of the mound should be

larger than the planned size of the fire to accommodate the spreading of coals.

- Build your fire on top of the mineral soil mound. Make sure it is thick enough to insulate the ground (and your ground cloth) from the heat. The heat of the fire still may be enough to kill grass or plants underneath, but it will not sterilize the soil, as would a fire built directly on the ground.
- After the fire is out, clean it up as described below. Return the mineral soil to its original location.

The Fire Pan

Another technique is to build your fire on something fireproof. Fire pans are metal pans originally developed for river running. The pan provides a site to build your fire and completely burn your wood. When finished, you just bury or scatter the ashes.

Fire Stoves

One step beyond fire pans are fire stoves, simple wood-burning stoves that cook more efficiently than an open fire. They confine or eliminate impacts to the ground beneath the fire, create a draft that concentrates heat, and provide a platform for pots to rest on. Some of these stoves evolved from research in developing countries to slow deforestation, a major issue in many areas where people still cook over open fires. There are a number of commercially produced fire stoves. They range from simple, collapsible boxes to units with battery-powered fans that perform as well as many petroleum-fueled stoves. Remember, using such stoves still requires firewood. If you are in an area where firewood is scarce, use a liquid-fuel stove.

FIREWOOD SELECTION

Select your firewood from small-diameter wood lying loose on the ground in order to ensure complete, efficient burning. Go by the rule of thumb—use only wood that is the diameter of the length of your thumb or smaller.

- No wood should be broken off standing trees, alive or dead. An area with discolored broken stubs and few branches within arm's reach loses much of its natural beauty.
- Saws and axes should not be used, as they leave unnecessary scars.
- If adequate wood is not available by acceptable means, use a stove. When in doubt, use a stove!
- Firewood is a valuable and often scarce resource, so it should not be wasted on excessively large fires. Build a small fire rather than a big fire, and just sit closer to it.

CLEANUP AFTER A FIRE

You should burn all wood completely. Plan ahead and stop feeding your fire long before you get ready for bed. Don't put a "night log" on your fire that will be only half-burned in the morning. For safety, never leave a fire unattended. When it's time for bed, the fire should be put out completely.

Let your fire burn down to white ash before dousing it thoroughly with water (untreated water is fine). Then stir all the way through the embers with a stick to make sure the fire is completely out. It should be cool enough to put your hand in the ashes when it's out. But *don't* put your hand in. White ashes mixed with water makes caustic lye, which can cause chemical burns (see Toxins, page 303).

The next morning, scatter as much of the ash as possible before burial to avoid an unnatural concentration of minerals in the fire pit. Bury the remaining ash. Scatter excess firewood before leaving your campsite.

AT THE END OF THE TRIP

All cans and plastic bottles that were used should be cleaned out and recycled after the trip. Cardboard containers from the original packaging should also be recycled. Depending on their condition, plastic bags or Ziploc bags can be washed out and reused. Medical waste should be disposed of properly.

CHAPTER 6
Wilderness Travel

Now that you're ready to hit the trail, this chapter will cover the basics of how to get around in the wilderness, from route-finding to river crossings. Let's start with the tools you will need to navigate.

MAPS AND MAP READING

A map is a two-dimensional representation of the three-dimensional world. All maps have some basic features in common, and map reading is about learning to understand this particular language. The most useful map for the backcountry is a *topographic map,* which uses markings called contour lines to simulate the three-dimensional topography of the land. The U.S. Geological Survey (USGS) makes quadrangle maps that cover areas in great detail. They are indispensable if you are traveling in a remote area because they are so specific. However, if the area has well-marked trails, local *trail maps* may be sufficient; they often have more accurate and up-to-date information on specific trails, making them easier to use. Below is a brief overview of the basic language of maps.

LATITUDE AND LONGITUDE

Maps are drawn based on latitude and longitude lines. Latitude lines run east and west and measure the distance in degrees north or south from the equator (0 degrees latitude). Longitude lines run north and south, meeting at the geographic poles. Longitude lines measure the distance in degrees east and west from the prime meridian (0 degrees longitude), which runs through Greenwich, England. The grid created by latitude and longitude lines allows us to calculate an exact point using these lines as X-axis and Y-axis coordinates.

Both latitude and longitude are measured in degrees (°), as follows:

$1° = 60$ minutes of arc
1 minute = 60 seconds of arc

Therefore:

$7\frac{1}{2}$ minutes = $\frac{1}{8}$ of 60 minutes = $\frac{1}{8}$ of a degree
15 minutes = $\frac{1}{4}$ of 60 minutes = $\frac{1}{4}$ of a degree

SCALE

All maps indicate their scales in the margin or in a legend. A scale of 1:250,000 (be it inches, feet, or meters) means that 1 unit on the map is the equivalent of 250,000 units in the real world. So one inch measured on the map would be the equivalent of 250,000 inches in the real world. Most USGS maps are either 1:24,000 (also known as 7½-minute maps) or 1:62,500 (known as 15-minute maps); the USGS is no longer issuing 15-minute maps, although the maps will remain in print for some time.

Map Size	Scale	Covers	Map to Landscape	Metric
7½ minute	1:24,000	⅛ of a degree	1 inch = 2,000 feet (⅜ mile) 2.64 inches = 1 mile	1 centimeter = 240 meters 4.16 centimeters = 1 kilometer
15 minute	1:62,500	¼ of a degree	1 inch = ~1 mile	1 centimeter = 625 meters

Standard USGS topographic maps are usually published in 7½-minute quadrangles. The map location is given by the latitude and longitude in the southeast (lower right) corner of the quadrangle. The date of the map is shown in the column following the map name; a second date indicates the latest revision. Maps are updated periodically from aerial photographs. Photo-revised maps have not been field-checked.

MAP COLORS

USGS topographic maps use the following colors to designate different features:

- Black—man-made features such as roads and buildings.
- Blue—water, lakes, rivers, streams.
- Brown—contour lines
- Green—areas with substantial vegetation (forest, scrub)
- White—areas with little or no vegetation; white is also used to depict permanent snowfields and glaciers
- Red—major highways and boundaries of public land areas
- Purple—features added to the map since the original survey: these are based on aerial photographs but have not been checked on land

MAP LEGEND

The map legend contains a number of important details. A USGS map includes latitude and longitude, as well as the names of the adjacent maps (depicted on the top, bottom, left side, right side, and the four corners of the map). The major features of the map legend are shown below.

- Map Name
- Year of Production and Revision
- General Location in State

- Next Adjacent Quadrangle Map
- Map Scale
- Distance Scale
- Contour Interval
- Magnetic Declination
- Latitude and Longitude

CONTOUR LINES

Contour lines depict the three-dimensional character of terrain on a two-dimensional surface. Just as isobars on weather maps depict lines of equal atmospheric pressure in the atmosphere, contour lines drawn on the map represent equal points of height above sea level.

Look at the three-dimensional drawing of the mountain above. Imagine that it is an island at low tide. Draw an imaginary line all around the island at the low tide level. Three hours later, as the tide has risen, draw another line at the water level and again three hours later. You will have created three contour lines, each with a different height above sea level. As you see in the figure, the three-dimensional shape of the mountain is mapped by calculating lines of equal elevation all around the mountain, and then transferring these lines onto the map.

On multicolored maps, contour lines are generally represented in brown. The map legend indicates the contour interval—the distance in feet (or meters) between each contour line. There will be heavier contour lines every fourth or fifth line, labeled with the height above sea level. The figure below illustrates how a variety of surface features can be identified from contour lines.

- Moderate slopes—contours are evenly spaced
- Steep slopes—contours are closely spaced
- Gentle slopes—contours are widely spaced
- Valleys—contours form a V shape pointing up the hill; these Vs are always an indication of a drainage path that could also be a stream or river
- Ridges—contours form a V shape pointing down the hill
- Summits—contours form circles
- Depressions—contours are circular with lines radiating to the center

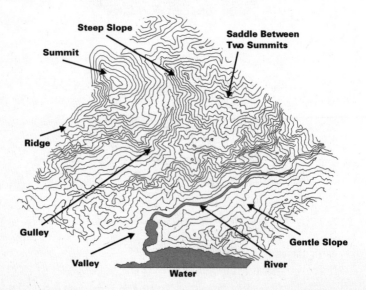

MEASURING DISTANCES

There are a number of ways to measure distance accurately on a map. One is to use a piece of string or flexible wire to trace the intended route. After tracing out your route, pull the string straight and measure it against the scale line in the map legend. Another method is to use a math compass set to a narrow distance on the map scale, such as ½ mile, and then "walk off" your route. It is a good idea to be conservative and add 5 to 10 percent of the total distance to account for features like switchbacks, which may not appear on the map. It's better to anticipate a longer route than a shorter one.

USING A COMPASS

The compass consists of a magnetized metal needle that floats on a pivot point. The needle orients to the magnetic field lines of the earth. The basic orienteering compass is composed of the following parts:

- Base plate
- Straight edge and ruler
- Direction of travel arrow
- Compass housing with 360-degree markings
- North label
- Index line
- Orienting arrow
- Magnetic needle (north end is red)

WHAT IS NORTH?

No, this is not a silly question. There are two types of north:

- **True North** Also known as geographic north or map north, this is marked as ★ on a topographic map. It is the geographic North Pole, where all longitude lines meet. All maps are laid out with true north directly at the top. Unfortunately for the wilderness traveler, true north is not at the same point on the earth as the magnetic North Pole, which is where a compass points.
- **Magnetic North** Think of the earth as a giant magnet (it is, actually). The shape of the earth's magnetic field is roughly the same shape as the field of a bar magnet. However, since the earth's magnetic field is inclined at about 11 degrees from the axis of the rotation of the earth, the earth's magnetic pole doesn't correspond to the geographic North Pole. Because the earth's core is molten, the magnetic field is

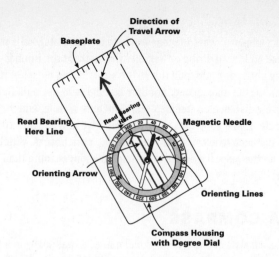

always shifting slightly. The red end of your compass needle is magnetized. Wherever you are, the earth's magnetic field causes the needle to rotate until it lies in the same direction as the earth's magnetic field. This is magnetic north (marked as MN on a topographic map that shows the magnetic lines for the United States). If you locate yourself at any point in the United States, your compass will orient itself parallel to the lines of magnetic force in that area. The following map shows some of the lines of magnetic force for the United States.

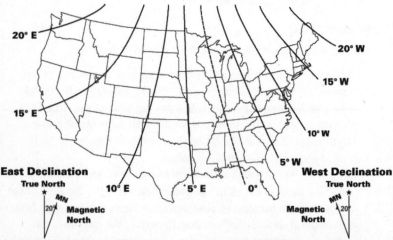

DECLINATION

As you can see in the illustration above, your location makes a great deal of difference in where the compass points. The angular difference between true north and magnetic north is known as the *declination,* and is marked in degrees on a map, as shown on the facing page. Depending on where you are, the angle between true north and magnetic north is different. In the United States, the angle of declination varies from about 20 degrees west in Maine to about 21 degrees east in Washington. The magnetic field lines of the earth are constantly changing, moving slowly westward (½ to 1 degree every five years), which is why it is important to have a recent map. An old map will show a declination that is no longer accurate, and all your calculations using that declination angle will be incorrect. As you will see, understanding this distinction becomes important when navigating with a map and a compass.

🍁 TRICKS OF THE TRAIL

Buy Your Compass for the Right Area In addition to the magnetic deviation east or west, compasses also show a vertical "dip" up and down. This dip varies in different parts of the world, and compasses are specially calibrated for that dip. Thus, a compass made for North America won't give accurate readings in South America.

USING A MAP AND COMPASS TOGETHER

In order to use your map and compass together, you need to know where you are in relation to magnetic north. You can find this information by looking on your map legend. If you look at the map of North America, you will see the line roughly marking 0 degrees declination. If you are *on* the line where the declination is 0 degrees, then you don't have to worry about this, since magnetic north and map north are equivalent. (Wouldn't it be nice if all your trips were on the 0 degree of declination line?) If you are to the right of that line, your compass will point toward the line (to the left), and hence the declination is to the west. If you are to the left of the line, your compass will also point toward the line (to the right), and hence the declination is to the east.

BEARINGS

The compass is used primarily to take bearings. A bearing is a horizontal angle measured *clockwise* from north (either magnetic north or true north) to some point (either a point on a map or a point in the real world). Bearings are used to locate your position or to reach a particular destination. If you are working from your map, it is called a *map bearing,* and the angle you are measuring is the angle measured clockwise from true north on your map to another point on the map. If you are taking a bearing from a real point on the landscape with a compass, you are using your compass to measure the angle clockwise from magnetic north to this point on the landscape. This is called a *magnetic bearing.* Remember that the bearing is measured clockwise. If you think of true north as 12 o'clock, then a bearing to the right of that (1 o'clock) is greater than true north, and a bearing to the left (11 o'clock) is less than true north.

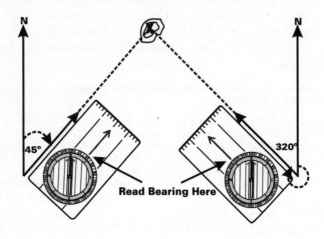

MAP BEARINGS AND MAGNETIC BEARINGS

Think of your map as an artist's rendition of the world. It displays true north, but it doesn't include magnetic fields as the real world does, so you need to make accommodations when going from your map to the real world. The real world doesn't have a true north, it's merely a construct of the map—so you have to make accommodations when going from the real world to your map. The basic principle is this: *to compensate for declination, you want the map bearing and the magnetic bearing to be equivalent.* If you are lucky enough to be on the line where the declination is 0 degrees, both are already equivalent. If you orient your map with your compass (see page 131) then you have made the two equivalent. If the map bearing and magnetic bearing are not equivalent, you will need to make your own bearing corrections by adding or subtracting the declination amount. That gives us four possible permutations to work with:

1. West Declination—Going from a Map Bearing to a Magnetic Bearing
2. West Declination—Going from a Magnetic Bearing to a Map Bearing
3. East Declination—Going from a Map Bearing to a Magnetic Bearing
4. East Declination—Going from a Magnetic Bearing to a Map Bearing

WEST DECLINATION

If your declination is west, then magnetic north is less than true north and the map bearing is less than the magnetic bearing. To make the two bearings equivalent, add or subtract the declination, as illustrated below:

- **Map Bearing to Magnetic Bearing** If you are taking a bearing from one point on your map to another point on the map with respect to true north, then you are working with the map bearing. To determine the magnetic bearing, *add* the declination to your map bearing to create the proper magnetic bearing. Map Bearing + Declination = Magnetic Bearing.
- **Magnetic Bearing to Map Bearing** If you use your compass to take a bearing from your current position to a point on the landscape, then you are working with the magnetic bearing. To determine your position on the map, *subtract* the declination from your magnetic compass bearing to create the proper map bearing. Magnetic Bearing − Declination = Map Bearing.

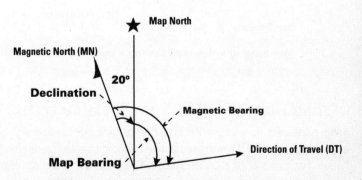

Map Bearing = Magnetic Bearing - Declination

EAST DECLINATION

If your declination is east, then magnetic north is greater than true north and the map bearing is greater than the magnetic bearing. As with west declination, you can make the two bearings equivalent by adding or subtracting the declination, as is illustrated below:

- **Map Bearing to Magnetic Bearing** If you are taking a bearing from one point on your map to another point on the map with respect to true north, then you are working with the map bearing. To determine the magnetic bearing, *subtract* the declination from your map bearing to create the proper magnetic bearing. Map Bearing − Declination = Magnetic Bearing.
- **Magnetic Bearing to Map Bearing** If you use your compass to take a bearing from your current position to a point on the landscape, then you are working with the magnetic bearing. To determine your position on the map, *add* the declination from your magnetic bearing to create the proper map bearing. Magnetic Bearing + Declination = Map Bearing.

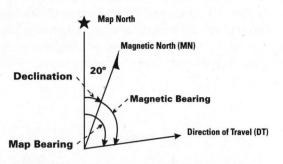

Map Bearing = Magnetic Bearing + Declination

ADJUSTING YOUR COMPASS FOR THE LOCAL DECLINATION

Some compasses have an outer degree ring that can be unlocked with either a set screw or a latch, allowing you to reset the compass to account for declination. For example, for a declination of 14 degrees east, rotate the degree dial to the right so that the magnetic needle points to 14 degrees instead of 360 degrees. Then you won't have to add or subtract for declination because your compass is aligned to true north. This means that when the compass needle is inside the orienting needle, the compass bearing that you read off your compass will be in relation to true north instead of magnetic north. If you have a fixed-ring compass, you can mark the declination angle on the compass ring with a piece of tape.

WILDERNESS NAVIGATION

Navigation in the wilderness means knowing your starting point, your destination, and identifying your route to get there.

CHECK YOUR POSITION REGULARLY

Keep your map and compass handy and refer to them every hour or so to locate your position (more often in low visibility). Keep track of your starting time, rest breaks, lunch stops, and general hiking pace. This will also give you an idea of how far you have traveled and whether you've planned your time accurately.

ORIENT THE MAP

You can eliminate the need to correct for declination if you use your compass to orient the map each time. As long as the map is oriented with respect to magnetic north, any bearings you take from map to compass or compass to map will be the same.

It is easiest to read a map if the map is oriented to the surrounding landscape. If you see a valley to your left, then the valley should show on the left on the map. You can do this by eye or with your compass.

Using Land Features

Lay the map on the ground or hold it horizontally. Rotate the map until recognized features on the ground roughly align with those on the map. This method is fine for general scouting of the area but not accurate enough for real navigation.

Using a Compass

1. Identify your declination from your map. If your declination is west of true north, subtract the declination from 360 degrees. If your declination is east of true north, add the declination to 0 degrees.
2. Set the compass at the correct declination bearing so that you compensate for declination.
3. Place your compass on the map so that the edge of the baseplate lies parallel to the east or west edge of the map, with the direction of travel arrow pointing toward the north edge of the map.

4. Holding the compass on the map, rotate the map *with* the compass until the north end of the magnetic needle points to the N on the compass housing (i.e., the red north end of the magnetic needle and the orienting arrow align). This is often referred to as "boxing the needle" since the magnetic needle is inside the "box" formed by the orienting arrow. The map is now oriented with respect to magnetic north. This means that the compass needle direction north is the same as true north on the map. You can also place the compass on the map so that the edge of the base plate lies along the magnetic north indicator line on the map legend at the bottom, and rotate the map as described above. This may give you a more accurate orientation for your map.

IDENTIFY TERRAIN FEATURES

With the map oriented, look around for prominent landscape features such as mountains, valleys, lakes, and rivers. Make a mental note of the geographical features you will be traveling along and seeing during the day. If you keep the terrain in your mind, you will have a general sense of your location just by looking around.

REAL-LIFE SCENARIOS

Below are some common backcountry scenarios. Let's see how you can use your map and compass to navigate you and your group.

SCENARIO 1—LOST IN THE FOG

After hiking along the trail, you bushwhack off to a nearby alpine lake to camp. When you wake up the next morning, you are fogged in. You know where you are on the map, but you can't seem to find your way out. Take a bearing on your map from your known campsite back to a known point on the trail that you can identify on the map, then follow your bearing through the fog. (You might also decide to wait out the fog if there is difficult terrain to traverse.) Should you decide to find your way out, here are the procedures:

Taking a Bearing from the Map (Map Not Oriented)

1. Lay the long edge of the compass base plate on the map, making a line from your starting point to your destination (from point X to point Y in the drawing). Since the base plate is parallel to the direction of travel arrow, the base plate can be used to set the direction to your destination.

2. Holding the base plate steady, rotate the compass housing until the compass orienting lines and orienting arrow are pointing to true north. You see the orienting lines and arrow are parallel to the line from A to B as well as the map gridlines.

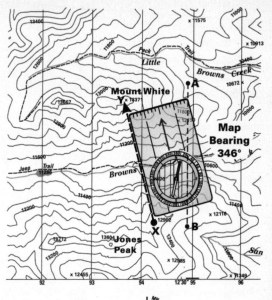

Map Bearing 346°

3. Read the bearing (in degrees) from the degree dial at the index line on the compass base plate (marked "Read bearing here"). In this case the bearing is 346 degrees.

Taking a Bearing from the Map
(Map Oriented to Magnetic North)

1. Orient the map with the compass (see page 129).
2. Lay the long edge of the compass base plate on the map, making a line from your starting point to your destination (from point X to point Y in the drawing). Since the base plate is parallel to the direction of travel arrow, the base plate can be used to set the direction to your destination.
3. Holding the base plate steady, rotate the compass housing until the orienting arrow coincides with the north end of the magnetic needle (known as "boxing the arrow").
4. Read the bearing (in degrees) from the degree dial at the index line on the compass base plate (marked "Read bearing here"). In this case the bearing is 338 degrees.

SCENARIO 2—HEADING TO THE SUMMIT

After hiking along the trail, you find a good campsite that is marked on the map. You see a summit ridge above the tree line that looks like a great place for photographs, but there's a valley thick with Douglas fir between you and the summit. Take a bearing from your current position to the summit and use that to travel through the forest. Here's your procedure:

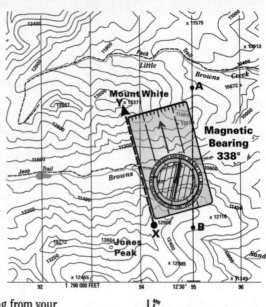

Taking a Bearing from the Land

1. Point the direction of travel arrow of the compass toward your destination on the land.
2. Rotate the compass housing until the north-orienting arrow of the compass housing lines up with the red magnetic needle. This is referred to as "boxing the needle," since you want the needle to be inside the box defined by the orienting arrow. The north-orienting arrow must be pointing in the same direction as the red (north) magnetic needle.
3. Read the bearing (in degrees) from the degree dial at the index line on the compass base plate (marked "Read bearing here").

Walking a Bearing Taken from the Land

1. After taking the bearing, as described above, hold the compass level and in front of you, so that the direction of travel arrow points to the your destination.
2. Rotate your whole body until the magnetic needle lies directly over the

orienting arrow. Make sure the north end of the magnetic needle points to N on the compass housing. The direction of travel arrow on the compass now points to your destination.

3. Keeping the needle "boxed," walk to your destination.

Walking a Bearing Taken from the Map

To walk a bearing taken from the map, you may need to correct for declination if you did not orient the map to magnetic north before you took your bearing. Once you have corrected for declination, follow the same procedure as indicated above for walking a bearing taken from the land.

Techniques for Walking a Bearing

Sometimes you can't see your final destination. One method for walking a bearing is to use line of sight.

- **Line of Sight** Walk to an obvious landmark—a tree or boulder that is directly on the bearing. Then take another bearing from that landmark to the next obvious landmark and walk to that. Keep it up until you reach your destination. By going to intermediate landmarks, you minimize the chances of veering off your bearing.

SCENARIO 3—RETRACING YOUR STEPS TO CAMP

You made it to the summit and took some great photos. Now it's time to get back to your campsite. You could just retrace your steps using a back bearing (see page 135) back to your location, but there is bound to be some error—when you hit the trail, where will you be in relation to your campsite? Your best bet is to intentionally aim off. Retrace your steps using a back bearing (see page 134). However, it's often hard to follow an exact compass course. You veer off course somewhat. This is known as lateral drift (see page 134). To prevent this problem, you can intentionally aim off to one side or the other of your target.

- **Back Bearings** Back bearings can be used either to retrace your steps or to check your position while hiking a bearing. Before you start to walk on your bearing, take a bearing 180 degrees off of the bearing you are going to walk. For example, if you are going to walk a bearing of 45 degrees, shoot a bearing directly opposite your course of 225 degrees. Locate a landmark along this opposite bearing. Walk a short distance along your bearing, then turn around and shoot a bearing back to the landmark along the opposite bearing. If you are on course, the bearing to the landmark behind you will still read 180 degrees off your bearing (in this case 225 degrees). If it doesn't, you are off course. Sailors and sea kayakers use back bearings all the time to check for lateral drift from wind or currents. Back bearings are also useful if you are heading out to a destination and then returning along the same line of travel. There are two basic formulas for calculating a back bearing:

When the Direction of Travel Bearing Is Less Than 180 Degrees

Back Bearing = 180° + Direction of Travel Bearing
BB = 180° + B
225° = 180° + 45°

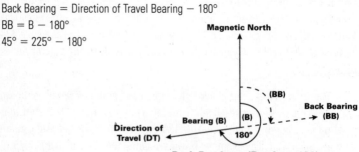

Back Bearing = (180 + Bearing)

When the Direction of Travel Bearing Is Greater Than 180 Degrees

If the direction of travel bearing is *more* than 180 degrees you use a different formula (otherwise you will have a back bearing greater than 360 degrees). If we reverse the example above, let's say your bearing is 225 degrees (which is greater than 180 degrees), then your back bearing works out to 45 degrees.

Back Bearing = Direction of Travel Bearing − 180°
BB = B − 180°
45° = 225° − 180°

Back Bearing = (Bearing - 180)

- **Aiming Off** It is almost imposble to walk a perfect bearing. In most cases your error can be anywhere from 3 to 5 degrees. This is known as lateral drift. Being off by just a few degrees can make a major difference after several miles. Therefore, rather than head straight for your target,

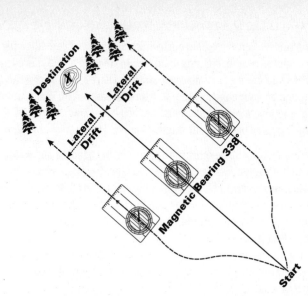

it's best to deliberately aim to the left or right side of your target. Then you will know whether to turn right or left and walk to the target.

• **Baselines** Baselines are helpful because they provide a large target. A baseline is a reference line that lies across your course. It can be a trail, cliff face, road, stream, or other feature. You can combine a baseline with aiming off to help navigate. Find a baseline near your destination, then aim off of it. When you hit the baseline, you'll know which direction to turn to walk along the baseline to your destination.

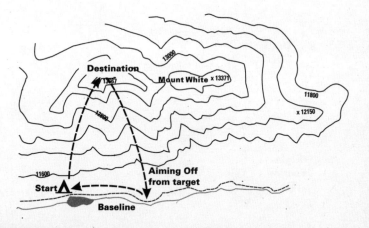

SCENARIO 4—THERE'S A SWAMP IN YOUR WAY

You're in the midst of an incredible bushwhack and you've been diligently
following a compass course, sighting from tree to tree. Up ahead there is a
clearing. When you enter it, you discover swamp. There's no way you can go
straight through on your compass course. The best method for maintaining
your course is to hike a rectangle around the bog by making a series of 90
degree turns from and back to your original course. Here's your procedure:

1. Set a new bearing 90 degrees from your original heading and walk
   along that until you have cleared the obstacle along that axis. Remember, whenever you turn 90 degrees to the right, add 90 degrees to your
   course. Whenever you turn to the left, subtract 90 degrees from your
   course. While walking, maintain a count of paces or track the distance
   you travel until your next turn.

2. You have passed the length of the obstacle, so go back onto your original bearing, parallel to your original course, until you clear the obstacle
   along that axis.

3. Now that you've passed the width of the obstacle, it's time to hike
   back to your original line of travel. Set a bearing 90 degrees back to
   your original bearing and walk the same number of paces as you did
   in step 1.

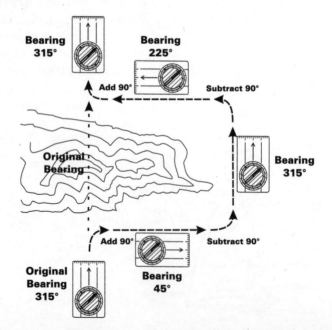

4. Once you have walked off the correct distance, you are ready for your last 90 degree turn. Now turn back to your original bearing. You will be along your original line of travel.

SCENARIO 5—NOW YOU ARE REALLY LOST

You're hiking off-trail through the broad alpine valleys, having a deep philosophical conversation about our connection with nature—so deep that you have lost some of your own connection with nature. Suddenly, you look around and realize you don't know where you are; this alpine valley looks a lot like the last one you came through. Okay, so you're lost.

Triangulation

Triangulation is used to locate your position when two or more prominent landmarks are visible. Even if you are not sure where you are, you can find your approximate position, as long as you can identify at least two prominent landmarks (mountain, end of a lake, bridge), both on the land and on your map (see figure on page 138). Here's your procedure:

1. Orient the map with your compass (see page 129).
2. Look around and locate prominent landmarks.
3. Find the landmarks on the map (preferably at least 90 degrees apart).
4. Take a compass bearing between you and the first landmark.
5. Place the compass on the map so that one corner of the base plate rests on the landmark.
6. Keeping the corner of the base plate on the landmark, turn the entire compass on the map until the orienting arrow and the compass needle point to north on the map.
7. Draw a line on the map along the edge of the base plate from the landmark. You can use the compass base plate to extend the line on either side of the landmark, intersecting the prominent landmark symbol. Your position is somewhere along this line. You've drawn a line from B through A.
8. Repeat this procedure for the other prominent landmark. The second landmark should be as close to 90 degrees from the first as possible. Draw a line from C to the other line. Your approximate position is where the two lines intersect at point A. This is only a rough approximation of your position.
9. To make it even more accurate, you can repeat this process a third time to show an area bounded by three lines. You should be located within this triangle.

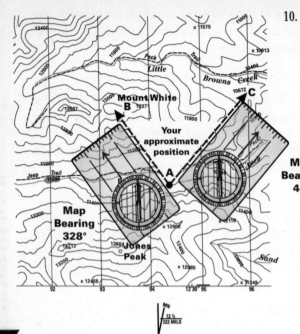

10. If you are located on a prominent feature marked on the map, such as a ridge, stream, or road, that feature can serve as a baseline and only one calculation from a prominent landmark should be necessary. Your position will be approximately where the drawn line intersects this linear feature or baseline.

OTHER NAVIGATION TOOLS

ALTIMETERS

An altimeter can be a useful navigation tool. It measures the local atmospheric pressure of the air, just like a barometer, expressed in inches or millibars of mercury. The altimeter displays the current altitude on a dial with a needle or a digital display. Since atmospheric pressure is constantly changing due to weather, you must calibrate the altimeter by first setting it when you are at a known elevation, preferably at the trailhead. As you hike, the altimeter shows the current altitude, and any increase or decrease in elevation. In order to maintain accurate readings, you should use your map to recalibrate your altimeter several times each day. One good trick is to recalibrate, or at least look at, your altimeter reading before you go to bed. If the altimeter reads higher the next morning, then the atmospheric pressure has gone up during the night, typically indicating stable or improving weather. If the altimeter reads lower, then the atmospheric pressure is falling, indicating potentially stormy weather.

You can use your altimeter in navigation as another source to help you locate your position. If you are hiking up a trail and it crosses a particular altitude (contour line) at only one point, then you know exactly where you are. In other situations, you know that you are somewhere along a contour line that lies at that altitude (elevation). Other clues may help you pin down exactly where you are along that contour line.

Inexpensive altimeters and altimeter watches are available for $50 to $200 but can be prone to inaccuracies owing to temperature. Let your altimeter adjust to the ambient air temperature before taking a reading. More expensive altimeters that automatically correct for temperature changes can run over $200.

WATCHES

Wearing a watch in the backcountry is a matter of personal wilderness ethics. Many people like to let nature set the pace of the day rather than wear a watch. I may not wear my watch, but I always bring one along. There are too many times when I have needed one: to get an accurate check on how fast I am hiking; to see if my time control plan is correct; and especially in first-aid and emergency situations, where timing vital signs and knowing the exact time may be essential in proper diagnosis and treatment. Watches can also be used to determine basic direction (see page 179).

GLOBAL POSITIONING SYSTEM UNITS

The Global Positioning System (GPS) is a network of satellites in orbit above the earth. A GPS unit is basically a radio receiver, available as a hand-held unit that's easily transportable in the backcountry. The satellites transmit to the GPS unit, which interpolates the signals into latitude and longitude data that are displayed on the unit. Typically, signals from three satellites are needed to identify a specific position (just like triangulation) and a fourth to interpolate altitude. GPS units are accurate to within a few hundred feet of your actual location. Although they can be used to determine your location very accurately and establish compass courses, don't rely on a GPS unit in place of knowledge of map and compass. Battery failure, damage to the GPS unit, or even leaving it behind at a rest stop could get you lost if you don't have good map and compass skills. GPS units are particularly useful in locations where there few landmarks (for example, long canoeing trips in the northern Canadian tundra).

BACKCOUNTRY TRAVEL

CONSERVING YOUR ENERGY

Over a long day of hiking, it is important to pace yourself and conserve energy. Fatigue can significantly increase accident potential (see page 193) and drain you of energy reserves that can be crucial in an emergency. Here are a few things to keep in mind:

- Each day you should examine your route to identify difficult stretches, schedule rest stops, and estimate travel time to spots along the route (see Chapter 1, "Trip Planning"). On a multiday trip, look at your estimates for previous days—how did your estimates compare with your actual travel time? If there is a significant difference, you may want to rethink your route.
- During the day, be aware of whether or not the group is moving according to schedule, and be prepared to alter the schedule if necessary.
- If possible, try to set your route to avoid difficult ascents or descents at the very end of the day when everyone is tired.
- Be especially cognizant of the least experienced or least physically fit hikers, and adjust the hike accordingly.
- Make sure that you leave enough energy (and time) to set up a good Leave No Trace camp at the end of the day.

SPLITTING A LARGE GROUP INTO SMALLER GROUPS

A large group can be fun, but also cumbersome and slow. Here are some considerations to help you determine ideal group size:

- **Traveling as One Large Group** *Pro:* Can be a positive group-building experience. Keeps equipment and human resources close at hand at all times. Minimizes chance of individuals getting lost. Good for groups with less experience. *Con:* Greater visual and noise impact on area and other hikers. Requires adjustment to a common pace (which could also be positive). Can compromise Leave No Trace travel, particularly if the area is pristine.
- **Splitting Into Smaller Groups** *Pro:* Reduces impact. Each subgroup still has its own equipment and human resources. Allows subgroups to form by common pace. *Con:* May need more equipment, such as first-aid kits, maps, and compasses. Each subgroup needs to have a higher level of backcountry skill. Need to establish rendezvous points and definitive backup plans in case subgroups get separated.

- **Traveling Alone** *Pro:* Unique wilderness experience. Reduces impact. *Con:* No other human resources immediately available if an emergency arises. May need more equipment, such as map and compass for each person. Each person must have good backcountry skills. Group may get too spread out.

Rendezvous Times

Whenever you travel in subgroups or alone, you need to establish clear rendezvous points and times, and stick to them. You may want to set a specific order within the group, such as having a lead person and a sweep person. Typically the sweep person carries the first-aid kit and has training in first aid. That way, the first-aid kit is always "moving toward" all of the group members.

PACE

A basic test for the right hiking pace is if you can keep it up all day with 5-minute rest periods every hour. If you find that you need to stop or slow down more often, then you are probably hiking too fast for the trail conditions, your pack weight, or the weather. When you are hiking as a group, you need to find a pace that everyone can handle.

Finding the right pace for a group of varying abilities can be a big challenge. Body metabolism, physical condition, age, experience, size, weight, and pack weight will all have an effect on the speed at which each individual can hike. Try to set a pace at an aerobic level that everyone can maintain over a long period.

Slinky Effect

What often happens is that faster people in a group gravitate to the head and slower people end up at the rear. This can be demoralizing to a slower person and difficult because she or he catches up to the group, which has stopped to rest, and then the group takes off again, "dragging" the slower person along so that person gets little or no rest (the "Slinky effect"). If the group gets too spread out, people in the rear may miss trail junctions or turns, and get lost, or people in front may take a wrong turn.

Modifying the Pace

It is generally better to have slower people in the front or in the middle of the group so that the group adjusts its pace to those individuals. You want to have everyone in the group hiking at a comfortable level of exertion. Faster

people should be sensitive to the pace of slower people and adjust themselves accordingly. Taking weight from a slower person and giving it to a
faster person helps to even out the pace.

REST BREAKS

All groups need to take regular rest breaks in order to hike effectively
throughout the day. A good schedule is about 5 minutes of rest for every hour
of hiking, which will minimize lactic acid buildup in the body. Lactic acid is
the by-product created when your muscles burn glucose while you exercise;
it's what causes your muscles to feel sore. When you stop, lactic acid continues to be produced and remains in the system. If you stop for less than 5
minutes, this buildup is not a problem. If you stop for more than 5 minutes,
you may begin to feel muscle soreness and tightening. In that case it is best
to extend the stop to 20 to 30 minutes to allow the excess lactic acid to be
cleared out of your system.

You should encourage everyone to rehydrate at every break. Make sure
that *every* break doesn't turn into a long one, or you will need to replan your
route for the day. Keep regular rest breaks in mind as part of your trip
planning.

HIKING TECHNIQUES

Rhythmic Breathing

Just as you need to balance the load in your pack to carry it properly, so you
need to balance the load on your cardiovascular system to hike efficiently
and without strain. Keeping an even breathing rate and pattern is one of the
best ways to monitor and control your energy output while hiking. You
should move at a pace that allows you to breathe comfortably and be able to
speak. If you are gasping for breath or if you can't keep up a conversation,
then you are hiking too fast.

The best way to control your pace is to synchronize the rhythm of your
walking with the rhythm of your breathing. As the cardiovascular load
increases from steep terrain, altitude, humid weather, or a heavier pack,
your breathing rate will increase. Slow your pace to regain that controlled
breathing rate. When the load is reduced, you can pick up your pace again.
This is the same principle that all endurance athletes use to maintain high
exercise output over a long period of time.

🍁 TRICKS OF THE TRAIL

Are You Pushing Yourself Too Hard? One good way to know how hard you are breathing is to determine the length of time it takes you to recover after you stop hiking. As soon as you stop, time your breathing rate and see how long it takes to slow down to what you would consider a resting rate (both in terms of breaths per minute and depth of inhalation). For most people (without cardiovascular or respiratory problems) 2 to 3 minutes or less is an average recovery time after moderate exercise. If it takes you significantly longer than this, then you are pushing harder than you should.

The Rest Step

The rest step is designed to rest the leg muscles, which are doing most of the work in hiking. As you shift your weight onto each leg, briefly lock the knee. While the knee is locked, your body weight is supported by your skeletal system rather than your leg muscles.

On very steep sections you can rest on the locked leg for several seconds or longer for greater rest. Keep in mind that the rest step should be used in conjunction with rhythmic breathing. Use the rest step to keep your breathing rate easy. If you go up steep sections too fast, your body won't get enough oxygen and you will switch from aerobic respiration to anaerobic respiration. High-altitude mountaineers take one rest step and hold it for 30 seconds or more in order to keep their breathing rate down. It is usually better to use the rest step and continue to push slowly up a short, steep incline than to stop in the middle and then need to get started again.

Walking Uphill

When going up a steep incline, stand up straight. This puts you in the best position to recover, should you lose your balance. Try to keep your steps small (aim for a maximum elevation gain of 6 inches per step). The energy expended on two small steps is less than that for one long one. If possible, avoid going up and down over rocks or logs in stair-step fashion. If an obstacle is large, go around it if possible (but don't step off the trail to avoid obstacles). Remember to use the rest step.

Walking Downhill

Walking downhill can be the most strenuous part of your journey. It is also more hazardous than walking uphill. Leaning backward with a heavy pack puts the hiker off-balance and places a lot of strain on legs, knees, and ankles. There is increased friction if your foot slides forward in your boot, which can lead to blisters. To help reduce friction, lace your boots up tightly, particularly around the ankle, before a long downhill stretch. Also, on steep downhills, improperly fitted boots can cause "toe jams" or "boot bang" where your toes smash repeatedly into the front of the boot, which can cause blood blisters and even toenail loss. Take small controlled steps. Try to avoid jamming your feet into the ground as you walk and keep your knees slightly bent to absorb the shock.

Much of the force in downhill hiking is absorbed in the knee joint, which must be prevented from flexing too far forward. This can cause knee pain and even long-term orthopedic problems. Some hikers use hiking staffs or a pair of trekking poles (like ski poles). This transfers some of the load onto your arms, relieving your knees.

❧ TRICKS OF THE TRAIL

How To Avoid Repetitive Stress Injuries A repetitive stress injury (RSI) comes from the accumulated stress of repeating the same action. When hiking with a heavy pack, loads on the body are magnified and simple actions that don't normally present a problem can lead to RSIs. Avoid such injuries by varying your actions. For example, I was on a backpacking trip on the Appalachian Trail in Pennsylvania, notorious for its rocks. In order to keep my balance I was constantly "hop-stepping" from rock to rock. The instinctive approach is to take a shorter "lead" step with the foot on your dominant side and then take a longer step with the other foot. So I was always taking the first, short step with my right foot, and then a longer step with my left. This meant coming down harder each time on the left leg. After many hours of this pattern, I developed pain and tenderness in the left knee. Now I know to vary my stepping pattern.

STRETCHES FOR HIKING

Hiking is just like any other sport. It is essential to warm up and to stretch muscles *before* using them to avoid stress and possible injury. Most of us forget to stretch. We are so busy breaking camp and trying to get going that we don't take 5 minutes to warm up. If it's early in the trip, you are probably using muscles that haven't been used for a while, and stretching makes them warm and loose. Stretching at the end of the day will keep your muscles from tightening up.

Keep the following in mind whenever you stretch:

- Before stretching in the morning, get your heart rate up by doing several minutes of aerobic activity—jog around camp, jump in place, swing your arms, do push-ups. It is important to have increased blood flow to the muscles *before* you start to stretch.

- Stretch slowly and smoothly; do not bounce or force stretches.
- Breathe in a controlled, slow rhythm. With each exhalation, let yourself move deeper into the stretch.
- Count during each stretch for concentration.

Everyone has his or her own repertoire of stretches. Go with your favorites and learn some from the other people on your trip. Here are a few good stretches for backpacking, from Robert Anderson's excellent book *Stretching*.

Squat

Quadriceps

Hamstrings

- **Squat** (lower back, shins, Achilles tendon) Squat with your heels 8 to 12 inches apart and toes slightly pointed out. Your knees should be over your toes and arms hanging down in the middle. Hold for 30 seconds. This may be done best on a downhill slant, with something supporting the midback, or by holding on to a tree.
- **Hamstrings** Sitting with one leg straight out, toes pointing up, and the other leg bent, slowly bend from the hip without curling back. Hold where you feel the stretch in the hamstrings. Do both legs.
- **Quadriceps Stretch** Stand on one foot. Grasp the ankle of the other leg with your opposite hand and pull the foot up to your butt. You should push forward with your knee so that the thigh stays vertical. Do both legs.

Hamstrings

Calf and Achilles Tendon

Groin

- **Calf and Achilles Stretch** Keep your toes pointing forward with the heel on ground and the knee straight. Keeping your back straight, lean forward onto a tree and stretch calf muscles and Achilles. This also feels good with a bent knee. Do both legs.
- **Groin Stretch** Lie on your back with your knees bent and the soles of your feet together. Let the pull of gravity do the stretching.

OFF-TRAIL HIKING

Off-trail hiking can be one of the most spectacular wilderness experiences. But it must be done thoughtfully and responsibly, maintaining the highest Leave No Trace standards. Don't hike off-trail to places reachable by trails; this only creates new trails, which damage the wilderness.

GENERAL BACKCOUNTRY CONDITIONS

When hiking off-trail, determine the best Leave No Trace approach for the area—should you spread the group out or hike together? Leave as few signs of your passing as possible. Also, determine if the off-trail area is an open vista where navigational landmarks will be easily seen or if it is dense forest or scrub where constant compass navigation may be necessary.

Consult the map carefully for landmarks, to minimize your chances of getting lost. Since the route may zigzag to avoid thicker vegetation, you may need to take repeated compass bearings. Be aware that hiking off-trail can be slow and exhausting. If you are truly bushwhacking through dense forest or scrub, hiking may take over twice as long as usual. Keep this in mind when estimating your travel time.

HIKING THROUGH THICK FOREST OR BRUSH

- Choose routes that offer the least resistance by constantly looking for openings ahead.
- Move slowly and deliberately, at well-spaced intervals.
- Remember that following one another too closely can result in people being slapped in the face by whiplashed branches.
- Part the limbs by pushing gently with your arms and shoulders instead of plowing through with your body and pack. This helps minimize damage to branches and foliage.
- Minimize loose gear hanging on the outside of your pack, which can get snagged on branches.
- Avoid breaking off limbs. Some off-trail hikes are used more than once,

and you rob others of the feeling of wilderness if they know people have been there before.

HIKING ON ROCKY SLOPES AND TRAILS

- **Minimize Rockfall Exposure** If there is a significant amount of loose rock on a slope, it is best to spread the group out. A rock kicked loose from above can be a dangerous missile heading toward hikers below. Try to avoid having one person hike directly above another (if the trail goes straight up or switchbacks up the slope, you may not be able to prevent this).
- **Yell Rock** If you kick loose a rock of any size, yell "rock," loudly. Even a small rock can hurt hikers below.
- **Duck** If you hear someone directly above you yelling "rock," try to turn and face downslope so that your pack is between you and the rock. Don't look straight up into the oncoming missile.
- **Take Your Time** If you are ascending or descending a rocky or boulder-filled slope, make sure that the rock you are stepping on is solid before you shift your full body weight onto it.
- **Vary Your Stride** There is a natural tendency to leap from rock to rock. Usually we take a short "feeler" step with the foot on our dominant side, and then take a longer step with the other leg. Vary the leg you use for takeoff and landing to prevent repetitive stress injury.
- **Trust Your Boots** When descending steep rock bands you want maximum friction, which you achieve by having the greatest surface contact between your boot soles and the rock. Try to keep your feet flat on the rock and bend heavily at the knees. Keep your center of gravity directly over your feet, with your back reasonably straight. When ascending steep rock bands, the same principle applies. Keep your feet as flat as you can. When the slope angle gets very steep, you won't be able to bend your ankles far enough forward to keep your feet flat. Using a diagonal traverse across the rock face instead of hiking straight up may decrease the angle, or you may have to climb more on the toes of your boots. Still, make sure that your center of gravity is over your feet. If you lean too far forward or too far back, you may fall over.

HIKING ON SNOW AND ICE

In many mountain areas there are permanent snowfields and glaciers, which can be very dangerous. If you are traveling to these areas, make sure you have the proper equipment and training to deal with hazards like avalanches, crevasses, and ice fall. A full explanation of hiking on snow and ice is beyond the scope of this book. Talk to rangers before you go, peruse the Bibliography for resources (see page 358), and get training.

- On steep snow carry an ice axe and know how to do a self-arrest. *Mountaineering: The Freedom of the Hills* by the Mountaineers offers a thorough explanation of this procedure.
- North-facing snow or ice slopes get less sun and stay harder longer during the day. They also tend to have snow later in the season. South-facing slopes melt out sooner. (Reverse these trends in the Southern Hemisphere.) Based on where you are going, the terrain, the extent of snow cover, and the time of day, one slope may be better than another to hike on.
- It's often best to climb in the early hours of the day before the sun has warmed the slopes too much, or you may find yourself up to your waist in soft, wet snow. Also, as the slopes get warmer, the snow softens and the risk of rockfall and icefall increases.
- The harder the snow or ice, the greater your chance for a fall. An ice axe and skill in self-arrest are essential for steeper areas or where the consequences of a fall are considerable (such as crevasses).

- On steep slopes, it may be too slippery to walk up flat-footed. If the snow is soft enough, you can kick steps into the snow. Kicking steps can be tiring, so make it as efficient as you can. Bend your lower leg at the knee and lift your heel to near 90 degrees. Let your foot drop and the weight of gravity will do most of the work of driving the toe of your boot into the snow. Test the step with some pressure before committing all your weight to it. This also compresses the step into a better platform. You will need to kick steps that are usable by everyone in the group, so take short steps. Periodically rotate the lead. The lead person stops, kicks steps to the side, and moves out of the way. The second person takes the lead and the previous leader falls in at the end of the group, for a well-earned rest.
- Avalanches aren't just a winter phenomenon. Warm conditions can often cause wet snow slides that can be extremely dangerous. Check with local rangers about avalanche hazard before you go. When you are on the trail, look for signs of slide activity. It's best to stay off slopes from 30 to 45 degrees.

CROSSING RIVERS

River and stream crossings can be one of the most potentially uncontrollable and dangerous situations during your trip. Fast-moving water and cold water temperature can lead to drowning or hypothermia. More backpackers are killed in stream crossings than die from snakebites. Great care must be given to planning and executing any swiftwater crossing. The two biggest factors affecting the potential danger of a crossing are the speed of the current and the depth of the river, but there are a number of other potential hazards:

- **Cold Water** can lead to hypothermia.
- **Foot Entrapment** occurs when a foot is caught on the river bottom and the person is pushed over by the force of the current. Often the force of the current keeps the person from being able to stand up and the individual is held under water—a potential drowning situation.
- **Strainers** are submerged branches that will hold a person swept against them—a potential drowning situation.
- **Undercut Banks and Rocks** are also places where you can be trapped by fast water—a potential drowning situation.

Making Judgments About River Crossings

You must examine the river carefully to determine what potential hazards exist in crossing. Base your decision whether to cross on a careful examination of the river, possible crossing sites, and the strengths and abilities of the people in the group. Don't let a desire to continue on a particular route push you to make a crossing that is too hazardous. Here are the questions you should ask about any river crossing:

- How deep is the water?
- How fast is it moving? (Test by tossing a stick into the main current.)
- What is the water temperature?
- Are there obstacles or hazards downstream?
- Will all members of this group be able to safely negotiate this crossing?

Red Flags for River Crossings

If you see any of these conditions, then the crossing is potentially dangerous and you should seriously consider not crossing at that location (look for another spot or don't cross at all):

- The river is in flood
- The river is moving very quickly and you can't determine its depth.

- The river level is higher than your knees and moving very swiftly
- The river has large floating logs and obstructions that could hit hikers
- There is a significant hazard downstream, near the crossing site (i.e., strainer, waterfall)

Choosing a Site to Cross

Hike up and down along the river to find the safest place to cross. Pick a wide, shallow stretch of water free from obstructions (boulders, partially submerged logs) and with gradual banks to facilitate easy entry and exit. Try to avoid crossing at a bend in the river, because the water is usually deeper and faster on the outside of the bend and the outside bank may be steep and difficult to climb. Outside bends are also often undercut by the current and are a prime location for strainers. The stretch of water *below* the crossing point should be long and shallow (a pool to drift into safely in case of mishap).

Important Crossing Considerations

- Keep your boots on (or change into sneakers or sandals, if available). They protect your feet and provide ankle support. Take your socks off to keep them dry.
- Keep your pack on, but *undo the hip belt and sternum strap* so that you can jettison the pack quickly if necessary.
- Move only one foot at a time while making sure that the other foot is firmly placed, and shuffle along rather than taking big steps. Keep moving slowly. Do not cross your legs. Feel the bottom before you commit your weight to the foot (to feel and avoid potholes).
- Use a hiking stick as a third leg, especially on the upstream side; walking sticks can be useful to test for dropoffs and rocks.
- Always *face upstream* while crossing solo. *If you face downstream, the force of the river could cause your legs to buckle underneath you.*
- If you feel your foot begin to get caught, fall over into the water to pull the foot out to avoid entrapment. Trying to stand may "set" the foot into the entrapment and place you at greater risk.
- If you lose your footing and are swept away, shrug out of your shoulder straps and jettison your pack. Float downstream on your back, feet first with toes on the surface. This position prevents foot entrapment. Use your legs as shock absorbers to fend off river obstacles. Actively swim to the shoreline. Do not let yourself be swept against logs or fallen trees, as you might be pinned against them. If you can't avoid being swept onto a river obstacle, try to clamber up onto it so that your head remains above water.

- Be extremely careful when walking on logs or boulder hopping. These places are likely to be slippery, and falls resulting in injuries are common.
- Baggy pants offer greater resistance to the water and increase your chances of being pulled over.
- In any deep river crossing, position someone below the crossing point as a safety backup. Remember the principles of basic lifesaving—reach for the person, throw her a line or floating object, and go in after her only as a last resort.

Crossing with a Rope

One end of a rope is securely anchored near the shoreline 5 to 6 feet (1.5 to 1.8 meters) above the river at a good crossing location. The other end is held by a strong member of the group. The first person to cross holds the end of the rope above the water as he or she crosses; *never tie into a rope.* The person crossing and the one on the shore should both try to keep the rope up out of the water to prevent drag. Upon reaching the other side, the crossing person anchors the free end to trees or rocks 5 to 6 feet (1.5 to 1.8 meters) above the river, creating a fixed rope across the river. Using the rope as a hand line, group members, standing on the downstream side of the rope, face upstream and, holding on to the rope, shuffle across the river. The last person (also a strong group member) unties that end of the rope and crosses as the first person.

Crossing Without a Rope

There are a variety of methods for crossing a stream without a rope:

- **Triangle Method** With three people you can create a "triangle of support." Each person faces inward and links arms at the shoulders, with their feet spread apart. The person who is downstream stays stationary while the other two rotate around that person. Then a new person becomes the downstream person and the triangle rotation continues.

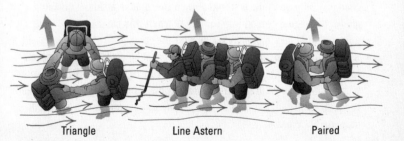

Triangle   Line Astern   Paired

- **Line Astern Method** Form a line with three or more people extending downstream. The line should face upstream, standing one behind the other, and give each other support by hanging on to one another's belts. The upstream person moves across first and stops, then number two, and so forth. If the current is extremely strong, the group moves simultaneously.
- **Line Abreast Method** Have the whole group form a line facing the opposite bank with arms linked, then walk across the river together.
- **Paired Crossing Method** Two people face each other and link arms, with the heavier person downstream. The upstream person serves as a "water break," and the downstream person, as support. The upstream person moves sideways first, supported by the downstream person, and then stops. Then the downstream person moves sideways into the "water break" or eddy created by the upstream person and the cycle continues across the river.

CROSSING ROADS

When we go to the backcountry, we do so to escape civilization, so we may forget that road crossings (even railroad crossings) can be part of the experience. This is especially true of long corridor trails like the Appalachian Trail and the Pacific Crest Trail. Like a river crossing, a road crossing can be hazardous, especially for a large group. Here are some things to think about:

- **Know Your Route** Know when and where you will be required to cross a road. When will road crossings occur—midday or dusk? Also, have an idea what type of road you will be crossing. Is it a backcountry road, rarely traveled, or a busy interstate?
- **Assess the Situation** Assess the road for the safest place to cross. You should have clear visibility down the road in both directions. If the crossing spot does not have such visibility, you may want to move to another crossing spot. If this presents a problem, locate a site that has good visibility and post a signal person there. Like a school crossing guard, the signal person lets you know when it is clear to cross. Signalers should be visible to cars, but off the road.
- **Know Your Signals** All trip members must be clear on what signals are used to indicate safe crossing. Similar to signals used by the American Whitewater Affiliation for paddlers, hikers use both arms overhead to mean continue, and two arms out horizontally and waving to mean stop, do not cross.

Walking Along Roads

Some trail routes require you to hike along a road, perhaps for several miles, before returning to the forest. This should be evident from your trip plan, but the exact nature of the road may not be. Assess the situation for the safest place to walk. Stay well off the road on the shoulder, if there is one. If there is a safer walking area on the other side of the road, you may decide to cross and walk there. If there is no shoulder on either side of the road, it is best to walk single file on the side of the road facing oncoming traffic. Be very careful at curves, where drivers may not be able to see you.

SETTING UP CAMP

If half the fun is getting there, the other half is being there. Here are some important considerations for setting up a campsite in the wilderness:

- Before setting off to hike, be informed of local regulations pertaining to camping and hiking—for example, no camping above 3,500 feet (1,066 meters).
- Try to plan your day so you arrive at a potential site with sufficient daylight to set up a good Leave No Trace camp. Know your route well enough to start looking for potential sites early.
- Find the most resilient site to set up a camp.
- In general, stay at least 200 feet (61 meters) away from trails, roads, water sources, and other campers.
- Try to avoid areas with rock faces, potential water runoffs, animal trails, and sensitive vegetation.

Your first priority in setting up a campsite is to establish activity areas. Some areas will get more traffic than others, so it is important to try to set up high-traffic areas in more resilient locations. For example, the cooking area is apt to get a lot of traffic, while the food-hanging area will get very little. Consider what "highways" will be established between high-traffic areas and try to minimize impact. Taking different paths each time from one activity area to another reduces "highway" impact.

The following are typical activity areas:

- **Water Source Area** The closest water source to your camp. Large collapsible water jugs will reduce the number of trips (and trampling) you do traveling back and forth to your water source. You should locate all the major areas of your camp at least 200 feet (61 meters) from your water source.

- **Sleeping Area** Look overhead to be sure that are no dead trees or branches above ("widowmakers"). The sleeping area should be upwind of the other areas, especially in bear country.
- **Cooking Area** Preferably downwind of the sleeping area.
- **Eating Area** In some cases you may want to set up an eating area that is separate from the cooking area. This can help keep large numbers of people from milling around hot stoves and boiling water, which can help reduce accident potential.
- **Food-Hanging Area** Preferably downwind of the sleeping area. It may be adjacent to the cooking area, since food odors will already be prevalent, or in another location.
- **Waste Disposal Area** This is for disposal of cooking and other waste water, and should be downwind of the sleeping area, at least 200 feet (61 meters) from any water source. It can be close to the food-hanging area, since food odors may be present.
- **Washing Area** This is an area for personal washing and should be an appropriate distance from the other areas.
- **Bathroom Area** If you are going to use a latrine for a group or set up a toilet to pack out feces, choose a designated site downwind of the sleeping area and at least 200 feet (61 meters) away from trails or water sources. If people will be using individual catholes or smearing, establish a general direction out of camp, preferably downwind. Individual sites should also be away from trails and at least 200 feet (61 meters) away from water sources.

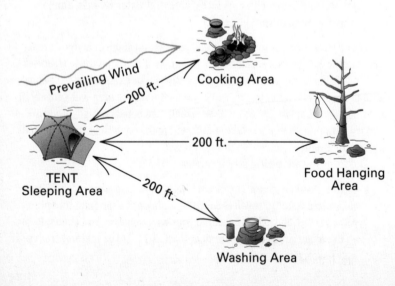

Set up the sleeping area, kitchen area, and food-hanging area in a triangular pattern, if possible, with about 200 feet (61 meters) on each side.

USING A TENT OR TARP

If you are using a tent, the setup will depend on whether the tent is freestanding or needs extensive guylines to hold it up. Make sure you are comfortable setting up your tent. (Imagine trying to figure it out in the dark when it's raining.) Check the prevailing wind direction. If rain is possible, locate your tent so that the door opens away from the prevailing wind. In hot climates—especially if you have two doors, or a window and a door—orienting the tent to the wind can provide refreshing cross-ventilation. You should have tent stakes appropriate for the conditions (stakes for dirt, sand stakes for dunes, or snow stakes for ice and snow).

Tarps can be extremely effective shelters, and are lightweight and inexpensive. The setup will depend on the availability of trees or other objects to which you can tie your tarp line. Check the prevailing wind direction. It is best to locate your tarp so that the door openings do not face the prevailing wind direction; otherwise, if it rains, water will come blowing in (see also page 35).

TRAVELING IN BEAR COUNTRY

When traveling in bear country, there are a number of special precautions that need to be taken. The first is to be aware of the type of bears you may encounter. The two species of bears in the United States are the black bear and the grizzly or brown bear. Grizzly bears can be significantly more dangerous than black bears. If you are traveling in grizzly country, talk with area rangers about special precautions and any restricted areas (for more information, see the Bibliography).

- Avoid any contact with bears.
- In grizzly country it is best to travel in groups of three or more.
- Wear "bear bells"—objects that hang from your pack and make noise to alert a bear that you are coming so it can leave.
- If a bear enters your campground, you may deter it by banging pots or making loud noises. You may also try assembling the group as a large mass, swaying your arms and making noise. Since bears have poor eyesight, they often shy away from an apparent foe that is larger than they are. If these measures fail, move well away from the bear. *Note:* If the

bear is habituated to humans, almost nothing you can do will drive it away if it is hungry.

- Keep human food away from bears (see How to Bearproof Your Camp, opposite). Keep a clean camp, and make sure cooking utensils are properly cleaned and packed away. Clean up and hang all excess or spilled food.
- Be aware that the odors of used tampons or pads will attract bears and other animals. After use, tampons or pads should be wrapped in aluminum foil with several crushed aspirin to absorb the odor and placed in a plastic bag, then hung up at night and packed out with other trash.
- Set up your cooking area downwind of your sleeping area so as not to attract a hungry bear through your camp.
- Be aware that bears and other animals tend to be more daring in areas people frequent. They become accustomed to finding food scraps left in camps by careless hikers. In particularly lean seasons, bears will seek meals wherever they can find them. Keeping a clean Leave No Trace camp helps prevent bears from becoming habituated to humans.
- In general, bears become a problem when they feel threatened (e.g., when they are cornered) or when they are traveling with their young. If you notice a cub traveling alone or with its mother, be especially cautious. Withdraw immediately.

BEAR ENCOUNTERS

If a bear charges or approaches you in an aggressive manner, it is most probably because the bear feels that you are a threat. Your actions should be designed to minimize that threat. Bear behavior is extremely complex and cannot be covered completely in this manual; if traveling in bear country, you should read a more detailed book, such as Gary Brown's excellent *Safe Travel in Bear Country*. Here are the important points that Gary recommends:

What to Do if Approached by a Bear

Your goal is to convince the bear that you are not a threat.

- Remain calm.
- Avoid abrupt movements.
- If possible, back away slowly, still facing the bear. Stop if this appears to further agitate the bear.
- Speak to the bear in a quiet, monotone voice.
- Do not look directly into the bear's eyes.
- Do not run away.

What to Do if Attacked by a Bear

- If you are wearing a pack, keep it on. It may protect you.
- Lie on your stomach facing the ground. Clasp your hands behind your neck with your arms tucked close to your head.
- Remain silent and motionless, even if the bear bites or claws you. If, despite being passive, the bear continues to maul you, you may have to fight back as a last resort. You should definitely fight back against a black bear.
- If the bear swats you, roll with the blow and return to your facedown position.
- Keep motionless and silent for at least 20 minutes or longer after the bear has left. Bears may move off and watch a victim for an hour, returning if they see movement.

🍁 TRICKS OF THE TRAIL

Pepper Spray There are a number of products on the market that spray a cayenne pepper derivative. Research indicates that such sprays are effective in deterring bears. In his book, *Safe Travel in Bear Country,* Gary Brown points out that such devices have limited range (15 to 24 feet/5 to 8 meters) and must be sprayed into the bear's eyes. Therefore it can only be used as a last resort when a bear is almost on top of you. Your best defense is to avoid bear encounters entirely and carry pepper spray, in your hand or on your belt, to use only in the event of an actual attack.

HOW TO BEARPROOF YOUR CAMP

The goal of bearproofing your camp is to minimize odors that might attract bears and to set up safe storage areas for food and garbage out of reach of bears and away from your sleeping area. The best way to do this is to start with a camp setup that facilitates these goals. In *Safe Travel in Bear Country,* Gary Brown describes a basic camp setup where the sleeping area is upwind of the kitchen and food areas, and all three are at least 300 feet (100 meters) apart.

Bear bagging is a general term used for hanging your food. There are lots of other animals (raccoons, opossums, coyotes, chipmunks, and skunks) that will go after human food. In some cases, you may be camped in locations where there are no bears, but still need to hang your food at night. Talk with local rangers about what the local critter population is and what precautions you will need to take. In areas with significant bear problems, there may be permanent food-hanging stands or containers provided by the park.

Hang up all food (except unopened canned food), pots, pans, cups, bowls, utensils, toothpaste, and garbage. In grizzly bear territory you should also hang up used tampons. On one backpacking trip in Shenandoah National Park, we diligently hung everything up. Around midnight a black bear came into camp and trotted off with someone's pack—he had left a tube of toothpaste in one of the outer pockets. Be sure your camp is clean of food scraps that may attract a bear. Suspend food and garbage in duffel bags, stuff sacks, or sealed plastic bags at least feet (5 meters) above the ground and at least 8 feet (2.4 meters) from the tree trunk. The bags should hang from a point where the tree can still support them but bears and other critters will have difficulty reaching them. Make sure the bags cannot be reached from the ground, either.

Be creative and sensible with your techniques for hanging food. A 75-foot (23-meter) rope (at least ¼ inch thick or 6 millimeters), two carabiners, and stuff sacks are helpful. When using stuff sacks, don't hang the sack directly from the drawstring. Instead, wrap the string around the neck of the sack and tie it, leaving a loop through which to clip a carabiner, which alleviates the stress on the drawcord by distributing the weight to the entire sack. Thus, the stuff sack is less likely to rip and spill its contents onto the ground. Below are two useful methods of bear bagging:

Counterbalance Method

1. Find a tree with a live branch. The branch should be at least 15 feet (5 meters) from the ground with no object below the branch that could support a bear's weight. The point at which you will toss the rope over the branch should be at least 10 feet (3 meters) from the tree. The branch should be at least 4 inches in diameter (10 centimeters) at the tree and at least 1 inch in diameter (3 centimeters) at the rope point (see illustration). (Be aware that no system is fool proof—a small bear

or other animal might still be able to climb out onto the branch and raid your food supply.)

2. Separate your food and other items into two bags of roughly equal weight.
3. Throw the rope over the branch. Attach one end of the rope to one of the bags.
4. Raise the bag as high as you can up to the branch.
5. Attach the other bag to the rope as high up on the rope as you can. Leave a loop of rope at the bag for retrieval.
6. Push the second bag up to the level of the other bag with a long stick.
7. To retrieve the bags, hook the loop of rope with the stick and pull it down. Remove the bag and then lower the first bag.

Marrison Haul System

The following simple but effective mechanical advantage hauling system was developed by Chris Marrison, one of Outdoor Action's Trip Leaders. However, some bears are smart enough to know that by cutting the diagonal rope tied to the tree, they can bring down the food bag.

1. Find a tree with a live branch. The branch should be at least 15 feet (5 meters) from the ground with no object below the branch that could support a bear's weight. The point at which you will toss the rope over the branch should be at least 10 feet (3 meters) from the tree. The branch should be a least 4 inches in diameter (10 centimeters) at the tree and at least 1 inch in diameter (3 centimeters) at the rope point.
2. Throw the rope over the branch. Make a trucker's hitch (see page 163) about 6 feet (2 meters) from the ground and clip carabiner 1 into the bight of the trucker's hitch.

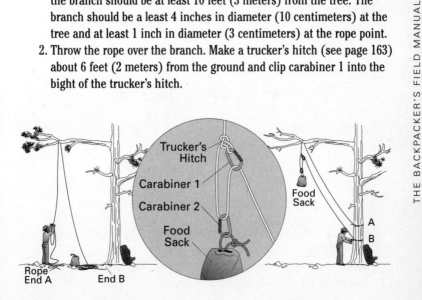

3. Feed the running end of rope end B through carabiner 2 and then through carabiner 1.
4. Pull the end of the rope end A to move carabiner 1 as close to the tree branch as possible. Tie off Rope End A to the tree.
5. Attach the food bag to carabiner 2 and haul the bag as high up as possible. Tie off rope end B.
6. To retrieve the bag, untie rope end B and lower the bag to the ground.

To haul the bear bag up, use a sturdy tree as a block around which to pull the rope. Protect the bark from friction in the rope by using a stuff sack or piece of clothing. Or find a sturdy dead branch on the ground and tie the end of the rope to be pulled to this branch. The branch serves as a yoke and allows more than one person to efficiently pull on the rope at once.

If the Area Is Treeless

If you are going to be traveling in a treeless area where bears are present, you will need to take additional precautions. You may want to store your food in bearproof plastic containers on the ground, away from your sleeping and cooking areas. Bears may still be able to smell the food, but they cannot open the containers.

KNOTS

A working knowledge of basic knots is as essential a backcountry skill as reading a map. Here are a few terms used in rope work

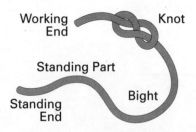

- Running end—the end of the rope that is the free end, commonly called the end.
- Standing part—the fastened part of the rope; may simply be called the line or the rope.

- Bight—a simple turn of rope that does not cross itself.
- Loop—a turn of rope that does cross itself.
- Half-hitch—a loop that runs around a shaft or another piece of rope, so as to lock itself.

TWO HALF HITCHES

This knot is useful for securing a rope back to itself after wrapping it around an object (e.g., a tree).

- Take the running end around the object and then around itself and back through to create a half hitch.
- Repeat the loop to add a second half hitch. You can pull a loop of rope through and leave the running end out to create a slippery half hitch (also known as a slip knot). One tug on the running end will pull out the hitch.

Half Hitch   Two Half Hitches   Slippery Half Hitch

BOWLINE

This knot is useful for tying one end of a line to something (e.g., one end of a tarp line to a tree).

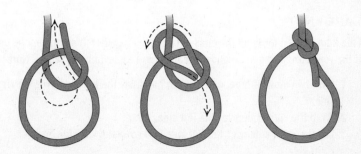

1. Form a loop of rope some distance from the end of the rope.
2. Feed the running end through the loop, back around the standing part of the rope and back through the loop.
3. To tighten, pull the running end and the standing part. Follow the old adage: "the rabbit comes out of the hole, around the tree, and back into the hole."

TAUTLINE HITCH

A knot that slides and "locks" on a rope, this one is excellent for the other end of a tarp line because you can adjust the tension of the rope. It can be used from one rope to itself or one rope to another.

1. Wrap the running end of the rope around the standing end with two complete wraps (additional wraps create greater friction).
2. From the lowermost wrap, bring the running end over itself, "bridging" the other wraps, back around the standing end, and then cinch the knot down.
3. When cinched, friction keeps the knot from sliding on the standing end. By loosening the "bridge" you can slide the knot up or down and reset it.

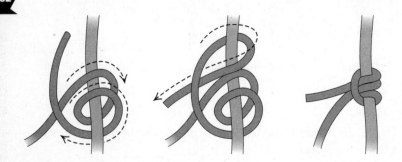

SQUARE KNOT

This knot is used for tying the ends of two ropes together. It should *not* be used if the ropes are going to be under great strain (e.g., climbing, rescue work).

1. With two ends of rope, one in each hand, lay the left side over the right side.
2. Wrap the right side over the left side.
3. Lay the right side over the left side and wrap the left side over the right side.

4. Cinch the knot down. It should be two loops of rope, each "strangling" each other. If not, you have created a granny knot, which is much harder to release after a load. The basic mnemonic is "right over left, left over right."

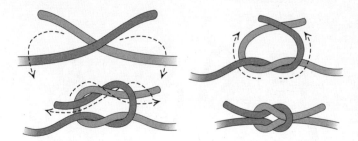

SHEET BEND

This knot is used to connect two different types (diameters) of rope. It should *not* be used if the ropes are going to be under great strain.

1. Create a bight in one rope. Feed the running end of the other rope through the center of the bight.
2. Bring the standing end back around behind the bight and back through the center, underneath itself.
3. Cinch the knot down by pulling on both ropes.

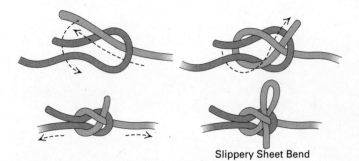

Slippery Sheet Bend

TRUCKER'S HITCH

This is useful for temporarily securing loads. It can be pulled tight and yet released immediately.

1. Create a loop of rope.
2. Pull a bight of rope from the running end up through the loop.

3. Wrap the running end around an object and feed it back up through the bight you created.
4. Pull down on the bight. This will give you a 2:1 mechanical advantage to pull the rope tight. Tie off the running end to some object or to itself with two half hitches.

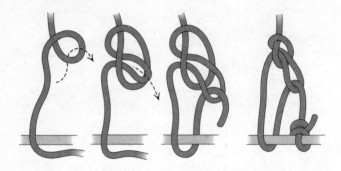

Note: There will be some stretch to your rope, and as you pull tension the bight will move down. Set the bight far enough away that when you have pulled tension, there is still a gap between the bight and the object.

Weather and Nature

We go to the wilderness in order to interact with the natural world. In spite of all our planning and equipment, nature ultimately sets the pace. That's why I find the backcountry such a rejuvenating experience—the longer I am there, the more I see and hear and experience. This chapter is designed to help you make better connections with the natural world.

Weather is a major part of the backcountry experience. Train yourself to be sensitive to weather. Watch those afternoon cumulus clouds build over the ridge on a hot, humid summer day, and think about what they might bring and where you should be if they come. With practice, you'll be able to predict fairly well what tomorrow's and even the next day's weather will be.

WIND

Major weather systems are caused by the interaction of air masses. In the continental United States, weather generally travels from west to east at about 500 miles (804 kilometers) a day, moved by the prevailing westerly winds. Local winds, caused by the differential effects of heating, are described below.

MOUNTAIN WINDS

- **Valley Breezes** These occur during the daytime. The mountains act like a heat sink and absorb lots of solar energy during the day. As a result, the mountains heat up more quickly than the valley. Air above the mountains is heated and rises, and is replaced by cooler air flowing up from the valley.
- **Mountain Breezes** These occur at night. The mountains act like the fins of a radiator giving off heat after the sun goes down, so they cool faster than the valley. Thus the air along the mountains cools and flows down into the valley, creating mountain breezes. At the same time, the valley gives off heat slowly and the air in the valley slowly rises, replaced by the cooler mountain air.

COASTAL WINDS

- **Sea Breezes** During the day the land warms faster than the ocean, so the air over the land heats up and rises while cooler (often moist) air from the water flows in to shore.
- **Land Breezes** At night the land loses heat more quickly than the water. The warmer air over the water continues to rise and is replaced by cooler air blowing from the shore.

CHANGES IN WIND DIRECTION

Changes in wind direction are an important clue to incoming weather.

- **Backing Wind** When the wind direction changes *against* the path of the sun—goes from west to east moving counterclockwise—this indicates a low-pressure system and potentially bad weather. I remember this by saying, "I'd better *back up* if the wind is *backing* because bad weather may be on the way."

- **Veering Wind** When the wind direction changes *to* the path of the sun—goes from east to west moving clockwise—this indicates a high-pressure system, typically associated with clear weather.

BEAUFORT WIND SCALE

The Beaufort Wind Scale is used to estimate wind speed based on normal observations. Each wind speed range is given a Beaufort number from 0 to 12. The specifications give you a visual clue to gauge the wind speed.

Beaufort #	MPH	KPH	KNOTS	International Description	Specifications
0	<1	<1	<1	Calm	Calm; smoke rises vertically
1	1–3	1–5	1–3	Light air	Direction of wind shown by smoke drift not by wind vanes
2	4–7	6–11	4–6	Light breeze	Wind felt on face; leaves rustle; vanes moved by wind
3	8–12	12–19	7–10	Gentle breeze	Leaves and small twigs in constant motion; wind extends light flag
4	13–18	20–29	11–16	Moderate	Raises dust, loose paper; small branches moved
5	19–24	30–39	17–21	Fresh	Small trees in leaf begin to sway; crested wavelets form on inland waters
6	25–31	40–50	22–27	Strong	Large branches in motion; whistling heard in telegraph wires; umbrellas used with difficulty
7	32–38	51–61	28–33	Near gale	Whole trees in motion; inconvenience felt walking against the wind
8	39–46	62–74	34–40	Gale	Breaks twigs off trees; impedes progress
9	47–54	75–87	41–47	Strong gale	Slight structural damage occurs
10	55–63	88–101	48–55	Storm	Trees uprooted; considerable damage occurs
11	64–72	102–116	56–63	Violent storm	Widespread damage
12	73–82	117–131	64–71	Hurricane	Widespread damage

CLOUDS

Recognizing different cloud types is an important part of predicting incoming weather. Parcels of air contain moisture in the form of water vapor. The amount of water vapor in the air is known as the *relative humidity,* which is expressed as a percentage of the total amount of water a particular temperature of air can hold. Cooler air can hold less water than warmer air, so as a given amount of air is cooled, the relative humidity increases. When the relative humidity of any parcel of air reaches 100 percent (the saturation point), clouds will form. Clouds are classified into two major categories based on how they are formed:

- **Cumulus Clouds** The typical "puffy" cloud, formed as small areas of rising air cool to the saturation point.
- **Stratus Clouds** Clouds in sheets or layers, formed when a large layer of air is cooled to the saturation point.

SPECIFIC CLOUD TYPES

Clouds are also classified by their altitude. There are two basic altitude prefixes: *cirro,* or high; and *alto,* or middle. The other prefix is *nimbo,* or rain. These prefixes are combined with the basic cloud categories, cumulus or stratus, to describe the major types of clouds.

High Clouds—above 25,000 feet (7,600 meters)
- Cirrus—"mare's tails"
- Cirrocumulus—sheets or layers of small globular clouds
- Cirrostratus—thin sheets; look like fine veils, give halos around the sun and moon

Middle Clouds—above 10,000 feet (3,000 meters)
- Altostratus—dense veils or sheets of gray or blue; sun or moon seen as through frosted glass
- Altocumulus—patches or layers of puffy, roll-like clouds, gray or whitish

Low Clouds—up to 6,500 feet (1,990 meters)
- Stratus—low uniform sheet, like fog with the base above the ground
- Nimbostratus—dark gray rain cloud
- Stratocumulus—irregular masses of clouds spread out in a rolling or puffy layer

Towering Clouds—up to 75,000 feet (22,800 meters)
- Cumulus—puffy; shapes change
- Cumulonimbus—thunderhead

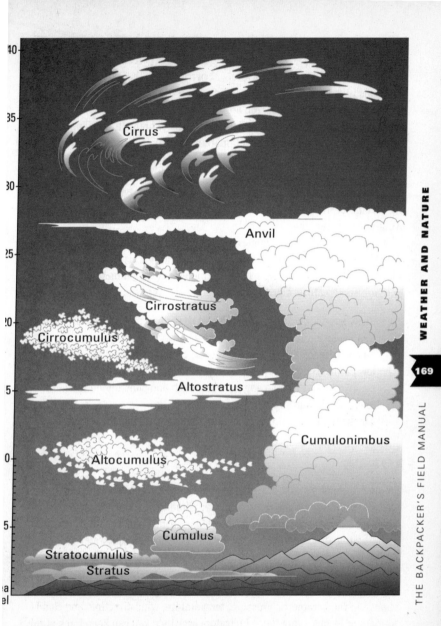

BAROMETRIC PRESSURE

Barometric pressure is the pressure of the weight of the air on the earth's surface. Air pressure decreases with altitude, so as you ascend to higher altitudes, the air pressure continues to decrease. At high altitudes the amount of gases in the air is less than at sea level, although the percentage of the gases is the same. At 10,000 feet (3,658 meters), for example, the percentage of oxygen in the air is still the same as at sea level (21 percent), but the *number* of oxygen molecules is approximately 70 percent of what it is at sea level. This means that for every breath you take, you are getting only 70 percent of the oxygen that you'd get at sea level. This is the major cause of high-altitude illnesses.

Barometric pressure is also an important indication of weather. Wet air is lighter than dry air, so rainy weather is associated with low-pressure systems and fair weather is associated with high pressures. A falling barometer indicates the arrival of a low-pressure system, possibly with bad weather. A rising barometer indicates the arrival of a high-pressure system, usually bringing clear weather.

If you are carrying an altimeter, you can set it for an altitude and check it later to see if it shows a higher elevation (indicating a rising barometer) or a lower elevation (indicating a falling barometer) (see Altimeters, page 138). Here are some natural signs of low or falling air pressure:

- Birds are not flying or are flying low. Lower barometric pressure means less dense air, which makes it harder to fly.
- Smells (especially bad ones, it seems) are more distinct because the low barometric pressure allows captive odors from plants to be more easily released. The saying is "when ditch and pond offend the nose, look for rain and storm blows."
- Smoke tends to curl downward and linger rather than dissipate.

FRONTS

Fronts are created at the boundaries of different air masses. When two air masses of different temperatures collide, a frontal boundary is created. Warm air rises up over cooler air, or cold air pushes underneath warm air, both causing air to be lifted up. As the air rises, it cools and water vapor in the air condenses to form clouds. If there is enough moisture in the lifted air, there will be precipitation. The type of precipitation (rain or snow) will depend on the temperature. As fronts move through, you will usually see a change in the barometric pressure, temperature, wind direction, and cloud formation. By observing these indicators over time you can keep track of the types of systems that move through your area. The chart on page 176 shows you how to predict what types of fronts are moving through and what weather you can anticipate.

WARM FRONTS

A warm air mass coming in over a cooler air mass creates a warm front.
A warm front usually covers 800 miles (1,280 kilometers) or more and
slants forward. It moves very slowly, providing an advance warning of rains
to come in 24 to 48 hours. Since warm fronts move slowly and often cover
large areas, rains can last for a long time—sometimes days. An approaching warm front is first indicated by high wispy cirrus clouds, lowering over
a period of one to two days into stratus clouds. The stratus cloud cover may
continue to lower and darken, forming nimbostratus clouds, resulting in
precipitation (see the following illustration). A look at the night sky can
provide early warning of a coming warm front. A halo around the moon
is caused by cirrus clouds; high cirrus clouds may also be indicated by
twinkling stars.

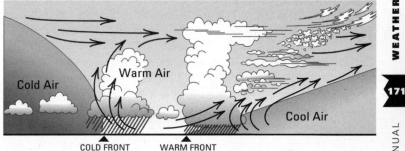

COLD FRONT   WARM FRONT

COLD FRONTS

A cold air mass pushing in under a warmer air mass creates a cold front.
Cold fronts generally cover 100 miles (160 kilometers) or less and move
much more quickly (20 to 30 mph or 32 to 48 kph) than warm fronts. Cold air
is denser and heavier, causing it to sink. As a result, friction against the
ground has a greater effect on the air mass. The leading edge piles up
steeply, while the trailing edge slants backward. This steep leading edge
pushes warmer air upward, ahead of the front. A cold front typically begins
with high cumulus clouds, which will lower to form layers of stratocumulus
clouds, possibly bringing precipitation. A strong cold front may push warm
air up very rapidly, creating cumulonimbus clouds (thunderheads) along a
narrow band called a squall line. After the cold front has passed, weather is
typically clear with drier, cooler air.

OCCLUDED FRONTS

An occluded front occurs when the faster-moving cold air catches up with slower-moving warmer air and lifts the warm air mass. In this case there tends to be a rapid progression of precipitation types, with nimbostratus clouds giving way to cumulonimbus clouds.

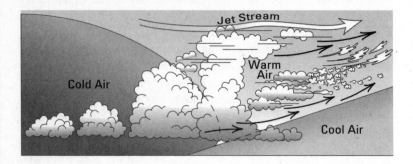

THUNDERSTORMS

Thunderstorms are the result of unstable moist air rising to form large cumulonimbus clouds. This can occur as part of a frontal pattern, as a cold front pushes in under a warm front, or as part of a local pattern of unstable air. Local thunderstorms begin when warm humid air rises from the ground, creating updrafts. As the air cools, it condenses to form a cumulus cloud. If the air is unstable, the updrafts continue, pulling in more warm, moist air. If enough moisture is present, the water vapor of the cloud will condense to form rain droplets. As water condenses from a gas to a liquid, it releases heat, which continues to fuel the updraft and pulls in more moist air from below. This cycle continues until significant amounts of moisture have developed. Rain and ice crystals begin to form within the cloud. When these become heavy enough, they fall, creating downdrafts within the cloud. These cool downdrafts may proceed out ahead of the storm. A sudden rush of cool air with darkening skies is often an indication of an oncoming thunderstorm.

The thunderhead continues to build in height and the top may reach as high as 11 miles (17 kilometers). High upper-atmosphere winds begin to flatten out the cloud top into a classic anvil shape. As the storm matures, the precipitation descending through the cloud (rain or snow) halts the updrafts, cools the cloud, and the storm eventually dissipates.

Thunderstorms are a common occurrence during the summer months in North America as the increasing heat of the summer sun and higher levels of moisture provide the fuel for frequent afternoon storms. Mountains are also a prime location for thunderstorms. As warm moist air hits the mountains, it is lifted up and over the mountains, creating updrafts that are fed by more warm moist air, beginning the cycle of thunderstorm development. In the mountains during the summer, be especially careful of afternoon thunderstorms.

THE PHYSICS OF LIGHTNING

If you remember basic physics, electrons are the tiny negatively charged particles that orbit around the atom. Most matter is electrically neutral, but you can create a charged object by transferring electrons from one object to another. This is what happens when you scuff your rubber-soled shoes across the carpet—you "scrub off" extra electrons from the carpet and develop a negative charge. Negatively charged objects are attracted to positively charged or neutral objects. If enough of a charge has built up when your hand touches a metal object, like a doorknob, a spark jumps across as the extra electrons flow from your body to the positive or neutral object.

In a mature cumulonimbus cloud, there are strong updrafts and downdrafts. These updrafts and downdrafts break raindrops and ice crystals apart, "scrubbing off" electrons and creating areas of positive and negative charges in different regions of the cloud. An area of strong negative charges is concentrated in the base of the cloud, while a layer of positive charges forms at the top. Since like charges repel each other, the negatively charged base of the cloud has an effect on the electrical charges on the ground beneath it, "pushing" the electrons on the ground away and leaving an area of positive charged ground directly beneath the cloud that follows the cloud as it moves.

Air is normally a poor conductor of electricity, but when the electrical potentials within the cloud become great enough, even air molecules will conduct electrical currents. The lightning flash is the flow of these separated positive and negative charges back together again along ionized air. Most lightning strikes (about 80 percent) occur within the cloud, flowing between the areas of positive and negative charges. You see this as cloud flashes, often referred to as *sheet lightning*.

Cloud-to-ground lightning, which accounts for only about 20 percent of lightning, starts as a thin stroke of negatively charged ions from the base of the cloud and begins to zigzag down toward the ground in a forked pattern known as a *stepped leader*. The forks are created as the electrons search for the path of least resistance to the ground. Meanwhile, the ground below is also busy. When the negatively charged stepped leader gets to within a few hundred feet (50 to 100 meters) of the ground, a leader of positive ions (the *return stroke*) leaps off the ground along a path of ionized air toward the stepped leader, typically from a tall object closer to the cloud, like a building or tree. Actually, there are many return strokes jumping upward, trying to make contact, but only one will win. Any object that is tall, like a mountain peak or a tall tree, is filled with positive charges trying to jump to the cloud. Being near any such object means that you are likely to be affected by the splash effect of the current as it hits the ground and dissipates (the *ground current*).

When the stepped leader and the return stroke meet, the circuit is complete and a rush of positive charges from the ground flows up into the cloud. This is the actual lightning flash that you see. Often there are several independent return strokes from the ground, which is why lightning seems to flicker. The stepped leader coming down from the cloud is much fainter and happens so quickly that all we see is the return stroke. The air around the electrical charge is heated to more that 43,000° F. (23,870° C), and expands violently and then contracts. This quick expansion and contraction of the air around the lightning causes air molecules to move back and forth, creating sound waves—thunder. Sound travels about one-fifth of a mile per second. So by counting the number of seconds from the lightning flash to the sound of thunder and dividing by 5, you'll have the approximate distance you are from the lightning strike. When lightning is 15 seconds or less away, the lightning is within three miles (4.8 kilometers) or less and *you should take immediate defensive action* (see Lightning, page 210).

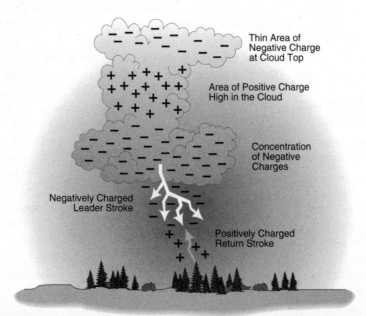

Thin Area of
Negative Charge
at Cloud Top

Area of Positive Charge
High in the Cloud

Concentration
of Negative
Charges

Negatively Charged
Leader Stroke

Positively Charged
Return Stroke

LIGHTNING DANGERS

Obviously, electrical storms can present significant accident potential. The primary dangers associated with cloud-to-ground lightning are direct hits and ground current. Once the lightning hits the ground, the electrical current dissipates along the ground following paths of least resistance. Injuries from ground currents are much more common than direct strikes, since they flow out over a much greater area. Ground currents can be as dangerous as direct hits if you happen to be in their path, and can result in thermal burns or cardiac arrest. (See CPR, page 245, and Thermal Burns, page 277.)

PREDICTING THE WEATHER

People have been making accurate short-term weather predictions long before satellites and Doppler radar. With a few regular weather observations throughout the day, you can gather enough data to make some reasonable guesses about incoming weather. Make this a part of your outdoor routine. An altimeter/barometer and a thermometer will help with your data gathering. It's best to make your observations around the same times each day: first thing in the morning, midday, and in the evening. Make your prediction for the next 24 to 48 hours, then check yourself and see how accurate you were. If you were way off, see if you can determine that cause of the day's weather. In his book, *Weathering the Wilderness,* William Reifsnyder provides a simple table to help you predict upcoming weather after you've made the following observations:

Cloud Formations

- What types of clouds were seen?
- What direction are they moving?
- How have the clouds changed during the day?

Wind Direction and Strength

- What direction was the wind blowing?
- What strength? (To estimate wind speed, use the Beaufort Wind Scale on page 167).
- Has the direction changed? Is it veering (indicating a high-pressure system) or backing (indicating a low-pressure system)?

Temperature

- Has the temperature gone noticeably up or down (beyond normal daytime fluctuations)?

Humidity

- Has the humidity changed? Increased or decreased?

Barometric Pressure

- Has the barometer changed (beyond any appropriate fluctuations for altitude changes)?

Your observation, when applied to the chart below, will help you predict upcoming weather patterns.

Phenomenon	WARM FRONT		COLD FRONT		OCCLUDED FRONT	
	Approach	Passage	Approach	Passage	Approach	Passage
Pressure	Falls steadily	Levels off or falls unsteadily	Falls slowly, or rapidly if storm intensifying	Sharp rise	Falls steadily	Rises, often not as sharply as cold front
Wind	SE; speed increases	Veers to S	S; may be squally at times	Sharp veer to SW; speed increases, gusty	E; may veer slowly to SE; speed increases	Veers to SW; speed decreases
Clouds	Cirrus; cirrostratus; altostratus; nimbostratus; thickening	Stratocumulus; sometimes cumulonimbus; clearing trend	Cumulus or altocumulus; cumulonimbus in squall line	Cumulonimbus; sometimes few clouds; clearing trend	Cirrus; cirrostratus; altostratus; nimbostratus	Slow clearing; stratocumulus; altocumulus
Precipitation	Steady rain or snow starts as clouds thicken; intensifies as front approaches	Precipitation tapers off; may be showery	None or showery; intense showers or hail in prefront squall line	Showery; perhaps thunderstorms; rapid clearing	Steady rain or snow starts as clouds thicken, intensifies as front approaches	Precipitation tapers off slowly
Temperature	Increases slowly	Slight rise	Little change or slow rise	Sharp drop	Slow rise	Slow fall
Humidity	Increases	Increases; may level off	Steady; or slight increase	Sharp drop	Slow increase	Slow decrease
Visibility	Becomes poorer	Becomes better	Fair; may become poor in squalls	Sharp rise; becomes excellent	Becomes poorer	Becomes better

Some natural indicators of changing weather can also be found in old sayings, which have evolved through a history of observation.

- *"Red sky at morning, sailors take warning; red sky at night, sailor's delight."* Redness in the *sky* (not redness in the clouds) is caused by light reflecting off moisture in the air. The red color is seen *opposite* the sun. If red is seen in the sky in the morning (in the west), it means that moist air is beginning to move over you, possibly bringing precipitation. If it is seen in the evening (in the east), it means that the moisture has moved past you.

- *"Rainbow in the morning is a warning, at night, a delight."* Rainbows are caused by sunlight reflecting off water droplets in the atmosphere, so they always occur *opposite* the sun. In North America, most weather systems move from west to east. A rainbow in the evening must be in the east, and is reflected light from wet weather already past. A rainbow in the morning must be in the west, and is reflected from wet weather moving toward you.
- *"When leaves show their underside, be very sure that rain betide."* A period of damp air softens leaf stalks and bends them more easily in the wind as a storm approaches. This is especially true with aspen and maple leaves.
- *"Rain before the wind, topsail halyards you must mind. Wind before the rain, soon will make plain sail again."* Rain falling ahead of a strengthening wind indicates a gale-force storm approaching. Wind ahead of a rain will die out as the rain arrives.
- *"No dew at night, rain by morning. No dew at morning, rain by the next day."* Dew is a sign of a fair tomorrow. On a clear night, without cloud particles, moisture is released from the air and collects as dew.

And here are some more natural indicators:

- **Fog** Morning fog is simply damp air condensed by the cold of the night. It will burn off with the heat of the morning. Fog at night or late in the afternoon is more often the result of cold rain or snow falling through the warm air upon which it condenses; this indicates a coming storm.
- **Animal Sounds** Crows, woodpeckers, and blue jays are typically very noisy before a storm, whereas insects stop making noise.
- **Rhododendron Act as Thermometers** At 60°F (15°C), the leaves are spread out. At 40°F (4°C), the leaves are drooped. At 30°F (−1°C), the leaves are curled. At 20°F (−6°C), the leaves are tightly curled.
- **Crickets** can also tell you the temperature. Count the number of chirps per minute. Subtract 40, then divide by 4. Add 50 for the approximate temperature in degrees Fahrenheit.

TEMPERATURE RANGES

In the temperate climate of the United States, the general temperature range from daytime low to daytime high is typically 20 to 40°F (11 to 22°C), assuming no new weather systems move in. This range increases in particular climates like deserts or at high altitudes, where the sun's heat has a greater impact on raising temperatures during the day. Weather systems also play an important role in temperature ranges. High-pressure systems are usually associated with few clouds at night, so daytime-accumulated heat dissipates. Clouds at night tend to hold in heat, decreasing the temperature swing. At high altitudes, the temperature drops about 3.5°F (2°C) for each 1,000 feet above sea level, so a warm 75°F (24°C) day at 5,000 feet (1,524 meters) in the valley turns into a cool 60°F (15°C) day up at 10,000 feet (3,048 meters). If you add a potential 30°F (16°C) temperature drop at night, it can be below freezing up on the mountain.

NATURAL SIGNS OF DIRECTION AND TIME

DIRECTION

There are a number of clues in nature that will help you determine your direction.

- **Polaris (North Star) Is Always Due North** The line formed by the two stars that shape the lip of the Big Dipper point to Polaris, which is the end star of the handle of the Little Dipper. It never moves, and all stars appear to revolve around Polaris (visible in the Northern Hemisphere only).
- **Stars Rise in the East and Set in the West,** as do the sun and the moon, except the stars around Polaris, which never set (Northern Hemisphere only).
- **Venus Can Be Seen in the West Three Hours After Sunset** Except for several months out of the year, Venus is the first to appear in the evening and the last to disappear in the morning. The nonappearance months vary from year to year.
- **To Determine Direction with Your Watch (in the Northern Hemisphere),** take (or imagine) an analog watch and point the hour hand at the sun. South is the direction halfway between that hour hand and 12 (in the Northern Hemisphere). Remember to compensate for Daylight Savings Time. This is often easier than trying to determine the east-west passage of the sun, especially during the middle of the day.

- **Shadow Compass** Another way to determine your direction is to make a shadow compass: Place a sharpened stick in the ground, point up. Mark the location of the tip of the shadow on the ground. Wait 15 to 20 minutes, and then mark the shadow tip again. Draw a line connecting these two points. This line will run east-west. Since the sun is always slightly south in the Northern Hemisphere, you can identify all four directions.

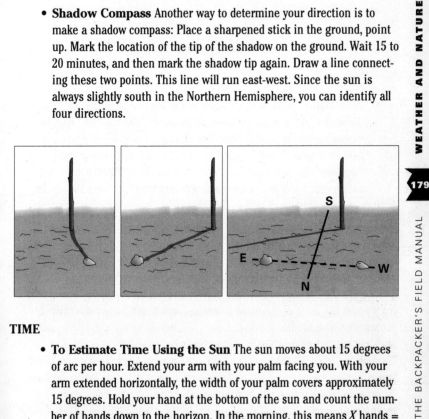

TIME

- **To Estimate Time Using the Sun** The sun moves about 15 degrees of arc per hour. Extend your arm with your palm facing you. With your arm extended horizontally, the width of your palm covers approximately 15 degrees. Hold your hand at the bottom of the sun and count the number of hands down to the horizon. In the morning, this means X hands = X hours from sunrise; in the evening, it means Y hands = Y hours until sunset. This will give you an idea of the number of daylight hours remaining. If you know the time of sunrise and/or sunset, it will give you an approximate time of day. If the width of your palm (four fingers) equals an hour, then the width of each finger represents 15 minutes.

For example, suppose it is afternoon and the sun is two hands above the horizon. This means there are approximately two hours until sunset. If you know the sun sets at 6:45 P.M., it is about 4:45 P.M.

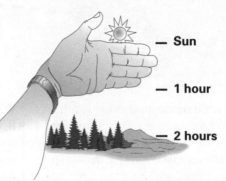

- **To Tell Time with a Compass,** orient the compass to north. Place a thin stick upright in the center of the compass and mark the degree number where the shadow from the sun hits. Consider that north is 12:00 P.M. on the "clock." Each 15 degrees off of north is the equivalent of an hour. Add or subtract accordingly from north (12:00 P.M.). If a shadow reads 330 degrees, for example, subtract 330 from 360 for 30 degrees or 2 hours; $12-2 = 10:00$ A.M.

COMMON TREES

Tree identification requires time spent in the woods with a reliable field guide (see the Bibliography). This section provides a short, key-based tool for identifying some of the more common trees found across the United States. The idea behind key-based identification is to identify particular features of the tree, such as leaf structure, and follow various options, or "branches," until you identify the tree. Since these keys are *not* complete, you will often run into a dead end when trying to identify a particular tree. Bring a thorough tree-identification book with you if you want to learn more about trees.

Trees commonly found in North America are divided into two major families, conifers and broadleaf trees. The basic differences between the two types of trees are described in the following chart. Broadleaf trees are most easily distinguished by the types of leaves and how they attach to the branch.

TREE TYPE	SEEDS	LEAF TYPE
Conifer	Have naked seeds, typically on a cone.	Most conifers are evergreen—they maintain their leaves all year. In order to reduce moisture loss through the leaves, conifers typically have long needlelike leaves with a waxy coating.
Broadleaf	Have seeds contained within an ovary.	Most broadleaf trees are deciduous—they lose their leaves once a year.

LEAF ATTACHMENT

- **Alternate** leaves are attached to alternating sites along the branch.
- **Opposite** leaves are attached to the branch directly opposite one another.

Alternate

Opposite

LEAF TYPE

Simple A single leaf blade is joined by a woody stalk to a twig.
- **Lobed** The leaf is divided into several separate lobes.
- **Unlobed** The leaf has no lobes.

Lobed

Unlobed

Compound A single leaf is composed of from three to several dozen leaflets that are joined to a midrib that is attached to a twig. There are two subtypes of compound leaves:
- **Palmate** Leaflets are attached to the midrib at one point.
- **Pinnate** Leaflets are attached at several points along the central midrib.

Palmate

Pinnate

TREE IDENTIFICATION KEY

Does the tree have needlelike leaves? If yes, go to Conifers, page 185. Otherwise go to Broadleaf Trees, following.

Broadleaf Trees

1. If the leaves are alternate, go to 2. If opposite, go to 3.
2. If the leaves are simple, go to 4. If compound, go to 5 (alternate).
3. If the leaves are simple, go to 13. If compound, go to 6 (opposite).
4. If the leaves are lobed, go to 8. If unlobed, go to 9 (alternate; simple).
5. If the leaves are pinnately compound, go to 7 (alternate; compound).
6. If the leaves are pinnately compound, go to Ashes. If palmately compound, go to Buckeyes.
7. If the leaves are toothed, go to Hickories.
8. If the leaves are toothed, go to 9. If smooth, go to 10 (alternate; simple; lobed).
9. If there are five main lobes and the leaf is star-shaped, go to Sweetgum. If the teeth are course and jagged, go to Sycamore.
10. If the leaf has more than four lobes, go to Oaks. If the tip of the leaf is notched, go to Tulip Tree. If the tree has some lobed and some unlobed leaves, go to Sassafras. Otherwise go to 11.
11. If the leaves are finely toothed and the stems are flat, go to Aspen, Quaking. If the bark is smooth or peeling, go to 12.
12. If the leaves are oval with sharp teeth and the bark is gray and smooth, go to Beech. If the bark is white or peeling, go to Birches.
13. If the leaves are lobed, go to 14. If unlobed, go to 15.
14. If the lobes are toothed, go to Maples.
15. Go to Dogwood.

Ash (Opposite; Compound; Pinnate) Ash grows up to 80 feet (24

 meters) with a very straight trunk. It has opposite compound leaves, each having three to eleven leaflets with toothed margins. Leaves are pale green and turn yellow in the fall. The fruits are single-winged seeds, which hang down in clusters. The bark is thick, furrowed or scaly, and usually ash colored on the branches. Examples: white ash, black ash, green ash.

Aspen, Quaking (Alternate; Simple; Unlobed; Toothed) The quaking aspen grows up to 70 feet tall (21 meters). The leaves are heart-shaped and toothed. The stems are flat and are easily disturbed by a light wind, causing the familiar "quaking." The leaves are bright green and turn golden yellow in the fall. The bark is a smooth greenish gray. Aspen are early colonizers after a fire.

Beech (Alternate; Simple; Unlobed; Toothed) The American beech grows up to 80 feet tall (24 meters). The beech often has a wide trunk and spreading branches. It grows well in low light so it is often a climax species. Offspring trees can sprout from the roots of a parent tree. Leaves turn yellow and then brown in the fall and may remain on the tree all winter. The bark is smooth and light gray.

Birches (Alternate; Simple; Unlobed; Toothed)

- **Paper Birch** Grows to 80 feet tall (24 meters). It has bright white, peeling bark with dark horizontal striations that gives it its "paper" name. The leaves are light green, heart-shaped, and toothed. They turn yellow in the fall.
- **Gray Birch** Grows to 30 feet (9 meters). The bark is dark gray and smooth and does not peel. The leaves are alternate and arrowhead-shaped with sharp teeth. The leaves turn yellow in the fall.
- **River Birch** Grows to 100 feet (30 meters). The leaves are diamond-shaped and the bark peels in many layers of thin flakes.

Buckeyes (Opposite; Compound; Palmate)

- **Horsechestnut** Grows to 80 feet tall (24 meters). Has seven to nine leaflets coming from a central rib.
- **Sweet Buckeye** Grows to 90 feet (26 meters). Usually has five leaflets coming from a central rib.

Dogwood (Opposite; Simple; Lobed; Smooth) Dogwood grows to 40 feet tall (12 meters). Dogwoods are known for their beautiful white blossoms in springtime. The bark is a scaly gray. The leaves are opposite and oval with curving symmetrical veins. Berries are red. The leaves turn deep red in the fall.

Hickories (Alternate; Compound; Pinnate; Toothed) Hickory leaves are compound, alternate, with a terminal leaflet. Each leaf has three to seventeen (depending on the subspecies) oval, pointed, and toothed leaflets. Flowers are three-branched, slender, drooping catkins. The fruit is a nut with a husk that splits into four sections when ripe. Examples: shagbark hickory, pignut hickory, bitternut hickory, mockernut hickory, and pecan. The nuts of the shagbark, pecan, and mockernut are edible.

- If the bark is smooth and gray and becomes very rough and scaly on older trees, peeling off into long "shaggy" strips, it is a Shagbark Hickory.

Maples (Opposite; Simple; Lobed; Toothed) There are numerous species of maple. In a few cases, the leaves are pinnately compound. Leaves turn a variety of brilliant colors in the fall. The seed is typically a pair of winged fruits in a U or V shape. Examples: sugar maple, red maple, and silver maple.

- If the notches between the lobes are U-shaped and the base of the leaf is curving, it is a sugar maple.
- If the notches between the lobes are V-shaped and the base of the leaf is not curving, it is a red maple.
- If the leaves are distinctly five-lobed and the notches between the lobes are deep, it is a silver maple.

Oak (Alternate; Simple; Unlobed; Toothed) There are numerous species of oaks. All have alternate simple leaves and the familiar acorns. Twigs usually have clusters of buds at the tips.

- If the leaves have rounded lobes and lack teeth, it is a white oak. Examples: eastern white oak, valley oak.
- If the leaves have pointed lobes and bristle-pointed teeth, it is a red or black oak. Examples: eastern black oak, scarlet oak, northern red oak.
- If the lower branches of the tree bend downward, it is a pin oak.

Sassafras (Alternate; Simple; Lobed; Untoothed) Sassafras grows to 50 feet (15 meters). The leaves are the most distinguishable feature. Each tree has both unlobed leaves and two-lobed and three-lobed leaves. When crushed, the leaves give off a pleasant odor.

Sweetgum (Alternate; Simple; Lobed; Toothed) The sweetgum grows to 100 feet (30 meters). It has star-shaped alternate leaves. The hanging fruits, a spike-covered ball, contains the seeds. The seeds are popular with some animals, especially the red squirrel, who may have a midden (a pile) of devoured sweetgum balls under its favorite perch.

Sycamore (Alternate; Simple; Lobed; Toothed) The sycamore grows to 100 feet (30 meters). It is easily recognized by its mottled bark. The smooth brownish bark peels off in irregular patches, leaving yellowish and whitish bark underneath. The fruit is a hairy ball that hangs from the tree. The leaves are simple, heart-shaped, with three lobes.

Tulip Tree (Alternate; Simple; Lobed; Untoothed) The tulip tree is a tall, straight tree that typically grows to 100 feet (30 meters). The flowers of the tree look like tulips. On mature trees you will notice no branches on the lower part of the tree. The tulip tree is a fast grower and often is an earlier colonizer in cleared areas.

Conifers

Most conifers are evergreen, keeping their leaves all year round. There are a few species of conifers that are deciduous, losing their leaves in the fall. These trees include the tamarack, the western larch, and the bald cypress.
1. If the needles are scalelike, go to 7.
2. If the needles are in bundles, go to 4.
3. If the needles are sharp and four-sided, go to Spruce.
4. If the needles are in bundles of two to five, go to Pines.
5. If the needles are flat with white bands underneath, go to 6.
6. If the cones are standing upright, go to Firs. Otherwise, go to Hemlocks.
7. If the foliage is in flattened sprays, go to Cedars.
8. If the foliage is in irregular sprays, go to Junipers.

Cedars (Scalelike Needles) The cedars found native in North America are in a different family from the true cedars found in Europe and Asia. Cedars are generally 40 to 50 feet tall (12 to 15 meters). They have tiny overlapping leaf scales typically arranged in flat sprays. Examples: western red cedar, northern white cedar.

Firs (Needles not Scalelike; Single Needles; Sharp and Four-Sided; Flat with White Bands Underneath) Firs are 60 to 130 feet (18 to 40 meters), with needles on two sides of the branch. The needles have two silvery white bands on the underside. The cones, rather than hanging down, sit erect on the branch and have scales that are wider than they are long. Examples: alpine fir, balsam fir, white fir. *Note:* The Douglas fir is not a true fir but a separate species.

Hemlocks (Needles not Scalelike; Single Needles; Sharp and Four-Sided; Flat with White Bands Underneath) Hemlocks grow from 65 to 200 feet (20 to 60 meters). The leaves have a definite fragrance. For a positive identificiation, just crush some of the round-tipped needles and smell. The needles are short, marked on the lower surface by two pale lines. The cones are oval, with scales as wide as they are long. Examples: eastern hemlock, western hemlock, Carolina hemlock.

Junipers (Scalelike Needles) Junipers have both tiny scalelike leaves and some small, pointed needles. They grow in height from 40 to 50 feet (12 to 15 meters). The fruit, found only on female trees, is a small, firm, bluish fleshy berry. Examples: eastern red cedar (which is in the juniper family), common juniper, Rocky Mountain juniper, western juniper.

Pines (Needles not Scalelike; Single Needles; Needles in Bundles of 2 to 5) Pines in North America commonly range in height up to 164 feet (50 meters). Pines are an evergreen with needlelike leaves in bundles of two to five. Species can be identified by the number of needles in a cluster and by the shape of the cone. The cones are usually longer than they are wide and contain the naked seeds on the hardened woody scales of flowers. There are two types of pine—soft and hard.

- If the needles are in clusters of five, the cones have a stalk, and the cones have scales without prickles, then it is a hard pine. Example: eastern white pine.
- If the needles are in clusters of two or three and the tree has cones with thick woody scales armed with spiny prickles, then it is a soft pine. Examples: Jack pine, longleaf pine, pitch pine, ponderosa pine.

Spruces (Needles not Scalelike; Single Needles) Spruces are tall, tapering trees that have a wide buttress of branches at the base. Size ranges from 100 to 164 feet (30 to 50 meters). The bark is thin and scaly. Leaves are stiff, sharp evergreen needles extending out on all sides of the branch in a spiral. The cones hang down from the branch and are egg-shaped, with thin woody scales.

PLANTS

There are far too many plants to cover in this manual—vines, shrubs, wildflowers, and grasses. You should take a good field guide along to help you identify plant species (see the Bibliography). There are a few basic things about plants that you should know.

WILD EDIBLES

If you are foraging for wild edibles, you need to be able to *clearly identify* the plant before eating it. Some species look very similar, and eating the wrong plant can make you very sick. Also, some wild edibles are edible only at certain stages in their development, and even then only certain parts of the plant are edible. *Know* your plant before you eat it—bring a good edible plants field guide with you.

Whenever you are collecting wild edibles, take only a few in any one spot and spread your collection out over a large area. Otherwise, you may reduce the population enough that it can't reproduce. In some locations or seasons, collecting wild edibles may be prohibited. Check with local rangers. And whenever you are collecting wild edibles, be aware of other animals that may be collecting the same thing. This is especially true in bear country. Berry patches, for example, can be sites for encounters with bears.

PLANTS TO AVOID

There are a few plants with toxins or stings that you should definitely be able to recognize and avoid. Here are the common ones found in temperate forests:

- **Poison Ivy** typically grows as a woody vine or small shrub. It has toothed leaves in groups of three and white berries. The leaves turn bright red in the fall. You may see it as a large hairy vine climbing high up the sides of trees (up to 1 to 2 inches in diameter or 5 centimeters).

It typically grows in wet areas. Remember the old saying "leaves of three, let it be." (*Note:* The box elder tree in the maple family has similar-looking leaves but has common winged seeds of the maple family instead of berries; poison ivy does not grow as a tree.)

- **Poison Oak** is similar to poison ivy except it always grows erect (no vines).
- **Poison Sumac** grows as a shrub or small tree (typically 6 to 20 feet or 2 to 6 meters). Like poison ivy, it contains a toxic oil that yields the same symptoms. It has compound leaves composed of 7 to 13 pointed leaflets that are not toothed. The berries are white.

Poison Oak

Poison Ivy

Poison Sumac

All parts of these three plants, at all times of year, contain a toxic oil in their sap called *urushiol,* which causes skin rashes on contact. The sap can be carried on your clothing or boots, causing contact dermatitis long after you have passed the plant. Be especially cautious of burning wood with hairy vines. Inhaling smoke with urushiol vapors can cause the same type of reaction to the sensitive tissues of the lungs, which can result in a serious medical emergency.

- **Stinging Nettles** are a 2- to 4-foot weed (0.6 to 1.2 meters) covered with coarse, stinging hairs. The hairs are on both the leaves and stem

Jewelweed

Stinging Nettle

of the plant. Brushing against it breaks off tiny hairs that lodge in the skin and can be quite painful. Interestingly enough, jewelweed (a.k.a. pale touch-me-not) often grows near stinging nettles. The milky sap from crushed stems and leaves of jewelweed soothes the sting from stinging nettles. Jewelweed grows 2 to 4 feet (0.6 to 1.2 meters) high and has pale yellow-orange pendant flowers.

SPOTTING WILDLIFE

For me, seeing wildlife, or signs of wildlife, is one of the great joys of being in the wilderness. It is also an important part of Leave No Trace camping. You must respect animals by being nonintrusive. Getting too close to animals can cause serious disturbances, including abandoned young, disturbed nesting grounds, and damaged foraging areas; it may even cause the animal's death. In winter, for example, many animals are under severe stress to gather enough energy just to stay alive. Escaping from a human could rob them of energy they need to sustain themselves. In some cases, breeding and nesting areas may be off-limits for backcountry travelers. Always remember that you are only a visitor to their habitat.

The best places for spotting wildlife are what are known as transition areas. These are the zones of transition between two types of environments such as a forest and a field, a field and a stream, or a forest and a stream. In these locations you will find a diverse plant population that provides both food and cover for herbivores. Wherever you have a high density of herbivores, you will also have carnivores.

The best times for spotting wildlife are during the early morning and early evening hours. These are prime feeding times for herbivores and, therefore, prime hunting times for carnivores. During the day most herbivores are lying low to avoid predators, so predators snooze as well. Night is also an active time for wildlife, although you will be more likely hear animals than see them.

TIPS FOR SPOTTING WILDLIFE

- Look for things that stand out from the environment around them. In a forest, most of the outlines are oriented vertically (trees, plants), whereas animals have mostly horizontal outlines. Look for horizontal lines against the vertical as the first sign of wildlife. Also, look for parts of the animal rather than the whole animal—for example, the corner of the deer's rump.

- Bluejays or crows constantly calling in an area are a common sign of a predator, such as a fox, hawk, or owl.

ANIMAL SIGNS

With a large group, it is often difficult to spot animals, but you can always find signs of their presence when you hike. Animal signs includes trails, tracks, hair, scat (feces), and gnaws and chews. In fact, most animal observation is based on finding signs. Be a detective: examine the signs and determine what animals are in the area. Knowing what's around will help you spot them, or avoid them if necessary. For example, if you are hiking out west, and you find a very large pile of fresh scat on the middle of the trail and a bear track, you know that you need to be very wary.

HAZARDS OF ANIMAL OBSERVATION

- Be careful not to get too close to animals, especially animals that appear very docile. This can be a sign of rabies (see page 306).
- Whenever you are examining animal signs, be aware of the possibility of disease transmission. For example, if you are examining animal scat, *do not* use your hands. Bacteria in scat can cause infections, and inhaled dried scat can lead to lung infections.

CHAPTER 8

Safety and Emergency Procedures

Emergency situations in the backcountry will tax all of your knowledge, experience, and judgment. Paul Petzoldt, the founder of the National Outdoor Leadership School (NOLS) and the Wilderness Education Association (WEA), once said, "Rules are for fools." He meant that you can't categorize situations into simple lists of problems and solutions. Each situation is unique, so as a backcountry traveler you need to assess the situation and make your own determination on the best response. This chapter identifies the issues that will help you in your assessment, but should not be taken as "rules" or the only responses. Your good judgment is what keeps you safe in the backcountry.

DEALING WITH EMERGENCIES—WHO'S IN CHARGE?

On some wilderness trips there may be organized trip leaders and participants. In this case, part of the trip leader's role is to take charge in the event of an emergency. Other trips may be a group of friends out for an adventure. In this case, there may be no assigned trip leader and everyone shares the load and the responsibility for making decisions. While this distributed leadership model works well when deciding where to camp or how long to hike on a particular day, it is not the best approach when there is a serious problem or emergency. In the event of an emergency, the best thing is for a few people (one or two) with the proper experience and training to take charge. *Before* the trip departs, the group should decide who has the skill and experience to take over in an emergency and/or whom the group is willing to delegate this responsibility to. Depending on the type of emergency, there might be different people who would take charge. In the event of a lost person, it might be the person with the most backpacking or search-and-rescue experience. In a first-aid situation, it might be the person with the highest level of formal first-aid or medical training. For the rest of this chapter, we will consider that, in an emergency, every group has a designated emergency leader or leaders, whom I'll call trip leaders.

Trip leaders must intimately understand certain realities about injuries and illness in the backcountry (serious or minor) if they are to deal with them effectively. Most trips are 2 to 24 hours or more from having professional medical help arrive at the accident site. The group depends on the trip leaders to take full charge of the situation—the trip leaders must care for the physiological and psychological needs of both the victim and the group. A trip leader who puts him- or herself in danger physically or emotionally for the "good of the victim" is a liability to the victim and to the group.

First and foremost, the trip leaders must stay calm and inspire confidence in the group and in each other that the situation is being handled in the best way. They should talk through every step confidently and out loud; this way the leaders can fill in each other's omissions and nothing will be rushed into. Depending on the nature of the emergency, it may be productive to ask the group for suggestions; they may have good ideas. However, there are also times when opening up discussion only slows people from taking necessary immediate actions.

Since each situation is unique, trip leaders must remain flexible in their responses. The key to properly responding to an emergency is to remain calm, assess the situation carefully before acting, and continue to reassess the strategy throughout. Here's a basic approach to handling emergency situations:

1. Assess the situation. Determine the nature of the emergency and what type of response is required (first aid, search for a lost person, etc.). Identify the number of people ill, missing, etc.
2. Develop a response plan based on the nature of the emergency and the potential risk to rescuers (first-aid treatment, initiate search, etc.). Neutralize risks to the best of your ability before proceeding. Do not initiate a rescue for which you are not properly trained. (Continue to reassess the situation and alter the response plan if necessary.)
3. Assume leadership of the group or select someone to head the group and delegate responsibility. Group members should assist in patient care if needed, locate position on the map, and so on.
4. Make the victim as comfortable as possible, maintain his or her body temperature, and protect the victim from the elements.
5. Make sure a trained first-aider is with the victim at all times.
6. Give the other group members something to do to get their minds off the situation and make them feel useful, such as setting up a temporary camp or preparing food and hot drinks for group members.
7. Make sure the other group members are okay. They may be suffering from shock or emotional difficulties; maintain group morale as much as possible.

HOW ACCIDENTS HAPPEN

Backcountry travel means recognizing that there are factors we cannot control, and that these factors impose potential risk. Recognizing and dealing with those risks is one of the challenges that make wilderness travel such a rewarding experience.

Accidents fall into two basic types: preventable accidents, which are by far the most common, and the more rare "acts of God," such as a tree branch falling on someone's head. In the early 1980s, Alan Hale developed the Dynamics of Accidents Model for explaining why accidents take place. His pioneering work has formed the basis of outdoor safety management ever since. Safety management is not just avoiding risk; it means taking a proactive stance to manage a safe environment. It's a philosophy that should be part of everything you do in the backcountry, just like Leave No Trace camping.

Hale determined that there were two basic factors that contributed to accidents. The first is *environmental hazards,* including things like terrain, location, and weather, as well as equipment and food, which create the "microenvironment" for each person on the trip. The second factor is *human factor hazards*—things like physical condition, medical condition, previous experience, and emotional state. When you combine these two types of hazards, you get an *accident potential.*

Let's take a simple example: Bill is extremely allergic to bee stings. If he goes into an area with lots of bees, his accident potential is very high. The effect of combining environmental hazards and human factor hazards multiplies the accident potential rather than simply being additive. That is, the greater the number of hazards, the more quickly the accident potential can rise. The greater the severity of a potential accident, the more essential it is to take the proper steps to prevent it.

ENVIRONMENTAL HAZARDS

The types of environmental hazards one may encounter are dictated by the following:

- **Activity** The activity you are engaging in establishes many of the parameters for the accidents that can occur. The hazards associated with backpacking, for example, are different from the hazards associated with whitewater canoeing or rock climbing. When you examine the particular activity, consider the environment in which the activity will take place. In some situations, the environment is static, relatively unchanging over time. In other activities, the environment itself may change too quickly to predict. Therefore, *static activities* are those in which the environment is relatively unchanging (e.g., hiking). *Dynamic activities* are those in which the environment changes very quickly in unpredictable ways (e.g., whitewater paddling). With a dynamic activity, you may need to provide a greater margin of safety because of the unpredictability of the environment.

- **Season and Climate** Weather, altitude, and the possibility of weather changes have a significant impact on the accident potential. Cold temperatures, hot temperatures, rain, snow, wind, and fog can create hazardous conditions for backcountry travelers.
- **Remote Locations** In remote locations, you need to exercise additional precautions. The distance from help means that you may be very much on your own if something goes wrong. You should factor this into your plans by reducing the difficulty level of your activities. For example, in whitewater paddling, rivers are rated from Class I (easy flatwater) to Class VI (extremely hazardous whitewater). Paddlers in remote locations will often increase the rating of a rapid to compensate. In this case, a Class III rapid (intermediate) in a remote location might be considered a Class IV (difficult) rapid. If you normally run only Class III, then you would plan to hike around this rapid. This helps you take into account the increase in accident potential and provides you with a greater margin of safety.

Other Common Environmental Hazards

Rocky trails   Overexposure to sun
Poison ivy   Exposed ledges
Stinging nettles   Bad weather
Bees, wasps   Contaminated water

Equipment Hazards

Improper clothing   Inoperative equipment
Faulty stoves   Missing equipment

HUMAN FACTOR HAZARDS

The different types of human factor hazards are usually determined by the group, and the number of people who are leaders and the number who are participants. Here are some examples of common human factor hazards that contribute to accident potential.

General

Age   Trying to "prove" oneself
Previous experience   Fatigue
Poor physical condition   Fear
Previous medical conditions   Limited outdoor skills
No awareness of hazards

Participants

Not interested in being on the trip

Poor communication skills

No willingness to follow instructions

Group lacks cooperative structure

Trip Leaders

Poor teaching ability

Inadequate skills to extricate self
and others from hazards

Poor judgment regarding safety

Inability to manage group

🍁 TRICKS OF THE TRAIL

Eating Disorders Be aware of whether there are individuals in your group who have eating disorders, such as anorexia or bulimia. If someone has a problem, they most likely will bring it with them on the trip. Look for people who either avoid eating (even though they are getting lots of exercise), who seem to binge-eat at some points and avoid eating at others, or who seem overly preoccupied with food, calories, or their weight. A person with an eating disorder may see a backpacking trip as an opportunity to "lose weight" through both exercise and abstention. If you suspect someone has an eating disorder, talk to the person confidentially about it and let him or her know of the serious safety risks involved, not only for the individual but also for the rest of the group. If you feel the person is not taking proper care of him or herself, or is putting the group at risk, consider evacuating the individual.

SAMPLE ACCIDENT SCENARIO

Read the following trip scenario and analyze it using the Dynamics of Accidents Model. What are the environmental hazards? What are the human factor hazards? What are the potential accidents? What can be done to reduce the accident potential? See page 224 to see how well you did with your analysis.

Sally is leading a group of ninth graders on the school's annual four-day wilderness trip. This is Sally's fourth such trip. Dan, the other teacher from the school, is new this year and doesn't have any backpacking experience. But it's hard to find teachers at the school who are willing to go. Dan is young and a good athlete and seems to be learning quickly.

It's early September in Shenandoah National Park and the group of eight students and two teachers has started their second day of hiking. The temperature has soared up to 90°F (30°C) with the humidity around 80 percent. The group slept in and cooked pancakes so they got a late start on the trail. After a 2-mile hike (3 kilometers), the group stops for lunch. Sally notices cumulus clouds starting to build. It's already after 1 P.M. and, eager to get on to camp, they finish lunch quickly and head off for a long descent down Little Devil's Staircase, a ledgy section of rocky trail along a deep stream gorge. The upper section is dry and the rock is slick and polished. As the afternoon progresses, the group is moving more slowly down the gorge. The smaller students are having trouble handling the steep sections with their packs. More than once Dan has had to take a student's pack as well as his own over the difficult sections. The clouds have now become thick thunderheads and the sky is darkening. They still haven't reached the bottom trail. The wind is picking up and large raindrops are spattering here and there on the rocks. Suddenly the sky opens up and the rain is falling in torrents. Dan, while carrying a student's pack, slips on the wet rock and falls backward, striking his head sharply against a boulder. Sally, picking the way down the trail in front, turns around as she hears one of the students scream. She drops her pack and scrambles up to Dan, who is unresponsive when she first arrives. She quickly checks for breathing and pulse and then Dan starts to open his eyes.

TEACHING THE DYNAMICS OF ACCIDENTS MODEL

On any wilderness trip, each individual is responsible for his or her own safety management, as well as the safety of the entire group. This is true even in situations where there is a defined trip leader. Unless you have one leader for each participant, it is impossible to supervise everyone all the time. So it is important that each group member accept a level of personal responsibility for maintaining a safe environment. Simply understanding the Dynamics of Accidents Model can significantly reduce the accident potential. The best way to accomplish this is to describe the model and give examples of environmental and human factor hazards at the beginning of the trip. This lets people know what to be careful of and sets a stage whereby individual and group safety is seen as an integral part of the trip. Reminding people during the trip that accident potential is rising and asking what can be done to reduce it is a good way to get the group to focus on the issue and take the appropriate safety management steps.

THE ENVIRONMENTAL BRIEFING

In order to prepare for the possibility of accidents, you need to anticipate what are the most likely accident scenarios on your trip. These scenarios should be part of your basic trip plan and should be communicated to all group members before or at the very beginning of the trip. If there is no defined trip leader, someone should be assigned the task of researching and presenting this information to the rest of the group.

REDUCING THE ACCIDENT POTENTIAL

In order to reduce the accident potential, determine the environmental and human factor hazards. Once identified, deal with those factors that you can change. If it is cold, rainy, and windy (environmental hazards) and people are hungry and tired (human factor hazards), the possibility for an accident like hypothermia is high. You can't change the weather, but you can make sure that people have dry clothes on, rain gear, and are well fed and hydrated. If, after attending to all of those things, you still have a significant accident potential, then it is time to take more decisive action, like setting up camp and getting everyone under shelter, putting people together in sleeping bags for warmth, and so on.

ACCIDENT ANALYSIS—CLOSING THE CIRCLE

What happens if you do have an accident or near miss on the trail? After it's all over, it is important to go back and examine what happened and why, so that you can be better prepared to avoid such an accident in the future. Analyzing close calls is also important, because there are far more close calls than real accidents.

If a serious accident occurs, the group members may have personal emotional issues to deal with. A supportive group environment and personal counseling may be required after a severe accident. The accident analysis may need to wait until the personal healing process has begun.

In an accident analysis, you want to examine issues like:

- What were the precipitating environmental and human factor hazards?
- Which hazards could have been reduced or altered?
- Did you have the right equipment?
- Did you have the right training and experience?
- Once the accident happened, how did you respond? What could you have done differently?

Books like *Accidents in North American Mountaineering* and *AWA River Accidents Summary* are useful guides to accident analysis (see the Bibliography).

PREVENTIVE MEASURES TO MINIMIZE ACCIDENT POTENTIALS

- Prepare a complete route plan.
- Notify the appropriate rangers or wilderness managers of your trip plans.
- Leave your trip route and return time with an "on call" person, with instructions about whom to call in case you are overdue.
- Preplan for emergencies. Determine who will be in charge in an emer-

gency and understand what emergency procedures you would follow in different situations. Have the necessary emergency phone numbers for your trip area (rangers, police, hospitals, etc.). Have a daily evacuation plan in case you need to hike out for help.

- Have appropriate equipment, both personal and group.
- Carry adequate water; treat water as needed.
- Know blister prevention and early treatment.
- Use good kitchen and personal sanitation to prevent gastrointestinal distress.
- Rest at regular intervals to prevent fatigue.
- Prevent hypothermia and hyperthermia.
- Know the allergies and medical histories of all trip members.
- Carry extra food, water, and clothing.
- Be prepared for a bivouac in case of an emergency.
- Don't push beyond the skills and fitness of any of the group members.
- Be in good physical shape and in good health. Don't go on a trip (or don't let someone else go) if suffering from a serious illness or medical problem. Wait until the medical issue is stabilized to avoid the complications and potential risks of an evacuation.
- Be cautious when using stoves and fuel. Never refill a hot stove; let it cool down first. Keep fuel refilled and fuel bottles at least 15 feet (5 meters) away from the actual stove in use (or from a fire).

SENDING FOR HELP

If a situation requires you to send for help (injury, illness, lost person), it is important to implement the following procedures:

1. **Where to Go for Help** From your pretrip planning you should be generally aware of where to go for help. Locate the nearest and/or easiest place to reach a house, ranger station, roadway, or phone. Keep in mind that reaching an isolated road in the backcountry may be just like being in the wilderness (no houses, no phones, no cars).

2. **People Staying Behind** You need to have a plan for what the group staying behind will do—stay where they are or move to a trail junction, shelter, or roadhead—and where *exactly* they will be. If the group does move, they should leave a note at their original location stating their planned route, destination, time they departed, and estimated time of arrival. This same information should be left at any trail junctions or major intersections the group passes.

3. **Enlist Outside Aid** If there are other hikers in the area, try to enlist their aid. This can include hiking out for help and assisting with first aid. Remember, someone still needs to be in charge. Asking other people for help means incorporating them into *your* emergency protocols. Make this clear at the outset—otherwise, these folks may just aggravate the situation. If someone in the other group has more experience (in first aid or emergency management), you might ask that person to take over. Always make sure that the transfer of responsibility is clear. If you feel that the person is not handling the situation properly, discuss it with the individual. If you don't reach an agreement, you may have an obligation to resume control of the situation.

4. **Hiking Out for Help** Preferably, at least three people should hike out. The people who hike out should have the necessary backcountry experience to do this safely on their own.
   - Determine on a map the *best* route to help—at a highway, gas station, town, store, ranger station, private home—*before* you depart! Keep in mind the terrain and potential obstacles. The best route out is *not* always the shortest distance out.
   - Determine what the group remaining behind should do if help does not arrive by a certain time.
   - The party going for help should have all the necessary equipment—map, compass, travel directions, food, water, clothing—to be able to travel quickly and should be prepared to bivouac. If you are far into the backcountry, hiking out could take several days.
   - Travel quickly, but do *not* run at breakneck speed on a trail and become another victim.
   - Do *not* split up the party going for help.
   - Conserve your strength in case you need to lead the rescue party back.
   - The people hiking out should contact the authorities and arrange for rescue assistance and also determine what they will do—stay where they are or hike back in with the rescue personnel.

5. **Collect Information** Have the following information with you if you need to send for medical or evacuation assistance:
   - Name, address, phone number, and age of victim.
   - A written record of the patient's initial condition and current condition (has it changed?); description of how accident occurred—date and time; description of injuries; vital signs; and first aid performed. (See SOAP Note, page 238.)
   - A copy of the Emergency Information Report (see page 356) with:

- Location of the group on a marked map; use compass bearings if necessary.
- First-aid equipment you have on hand.
- Type of rescue or medical support you need.
- First-aid equipment needed.

EVACUATION PROCEDURES

Evacuation is a general term for transporting someone from a trip. In most cases we think of this as the result of a medical problem. It can also be caused by psychological problems, a family emergency, or the assessment by the trip leaders that the person's behavior poses a threat to him- or herself or others in the group. (Specific evacuation protocols for first-aid situations are covered in Chapter 9.)

If someone needs to be evacuated as the result of an injury or illness, the primary concern is for the safety and health of the patient, and the secondary one is the safety and health of the other members of the group. When assessing the need for an evacuation, think both of the patient's condition and how rapidly medical attention is needed. For example, it may take two hours for the patient to walk out on his or her own, whereas to send two people out for help (2 hours), get a rescue squad to the trailhead (1 hour), hike back in (2 hours, unless driving in is possible), and hike back out (2 hours+) will mean over seven hours before the patient is evacuated. The injury may need treatment sooner than that. Carefully evaluate your resources: do you have the necessary equipment, manpower, and experience to *safely* evacuate the person, given the current trail and weather conditions? If you do evacuate the person, take the time to plan the best route out, keeping in mind the patient's condition, the distance, and the terrain. Depending on the situation, you might choose the shortest route, the quickest route, or a longer route that poses less threat to the patient. Use the evacuation scenario list below to determine how to deal with an evacuation situation.

POSSIBLE EVACUATION SCENARIOS

1. **Person Can Walk Out on His or Her Own Power** The person's medical condition would not be compromised by walking out. This may necessitate taking all the person's equipment. Example: Stomach ailment, mild allergic reaction, minor laceration.
2. **Person Can Walk Out with Assistance** If the distance is not too great, the person may be able to hike out if carrying little or no weight

and with assistance. This is to be attempted *only* as long as it does not aggravate the individual's condition. The person must be constantly monitored. Example: Stable ankle sprain, fractured forearm.

3. **Person Cannot Walk Out** The injury or illness would be aggravated by walking out or movement is contraindicated. In this case a litter evacuation is required. Do *not* attempt a litter evacuation unless you have the necessary equipment, experience, and manpower; otherwise you risk additional injury to your patient as well as placing other members of the group at risk. In this case, a litter evacuation by skilled rescue personnel (rangers, first-aid squad) is required. Send for help. Example: Head injury, lower leg fracture, spinal injury.

CHOOSING TO EVACUATE

If you have determined that it is medically appropriate to evacuate your patient, you need to determine whether or not you have the skills, the time, and the manpower to perform the evacuation safely. Ask yourself these questions:

- How much daylight do you have?
- What is the weather? Is it changing? For the worse?
- Can you continue to provide the necessary first-aid treatment and monitoring during the evacuation?
- Do you have the necessary equipment to properly package and transport the victim?
- What if your patient's condition deteriorates? Would it be more difficult to treat him or her once you start hiking out?
- How many people do you have to do the evacuation? For a litter evacuation over any long distance you should plan to have a minimum of three teams of six to eight people rotating through the litter carry.

WHAT TO DO IF SOMEONE GETS LOST

Getting lost can be as simple as heading out from camp to go to the bathroom and getting disoriented or following an incorrect compass course for hours. Keep calm and try to gather enough information to determine where you are. If you panic, the possibilities of getting more lost increase and your accident potential rises dramatically.

IF THE GROUP GETS LOST

If your entire group is lost, it may be embarrassing and inconvenient, but it's not that dangerous (unless you are in a dangerous location, such as an exposed ridgeline in a lightning storm). You have all your human resources and equipment, so if you came properly prepared, you should be able to deal with the basic survival issues and then work on identifying your location.

GENERAL GUIDELINES

- Identify your *last known position*. Mark the current time. Check with all group members about what they remember since that point, including landmarks, trail junctions, and signs.
- Determine how long it has been since your last known position. Subtract the time for any lunch or meal breaks to calculate your total hiking time since your last known position.
- Estimate your hiking speed and try to include time for descents and ascents (see Estimating Travel Times, page 9).
- Using your last known position and the estimated elapsed hiking time, you should be able to determine how far you could have traveled—a radius of travel. Draw a circle with a slightly larger radius (to account for inaccuracies in your estimates) on your map. This represents the possible area that you are in. You may be able to eliminate certain possibilities based on the topography. For example, there may be obvious baselines such as rivers and roads. If you have not crossed these, then at least you know where you have not been. Systematic elimination of where you aren't helps identify where you are.
- Look for any major landmarks or terrain features around you. See if you can locate those features on the map. With the map oriented, you may be able to determine a rough location with respect to local landmarks. It's essential that you be sure about your landmarks. For example, in an extremely mountainous area, it may be difficult to tell which peak is which.
- If a rough landmark examination does not work, you may be able to locate your position using map and compass through triangulation (see page 137).

IF YOU OR AN INDIVIDUAL IN THE GROUP GETS LOST

If you are a member of a group, and you get separated or lost from the group, it is important to follow these guidelines. All group members should be briefed on these procedures at the start of the trip.

- *Don't panic. Stay calm.* Your attitude is the most important factor in reducing the accident potential.

- *As long as you are not in any immediate danger, stay right where you are!* As soon as the group notices that you are gone, they will begin search procedures. It is best not to wander further. This only increases the size of the area people will have to search for you.
- In a short time it will be noticed that you are missing and people will begin searching for you. Look and listen for the signals of rescuers and be prepared to make your own signals. Three of anything (whistles, shouts, flashes of a flashlight) are the universal distress signal (see Signaling for Help, opposite).
- If for a safety reason you need to move, it is best not to move far. Go only as far as it takes to remove yourself from the immediate hazard (lightning, rockfall, avalanche, etc.). If possible, leave a note or other indication that you were there and where you went (rock cairns, arrows on the ground).
- Take stock of your resources, equipment, water, any food. These can be important. Do *not* leave any equipment.
- It is essential that you conserve body heat and energy. Be watchful of hypothermia. Put on all of your layers of clothing before you begin to get cold. You can increase your insulation by stuffing dry leaves into the open spaces in your clothing. A survival shelter may also be useful (see page 219).
- When it gets dark, sit down and rest. If possible, build a safe fire. This will keep you warm and serve as a signal for rescuers.

IF YOU ARE HIKING SOLO AND GET LOST

This is a situation where good, careful judgment is essential. In some situations, your best move is to wait until you are overdue and people come looking for you. In other situations, you may be better off traveling to try to locate yourself. There are no rules. One thing to keep in mind is not to move during extreme weather conditions, as you only increase your risk of hypothermia and of getting more lost. Take shelter and keep warm until the bad weather has passed. Then begin your exploration to discover where you are. Follow the General Guidelines given on page 203. If you still have no idea where you are, and it is not appropriate to wait for help, use the Square Spiral technique described by David Seidman in *The Essential Wilderness Navigator:*

- Look around you and carefully make note (in writing) of the area that you are in. This is your "home base." Mark this area somehow with a stick in the ground or a rock cairn so that you can recognize it if you return.
- Now do a quick search for landmarks to identify your location. Taking

your gear with you, follow a short straight-line compass course out from home base along the cardinal compass points (N, S, E, W) and then the intercardinal compass points (NE, NW, SE, SW). Go out on each line for 5 minutes, looking for landmarks. Write down any landmarks you find, then return to your home base.

- Look at your collected landmarks and your map to see if you can identify your location. If this short compass bearing walk turns up no landmarks to identify your location, you need to start a search pattern. Here's how to do a more extensive search:
- From home base, head in one cardinal direction (N, S, E, or W). Write it down. Walk for about 30 minutes along that bearing (about 1 mile/1.6 kilometers), writing down any landmarks.
- After 30 minutes, stop, turn 90°, and walk another 30 minutes (write down your new direction), slowly spiraling out from your home base looking for prominent landmarks. Continue your square spiral until you arrive back at home base. If you found any recognizable landmarks, use those to help determine your position by map reference or triangulation. If you did not find any recognizable landmarks, pick another cardinal direction and create another square spiral out from there. If needed, you can always retrace your steps by reversing your bearings back to your home base (see Back Bearings, page 133).

SIGNALING FOR HELP

Signaling for help is essential to increasing your chances of being located quickly. Here are some techniques for signaling rescuers:

- A series of three anything (whistles, flashes) is the universal signal for distress.
- Fires—during the day the smoke will be more visible. At night, the flame will be your best signal. Be careful if the fire danger is high.
- Mirrors can reflect sunlight beyond the horizon up to 7 million candlepower. Hold the mirror in your hand with your arm outstretched. Sight along your arm to aim the mirror flash at particular points along the horizon. Send three flashes. Some rescue mirrors actually have a sighting hole to let you focus on a target.
- Flashlight—use in a series of three flashes.
- Strip signals on the ground. These can be built of rocks or tree branches or dug in the ground, and are designed to be seen from the air. Make your signal big (20 feet long or 6 meters) so that it can be seen from a distance, and select a highly visible location. The universal signals are shown on page 206.

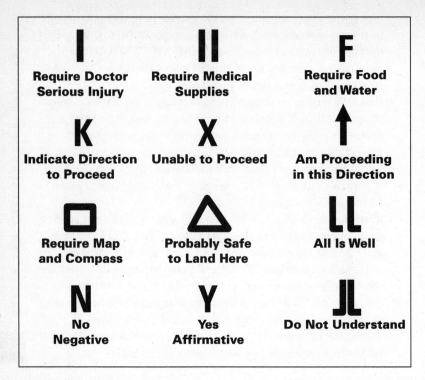

I
Require Doctor
Serious Injury

II
Require Medical
Supplies

F
Require Food
and Water

K
Indicate Direction
to Proceed

X
Unable to Proceed

↑
Am Proceeding
in this Direction

☐
Require Map
and Compass

△
Probably Safe
to Land Here

LL
All Is Well

N
No
Negative

Y
Yes
Affirmative

JL
Do Not Understand

LOCATING LOST PERSONS

Hiking as a group means keeping track of people. If you are thinking about separating your group (for Leave No Trace reasons or other considerations), you need to be sure that each person or subgroup has the necessary skills, equipment, and judgment to reach the intended campsite. If you aren't sure this is the case, don't split up the group. If you discover that someone is missing, you should take the following steps:

1. **Gather Information** Establish when the person was last seen, what direction he or she was heading, whether he or she said anything about where he or she was going. The last time the person was seen, as compared to the current time, will give you an indication of how far the person *could* have traveled. Estimate the hiking speed of the person and determine how far he or she could have walked. Use this estimate for the radius of your circle from the point last seen. This establishes your general search perimeter.

2. **Make a Quick Check of Area Last Seen** If you are near the point where the person was last seen, make a quick check of the area. Shout the person's name and look around.

3. **Make a Hasty Search** If shouting does not bring a response, group members in pairs should perform an organized *hasty search* by quickly sweeping the area, nearby trails, lookout points, nearby streams or lakes, and any other obvious places the person might be. Search for approximately 20 to 30 minutes. Take time to plan out where searchers will go on the hasty search before sending them out. Look particularly in any areas that seem *probable* based on your earlier information gathering (i.e., the person was heading south out of camp, wanted to see the sun set, etc.). Look for signs of the person, such as clothing or belongings. Shout for the person repeatedly. Listen *carefully* for a response. The person may be injured and be unable to respond loudly, if at all. Look for visible signs in case the person is unable to answer.

🍁 TRICKS OF THE TRAIL

Cell Phones and Radios There is a great deal of discussion in outdoor programs about the use of cellular phones and radios. Some people feel that these are essential backcountry safety devices, some feel that they intrude on the experience of being in the wilderness, and others feel they are mistakenly used as a crutch. They can be useful tools in an emergency situation. However, it is important to recognize that none of these communication technologies works (yet) in every location, and therefore shouldn't be relied upon completely. Any electric device can run out of power or break, so never rely on it in place of first-aid training, knowledge of the area, or a good trip plan. In the next few years, as satellite coverage comes on-line for cellular phones, it will be possible to call from anywhere. At that point I expect that more and more people will begin to carry them. But if you carry a cellular phone or a radio, don't delude yourself that help is only a phone call away. Even with a phone, it still may take rescue personnel hours or even days to get to you, so you must be prepared to deal with the situation.

At a conference on wilderness safety someone told the story of a fellow who went hiking with his cell phone. He got lost and called the rangers to tell him where to go. They asked him what landmarks were nearby and there weren't any obvious ones. It turned out he had no map or compass and had absolutely no idea where he was. He assumed that because he had a cellular phone, all he had to do was call and ask for directions. But the rangers couldn't figure out where he was or how to help him find his way back.

---

4. **Secondary Search** If the hasty search does not bring results, a more systematic *secondary search* should be initiated by teams covering nearby trails, roads, water areas, and cliffs. Based on the elapsed time since the person was last seen, determine a general search perimeter, assuming an average walking speed for that person. Based on your

location and resources, you will need to determine how long it will take to do a secondary search. Take time to plan out where searchers should go to cover all likely locations before sending them out. In case of darkness, all searchers should be equipped with flashlights and should always be within sight of the next searcher. Make sure that these teams are properly equipped and have the experience to prevent themselves from getting lost.

5. **Go for Help** If the secondary search does not bring results quickly (within 1 hour or so), or the possible search perimeter is too large for you to cover, you may need to send for help in order to bring in rangers or other rescue personnel for a more extensive search (see Signaling for Help, page 205). This of course depends on where you are and how far away help might be. If you decide to go for help, *don't delay or "wait another hour."* Fill out the Emergency Information Report (see page 356) and follow the instructions for groups hiking out for help. As a team goes out for help, the other members can continue the secondary search. If the person is found after the team goes for help, determine how long the help team has been gone and how long it was expected to take them to get out. *Do not* try to chase down the team if they have too much of a head start; rushing out could lead to another accident. You may need to wait for the rescue personnel to return with the team.

6. **Make a Line Search** If the secondary search is not effective, the search perimeter is not too large for you to cover, your next option is to perform a more detailed line search. If you have reached the point of needing to do a line search, you are probably going to need outside help. Chances are the person has wandered a significant way from your location, creating a search zone that is probably too big for you to search; or the person is possibly injured and unable to respond.

Line searches should be performed once you have some clues as to the person's location—the point last seen, a piece of clothing or gear, footprints, and so on. The line search requires the group to spread out in a line. Searchers should be close enough together (for that particular terrain and vegetation) to be able to see all the ground between themselves and the people next to them. Someone must take the role of the search commander and start the group moving forward at a controlled pace. Look for the lost person and for any clues to his or her whereabouts. Look behind you regularly for clues that might be behind rocks or trees. At any sign of a clue, the entire group should be told to stop while the clue is examined, and if possible identified as belonging to the missing person, and recorded in writing. Then the search line should continue. The search commander keeps track of areas searched and moves the search line as needed.

Halting a Search

Choosing to stop a search is a highly emotional decision. With outside help, you can rely on experts in search and rescue to take charge and bring their experience and more advanced resources to bear (such as helicopters, search dogs, and advanced search data analysis). If you are on your own, you will need to decide how long to continue the search. Bad weather, difficult terrain, or lack of sleep can place the searchers at significant risk, and you do *not* need another victim. You may need to call off your search, rest, and resume later. If the risk to others is significant, you may need to discontinue the search. At this point, you should contact local rescue authorities. They may be able to restart the search, or determine that the search should be terminated.

EXTREME WEATHER CONDITIONS

If your group is hit by severe weather conditions, your major concern is to maintain warmth and keep people dry (wet clothing can quickly lead to hypothermia). Here are the basic steps you should take:

- Concentrate immediately on everyone being properly clothed to minimize possible hypothermia and/or frostbite.
- Find shelter or set up camp to get out of the bad weather.
- Get people together under shelter with sleeping bags and have the group share the bags for warmth.
- If possible, get a stove working for hot drinks. Definitely have everyone eat food to restore energy and help them maintain body temperature.
- Do *not* try to hike out in the midst of a serious storm. The possibilities for injuries or having people (or the entire group) get lost are too great. You may need to move the group a short distance to a more sheltered location.
- If there are strong winds, try to locate a shelter site in a protected area away from dead trees or trees with dead branches that may fall.
- In severe lightning storms, there is danger from both direct hits and ground currents. When lightning is close, separate the group and have people assume the lightning position (see Lightning, page 210) until the storm has moved away.
- Wait until the storm has abated before moving camp or hiking out. Be careful of broken tree limbs that may fall after the storm.

LIGHTNING

Lightning can be a serious hazard in the backcountry. Before going on your trip, you need to include an assessment of general weather patterns and the potential for lightning or severe thunderstorms into your trip plan. In certain locations or at certain times of the year, thunderstorms are common. For example, summer afternoons in the Rocky Mountains often bring thunderstorms as warm moist air rises over the mountains. Being high on an exposed ridge in the late afternoon can be extremely hazardous. (For information about weather and the causes of lightning, see page 173.)

Warning Signs of Lightning

There will always be signs of an impending storm that contains lightning. Storms must build in order to develop enough electrical current for lightning. Any or all of the following may indicate the possibility of imminent lightning:

- Thunder, even without any visible lightning
- A sudden cloudburst of enormous raindrops or huge hailstones
- A fast-moving cold front; these often trigger thunderstorms along a squall line ahead of the front as it pushes warm moist air upward. A change in wind direction with a sudden blast of cold air is often an indication of an incoming cold front.
- Signs of highly ionized air—highly ionized air is essential for the development of lightning; any of the following signs is an indication of serious lightning potential: hair standing on end or crackling; crackling noises or buzzing in the air; small sparks given off around metal objects; bluish glow around objects, known as Saint Elmo's fire.

Storm Distance

Lightning often strikes out ahead of the storm, so just because the storm is not yet directly over you, don't assume that you aren't in danger. The distance of approaching lightning storms may be calculated by timing the interval between the lightning flash and the following thunder. Sound travels about one-fifth of a mile per second, so count the number of seconds between the lightning flash and the thunder and divide by 5 to find the distance. (For kilometers, sound travels about one-third of a kilometer per second, so divide by 3.) If the thunder is within 15 seconds from the lightning, then the storm is within three miles (5 kilometers) from your location and *you should take immediate defensive action.*

A Direct Strike

Direct lightning strikes are rare, but they do occur. Golfers are probably the single most identifiable group of strike victims—they are out on an open field, usually the tallest objects around, and often have metal golf clubs in their hands. Almost anything can send up a return leader. Typically the leader that "wins" will come from the point with the least resistance to conducting electricity and/or the closest point to the stepped leader from the cloud—high and relatively sharp points like radio antennas, mountain summits, sharp ridgelines, trees, or a standing person. Direct lightning strikes typically cause the heart to stop and cause serious electrical burns.

Ground Currents

The electrical current that strikes the ground does not dissipate at the point of the direct hit; it splashes outward in numerous directions and flows along the paths of least resistance. This is known as ground current and is the more frequent danger to backcountry travelers. Ground current pathways include cracks and crevices filled with water, wet rock, wet climbing ropes, root systems, and cables along the ground. In some cases the easiest path may be to "jump" across a gap of ionized air. This is known as a *spark gap,* and it's the same principle as scuffing your feet across the carpet with a wool sweater on and then coming close to a metal lamp—you have so much built-up electric charge that it jumps through the air and leaves a spark. This can occur at the openings of caves or under overhangs, where it is easier for the current to jump across the gap than to travel all the way around. If you are between the two sides of the gap, the current will flow right through you, so hiding in caves may be more hazardous than being out in the open.

Physiological Effects of a Lightning Strike

Electrical currents can cause the heart to stop, respiration to cease, thermal burns, muscle spasms, brain and nerve damage, and initial blindness. The extent of injury depends on the amount of current, the duration of the current, and the current's path through the body. With a direct strike, the current is usually so large that the results are fatal. Ground currents can be significantly less powerful, and the current path makes a major difference. For example, current entering in one hand and out the other hand will pass through the heart, spinal cord, and vital organs. Current passing from the foot to the knee on the same leg is not nearly so damaging. Be prepared to administer CPR, and treat for shock and electrical burns.

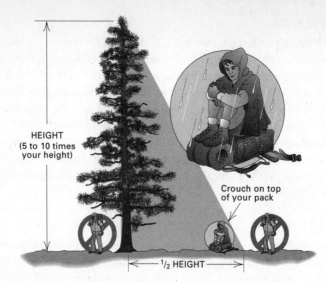

HEIGHT
(5 to 10 times
your height)

Crouch on top
of your pack

1/2 HEIGHT

Protection from Lightning Strikes

Your goal is to find the location that is least likely to send up a return strike. Obviously, the major sources for strikes are things like mountain peaks, exposed ridges, and tall trees. You want to get away from these objects, but if you get too far away—out into an open field, for example—you may set yourself up as another likely target. If you are caught in an area where a lightning strike seems possible, you may be safest inside the "safety shadow" of a potential lightning target. That means far enough away that you are relatively safe from the direct strike and ground currents, but not so far away as to become a target yourself. For example, if you are near a pinnacle, stay inside a zone where your horizontal distance from the pinnacle is about one half less than the pinnacle's height above you. It is best if the pinnacle is 5 to 10 times your height to get a reasonable distance away from the potential strike location.

Locations That Can Receive a Direct Strike

- Get off of ridges or pinnacles. Even a few yards (meters) may offer some protection.
- Stay away from taller trees. If you are in a forest, try to find a group of lower trees that are less likely to be a strike site.
- Get off the water.

Locations Where Ground Currents Can Easily Travel

- Stay out of depressions, gullies, or drainages that may have water flowing in them.

- Find a position partway down a slope. Dry or well-drained ground is best.
- Avoid caves and overhangs unless they are *clearly dry* and *spacious.* These are usually part of a larger system of cracks and fissures, which are likely conduits for ground currents, especially if they are wet. Don't seek shelter in caves, under boulders or overhangs, or in bunkers unless they are dry and unless you have at least 15 feet (5 meters) of headroom and 4 feet (2 meters) of space on every side.

Where You Want to Be

- Crouching on top of your pack
- Crouching on top of a boulder that is resting on top of other rocks
- Inside the safety shadow of a pinnacle or tree

🍁 TRICKS OF THE TRAIL

Lightning Strikes Our instinctive response in a thunderstorm is to get into a shelter, but sometimes the shelter can be more dangerous than staying outside. In July 1994, while I was sea kayaking in Maine, a severe afternoon thunderstorm developed. Luckily we were able to get off the water before it hit. Nearby, another group of kayakers was caught out in the storm. They headed for an island in the harbor and sought shelter in a concrete WWII bunker. Unfortunately, the bunker was elevated above the water and was filled with steel reinforcement. The bunker took a direct strike. Tragically, one person was killed and three others were seriously injured. The three who survived all required CPR to revive them. Understand the dynamics of lightning, including the spark gap effect. Don't seek shelter in caves, under boulders or overhangs, or in bunkers *unless* the area is dry and you have at least 15 feet (5 meters) of headroom and 4 feet (2 meters) of space on every side.

What to Do in a Severe Lightning Storm

Most lightning storms move away fairly quickly. With good rain gear, you should be able to stay relatively dry until the storm has passed, even out in the open. Hypothermia could be a problem if you become wet, but that's a secondary problem compared to the imminent lightning danger. Here is what you should do if you are in immediate danger from lightning:

1. **Spread Out** If the group is in an area of high lightning danger, the group should *not* wait out the storm huddled together. Split up but still be within sight of each other—30 feet (9 meters) apart or more— unless this puts some people in a site with a higher strike potential. The survival of one person whose heart or breathing has stopped as a result of a strike may depend on prompt action by companions (*know*

CPR). It is quite unlikely that everyone would be knocked unconscious simultaneously if the group is sufficiently separated.

2. **Assume the Lightning Position** Anytime thunder is *15 seconds* or less from the lightning, and the storm is within 3 miles (4.8 kilometers), you should assume a crouch position with your feet close together and your butt off the ground. Your hands should be on your knees. If possible, you can crouch on top of a dry, insulating material like a foam pad. This position means that if you were in the path of a ground current, it would go up one leg and out the other, minimizing the parts of the body affected. If a hand is on the ground, the current could flow through the arm, through all the major organs (potentially causing significant damage), and out a leg.

3. **Set Aside Metal Objects** Contrary to popular belief, metal objects (pack frames, ice axes, climbing hardware) on the ground do not *attract* a lightning strike. There are usually much better objects for a return stroke. However, metal in contact with the body can provide a path of least resistance for *ground* currents. It is best to set metal objects like pack frames and ice axes away from your body, to create a more attractive path *past* you rather than *through* you.

FOREST FIRES

When traveling in the backcountry, it is important to be aware of fire hazards. Just like avalanche forecasts in the winter, many wilderness areas post fire danger levels. Check with local rangers to determine the fire danger before you go out. If the fire danger is high, you may have to reduce fire or stove use, or even reroute your trip. Fire is a complicated aspect of wilderness management. In some ecosystems, natural fires from lightning strikes are part of the forest ecosystem—some pinecones open and release their seeds only at temperatures of 120°F (49°C).

Natural fires are caused primarily by lightning strikes. However, most of the fires in the United States are caused by human activities, including campfires, smoking, debris burning, toilet paper burning, and equipment use. Assess the fire danger in an area before you go in, avoid inadvertently starting a fire, and know how to evacuate yourself to safety in the event of a fire.

THE DYNAMICS OF FOREST FIRE

Any substance that will ignite and combust is potential fuel for a fire. For a living plant, more than half of the plant's weight is water, so living plants are relatively resistant to burning. Most fires start with dry or dead fuel. Fine fuels, like dry grasses and twigs less than ¼ inch (6 millimeters) across, are easy to combust; once burning, they can carry the fire to the larger fuels. As the fire spreads outward, the heat from the fire dries out the surrounding fuel and increases the likelihood that this fuel will begin to burn—this is known as *preheating*. Once a fire is blazing, it can preheat and then burn live plants and trees.

In the forest, there are three basic types of fires, and most fires are some combination of these types:

- **Surface Fires** burn litter on the surface, such as grasses, small plants, shrubs, small trees, and downed limbs and branches.
- **Ground Fires** burn the duff and organic layer in the soil beneath the surface litter.
- **Crown Fires** burn the tops of trees and shrubs.

How Fire Moves

Depending on the conditions, fire can spread slowly (¼ mph or 0.4 kph) or fast (5+ mph or 8+ kph). Understanding how a fire is moving will help you determine which directions are safest and which directions are most dangerous. From the point of ignition the fire spreads in three directions.

- Head (forward)—Fire rapidly spreads in the direction the wind is blowing.
- Flank (at the sides)—Fire spreads less rapidly at right angles to the direction of the wind.
- Rear (rearward)—Fire moves slowly into the wind (a.k.a., a backing fire).

Effect of Terrain on a Fire

If the ground surface is basically flat, the flames from an already ignited area can preheat only a few trees at a time and the fire spreads slowly. On a steep slope, flame can preheat many more trees above it and the fire spreads much more rapidly upslope. At the top of a peak or a ridge, the flame cannot preheat trees on the downslope side away from the fire, so it rapidly uses up existing fuel and may die out.

Effect of Wind on a Fire

Any wind can significantly enhance the spread of the fire up the slope by bringing the flame closer to unburned trees and preheating them. A strong wind can do this on horizontal surfaces and steep slopes. At a peak or ridgetop, wind may actually bend the flame down the far side of the slope, preheating more fuel and allowing the fire to continue down the far side of the ridge. Winds may be part of the local weather pattern; however, a large fire often creates its own winds. As air above the fire is heated, it rises, creating convection currents (air flowing in to replace the rising air). The hotter the fire, the more air may be sucked into it, fanning the flames.

FIRE SAFETY PLAN

Fire Prevention

If the fire danger in the region is high, use the local guidelines set by the rangers. As the fire danger increases, you may need to modify your activities, which could mean no campfires of any kind, no stove use, or no burning of toilet paper.

Fire Evacuation

In order to escape a fire, you first must be sensitive to signs of fire. Here are general procedures for escaping a forest fire:

- Be aware of any smoke. Smoke may be evident long before the fire is actually visible. If smoke is present, ascertain the wind direction and try to locate the fire.
- If you see fire, estimate the spreading intensity, the direction of the fire, and the extent of the fire, including the effects of the wind speed, wind direction, and terrain. Keep in mind that mountain ridges often have their own up-currents and down-currents that may be moving differently from the general weather pattern of winds.
- Once you have determined the general location of a possible fire, decide if you are upwind or downwind of it. Identify as best you can the fire area on your map. Look for the nearest trailhead, road, or other connection with civilization that does *not* take you toward the fire. If

you must move toward the fire, move along the *flank* or *rear* of the fire. The expansion of the fire is much slower there and you may have enough time to evacuate your group past the fire.

- When you have reached civilization, contact local rangers and emergency personnel. Provide them with as much detail as you can about the size and type of fire and its location. Give them your exact location and arrange for any additional transport your group may need. Also, make sure that the parking area for the vehicle is not at risk. If so, ask the rangers what they can do to help you get to and move your vehicle.

Burn Injuries

When we think of fire, we typically think of the damage caused by burns from the actual flames. However, more than just the flames are dangerous. In a forest fire, air temperatures are extremely hot. Injuries and burns can occur simply from contact with this superheated air. Inhaling this heated air can cause serious burns to lung tissue. Smoke inhalation and lung damage are also serious concerns in a fire (see Burns, page 277).

Fire Survival

If you are unable to escape an oncoming fire, there are only a few alternatives.

- Do your best to locate the fire and move perpendicularly away from the *flank* of the fire.
- If the surface fire is severe or approaching fast and crowning, look for the nearest large body of water and take shelter in the water. You are safer in the water, but be aware of the possibility of hypothermia from prolonged exposure to cold water.
- Go to an area with little fuel, such as a creek bed (even a dry one) or rockslide.
- Go to an area that has already burned (and hence is devoid of fuel).

Fighting Fires

In some situations, a fire may start right near your location. At the initial ignition stage, you *may* be able to contain a small surface fire. Deny the fire access to additional fuel by clearing downed branches, shrubs, and duff from its path. Once you have removed the fuel source, then the fire will either burn itself out or you may attempt to extinguish the flames with water or dirt. This may be possible, *but only if the fire is very small.* Without special training in fire fighting and the proper equipment, it is extremely difficult to put out anything but a *very* small surface fire. *Do not attempt to do* so if it means placing your group in danger (see How Accidents Happen, page 193).

WILDERNESS SURVIVAL

Many years ago, I took a wilderness survival course given by Tom Brown. From this course and from Tom's book, *Tom Brown's Field Guide to Wilderness Survival,* I learned the basic tools necessary in a wilderness-survival situation. If you find yourself in an emergency situation where you are cut off from help for an extended period with limited resources, don't panic. Most of the tools that you need to survive are all around you. Learning a few basic techniques and maintaining a positive attitude will cover your immediate needs for a few days to a week. Here's what to do:

- Attend to any immediate dangers—avalanche, fire, etc.
- Thoughtfully recognize the hazards of your situation and remain calm.
- Calmly assess all of your resources.
- Attend to the basic elements of survival.
- Signal for rescue.

THE FIVE ELEMENTS OF SURVIVAL

Once you acknowledge that you are in a survival situation, you should take inventory of all the food and equipment you have on hand—you may need everything. Then attend to the basic priorities of survival. In *Tom Brown's Field Guide to Wilderness Survival,* Tom Brown describes five basic survival priorities you should attend to:

1. **Attitude** Maintaining a positive attitude is essential. You *can* survive if you stay calm, use all your available resources, and prioritize your basic needs.
2. **Shelter** A shelter is designed to provide protection from the weather and, depending on the conditions, to protect you either from heat or cold. Hypothermia or hyperthermia are two of the greatest dangers in a survival situation. A proper shelter can prevent these situations. In a desert scenario, for example, your goal is to stay under a shelter, shaded from the effects of the sun. In cold weather situations, the shelter provides insulation from the cold.
3. **Water** Water is the most essential "nutrient" for the human body. With adequate shelter and water you can survive for weeks.
4. **Fire** In a survival situation, fire provides heat and light, and signals to rescuers.

5. **Food** Individuals in good physical condition and with extensive survival training can go for up to 2 to 3 weeks without food. Your goal in a wilderness survival situation is to be located in a matter of days, so in most cases you will be located long before food becomes a major survival issue. Obtaining food is 90 percent of wilderness survival and is beyond the scope of this book. This includes knowledge of edible plants, tracking, hunting, stalking, trapping, and so on. (If you are interested in learning these skills, see the Bibliography.)

SHELTER

If you are in a survival situation, your first priority is to construct a shelter to protect you from the elements. Wetness, cold, and heat are your main enemies. Natural shelters, such as caves, overhangs, and rock outcrops, may protect you from rain but don't provide any insulation. They should be used only temporarily, in sudden inclement weather, until you can build a survival shelter.

The Debris Hut

Tom Brown, in his book *Tom Brown's Field Guide to Wilderness Survival,* describes the debris hut as the most basic survival shelter that can be built almost anywhere. If you've ever seen a squirrel's nest up in a tree, then you understand the basics of creating a survival shelter. The nest is a ball of leaves creating dead air space. In cold conditions, this holds in body heat; in hot conditions, it keeps cooler air trapped inside. You should build your debris hut *first* so that you are prepared for any bad weather—rain, a sudden temperature drop, scorching heat—and can avoid hypothermia or hyperthermia. The following are some good places to build a debris hut:

- In a high, well-drained area, raised off the general ground level.
- In a protected area (wind makes it difficult to build a debris hut and convection can rob you of stored hot or cool air).
- Where there is good shelter building material close at hand. This conserves energy needed for survival. Building a shelter is the most energy-demanding survival activity, so you need to do it efficiently.
- No closer than 50 to 100 feet (15 to 30 meters) to water. The humid air near a water source will make you feel warmer in hot weather and colder in cool weather. However, the moist air also makes it difficult to dry out the insulating materials of your debris hut, thereby reducing the maximum insulative efficiency of your shelter.
- At least 6 feet (2 meters) from your fire. A debris hut is actually a giant tinder bundle, so you need to be very careful with fire.

Constructing a Debris Hut

The debris hut consists of a central ridgepole with one end on the ground and the other lashed to a tree or propped against a stump. The ridgepole should be long enough so that you can lie completely under the length of the pole without your feet being smushed. Two angled poles come from the highest point of the ridgepole to the ground in an A-frame and form the opening. The front of the ridgepole should be high enough so that, while lying on your side, you can just barely touch the ridgepole. With this general frame in place, line branches across the ridgepole from the ground on either side for ribs. Over a good layer of branches, pile light and airy brush (pine boughs, moss, sagebrush, leaves) to act as an insulative layer. Cover the outer layer with a few light branches to keep the insulating layer from blowing away. The hut will eventually look like a dome of debris with a tri-angular door (see preceding illustration). Once the hut has been built into a dome, stuff the inside with more insulative material—dried leaves, pine needles, dried grasses. You are creating a massive dead air space to provide insulation for your body. Crawl in and pack more dried materials around your body. In effect, you are creating both an insulated shelter and a sleeping bag in one.

For insulation materials, the best sources are dry vegetation such as dried grasses, ferns, and leaves. If none are available, you can use green plants. (You should *only* use green plants if you are in a true survival situation.) Green plants are mostly water; just like wet clothing, a wet plant will conduct heat 25 times faster than a dry one. If the material you are using is green, you should increase the overall thickness of the hut by about $\frac{1}{3}$ to compensate. The actual thickness of your debris hut will depend on the temperature. In the summer, the wall should be as thick as the distance from your outstretched finger to the middle of your upper arm; in the fall ($40°F$ or $4°C$), the wall thickness should measure from your fingertip to armpit; and in the winter ($17°F$ or $-8°C$), the wall should be 4 to 5 feet (1.2 to 1.5 meters) thick.

If you are experimenting with a debris hut, be aware that in certain regions, small critters like ticks and brown recluse spiders may end up in your hut with all the leaf litter. In a real survival situation, the idea that you might get Lyme disease from a tick is a minimal risk compared to the possibility of death from hypothermia. In a non-emergency situation, you should be aware of these other risks.

🍁 TRICKS OF THE TRAIL

In winter conditions, a debris hut may not be possible, in which case your best insulator is going to be the snow around you. Snow is a great insulator—all the interlocking snow crystals create excellent dead air space. For a true survival situation, build a structure quickly and with little energy expenditure, and remember to poke a ventilation hole into the roof for air flow. Keeping a stick in this hole and shaking it every so often will keep the hole open.

WATER

Water is your single most important "nutrient." You can *only* go for 24 to 72 hours without water before the effects of dehydration become apparent: impaired judgment, loss of strength and motor coordination, and increased susceptibility to hypothermia and hyperthermia. Dehydration ultimately leads to death. That's why staying hydrated is the second priority if you are in a survival situation. Whatever the water source, it is essential to *know about the purity of the water you are drinking.* It may sound strange, but drinking contaminated water can be as dangerous as not drinking at all. If you get a major gastrointestinal infection from contaminated water, you can lose so much water from diarrhea or vomiting that you may die. In a survival situation you often will need to look for multiple sources of water. If safe water is not readily available, structure your day to conserve water. Work during the cooler morning and evening hours and rest during the hot part of the day in the shade to reduce sweating and water loss.

In his book *Tom Brown's Field Guide to Wilderness Survival*, Brown identifies a number of sources for obtaining water in a survival situation.

Rivers, Lakes, and Streams

Before going into an area, it is important to check with local rangers about water quality. The water should be clear and running quickly; standing water becomes stagnant and contaminated with microorganisms. Ask yourself what's upstream—a town, cattle ranch, campers—that could be contaminating the water source. You should assume all water is contaminated and purify it (see Water Purification, page 83).

Areas devoid of vegetation may indicate contaminated or toxic water. Dead animals in the water upstream can cause contamination that will not be apparent. Observe what animals are doing—are they drinking the water? If so, it *may* be okay. But keep in mind that animals are resistant or immune to many microorganisms that we are not. It's best to get water upstream of animal drinking areas to avoid their possible contamination of the water from things like *Giardia* (see Gastrointestinal Infections, page 316). Be aware where animals *don't* drink. This water is best to avoid.

Natural Caches

Natural caches are depressions in rocks, hollow tree stumps, and such that collect rainwater. These are less desirable than moving water, but *may* be okay if the water has recently collected. The big question is, how long has the water been sitting there? In many cases you won't know. Water that has been standing for some time often becomes stagnant and contaminated with microorganisms. Look at the water in the cache. If it is cloudy, assume it is contaminated and do not drink it *unless* you can boil or purify it. Even clear water can be contaminated, so it's best to purify all water unless it is fresh-cache rainwater. Try to avoid stirring up debris as you get water. Put a cloth in to soak up water and wring it into a container or your mouth. You can create your own rainfall caches using pots or water bottles.

Soaks

There is always water underground, even in the desert. The question is how far down and how much energy (and fluid from sweat) would be expended to reach it. In many situations, water may be close enough to the surface for you to tap it.

Look to see where there is runoff, for areas of vegetation where "watery" plants are very thick, and for moist depressions in the soil. Dig a hole in the ground at these sites and see if it fills with water. If so, you may be able to scoop the top layer. You can also stick a reed or straw into the hole. The capillary action of the reed will bring the water up, leaving the debris behind.

Solar Still

You can create a solar still almost anywhere to make fresh drinking water. The solar still uses the sun's energy to extract moisture from plants or other water sources through condensation. Since the water recondenses from vapor, any microorganisms are left behind in the original water source, creating microbiologically pure water (it does not remove chemical contaminates). You need a 5 × 5-foot (1.5 × 1.5 meters) piece of clear plastic sheeting and 6 feet (2 meters) of surgical tubing.

- Dig a pit about 3 feet deep and 4 feet across (1 meters × 1.2 meters) in an area with good sun exposure. Place a wide-mouthed collection container in the middle of the pit.
- Place one end of the tubing in the container and the other end on the ground next to the pit. Place the clear plastic over the entire pit and cover the edges of the plastic with dirt to seal off the pit.
- Place a rock in the center of the plastic over the container to create a depression in the plastic. The angle of the depression should be fairly steep, about 45 degrees. The low point of the plastic sheet should be about 3 inches (8 centimeters) above the container and centered over the container so that the water will drip into it. As the sun heats up the sealed environment, the water from the ground becomes water vapor. This water vapor rises and hits the underside of the plastic sheet, where it condenses and forms droplets that roll down and drop into the container (see illustration below). The tube serves as your drinking straw.

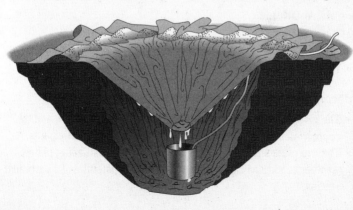

It will take some time to build up enough moisture in the still to start the process. The surgical tubing allows you to suck water from the container without taking the system apart, which would just mean more time for additional water production. A solar still in a damp area will collect water for four to five days. Then simply dig a new hole and start the process again.

To increase the water production, you can "add water" to the system. Place cut green plants in the pit around the container. The sun's heat will cause their moisture to evaporate. Use edible, or at least nonpoisonous, plants—otherwise the water that condenses may contain chemical toxins. You can also pour biologically contaminated water (like that found in an old water cache) around the edge of the pit. The water will be filtered by the dirt and distilled into biologically pure water. This technique allows you to use one still and continually "prime" it with new water.

ACCIDENT SCENARIO ANALYSIS

Here is the analysis of the backpacking scenario given at the beginning of the chapter.

Environmental Hazards

- Rocky trail
- Wet trail
- Lightning
- Heat
- Humidity
- Dehydration

Human Factor Hazards

- Age of kids—their physical abilities and experience
- Dan's inexperience
- Limited group resources in an emergency

Possible Accidents

- Fall
- Heat exhaustion, heat stroke
- Lightning strike

Reducing the Accident Potential

- The group should have had better knowledge of the terrain and the appropriateness of the route to the age group of the participants.
- The trip route should also have included an understanding of how weather conditions can increase the accident potential of a particular section.

- The group could have had a better plan for the day in terms of mileage, when to leave camp, rest breaks, lunch breaks.
- The group should have had a plan for "bail out" in case of bad weather.
- There should have been more experienced trip leaders.

Sample Environmental Briefing

Here is a sample environmental briefing based on the sample above. Sally could have covered these topics with the group before the trip. Simply understanding the Dynamics of Accidents Model can significantly reduce the accident potential.

Sally: "Here are some of the possible environmental hazards we all should be aware of: hot temperatures, dehydration, afternoon thunderstorms, wet, slippery trails, and steep trail sections."

CHAPTER 9

First Aid and Emergency Care

BACKCOUNTRY FIRST AID

Performing first aid in the backcountry may be the greatest challenge you encounter. You may be far from help and have limited first-aid supplies. Your ability to carefully examine a patient, determine a problem list, and develop a workable treatment plan may be the thing that keeps this person alive until more advanced rescue and medical care arrives.

🍁 IMPORTANT NOTE

The information in this chapter is designed as reference material only, to help people who have *already* taken a wilderness first aid course and CPR training. It is not a substitute for training and certification in first aid and CPR. If you have not been properly trained in these procedures, you can cause more harm to your patient by treating him or her.

If you haven't taken a first aid or CPR course, take one before you go into the backcountry! Even a simple day trip can lead to a serious medical emergency. For a list of some organizations that offer training in wilderness first aid, see page 335. There are also a number of excellent books specifically on backcountry medicine listed in the Bibliography.

THE WILDERNESS CONTEXT

In recent years there has been new appreciation for the challenges of providing first aid in the backcountry. Minimal equipment, no access to advanced medical care, potentially extreme weather, and the possibility that it may be hours or days until advanced medical care arrives all create a situation comparable to "combat first aid."

In order to respond to these challenges, the Wilderness Medical Society and other organizations have recognized that there is a significant difference between urban first aid, where advanced medical care is often only a 911 call away, and wilderness situations. The society defines a *wilderness context* as one that occurs more than two hours from *definitive medical care*, typically defined as a hospital emergency room or mobile paramedic emergency unit. Physicians recognize that with certain injuries or illnesses, failure to treat a patient within two hours can be life threatening or can lead to significantly greater injury. As a result, certain treatment procedures have been approved for use in the wilderness context, but *only* by those who have received instruction from an authorized source.

GOOD SAMARITAN LAWS

Whenever you talk about first aid, it is important to understand the issues of treatment and liability. If you are a licensed health-care professional (paramedic, EMT, nurse, or physician), then your license establishes the parameters of what treatments you are allowed to perform and what you are not allowed to perform.

For the nonprofessional, Good Samaritan laws provide protection to render first aid *to the level of their training*. The Good Samaritan laws were designed to encourage people to help someone in a medical emergency without fear of being sued if something bad happens to the patient. If you have been trained in CPR or wilderness first aid and you treat someone within the guidelines of what you have been taught, the Good Samaritan laws generally protect you from a lawsuit. However, if you stray outside of that training you expose yourself to liability. For example, if you carry medications in a first-aid kit, as a nonprofessional you are technically not permitted to give someone else a medication. This would be considered prescribing medication for someone. You can, however, inform the person of available medications that they could take, and then the person can self-administer the medication.

In a wilderness first-aid course, you may be taught techniques to use in a wilderness context that even a health-care professional, like an EMT, is not authorized to do in an urban context. However, you must be extremely careful to apply your level of training to the medical context you are in. For example, if you have been properly trained in how to recognize and reduce a shoulder dislocation in a wilderness setting, you are *only* authorized to do so when you are in a wilderness context. Reducing a shoulder while you are in an urban setting is *not* appropriate since advanced medical care is less than two hours away, and doing so could place you at a significant liability risk.

The bottom line is, if you are going into the backcountry, you should have solid training in wilderness first aid. Don't take a basic first-aid course designed for the urban environment. Such a course will teach you only rudimentary skills like how to bandage a wound and call 911. You need the advanced skills of patient assessment, treatment techniques, and how to maintain someone for an extended period of time until advanced medical care can be reached. Using treatment procedures developed for the wilderness context is only covered by the Good Samaritan law if you have been trained in those procedures by an authorized Wilderness First Aid training program. If you have not been formally trained, then you must make the decision about how to treat your patient. Remember that the physician's motto is "do no harm." If you are not sure of what you are doing, don't blunder around, or you could cause greater injury to the patient.

PATIENT ASSESSMENT

Patient assessment is the key to all medical care. You need to evaluate your patient's condition, determine what is or may be wrong, and implement an appropriate treatment plan with the equipment available. Then you need to make a judgment about whether the person can continue on the trip or whether he or she needs to be evacuated to definitive medical care (see Dealing with Emergencies—Who's In Charge?, page 192). When in doubt, be conservative and assume the worst.

The patient assessment system (PAS) is designed to provide a comprehensive approach to evaluating a patient's condition, from a minor cut to multiple traumatic injuries. Patient assessment is a complex skill that can be done well only with practice. Although the general principles of patient assessment are identical, they must be adapted to each situation. The general outline appears below.

ASSESS THE SCENE

Remember, *rescuer safety first.* Before approaching a patient, make sure that the scene is safe. You don't want more victims because people rushed foolishly into a dangerous situation. This may mean waiting for avalanche debris to settle, floodwaters to recede, etc.

- Once the situation is stabilized, approach the victim. If you cannot ensure the safety of the scene, you may not be able to treat the patient.
- Make sure that no one else is in any danger.
- Account for all victims.
- If the patient is in *imminent danger* (for example, a dangerous forest fire), you may need to move the person to another location before starting your assessment.
- Take proper precautions to maintain your safety at the scene, including wearing latex gloves (see Universal Precautions for Working with Blood and Body Fluids, page 244).
- Look for clues to the cause of injury.

PRIMARY ASSESSMENT

The goal of the Primary (or Initial) Assessment is to identify any potentially life-threatening situations that must be dealt with immediately. The Primary

Assessment is prioritized and should be performed in the following order: A (Airway), B (Breathing), C (Circulation), and D (Disability). If you find any problem in the Primary Assessment, stop the assessment and treat the patient immediately. The Primary Assessment may last only a few seconds if the patient is alert, walking around, and speaking to you. Here are the basic problems to look for during a Primary Assessment:

A = AIRWAY	
Problem	Airway blocked.
Assessment	Check for a clear airway. Open the airway in accordance with your training in CPR. Look, listen, and feel for breathing.
Treatment	If not breathing, clear airway and provide Basic Life Support.
B = BREATHING	
Problem	Patient not breathing or distressed breathing.
Assessment	Is air going in and out normally?
Treatment	If not, make sure airway is clear; provide rescue breathing.
C = CIRCULATION	
Problem #1	No pulse.
Assessment	Check for a pulse at the carotid artery.
Treatment	If there is no pulse, begin CPR.
Problem #2	Severe bleeding.
Assessment	Look for any signs of severe bleeding, especially under body, where blood can pool in sand or dirt.
Treatment	Control major bleeding.
D = DISABILITY: Possible damage to spinal cord leading to paralysis or death.	
Problem	Possible spinal injury.
Assessment	• Mechanism of Injury: a fall or impact force that could have injured the spine. If there is no mechanism of injury (for example, the person cut her hand with a knife), you can rule out a possible spinal injury.
	• Unreliable patient. If the accident is unwitnessed and the person is unresponsive, lethargic, or combative—in essence, you cannot rely on her answers as truthful or accurate—you cannot rule out the possibility that there was a mechanism for spinal injury.
Treatment	Stabilization. For any patient with an unwitnessed injury or any possible mechanism for a spinal injury such as a fall, you should initially assume that an injury exists and treat as such.
	• Ask the patient not to move her head and stabilize the head with your hands to maintain the head and neck in a neutral, in-line position (aligned with the midline of the body).
	• Keep the head and neck in a stabilized position until spinal injury can be ruled out and/or professional rescuers arrive on scene for transport.

SECONDARY ASSESSMENT

Once all life-threatening conditions have been addressed, the rescuer should perform an in-depth, head-to-toe physical exam, record the patient's vital signs, and ascertain his or her medical history.

Patient Exam

With some practice, the rescuer can accomplish an effective and thorough exam in minutes. Except in cases of imminent danger, avoid moving an injured patient until the exam has been completed. Make the patient as comfortable as possible with your professional manner, and protect him or her from inclement environmental conditions. It is best if the examiner is of the same gender as the patient; otherwise having an observer of the same gender can help make your patient feel more comfortable. It is often convenient to have a note-taker record the findings of the patient exam, vitals, and medical history, allowing the rescuer to concentrate on the exam. For the patient exam, keep the following principles in mind:

Principles in the Patient Exam

- Identify yourself; talk to the patient; keep a calm voice; let him or her know what you are doing.
- Develop a relationship with your patient as the only person performing the exam and any necessary treatment.
- Avoid moving the patient unnecessarily.
- Watch the patient's face for signs of pain or discomfort.
- Be professional.
- Keep the patient involved—ask questions about medical history and self-assessment. Give the patient a sense of control.
- A typical exam starts at the head, proceeds down the torso to the toes, and then returns to the arms.
- Observe for cuts, bruises, burns, or deformity. Look for discoloration and wetness. Listen and smell for anything abnormal.
- Examine the skin, muscles, and bone by feeling gently with your hands. Check for abnormalities, wetness, and tender areas.
- Compare symmetric body parts, such as hands and feet (especially useful to detect swelling).
- Flex the joints gently to check for mobility. Be sensitive to potential injuries and stop if there is any sign of pain.

As you examine your patient, here are some of the signs and symptoms to look for, and the possible implications of those findings.

Head and Neck

Examination	Signs and Symptoms	Possible Implications
Palpate scalp	Deformity, bleeding	Bump on head; skull fracture
Check face	Bruises, bleeding	Facial fractures; skull fracture
Ears and nose	Fluid; bruises behind ears	Bloody nose; skull fracture; increasing intercranial pressure (ICP)
Pupils	Equal in size? Responsive to light?	Increasing ICP
Palpate face and jaw	Bruises around eyes	Increasing ICP
Check inside mouth	Broken teeth; vomit; bleeding	Airway concerns
Lymph nodes	Swollen	Infection
Trachea	Deviation of the trachea or neck, veins bloated and visible	Chest wall and/or lung injury; pneumothorax

Upper Torso

Examination	Signs and Symptoms	Possible Implications
Palpate neck and back vertebrae	Tenderness or guarding?	Spine fracture
Palpate shoulders, shoulder blade and collarbone	Stable? Pain?	Fracture or dislocation
Press on rib cage from top, sides, sternum	Unstable, pain, grating sound	Chest wall injury
Breathing	Does chest wall rise symmetrically?	Flail chest

Lower Torso

Examination	Signs and Symptoms	Possible Implications
Palpate four quadrants of abdomen and back under ribs	Rigidity, pain (local/general, dull ache, stabbing, burning)	Abdominal injury or illness
Examine skin	Color; bruising; lacerations	Abdominal injury or illness
Pelvis/hips	Push from top, sides, rocking. Unstable? Pain?	Pelvic fracture; volume shock
Genitals	Bleeding, tenderness?	Soft tissue injury; urinary tract or yeast infection

Extremities

Examination	Signs and Symptoms	Possible Implications
Arms, legs, hands, and feet	Unstable, decreased range of movement? Inability to bear weight, weakness? Tenderness, pain? Abnormal circulation, sensation, and movement?	Fracture; dislocation; sprain; strain; soft tissue injury

Performing an Abdominal Exam

The key to performing a physical exam of the abdomen is to ensure that the patient is as relaxed and comfortable as possible. Have the patient lie down in a sheltered spot, then remove or pull back any clothing covering the area. Make sure that your own hands are as warm as possible before beginning. The exam itself involves nothing more complicated than gently feeling, with fingertip pressure, all four quadrants of the abdomen (above/below and left/right of the navel).

A basic understanding of anatomy is all you need to get useful clues from this exam. Compare your findings from the patient to the way your own body feels. A normal stomach should feel soft—rigidity indicates internal bleeding. Attempt to localize areas of tenderness exactly. Pain that can be specifically located is more suggestive of a serious condition than general and diffuse pain. Attempt to distinguish between deep pain and pain at the surface—that is, muscle pain or shallow bruises. If you are uncertain of your findings, assume the worst until proven otherwise and proceed accordingly.

Liver
Right Kidney
Colon
Pancreas
Gall Bladder

Colon
Small Intestine
Ureter
Appendix
Major Artery
and Vein to
Right Leg

Liver
Spleen
Left Kidney
Stomach
Colon
Pancreas

Colon
Small Intestine
Ureter
Major Artery
and Vein to
Left Leg

Vital Signs

Measure and record vital signs every 15 minutes. Changes in vitals provide critical information on the condition of the patient. While each individual will have differing resting vital signs, it is the change in vital signs over time that may indicate injuries or illnesses. Vital signs include the following:

- **Pulse** Record rate and strength (typical adult: 60 to 80 beats/minute).
- **Respiration** Record rate, strength, and any unusual smell (typical adult: 12 to 20 respirations/minute).
- **Skin** Assess skin color (pale/normal/red), temperature (cool/normal/hot), and moisture (dry/normal/clammy/sweaty).
- **Level of Consciousness** Use the AVPU scale:

  A = Alert—responds to questions and is completely oriented to time and place

  V = Verbal—responds to questions, but not completely oriented.

  P = Pain—responds to painful stimuli. Rub your knuckles on the sternum.

  U = Unresponsive—does not respond even to painful stimuli.
- **Temperature** Record temperature. To ensure an accurate reading, shake down the thermometer to push the mercury below the degree markings.
- **Circulation** Blood pressure is a measure of how well the body is being perfused with blood. Without a blood pressure cuff, you cannot get an exact reading. However, checking for a pulse in the distal extremities, such as at the wrist and the ankle, gives you a general assessment of how well blood is circulating (perfusing) in all four limbs. Typically if you get a pulse at the wrist, the systolic blood pressure should be 80 or above.

Patient History

The purpose of the patient history is to get as much information as you can that will give you clues as to the nature of the problem. Use the acronym SAMPLE to remember the categories to cover. Record everything on the SOAP Note (see page 238).

S = **Symptom** Is there pain or discomfort? When was the onset of the pain? Was the onset sudden or gradual? Describe the pain: Crampy? Stabbing? Generalized? Burning? Intermittent? What aggravates it? What alleviates it? Are there nonpain-related symptoms—tiredness, weakness, dizziness, nausea?

A = **Allergies** Any allergies to foods and medications, as well as urgent allergies like bee stings?

M = **Medications (prescription and over-the-counter)** What is the patient currently taking and for what conditions? When did she last take it? Keep the medication with the patient in the event of an evacuation.

P = Past Relevant History Has anything like this ever happened before? People with chronic problems often know their best treatment. Check any trip documentation, such as health history form or a medic alert tag.

L = Last Meal What and when did the patient last eat and drink? How much? This can be very important in many cases (e.g., diabetic emergencies, heat exhaustion, hypothermia, abdominal problems).

E = Events Leading Up to Accident What happened?

Obviously many parts of the patient exam, vital signs, and history can be done at the same time, and each situation will determine the most important questions to ask and action to take. For example, if someone is complaining of diarrhea and has not fallen, it is probably not necessary to extensively check the legs for fractures.

Assessing the Patient's Pain

In their book *The Outward Bound Wilderness First-aid Manual,* Jeff Isaac and Peter Goth define the acronym OPQRST as a useful framework for assessing pain.

O = **Onset** When did the pain begin?

P = **Provoke** What provokes the pain (i.e., moving, eating)?

Q = **Quality** What exactly does the pain feel like? Dull? Stabbing? Cramping?

R = **Radiation** Does the pain spread to other parts of the body?

S = **Severity** If 10 is the worst possible pain and 1 is very mild pain, how does this pain rate from 1 to 10?

T = **Time** Does the pain change over time? Is it constant, or does it come in waves?

TREATMENT AND DOCUMENTATION

TREATMENT PLAN

After you have finished your thorough examination, you must assess the patient's condition. Your examination establishes the basic problems and sets a baseline of the condition. You must decide, based on all the information you have been able to gather, what may be wrong and what plan of action you can take in the field to treat it. By continuing to monitor and note changes, you may discover problems that were not initially apparent. As a result, it is imperative that you document all findings, including things you looked for but did not find. The most common organization for this information is called the SOAP Note. The SOAP acronym stands for the four major headings below. In case of evacuations, SOAP Notes are crucial in relaying information to outside rescuers and medical professionals. (See the sample SOAP Note form, page 357.)

S	Subjective	What the patient tells you	The patient's chief complaint, the events leading up to the accident, and medical history.
O	Objective	What you found	All findings of the patient exam, vital signs, and observations of the rescuer.
A	Assessment	What you think is wrong	A list of all problems in order of importance. For example, "probable broken ankle" or "possible appendicitis." Also includes any anticipated problems, such as "possible volume shock due to blood loss from lacerated leg."
P	Plan	What you intend to do	Document all treatment given and plans for evacuation.

Definitive Care

The definitive care you provide depends upon your assessment of the patient's condition, your level of training, and the equipment you have on hand. If you are unsure about your problem list, you should assume the worst and respond accordingly. Any serious condition will require professional medical attention. In some cases this means bringing that care to the patient; in other situations you may have to evacuate the patient to medical care.

GENERAL FIRST-AID PRINCIPLES

There are a number of general principles that repeat themselves in different injuries and illnesses. Understanding these basic physiological and treatment principles will help you understand the dynamics of treating your patient.

SHOCK

The minimum requirement for keeping a human body functioning is the supply of oxygenated blood to all body tissues, known as perfusion. There are three primary components needed to maintain perfusion: enough *fluid*—blood—to provide the pressure needed to circulate to all parts of the body; a *pump*—the heart—capable of circulating the blood; and *pipes*—arteries, veins, and capillaries—that can carry the blood from the heart to the rest of the body. Failure of any one of these components will compromise the body's ability to keep up perfusion. Regardless of the specific cause, any condition resulting in inadequate perfusion will result in an identical set of signs and symptoms, known as shock.

Vital Signs in Shock The body attempts to compensate for decreased perfusion by increasing the pulse and respiration rates. The body also may decrease blood flow to the periphery (skin, arms, and legs) in order to save blood for the vital organs (see Shell/Core Response, page 241). Look for the following:

- Pulse—increased (above 100/minute in adults), weak
- Respiration rate—increased, shallow
- Skin—pale, cool, and clammy
- Blood pressure—decreased in later stages
- Level of consciousness—patient in shock will generally be anxious and agitated in early stages, and become progressively less responsive as condition worsens
- Nausea and/or vomiting

Types of Shock There are several different types of shock:

- **Volume Shock (fluid failure)** There is not enough fluid to provide adequate perfusion. The most typical causes are the result of blood loss from a wound or from dehydration (from inadequate drinking, from sweat loss due to heat, or diarrhea).
- **Vascular Shock (pipe failure)** Not enough fluid pressure to provide adequate perfusion. Caused by massive dilation of the blood vessels. In the wilderness, common causes are an acute allergic reaction (anaphylaxis) or a spinal injury.
- **Cardiogenic Shock (pump failure)** A damaged heart that is not able to pump blood through the body adequately. This can be a chronic problem from heart disease or an immediate problem from an acute injury.

Treatment for Shock Shock does not just happen—it must be caused by something. Identify the cause, and treat that as best you can (see Anaphylaxis, page 312; Bleeding, page 241; Fluid Balance, page 285). Remember, all major injuries left untreated can result in shock. In many cases, it may be shock more than the precipitating injury that can lead to death. In their book *The Outward Bound Wilderness First-aid Handbook,* Jeff Isaac and Peter Goth define the acronym PROP as the basic treatment for any type of shock:

P = **Position** Keep the person in a comfortable position and maintain body warmth. You may keep the person lying down with feet elevated 6 to 10 inches (15 to 25 cm). This helps blood return from the legs to the heart. Do *not* elevate the legs if the patient has a possible head injury, spinal injury, or a leg injury that would be compromised by raising the leg.

R = **Reassurance** Reassure the patient.

O = **Oxygen** Provide supplemental oxygen if available to increase the oxygen level in the blood.

P = **Positive Pressure Ventilations (PPV)** You can increase available oxygen by giving PPV (rescue breathing), even to a conscious person.

SWELLING

Swelling (edema) is the body's universal response to injury and tissue damage. It serves to both increase blood flow to injured areas and isolate those areas from surrounding tissue. All swelling, regardless of cause or location, follows roughly the same pattern. Swelling occurs quickly for the first 6 hours after an injury, and continues at a somewhat slower pace until approximately 24 hours after injury. Additional swelling is negligible after 24 hours. Extensive swelling can result in ischemia and tissue death. Swelling from certain injuries can be life-threatening, such as injuries to the brain, where the swelling takes place in an enclosed space (the skull).

ISCHEMIA

When blood flow (oxygen and nutrients) is cut off to body tissue, the result is ischemia. In its early stages, ischemia amounts to having an arm or leg fall asleep—the patient may feel tingling or numbness, and will eventually lose sensation and movement in the limb. If ischemia continues, it ultimately results in the death of that tissue. Anything that impedes or cuts off blood flow to an area can result in ischemia, including swelling of a part of the body, damage to a blood vessel (lacerations or twists in the vessel), or a tight bandage or splint. You should always check the tissue distal to a splint or bandage (farther from the heart) for signs of ischemia.

Checking Distal Circulation, Sensation, and Motion (CSM) One important technique for evaluating whether a peripheral area is being properly perfused is to check for circulation, sensation, and motion (CSM) at the distal end (away from the heart) of the extremity. For example, with an arm fracture, you would want to check CSM at the fingers.

- **Distal Circulation** You can check distal circulation by checking for a pulse or by checking for capillary refill. Check capillary refill time by pressing the nail beds to blanch a spot. In healthy individuals, the blood returns and the white skin at the blanch site becomes pink within 2–4 seconds. If it takes significantly longer than this, then you know that peripheral circulation is impaired. If the person is experiencing a shell-core response (see below), you will see a longer capillary refill time.

- **Distal Sensation and Motion** You can check distal sensation by rubbing something gently along the skin and by gently poking the skin with a sharp object. You can check for motion in a number of ways, as long as moving the extremity will not compromise the injury.
  - **For fingers** Ask the person to wiggle the fingers, squeeze your hand, and spread her fingers open with resistance from your hand.
  - **For toes** Ask the person to wiggle her toes, try to lift her toes up against resistance from your hand, and try to push her toes down against resistance from your hand.

SHELL/CORE RESPONSE

One adaptation of the human body is the natural response to protect the vital organs in the torso and head by cutting off blood flow to the extremities. In volume shock, the shell/core response minimizes blood flow to the extremities by constricting peripheral blood vessels to maintain perfusion of the vital body organs—the heart and the brain. In hypothermia, the shell/core response conserves heat and oxygenated blood in the vital body organs, at the expense of the relatively resilient and expendable body shell (arms and legs). Patients undergoing a shell/core response will have pale and cool skin, as blood withdraws from the outer layers toward the core. Shell/core response is not, in and of itself, a medical problem, but rather indicates that the body is undergoing extreme stress from some source. As such, there is no direct treatment for the shell/core response itself. Try to determine the cause, and treat the underlying problem.

BLEEDING

Bleeding can be controlled by using the following techniques:

- **Direct Pressure** Most bleeding can be controlled by applying well-aimed *direct pressure* to the site of the wound. Using a gloved hand and a piece of sterile gauze (if available), apply firm pressure to the wound. It may take up to 15 minutes for bleeding to stop completely. It is absolutely essential that the site of the bleeding be located exactly when applying direct pressure. This may require cutting away clothing or wiping away blood until the wound can be seen clearly. If you can't see the wound, you can't control the bleeding. When bleeding continues, most often it is due to pressure not being applied directly over the wound. You may have to remove your hand, reassess where the wound is, and reapply the direct pressure.

- **Elevation** Elevate the wound above the heart, thereby decreasing the local blood pressure.
- **Other Techniques** In most cases direct pressure and elevation will stop the bleeding. If it does not, you may need to use these techniques in addition:
  - **Pressure Points** Generally considered to have very limited applicability. The pressure points for blocking the major arteries to the limbs are located under the armpits and in the groin.
  - **Pressure Bandages** For rare situations when the rescuer has difficulty holding sustained direct pressure, such as with a very large laceration. Use a circumferential gauze dressing. It must cover a wide area so as to avoid impinging blood flow to the entire limb.
  - **Tourniquets** Rarely necessary except in situations of amputation. You should resort to a tourniquet only when *all* other techniques have failed and continued blood loss will cause death. Anytime you use a tourniquet, you risk ischemia to the tissues below the tourniquet and potential loss of the limb. If it's "life or limb," consider a tourniquet.

WOUND CARE

Cleaning a Wound Make sure the bleeding has stopped. Clean around the wound with soap and water or use a dilute povidone iodine solution. (To make the iodine solution, add approximately 1 inch (2 cm) of iodine ointment to 1 liter of water and allow to dissolve.) Irrigate the wound itself with a forceful flow of sterile water or povidone iodine solution, using a plastic bag with a small hole in the end or a large syringe. (Do not use 2 percent tincture of iodine; this causes burns.) Such rinsing helps remove any foreign material and does not damage tissues. Any foreign material, dead tissue, or even clotted blood left in the wound virtually ensures infection. For puncture wounds, bleeding should be encouraged to help remove bacteria and debris. We all know that alcohol stings when it gets in a wound. Antiseptics such as alcohol or tincture of iodine can damage tissues and *should not be used directly on the wound.* Antiseptics are used primarily for cleaning *around* a wound, like an alcohol swab on your skin before you are given an injection.

Wound Dressing and Bandaging Never close a wound with tape; this increases the risk of infection. Instead, dress and bandage a wound. A bandage is usually composed of three layers, each with different functions.

- **The Inner Layer** This layer of the bandage should be made of a thin, sterile material that does not stick to the wound, such as Tefla. This allows the bandage to be changed relatively painlessly without aggravating the injury. You can also use plain gauze covered with antibiotic ointment or petroleum jelly. Do *not* place ointments directly on the wound.

- **The Dressing** The dressing should be sterile and bulky, such as simple gauze pads that have been opened and crumpled to increase their bulk, allowing them to absorb blood and fluid.
- **Outer Wrappings** The outer portion of a bandage holds the dressings securely in place. Materials that have some elasticity are easier to use and stay in place better than plain gauze. If protection from water is not a concern, porous tape should be used to hold the bandage in place. When the bandage is changed, the tape should be clipped off at the skin edges and new tape placed on top of the old to avoid the skin irritation that results from repeatedly stripping off the old tape.

To Dress and Bandage a Wound

1. Apply antibiotic ointment to the inner layer. The ointment should be applied to the dressing rather than directly to the wound. This will prevent contamination of the remaining antibiotic in the tube or bottle.
2. Apply an inner layer of nonstick gauze.
3. Apply dressing layers as needed (this may depend on the amount of bleeding and the size of the wound).
4. Apply the bandage. It should be tight enough to hold the dressings in place but not so tight as to impede circulation. Check CSM—circulation, sensation, and movement—distal to the wound to make sure the bandage is not too tight. Be aware that swelling may occur up to 24 hours after the injury occurred.
5. Change the dressing daily and check the area for signs of infection.

WOUND INFECTION

It takes time for bacteria to infect a wound. A wound that is healing normally may appear red and swollen for 24–48 hours after the injury. Wound infection generally sets in 2 to 4 days after the injury. Any wound that remains red and swollen after 48 hours, or that becomes more swollen and painful, should be considered infected. In *The Outward Bound Wilderness First-aid Handbook,* the authors define the acronym SHARP to describe the common signs of a local infection:

S = **Swelling** The area will be swollen.
H = **Heat** The area will be hot to the touch.
A = **Ache** The area will be painful.
R = **Redness** The area will be red.
P = **Pus** The wound may show pus drainage.

High-Risk Wounds for Infections

- Animal or human bites
- Crushing wounds
- Wounds near or on joints
- Punctures
- Impaled objects
- Open fractures

If a wound becomes infected, remove all dressings and reclean the wound exactly as in the initial cleaning described above. Rebandage the wound. Be aware that you may need to evacuate the patient to medical care.

Signs of the Infection Spreading These are signs that the localized infection around the wound is spreading to the rest of the body. This type of systemic infection is *extremely serious and can lead to death.* Anyone showing signs of a systemic infection from a wound should be evacuated immediately. Here are the signs:

- High fever that develops after a wound
- Red streaks on the skin moving away from the wound and toward the heart

UNIVERSAL PRECAUTIONS FOR WORKING WITH BLOOD AND BODY FLUIDS

As first-aiders, all of us at one time or another will likely be exposed to blood and body fluids while treating a patient. There are a variety of diseases that can be transmitted from these fluids to the rescuer through contact with open cuts or mucous membranes. These include the HIV virus and hepatitis, both of which can be fatal. The basic principle of universal precautions is to always have a protective layer between you and the body fluid.

What Body Fluids Are Dangerous?

- Blood
- Blister fluid (may contain blood)
- Vaginal secretions
- Semen
- Vomit—dangerous only if the individual is vomiting up blood

What Precautions Do I Take? The following set of universal precautions are used by hospitals and health-care organizations around the world to protect people who are exposed to body fluids. The best way to protect yourself and others is to assume that *all* body fluids are contaminated. This means *always* wearing gloves and handling contaminated items carefully. Wear disposable gloves whenever you may come in contact with body fluids. These should be bagged as described below:

- Anything contaminated with body fluids (bandages, clothing, medical instruments) should be rinsed with a chlorine bleach solution (1 part bleach to 10 parts water). This will kill both HIV and hepatitis. Double-bag the items in two plastic bags. Do not throw out any blood-contaminated items that are sharp (e.g., epinephrine syringes with needles). Owing to the risk of someone sticking him- or herself, these items are considered medical waste. Sharp objects should be sealed in a rigid container and labeled "Medical Waste." Dispose of all medical waste properly after the trip.
- Any blood at the scene (on the ground or tarp) should be sprayed with chlorine solution.
- If you are changing a dressing, it should be considered contaminated. Dressings that have been contaminated by puslike drainage should be handled with great care to avoid spreading infection.

What About CPR?

If you need to do CPR on a patient, you should protect yourself from body fluids. Blood in the mouth, or a person vomiting blood, can be dangerous to the rescuer (and people frequently vomit during CPR). You should use a one-way valve CPR mask. The one-way valve will prevent you from inhaling or swallowing fluids from your patient.

BASIC LIFE SUPPORT

Basic Life Support (BLS) is the fundamental skill of maintaining blood circulation and respiration for a patient whose breathing and/or heart has stopped. If there is a near-drowning, respiratory failure, heart attack, or lightning strike, the *only* thing that will keep that patient alive until definitive medical care arrives is your ability to do CPR. CPR must be initiated within minutes (in cases of immersion hypothermia and cold water, you may have longer before any permanent damage occurs). You should take a CPR course from the American Red Cross or the American Heart Association on a regular basis to keep your skills current. This brief review is *not* designed to replace a course and assumes that you already know the basic skills and terminology. Always follow Universal Precautions, such as using a one-way valve mask, when giving CPR.

1. Is the Victim Unconscious?
- Tap the person and ask, "Are you OK?"
- If no response, call for help.

2. Open the Airway.
- Use a Head Tilt and Chin Lift. If you suspect head or spinal injuries, use the jaw thrust method only.
- Look, listen, and feel for breathing.
- If there is no breathing, go to #3.

3. Give Four Quick Breaths.
- Pinch nostrils closed. Give four quick breaths. Try to ventilate.

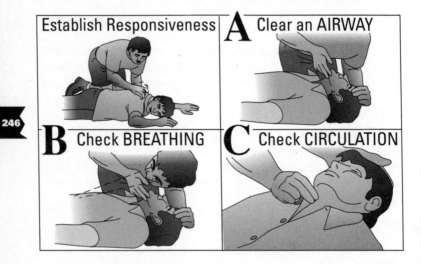

- If air does not go in, reposition the head to open the airway. If air still does not go in, straddle the patient and do 4 abdominal thrusts. Use a finger sweep to clear any foreign object, and attempt to open the airway again with chin lift or jaw thrust. Continue #2 and #3 until air goes in.

4. Check the Pulse.
- Check the pulse for at least 10 seconds (up to 1 minute if the person is severely hypothermic).
- If there is a pulse but no breathing, proceed with rescue breathing.

- Rate is 2 breaths every 15 seconds. (Count one and two and three and four . . . and fifteen, breathe, breathe.)
- If there is no pulse or breathing, go to #5.

5. **Locate the midsternum.**
   - Slide two fingers up the rib cage to the xiphoid process. Go two fingers up from that to the midsternum.
   - Interlace your fingers and place the heel of your lower hand against the midsternum.

6. **Chest Compressions and Breathing.**
   - Push straight down without bending your elbows. Push down 1½ to 2 inches (centimeters) for an adult.
   - For one rescuer the rate is 15 compressions and 2 ventilations (count to yourself: one and two and three and four . . . and fifteen, breathe, breathe).
   - For two rescuers the rate is 5 compressions and 1 ventilation (count one and two and three and four and five, breathe).

MOVING A PATIENT

There will be times when you need to move a patient, either to treat her or to quickly move her away from a dangerous situation. In many cases, you may be concerned about a possible spinal injury, so it is important to move the person as a unit, keeping the spine from bending or twisting.

When Moving a Patient
- Move a patient in small steps.
- One person should stabilize the patient's head, and call when movement should occur. Make sure all rescuers are ready.
- If possible, have one person at each of the major weight centers of the body to control that area—shoulders, hips, and legs.
- If you have to "unkink" a person, move only one body weight center at a time. Move each weight center slowly, and in increments, until the body is in a normal axial position.
- If you have to move the person some distance, if possible get her into an axial (lengthwise) position and then move her along the body's long axis.
- If the person is suspected of having a spinal injury, you should immobilize the neck using a cervical collar and the spine with a backboard (if possible) before moving.

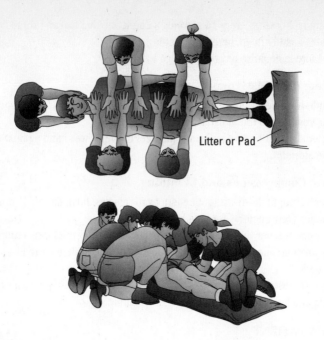

Litter or Pad

The In-line Drag The in-line drag can be used to move a person a short distance.

1. Have one person at the head and at least one person at each of the major weight centers (shoulders, hips, legs).
2. The person at the head checks to see that everyone is ready, and on her command the group lifts the patient to the same level and moves slowly forward. Depending on the distance to be moved, this may be a drag just above the ground, or the group may need to stand up and carry the person over a longer distance.

The Log Roll The log roll is used to roll a patient onto her side or onto a backboard.

1. Rescuer 1, at the head, stabilizes the head throughout the log roll and gives all commands about when to move.
2. Rescuer 2 kneels at the patient's chest and reaches across to the shoulder and upper arm of the patient.
3. Rescuer 3 kneels beside the patient's waist and reaches across to the lower back and pelvis.

4. Rescuer 4 kneels beside the patient's thighs and reaches across to support the legs with one hand on the patient's upper thigh, the other behind the knee.
5. Rescuer 1 gives the command, "Roll on 3; 1, 2, 3," and the rescuers slowly roll the patient toward them, keeping the body in alignment. Rescuer 1 supports the head and maintains alignment with the spine. Once the patient is on her side, a backboard or foam pad can be placed where the patient will be lying when the log roll is complete.
6. Rescuer 1 gives the command, "Lower on 3; 1, 2, 3," and the procedure is reversed. The patient is slowly lowered back while the rescuers keep the spine in alignment.

Log rolls can be done with fewer than four rescuers, if necessary. It is important to make sure that the entire spine is kept in line as the patient is rolled.

MAJOR BODY SYSTEMS

In order to properly evaluate a patient's medical condition, you should have a basic understanding of the three major body systems: how they function normally, what can go wrong with them, how to perform basic assessments, and what are the basic treatment protocols:

RESPIRATORY SYSTEM

Goal	Gas exchange: Oxygen in and carbon dioxide out.
Problem	Respiratory failure
Mechanisms of Injury	Airway obstruction—foreign objects (choking) or swelling (allergic reaction or asthma).
	Chest wall injury
	Respiratory drive loss
Assessment	Is air going in and out? If not, begin rescue breathing.
	Rate and quality of respirations (easy or labored)
Treatment	General treatment for respiratory problems goes by the acronym PROP:
	Position: Encourage the patient to rest in the position most comfortable for her. Most patients will do this on their own. If the patient is unconscious, roll her onto her side to keep the airway open.
	Reassurance: Breathing difficulty is always a terrifying condition. Encourage the patient to relax, and coach her in breathing slowly and deeply.
	Oxygen: If available, supplementary oxygen will increase the effectiveness of the patient's attempts to breathe.
	Positive pressure ventilation: It may be necessary to assist the patient's efforts at breathing by blowing a breath into her mouth (as per rescue breathing) as she attempts to inhale.
	Specific treatment of the underlying problem will vary widely. Airway obstructions should be dealt with according to your own training in basic life support (i.e., the Heimlich maneuver). If the patient is having difficulty breathing due to chest injury, turning the patient so that she is lying on the injured side often helps relieve some respiratory difficulty.

CIRCULATORY SYSTEM

Goal	Provide an adequate supply of oxygenated blood to all body tissues (perfusion).
Problem	Shock = inadequate perfusion.
Mechanisms of Injury	*Types of shock:*
	Fluid problems (loss of volume)—inadequate blood in circulation.
	Pipes problems (e.g., anaphylaxis)—problems with blood vessels
	Pump problems (e.g., cardiac arrest)—problems with the heart muscle
Assessment	Check for carotid pulse—if absent, begin CPR.
	Check for and control major bleeding.
	Secondary assessment—check distal capillary refill.

Signs and symptoms of volume shock:

> Increased pulse (≥100)
>
> Increased respiration (≥24)
>
> Pale, cool, and moist skin (as the problem progresses)
>
> Possible loss of major quantities of body fluid

Treatment	Volume shock is a primary life-threatening issue in the backcountry. Volume shock does not spontaneously improve, nor can it be definitively treated in the field. The amounts of fluid lost in these cases often cannot be replaced orally: IV fluid replacement may be necessary. Evacuation is always required.
	Loss of any body fluid is ultimately reflected in reduced blood volume. Sweat, burns, vomiting, and diarrhea all lead to the same ultimate problem as bleeding. Losses from any of these sources result in exactly the same pattern of symptoms (as listed above).
	Field treatment for volume shock (until the patient can be evacuated) is simple: Stop the leak. Reduce or remove the underlying cause of the volume loss, i.e., control bleeding with well-aimed direct pressure. Replace fluids if possible.

NERVOUS SYSTEM

Goal	Voluntary and involuntary control of body functions
Problem	Inadequate perfusion to the brain
	Increasing intracranial pressure
	Spinal cord injury
Mechanisms of Injury	Medical problems or trauma leading to swelling, inadequate perfusion
Assessment	Level of consciousness—see AVPU scale, page 236
	Is there a mechanism for spinal injury?
	Due to the tremendous potential for damage and the extreme difficulty in correctly assessing nervous system problems, any decrease in a patient's level of consciousness (anything below A on the AVPU scale) warrants evacuation.
	Other less dramatic changes in mental status (i.e., lethargy or irritability) require a bit of detective work to determine a cause, and may be treatable in the field.
	Wilderness Medical Associates defines seven general factors (STOPEAT) that commonly affect brain function:
	Sugar—lack of blood sugar in the brain (especially an issue for a person with diabetes)
	Temperature—overheating or overcooling in the brain (see Heatstroke, page 292, and Hypothermia, page 293)
	Oxygen—lack of oxygen in the brain
	Pressure—increasing intercranial pressure (see Head Injuries, page 267)
	Electricity—electric shock, such as a lightning strike
	Altitude—high altitude (which can cause lack of oxygen to the brain and brain swelling, see Altitude Illnesses, page 323)
	Toxins—various toxins (inhaled, ingested, see Toxins, page 303)
Treatment	Ascertain the cause of the nervous system problem and treat accordingly.

THE MUSCULOSKELETAL SYSTEM

Injuries to the musculoskeletal system—strains, sprains, fractures, and dislocations—are the ones you are most likely to see as accidents in the backcountry. Fortunately, they also represent the area where a rescuer with minimum training can provide a great deal of help. The generic treatment for a musculoskeletal injury is to immobilize the area and to limit usage.

Assessment of the severity of an injury is more complicated. It's often hard to distinguish between an ankle strain, sprain, or minor fracture, especially initially when it hurts like hell and you don't want to put any weight on it. You may need an X ray to be really sure. So instead of trying to determine something you can't in the field, first determine whether the injury is stable or unstable. A *stable injury* may be a strain, sprain, or stress fracture that doesn't prevent use. The person may be able to hike out on her own or with assistance. An *unstable injury* is a fracture or dislocation that will require splinting (see General Fracture Treatment, page 255) and may require a litter evacuation.

STABLE AND UNSTABLE INJURIES

Both stable and unstable injuries will show the following common signs and symptoms:

- Pain
- Tenderness
- Swelling
- Bruising

Pain is the best indicator of the appropriate level of use. If an ankle hurts too much to bear weight, then the patient should *not* be walking on it. You may need to wait for the initial pain to subside in order to determine the severity of the injury. Here are the criteria that Wilderness Medical Associates uses to evaluate stable versus unstable injuries.

Signs and Symptoms	Stable Injury	Unstable Injury
Mechanism of Injury	Yes	Yes
Ability to Bear Weight	Yes	No
Normal Range of Motion	Yes	No
Feeling of Instability	No	Possibly
Deformity or Angulation	No	Possibly
Crepitus—grating sound caused by broken bone ends rubbing together	No	Possibly
Point tenderness—tenderness at a specific point on the bone.	No	Possibly
Patient felt or heard something snap or break	No	Possibly

BASIC STABLE INJURY TREATMENT

The goals in treating a stable injury are to reduce swelling and limit use. The basic treatment (called RICE) is to limit activity to that which does not cause pain, and administer anti-inflammatory medications (aspirin, ibuprofen—see Medications Profiles, page 328).

R = **Rest** Rest the area and limit use.

I = **Ice** Apply ice or another cold source immediately after the injury occurs—15 minutes on, then 15 minutes off, for up to 48 hours to reduce internal bleeding and control swelling. Avoid direct ice contact to the skin.

C = **Compression** Add light pressure. An elastic bandage is often helpful for sprains because it partially immobilizes the sprain and also provides some compression to limit swelling of the joint.

E = **Elevation** Elevating the sprain will limit the swelling, as this increases the reabsorption rate of blood and edema fluid.

STRAINS

Strains are minor muscle or tendon injuries usually brought on by sudden stress or prolonged use of a particular muscle group. Pulled muscles and tendonitis are both forms of strains. Pulled muscles tend to have a sudden onset, while tendonitis is characterized by a gradual onset of pain and stiffness. Having limber muscles is the best way to avoid such injuries. People should stretch every morning before starting the day and also stretch after long rest breaks or lunch stops.

TENDONITIS

Tendonitis is caused by the swelling of tendons or surrounding tissue. The onset is usually gradual and results from repeated use, which causes inflammation over extended periods of time. A common scenario for hikers is tendonitis of the Achilles tendon (which runs up the back of the ankle), caused by stiff or tight high-top boots that constrict the tendon, causing inflammation and swelling.

Treatment Moist heat, massage, and anti-inflammatory medications (aspirin, ibuprofen) as appropriate. Also, regular stretching is beneficial. Splinting can help in the short term. Tendonitis symptoms in the Achilles tendon can sometimes be relieved by the insertion of a foam heel pad in the boot. Stretching the leather of the boot in the Achilles area may reduce the risk of inflammation.

Ankle-Stabilizing Straps If someone has sprained an ankle and it is a stable injury, she can walk out on it. To keep her from spraining it again, create an ankle-stabilizing strap with two sleeping bag straps. First, make an ankle collar by wrapping one strap around the ankle just below the top of the hiking boot. Take the other strap and run it underneath the sole of the boot, up both sides of the boot between the boot and the ankle collar, and over the ankle collar on both sides to create a stirrup. Take the strap back down under the heel and secure it on the outside of the ankle by tightening the strap. This creates a rigid webbing strap that will help prevent sideways ankle flex but still allow flex front and back. Make sure that the straps aren't so tight that they inhibit circulation.

SPRAINS

A sprain is a severe stretch or tear of the tendons and/or ligaments around a joint. Sprains can be associated with fractures and/or dislocations. A sprain has symptoms similar to a fracture: pain, swelling, discoloration, and pain on use. Ankles, knees, and wrists are all commonly sprained. If you are unsure if it is a sprain or a fracture, treat it as if it were a fracture.

Treatment The first aid is the same for any sprain—RICE, pain-free activity, and anti-inflammatory medications. Splinting also helps. Sprained ankles are most common and can be treated either with a figure-eight bandage over the foot or by taping the ankle. In either case, the goal is to achieve lateral stability. The patient should place her foot in a normal position as if she were standing up straight. The figure-eight is wrapped around the back of the heel, crosses under the sole of

the foot, and crosses again on top of the foot. To tape an ankle, alternate pieces of tape that go under the heel and straight up the leg with ones that go from behind the ankle around to the top of the foot.

GENERAL FRACTURE TREATMENT

There are several general principles that apply to all splinting, regardless of the location of fracture.

- If you are unsure whether it is a fracture or a sprain, assume it is a fracture.
- If the fracture is between two joints, you should immobilize the joints above and below the fracture site. If the fracture is on a joint, you should immobilize the joint above and below the fracture site.
- Immobilize the fracture in a comfortable position of normal use by creating a rigid, well-padded splint in the most comfortable position.
- Ensure that you will have access to hands or feet distal to injury and to be able to monitor distal CSM.
- Make sure you have splinting materials available before you begin treatment.

FRACTURE SITES AND BASIC SPLINTS

- **Skull and face** Monitor ABCs closely. There is a possibility of head injury (see page 267) and spinal injury. Cervical collar and backboard (see Spinal Injuries, page 264).
- **Neck** Cervical collar and backboard (see Spinal Injuries, page 264).
- **Jaw** "Toothache bandage." Beware of vomiting.
- **Collarbone** Sling and swathe.
- **Shoulder** Sling and swathe.
- **Back** Cervical collar and backboard (see Spinal Injuries, page 264).
- **Ribs** Sling and swathe (firmly)—monitor breathing (see Chest Injuries, page 272).
- **Upper arm/elbow** Sling and swathe or board splint.
- **Forearm, wrist, and hand** Board splint and sling and swathe.
- **Pelvis** Backboard with lots of padding—watch for shock (see Shock, page 238).
- **Femur** Traction splint—watch for shock (see Shock, page 238).
- **Knee** Splint at angle found with lots of padding.
- **Lower leg** Splint straight with ankle at 90 degrees.
- **Ankle/foot** Splint with the ankle at 90 degrees with big, soft splint.

SPLINTING

The purpose of a splint is to immobilize the injured area and prevent further movement and possible damage. It also helps reduce pain and swelling. Here are some splinting basics:

- Check circulation, sensation, and movement (CSM) below the fracture before you begin treatment. If you find impaired CSM, then you know that the fracture is affecting blood vessels or nerves.
- Use traction-in-position (TIP) to pull the bone back into its normal alignment. From the position the bone is in, pull gentle traction and move the broken bone back into its normal anatomical position.
- Stop traction-in-position (TIP) if you find increased resistance or significant increase in pain.
- Maintain the traction using hands-on stability.
- Apply the splint.
- Recheck circulation, sensation, and movement below the fracture site after treatment. If CSM was impaired before and is now improved, your traction-in-position and splinting has helped. If CSM was fine before and is now impaired, your splint may be too tight or the splint may be cutting off blood flow or nerve transmission.

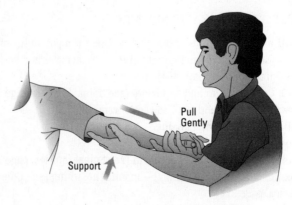

Pull Gently

Support

- Treat for shock (see Shock, page 238). Fractures often result in blood loss, which can lead to shock.
- Prepare to evacuate your patient.

SAM Splint Guidelines The SAM Splint is a foam-covered sheet of pliable aluminum that may be molded into an effective splint for a number of injuries. Owing to its versatility and minimal weight, it is commonly used in wilderness first-aid kits. Using a SAM splint effectively requires some basic instruction. If the splint is flat, it has little strength. However, by creating bends in the splint, such as a fold along the long axis, it becomes quite rigid. It is best to practice molding the splint to an uninjured limb first and make sure you have a good fit so you don't have to jostle the injured limb.

- **Ankle** There are two different methods of using a SAM splint on an ankle; both require additional stabilization with a larger splint. Bend the SAM splint from the sole of the foot up the sides of the leg in a U shape. Pinch a tuck at the bottom of the foot to tighten the splint and stabilize the injury. Another method is to start with the middle of the splint on the sole of the foot. Wrap the splint over the top of the foot and around to the back of the ankle in a figure eight. If two SAM splints are available, it is advisable to use both of these methods in conjunction. Additional padding can be achieved by wrapping a rolled foam pad around the lower leg. You can also create a solid ankle splint using a rolled foam pad or well-padded sticks.
- **Wrist/Forearm** The SAM splint should be folded in half lengthwise. One end of the splint should be rolled up to create a rest for the hand. Mold the SAM splint to the curvature of the arm, and pad between the split and the arm. Wrap with gauze or elastic bandage. This splint can be finished with a sling and swathe.

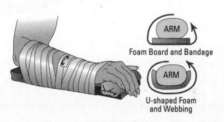

Foam Board and Bandage

U-shaped Foam and Webbing

- **Elbow** The elbow should be splinted in the mid-range position. The splint can be molded so that the elbow rests in the middle of the splint. The curvature of the splint can be maintained by taking tucks in the sides of the bend. Pad between the splint and the arm and wrap with gauze or an elastic bandage. Apply a sling and swathe.

Sling and Swathe The sling and swathe is used on a number of different fractures, including collarbone, shoulder, ribs, upper arm, and to secure a lower arm splint. With the sling and swathe, it is important to immobilize

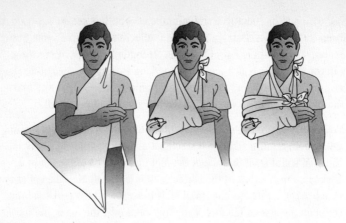

the arm while maintaining comfort. Be sure to pad the neck and keep knots off the back of the neck.

Lower Leg Splint Splinting a leg, such as for a lower leg fracture, requires long rigid materials. Place one rigid support on each side of the leg. This can be accomplished with multiple SAM splints, or with a rolled-up or folded foam pad and a rigid object such as branches, tent poles, or ice axes.

FRACTURES AT JOINTS

Fractures at joint sites can also include dislocations. Attempting to pull traction-in-position (TIP) can create additional damage at the joint.

Treatment Check distal circulation, sensation, and movement (CSM). If present, these fractures should be splinted in the position they are found. Do *not* use traction-in-position (TIP) to attempt to realign the bone to its normal anatomical alignment. If distal CSM is *not* present, use TIP *only* until distal CSM returns. Then splint in this position. Stop traction-in-position (TIP) if you feel increased resistance or significant increase in pain.

ANGULATED FRACTURES

Angulated fractures are fractures of the extremities in which the bone has been broken and is now lying at an abnormal angle. These fractures present a special problem because they are almost guaranteed to interfere with normal circulation and neurological function below the fracture site. If the broken bone is not brought back to the position of normal use, the fracture may act as a tourniquet, causing ischemia and ultimately tissue death below the break.

Treatment These fractures should be brought back to a position of normal use by pulling traction-in-position (TIP). Grasp the bones on each side of the fracture and slowly pull in line with the bone, no matter what angle they are lying at. This procedure is best done with two people—one person holds the bone above the fracture steady while the other one slowly pulls traction. Remember, pain from a broken bone arises from uncontrollable muscle contraction, so traction should reduce the pain.

After you have held traction for 10 minutes or more, the muscles should be fairly fatigued. Then slowly move the bone back into a position of normal use. Let the your patient be your guide. If he says the pain is increasing, stop, hold traction, and wait until he is ready before you move again. You are in no great rush. Remember also that all of the major blood vessels and nerves are surrounded by a highly sensitive layer of tissue, so you will inflict pain before you do any real damage. Your patient is relatively safe as long as you let him be your guide. Once the bone is in a position of normal use, it can be splinted like a normal fracture. Prepare to evacuate your patient.

OPEN FRACTURES

When the broken bone ends break the skin, it is called an open fracture. Open fractures may result in significant blood loss from bleeding, since the sharp bone ends may tear major blood vessels. You need to be prepared to treat for shock (see page 238). Open fractures pose significant additional complications due to the high risk of wound infection, especially if the bone is actually sticking out of the open wound.

Treatment Treatment decisions such as whether to apply traction-in-position (TIP) should be based on the need to control bleeding. If bleeding is severe, your primary concern must be to control the bleeding to prevent volume shock. Use TIP to pull the bone ends back in, which should help control the bleeding. If you decide to draw the bones back into the body, flush them with a povidone-iodine solution or clean water first to remove all foreign material and reduce the risk of infection. (See Wound Care, page 242.)

If bleeding is not severe, you should *not* pull to draw the bones back in. Without severe bleeding, the major danger is from infection and drawing the bones back in will draw bacteria and dirt into the wound. Instead, use large, bulky padded dressings so as not to aggravate the fracture sight. If the bone is sticking out of the wound, bleeding can often be controlled by making a "donut bandage" and applying this around the wound. (To make a donut, use at least two cravats. Wrap one around your hand several times to make a large loop. Then take the other bandage and wrap it around the first bandage.) Place the donut around the wound and secure it tightly with a wide cravat. Do not pick at, or try to push back, any exposed bone. Splint the injury as it lies. Keep in mind that you are dealing with two injuries: a fracture and a serious wound. Prepare to evacuate your patient.

FEMUR FRACTURES AND TRACTION SPLINTS

Femur fractures must be handled slightly differently than regular fractures. The large muscles of the leg will be in spasm, causing the broken bone ends to override each other, cutting and damaging tissue. There is major risk of damage to nerves and blood vessels, including significant bleeding and shock should always be anticipated. In order to minimize this risk, a traction splint is used to overcome the effect of the muscle spasm and pull the bone ends back into their normal position.

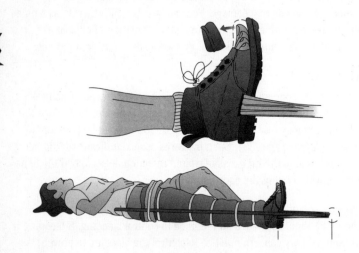

Treatment

1. Roll up a foam pad lengthwise and wrap it around the leg as a splint. Secure it in place with cravats or tape.
2. To prepare for applying traction, attach traction straps over the boot or padded ankle (see illustration). Fold two cravats into long narrow bandages. Fold lengthwise, and pass one over and one behind the ankle, making sure the ends of each bandage fit snugly and flat against the

ankle. The toes should remain visible or at least accessible for assessing distal circulation, sensation, and movement.

3. To construct the traction splint you need a long a polelike object (tent pole, hiking staff, ski pole, canoe paddle). It should extend from the top of the hip at least one foot (30 cm) beyond the bottom of the foot. Anchor the pole to the leg using a well-padded strap over the thigh at the hip. The distal end of the pole will need a strap that can be attached to the ankle hitch and tightened to create traction on the leg. (Practice this system on a noninjured person *before* applying it to your patient.)

4. Apply traction on the thigh by pulling the traction straps. Maintain traction by securing the traction straps to the end of the pole. Tie the traction splint to the foam pad splint already on the leg.

5. Once you have begun to pull traction on the leg, *don't* release traction. This will only result in increased injury to the surrounding vessels and tissue. Prepare to evacuate your patient.

DISLOCATIONS

The signs of dislocation are similar to those of a fracture: pain aggravated by motion, tenderness, swelling, discoloration, limitation of motion, and deformity of the joint. Comparison with the unaffected joint may help identify the problem. Dislocations should be treated as fractures and splinted in a comfortable position. There are three types of dislocations that can be reduced successfully in the field: shoulders, knees, and digits (fingers and toes). Keep in mind that reducing any dislocation can result in additional injury at the joint site and below. In some cases, you may not be able to distinguish between a dislocation and a fracture dislocation. Reducing a fracture dislocation can create other medical problems. Fracture dislocations are usually caused by a direct blow to the joint in question, and therefore you should *never* try to reduce a dislocation that has been caused by a direct mechanism. Only attempt to reduce a dislocation if *all* the following conditions are true:

- The dislocation is at the shoulder, knee, or fingers.
- The dislocation was caused by an indirect mechanism (a force was applied distally to the extremity and the proximal end joint was levered out of position). Imagine grabbing the end of your finger and levering the joint out at the knuckle—this is an indirect force. Do *not* reduce the joint if a direct force caused the injury, such as the impact from a fall (the underlying bones may also be fractured).
- There is a lack of circulation, sensation, and/or movement (CSM) of the extremity below the injured joint.

- You are more than 2 hours from more advanced medical assistance.
- **You have been *properly trained* on how to reduce a dislocation *and* feel competent to attempt the procedure.**

If *all* these conditions are true, field reduction is appropriate and usually successful. If reduction is delayed for more than 2 hours, the nerves and tissue below the injury are at risk. Failure to relocate can result in permanent tissue damage. After reducing the dislocation, check again for circulation, sensation, and movement (CSM) of the extremity below the injured joint. If CSM has returned, then the act of relocation has helped save distal tissue. If not, the person is probably no worse off than before.

SHOULDER DISLOCATIONS

Shoulder dislocations can be caused either by a direct force, such as the impact of a fall onto the shoulder, or by indirect force, such as a levering force applied to the arm. Anterior shoulder dislocations are the most common (about 98 percent of all shoulder dislocations) and are characterized by moderate to extreme pain and an obvious displacement of the arm forward from the shoulder socket. The displacement will give the shoulder a "stepped" appearance. The victim usually cannot bring the arm in against the chest. If this is not treated quickly, the pain will worsen and the joint will begin to swell, causing additional complications later. You should *not* attempt to reduce a posterior shoulder dislocation.

Treatment If a shoulder dislocation has been caused by a direct mechanism, then field reduction should *not* be performed, since the possibility for a fracture dislocation is high. In this case, the arm should be splinted and evacuation must be initiated. Normally the most comfortable position for splinting is to secure the patient's hand to her head. To make this more comfortable for the patient, a rolled-up blanket can be secured under the armpit of the dislocation using a figure-eight bandage. If the dislocation is from an indirect force, there are several methods for reducing an anterior shoulder dislocation.

- **Hanging Weight Technique** The hanging weight technique is relatively simple but gives the rescuer little feedback during the process. Have the patient lie facedown on some object that is 4 to 5 feet off the ground (1.5 meters), like a rock or fallen tree. Have her dangle her injured arm down along the edge. Secure a weight to her hand (10 to 15 pounds or 4.5 to 6.8 kilos). The amount of weight depends on the musculature of the victim. The passive pull of the weight will eventually exhaust the shoulder muscles that are in spasm. It is these spasming muscles that are keeping the bone out of the socket. When the muscles are exhausted, the arm will slip back into normal position.

- **Baseball Pitch Technique** This technique takes considerably less time than the hanging weight. Have the patient lie on her back with the injured arm along her side. While another rescuer holds on to the patient's body, pull steady, gentle traction on the arm at the elbow. Once traction has been started, *do not release* it until the dislocation has been reduced. Continue traction and slowly swing the arm so that the upper arm is in line with the shoulders. Then rotate the forearm until the arm is in the "baseball pitcher" position. At this point, the shoulder should reduce with a noticeable decrease in pain. The key to this method of reduction is to go slowly. It can sometimes take up to an hour or longer for reduction to occur. Let the patient be your guide as to how quickly to move. If there is any increase in resistance or a significant increase in pain, *stop.* Maintain the arm in that position, with traction, until the pain subsides, then continue to move the arm, this time more slowly.

- **Hands on Forehead Technique** This technique does not require active rescuer assistance. Tell the patient to place her hands on her forehead. Then ask the patient to lie back and spread her elbows (trying to get both elbows to touch the ground). Do not physically force the patient. If the patient can get the elbows back, the shoulder most likely will suddenly pop back into place with a tremendous relief of pain.

Once the shoulder is back in the socket, be aware that the shoulder is unstable. Immobilize it as quickly as possible using a sling and swathe (see Sling and Swathe, page 257). There can be further complications associated with a dislocation, and evacuation is strongly encouraged for any dislocation.

KNEECAP DISLOCATION

The kneecap, or patella, is the bony plate that lies over the knee joint. It usually dislocates laterally; that is, it slips to the outside. Due to the structure of the knee, it might appear as if the patella has dislocated proximally (to the inside), but an examination of the lateral side of the leg will usually reveal that this is not the case. A dislocated patella is extremely painful and can be treated quickly and effectively in the field.

Treatment Have the patient sit down with her knee bent. Place one hand below the knee with your thumb underneath the patient's kneecap (which has moved to the outside of the knee). Grasp the patient's ankle with your other hand, and in one motion, straighten the leg and push firmly on the outside edge of the kneecap. The kneecap will pop back into place with a sudden relief of pain. Patients may feel fine afterward, but discourage them from walking. Treat it as a severe sprain (see Sprains, page 254). Since it is possible that the kneecap will dislocate again, evacuation is recommended. *Note:* Dislocations to the knee joint itself (not the kneecap) can be very damaging to the complicated structures of the joint. Do *not* attempt to reduce a knee dislocation. Splint the joint in a position of comfort and evacuate the patient.

DIGIT DISLOCATION

Fingers and toes can dislocate. When this occurs, the distal end of the digit in question will be angulated with respect to the rest of the digit. Make sure that this is a dislocation and *not* a fracture or fracture dislocation before reducing.

Treatment Grasp the digit (finger or toe) at the base with one hand and just distal of the dislocation with the other hand. Gently pull traction and pull the dislocated end of the digit back into anatomical position. The digit should then be splinted by taping it to an adjacent, uninjured digit (finger or toe).

SPINAL INJURIES

If a traumatic injury has occurred, especially something like a fall or severe impact, immediately suspect a spinal injury until you can prove otherwise. During your patient assessment you should be looking for the following:

- Mechanism of injury (fall, sudden impact, or other trauma)
- Numbness or tingling in the extremities
- Weakness in extremities

- Pain or tenderness anywhere along the spine
- Deformity anywhere along the spine
- Paralysis

The only way to rule out a spinal injury is if *all* of the following are true:

- You have been properly trained and certified by an authorized medical authority to evaluate spinal injuries
- The patient is conscious and reliable
- The patient has no sign of neurological problems (see Patient Assessment, page 231)
- There is no indication of any of the symptoms described above

If you are unsure, you must assume a spinal injury has occurred. The primary treatment goal for spine injuries is to stabilize the spine to prevent further damage. This can be difficult in remote settings. Professional rescue personnel will often need to be brought in to immobilize the patient's spine on a backboard and transport her.

Treatment Ideally, the victim should not be moved unless there are serious environmental or life-threatening hazards (airway, breathing, or severe bleeding). In this case, move the person as a unit, supporting the neck at all times.

1. The spine must be stabilized. One person should always be at the head of the patient, using traction-in-position (TIP) to maintain the neck in a neutral position (the position the head normally sits in relation to the spine, neither bent forward or backward). A cervical collar can be improvised with a SAM splint, foam pad, or by filling a stuff sack with sand or dirt to form a moldable but rigid cradle.

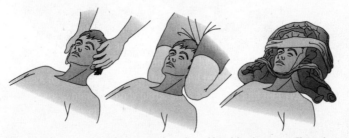

Use hands ... or use knees so hands are free for other care....

Use blankets, stuff sacks weighted with sand, etc. Stabilize forehead and chin with straps.

2. Before moving the patient, she must be placed on a rigid backboard, which serves as a splint for the entire spine. It may be difficult to fashion a proper backboard in the wilderness. External and internal pack frames may be used to create a backboard. If you can't create a proper backboard, you may need to wait until professional rescuers arrive.
3. In the event that the person needs to be moved, you should use the log roll or the in-line drag (see pages 247–48).
4. Treat the patient for shock and monitor until professional medical support arrives. Prepare to evacuate your patient.

CERVICAL SPINE INJURIES

Cervical spine injuries warrant special attention. A fractured cervical spine can damage the spinal cord, causing partial or complete paralysis or death. The nerves that control the diaphragm originate below the fourth vertebra of the neck (C4). If there is a cervical spinal fracture above the fourth vertebra, and the fracture leads to damage or severing of the spinal cord, the patient will no longer be able to breathe on her own ("above C4, breathe no more"). This means the patient will require rescue breathing or CPR. Remember that a person with an unstable cervical spine injury may not have any damage to the spinal cord until you start moving them!

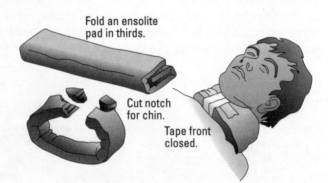

Fold an ensolite
pad in thirds.

Cut notch
for chin.

Tape front
closed.

Treatment Cervical spine injuries should be treated as described for general spinal injuries. The important point in treating a suspected cervical injury is to avoid moving the patient's neck. Apply a cervical collar to maintain the neck in a neutral position, but avoid any unnecessary movement of the patient. A cervical collar can be improvised with a SAM splint or foam pad. If applying a collar may cause unnecessary neck movement, try stabilizing the head with "sandbags"—sacks filled with sand or dirt. These can be laid on either side of a prone patient's head and secured to prevent movement. Prepare to evacuate your patient.

INJURIES TO THE CENTRAL NERVOUS SYSTEM

Any patient who has recently suffered a blow to the head or any period of unconsciousness should be examined carefully.

FAINTING

Fainting is a temporary loss of consciousness that does not occur as the result of a blow to the head. This is most often the result of a sudden and temporary drop in blood pressure for any one of a number of reasons. Fainting commonly occurs in hot environments due to a combination of immobility and mild dehydration—the classic case is the soldier who faints while standing at attention.

Treatment Fainting is, in and of itself, not a serious condition. Allow the patient to rest until she feels well enough to continue on. Provide fluids if dehydration is a possibility. Do a thorough assessment to make sure that a more serious problem is not the cause of the fainting.

HEAD INJURIES

The term *head injury* refers to some form of damage or trauma to the brain itself. Injuries to the brain result in swelling or internal bleeding from broken blood vessels. However, there is no extra space inside the skull to accommodate this swelling. As the brain tissue swells, it is squeezed by the skull, causing an increase in intracranial pressure (ICP), a potentially fatal injury. All swelling follows the same general pattern: swelling is fastest in the first 6 hours, continues more slowly until 24 hours after the injury, at which point it generally stops. The patient's condition will deteriorate continuously until swelling stops, so the fastest possible evacuation—preferably in the first 6 hours—is called for with any concussion. Anyone who has suffered a severe blow to a head, particularly when associated with severe headache and vomiting, should be expected to deteriorate rapidly.

Any type of severe blow to the head is likely to cause a head injury. Similar kinds of damage can occur from a medical problem such as stroke or an aneurysm. Look for a mechanism of injury that could have caused an impact to the brain. Also remember that severe head injuries may also be associated with a spinal fracture. If you cannot rule out a spinal injury, the person should have her head and spine immobilized.

Head Injury Assessment Look for tenderness and pain around the skull; for dark marks behind the ears (battle signs); and for dark rings that go all the way around the eyes (raccoon eyes). Each of these is caused by blood pooling under the skin and is a sign of a skull fracture. Also look for a clear or bloody discharge from the nose and/or ears, which may be cerebral spinal fluid leaking from a fractured skull. Do not be distracted by scalp lacerations. They bleed a lot, but are minor.

If a person strikes her head and suffers from a temporary loss of consciousness, altered mental status, or amnesia, she has suffered a concussion and is at risk for increasing intracranial pressure (ICP). If the person did not suffer a concussion, then she is probably just suffering from a minor head wound. Increasing ICP is a serious condition and has the following signs and symptoms:

Early Signs

- Severe headache
- Dizziness
- Nausea or vomiting
- Decreasing pulse rate
- Increasing respiration rate
- Decreasing mental status (look for an overall decrease down the AVPU scale)

Late Signs

- Changes in pupil size and reactivity to light
- Seizures
- Cerebrospinal fluid discharge

The major thing to watch with a head injury is the level of consciousness, which will change as the intracranial pressure goes up. The patient will be disoriented, irritable, confused, and/or obnoxious. One test is to ask the person to count backwards by nines from 100; if she can't do it, you know that some part of her higher brain function is being impaired. Eventually the level of consciousness will decrease (see Patient Assessment, page 231). You may also see deeper and faster breathing, slower pulse, flushed and warm skin, and unequal pupils. The one thing that can and must be done in the field is to carefully monitor the patient's mental status. This information is essential for proper medical treatment and should be routinely obtained and recorded about every 15 minutes. Persons going for help should take a copy of this information for the rescue authorities (see SOAP note, page 238).

Evaluating Possible Increasing Intracranial Pressure These are the best ways to monitor for increasing ICP.

- Level of consciousness—monitor LOC for changes in personality, decreased mental status, and any decrease on the AVPU scale.
- Loss of ability to stand with eyes closed or walk a straight line— "sobriety test"
- Muscular weakness—compare movement at the hands and feet on both sides of the body (see Checking Distal Circulation, Sensation and Motion, page 240)
- Loss of sensation—compare sensation at the hands and feet on both sides of the body.

General Treatment There is no specific field treatment for a brain injury and increasing intracranial pressure (ICP) except to get the person to advanced medical care. Monitor her vitals, especially level of consciousness, closely. Whenever there is a severe blow to the head, assume there is a neck injury and splint the neck. The person should be placed flat because of the likelihood of cervical spine injuries. Vomiting is common, so monitor the patient's airway and take precautions to prevent aspiration of vomit. If the person begins to vomit, you will need to log-roll her onto her side (see The Log Roll, page 248). Head injuries alone do not cause shock; however, other injuries sustained may. Treat for shock but do *not* elevate the legs, as it may increase intracranial pressure. Prepare to evacuate your patient. When evacuating, take into account how swelling will change over time.

CONCUSSION

A concussion is generally a mild brain contusion caused by an impact force to the head. Anyone who has experienced a blow to the head and who shows any of the following symptoms is considered to have a concussion.

- Loss of consciousness
- Amnesia (from before the event or after)
- Altered mental status

Anyone who has had a concussion may develop increasing intercranial pressure (ICP), a potentially life-threatening injury. This person must be monitored carefully for any signs of increasing ICP.

Treatment Generally, no specific treatment is possible for a concussion. Monitor carefully for the next 24 hours for signs of increasing ICP from swelling or internal bleeding. The person does *not* need to be constantly kept awake, but must be woken every hour or so to be assessed. Evacuation may be required.

SKULL FRACTURES

Skull fractures may be very difficult to diagnose and may occur with significant, little, or no brain injury. The typical signs of a fracture—pain, tenderness, swelling, and discoloration—may be masked or mimicked by contusions or lacerations in the scalp tissue overlying the skull. Fractures of the base of the skull often produce bleeding or a flow of clear fluid (cerebrospinal fluid) from the ears or nose. Make sure that any fluid is, in fact, coming from *within* the ears or nose and is not blood from a laceration of the surrounding skin. The safest course is to assume that any head injury resulting in unconsciousness has also fractured the skull.

Treatment No specific treatment for skull fractures can be given in the field. Maintain an airway and contact rescue authorities for evacuation. Monitor for possible increasing ICP. Prepare to evacuate your patient.

Evacuation Guidelines Severe concussions and possible skull fractures always require a litter evacuation; minor concussions and surface wounds do not. When in doubt, send for help to evacuate the patient.

SEIZURES

Seizures can be caused by a wide variety of reasons, including epilepsy, and may occur without any prior history. If anyone on your trip has a history of seizures, make sure that she takes her medications if appropriate (most seizure patients are good about this), and remind her that physical stress and the dietary changes of a trip can contribute to the likelihood of having a seizure. In addition to epilepsy, the acronym STOPEAT indicates the other potential causes of seizure activity.

S = **Sugar** Lack of blood sugar in the brain (especially for a person with diabetes)

T = **Temperature** Overheating or overcooling in the brain (see Heat Stroke, page 292, and Hypothermia, page 293)

O = **Oxygen** Lack of oxygen in the brain

P = **Pressure** Increasing intercranial pressure (see Head Injuries, page 267)

E = **Electricity** Electric shock, such as a lightning strike

A = **Altitude** High altitude (see Altitude Illnesses, page 323)

T = **Toxins** Various toxins inhaled or ingested (see Toxins, page 303)

Seizures in general have three phases: the aura, the seizure, and the postictal phase. In the aura phase, the patient can become dazed, have a glassy look in her eyes, and seem lost. Some patients can recognize this as a warning for a seizure and will try to communicate it to you, but may not be able to speak. If you see this coming, have the patient lie down and remove everything in her way. The seizure itself may not be noticeable (person simply lies there) or it may be a grand mal (violent) seizure. Your only concern is to prevent the patient from hurting herself by removing anything that could be in the way.

- Do *not* try to restrain a person having a seizure.
- Do *not* try to stick anything in her mouth.
- Do *not* worry if the person's jaw is clamped shut. The notion that she will choke on her tongue during a seizure is a myth. She probably isn't breathing during the seizure and her jaw will relax and breathing will resume when the seizure has subsided. After the seizure, make sure the patient has an open airway and has resumed breathing; otherwise, begin rescue breathing (see Basic Life Support, page 245).
- After the seizure, the patient will enter the postictal phase. She is usually very confused and lethargic, but her level of postictal consciousness will slowly return to normal.

Warning: Some postictal patients are extremely violent. They are often very disoriented and may see everything as a threat, so treat them carefully. These patients will be difficult to reason with because they are not truly conscious, although they may be screaming at you. These patients should be kept from running around, as they have no natural sense of danger and can easily hurt themselves. Use physical restraint *only* if absolutely necessary to prevent the patient from harming herself, but do so with the utmost care. Any postseizure patient should be examined at a medical facility. Prepare to evacuate your patient.

CHEST INJURIES

Chest injuries are typically the result of trauma. The major danger of chest injuries is the potential for damage to the underlying organs—heart, lungs, liver, kidneys, spleen, and others—which can result in life-threatening internal bleeding. Any internal injuries will be difficult to diagnose. Monitoring for changes in vital signs may be your only indication.

Basic Treatment Any chest injury may have an impact on the person's ability to breathe. Basic first aid includes maintaining an airway and assisting the patient in breathing with PROP (see page 239).

BROKEN RIBS

Broken ribs are usually caused by a blunt trauma to the chest cavity. Due to the connective tissue and muscle surrounding the ribs, they are likely to remain in position. The patient will complain of sharp pain at the site of trauma that increases upon inspiration. Make sure that the patient's breathing is not impaired. Be wary of the possibility of a sucking chest wound (pneumothorax; see below). Also, watch for internal bleeding, as the force of breaking the ribs may also have damaged the nearby internal organs, such as the liver, kidneys, and spleen.

Treatment Rib fractures cause painful breathing. As long as the pain can be controlled with normal analgesics (see Medications Profiles, page 328), the ribs need not be splinted. If the pain cannot be controlled, splinting the chest will help stabilize the broken ribs. Either swathe the chest with broad firm cravats or tape the chest with wide pieces of tape that run parallel to the ribs and go from the sternum to the vertebrae. Monitor the vitals, especially respirations. Prepare to evacuate your patient.

FLAIL CHEST

In some cases, if several ribs are broken in multiple places, an entire section of the chest wall can come loose. This is called a flail chest, characterized by *paradoxical breathing,* or having part of the chest go in when the rest is expanding, and vice versa. This will cause extreme respiratory difficulty, and hence is an immediate life-threatening emergency.

Treatment A temporary treatment can be achieved by having the patient lie in the semiprone position and padding underneath the injury to prevent the movement of the flail chest. A longer-term treatment can be achieved by firmly tying down the ribs with bulky dressings or tape. If the patient is lying on her back, a bag of sand or well-padded rock can be placed on the flail chest to prevent the paradoxical movement. Assist respirations with positive pressure ventilation if possible. Prepare to evacuate your patient.

SUCKING CHEST WOUND

A sucking chest wound is caused by a hole left by an impaled object in the chest. This can be caused by a broken rib or by a deep chest wound. It gets its name from the sound of air rushing through the chest wall. If not treated immediately, air will begin to fill the space between the lungs and the chest wall (pleural space), causing the lung on that side to collapse. *This is an immediate life-threatening emergency.*

Treatment The goal of treatment for a sucking chest wound is to create a one-way valve so that air can exit but not enter the cavity between the lungs and the chest wall. Find the hole, cover it with a small, square piece of plastic bag or aluminum foil, and tape three sides of the square so that air can escape the chest cavity but not enter (leave the bottom end open for drainage). As the patient inhales, the plastic is sucked against the hole, sealing it off and preventing further air from entering. As the patient exhales, air is pushed out, and the one-way valve opens, allowing air to escape. If the patient's breathing becomes *more* labored after applying the one-way valve dressing, then seal it completely on all sides. Lay the patient on her affected side (unless spinal injury is suspected) and send for help. Prepare to evacuate your patient.

PNEUMOTHORAX

A *pneumothorax* is similar to a sucking chest wound in that the space between the lung and the chest wall (pleural space) fills with air from a punctured lung. The difference is that a pneumothorax is a closed injury—there is no open hole to the outside. It is often caused by blunt trauma to the chest, like a fall onto a rock. *This is an immediate life-threatening emergency.* It may be harder to diagnose than a sucking chest wound since no "hole" is evident. Look for bruising on the chest wall, difficulty breathing, pain upon inspiration, and pain upon palpation. In extreme cases, the pressure of the collapsed lung pushes the trachea or heart off center (trachial deviation).

A *hemothorax* is a similar condition but involves internal bleeding that causes the lung to collapse. A *hemo-pneumothorax* is both air and internal bleeding. Treatment for all three conditions is the same.

Treatment Lay the victim on her affected side (this helps limit the amount of air escaping from the lung into the pleural space). Keep in mind that an open or closed pneumothorax is often caused by a large force that might also cause spinal injury. If spinal injury is suspected, do not place the patient on her side. Monitor the vital signs. Assist respiration with positive pressure ventilation, if necessary. Prepare to evacuate your patient.

IMPALED OBJECT IN THE CHEST

If an object is impaled deep enough in the chest, the object may cause a sucking chest wound or pnuemothorax or may damage other internal organs.

Treatment Don't remove an impaled object in the chest unless you need to do so to evacuate the patient (see Impaled Objects, page 279). The object may be serving as a cork, preventing major bleeding. Stabilize the impaled object and send for help. Monitor the vitals. Treat for shock and give PROP (see page 239). Prepare to evacuate your patient.

SOFT-TISSUE INJURIES

Soft-tissue injuries encompass any injuries to the soft tissues of the body—skin, muscles, internal organs, and so on. The primary treatment for soft-tissue injuries is to stop bleeding and properly clean and bandage the wound to minimize infection. Any more serious complications from the injuries will need to be treated by advanced medical care.

LACERATIONS

Lacerations and other wounds may be treated in the wilderness or may need advanced medical care.

Treatment Stop the bleeding (see Bleeding, page 241). Properly clean and dress the wound. Keep the dressings clean and dry. Change them every 24 hours as needed. Monitor for infection. Be prepared to evacuate your patient under the following circumstances:

- If there is a large initial blood loss.
- If there is any sign of major infection.
- If there appears to be a need for stitches—a gaping cut over ½ inch long (1.2 centimeters). Stitches should be applied within 8 to 12 hours, otherwise the physician is likely to leave the wound open.

- If there is a laceration to the face, hands, or over a joint.
- If there is any injury to a blood vessel, ligament, or tendon.

BLISTERS

Blisters are actually highly localized second-degree burns caused by the heat of friction. They are usually found on the feet and may be the most common cause of evacuation on trips. If people pay attention to their feet and take proper precautions, most blisters can be avoided, or at least caught and treated before they become serious enough to impact your trip.

Prevention Make sure everyone's boots fit properly and are broken in *before* the trip starts. Wear more than one pair of socks; the best combination is a thin polypropylene liner sock with wool or synthetic outer socks. Wearing two pairs of socks keeps the friction between the socks and not against the skin. Polypropylene also helps transfer moisture away from the feet. To keep your feet dry, change liner socks as necessary, or use foot powder. Keep socks from bunching up—heeled socks are better than tube socks for this reason. Keep boots laced up snugly, especially on hills to keep the foot from sliding forward into the front of the boot.

Get into a routine of checking for "hot spots"—the first sign of blisters—and make sure people know that anyone can get blisters. If you know you are susceptible to blisters in a certain spot, put moleskin or tape over that area *before* you start hiking. Tincture of Benzoin can be used both to help tape stick to feet (apply before your feet start to sweat) and to toughen up the skin (which may help prevent blisters).

Treatment for Hot Spots Before a blister forms, there will be a hot spot—a small reddened area that is essentially a first-degree burn. The hot spot should be covered with a thin layer, such as Spenco Adhesive Kit, moleskin, or tape. Keep an eye on the area to make sure a real blister doesn't form. Tincture of Benzoin may be helpful to apply to the skin to keep the tape attached.

🍁 TRICKS OF THE TRAIL

Round Your Corners If you place a rectangular piece of tape or moleskin on your skin, it will tend to peel up at the sharp corners. Round off the corners with scissors before you put it on and it will stay in place better.

Treatment for Blisters If the friction on a hot spot continues, eventually the top layer of skin becomes separated from the layers below. The space between the layers fills with fluid. This fluid is sterile, and so as long as the blister remains intact, you have a closed wound that does not have any risk of infection. Once the blister has popped, you have an open wound, prone to infection.

The blister may be filled with fluid or it may have popped on its own. Since a popped blister is more prone to infection, you should *not* pop a blister unless the person cannot walk with the blister or walking would pop it anyway. If you must pop a blister, sterilize a needle in a flame or with alcohol and lance the blister on the edge nearest the ground, so it will drain easily. Try to have the patient do this herself. Drain the fluid and then treat it as any other open wound. Use universal precautions since blood maybe present (see Universal Precautions for Working with Blood and Body Fluids, page 244).

To protect the blister area, build up a donut of padding around it out of moleskin or molefoam. Use as many layers as you need to keep pressure off the blister. If the blister is popped, place antibiotic ointment inside the donut hole and tape over the top of the donut. Blisters may need to be redressed on a daily basis. Be careful of infection. Blisters usually do not require evacuation unless infection sets in or the person no longer feels comfortable walking.

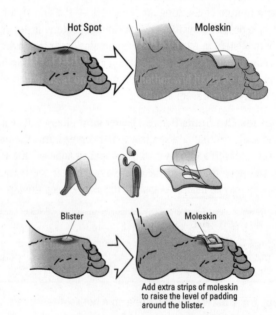

Hot Spot · Moleskin

Blister · Moleskin

Add extra strips of moleskin to raise the level of padding around the blister.

THERMAL BURNS

Burns are always a possibility when stoves and fires are used, so special precautions should be taken when working around them. Burns are categorized based on the depth of the tissue damaged (first, second, and third degree) and the percentage of the body burned. (See also Eye Injuries, page 281.)

Principles in Treating Burns

- Put out the fire. Drop and roll in a blanket, if possible.
- Monitor the airway and breathing. Be very suspicious of burns to the face and neck, including soot in the mouth and nose and singed nasal hair. Burned airway tissues will swell and may block the airway. Burns to the lungs (inhaled hot gases) can cause swelling and fluid buildup in the lung tissue, which can lead to respiratory failure. Treat with PROP (see page 239) and prepare for immediate evacuation.
- Apply cold to reduce tissue damage using ice, cold water, or Cold Pack. Do *not* place ice directly onto the burn site. Wrap it in a cloth; otherwise you may actually freeze the tissue, causing further damage.
- Do not apply ointments to a burn; they can trap heat in the skin, causing additional damage.
- Treat for shock and monitor the patient's vitals.
- Gauge the depth of the burn (first, second, or third degree) and percentage of the body area that has been burned.

FIRST-DEGREE BURNS (SUPERFICIAL BURNS)

Only the top layers of skin are affected. Tissue is red and painful (nerve sensation is intact). Sunburn is a typical first-degree burn.

Treatment Local application of cold.

SECOND-DEGREE BURNS (PARTIAL-THICKNESS BURNS)

Deeper layers of tissue are damaged. Tissue is red and very painful (nerve sensation is intact). Blisters may form.

Treatment Local application of cold. If blisters are present, they should be left intact. Gently clean the area and apply a sterile dressing. Nonstick pads such as Tefla are best for this, covered with roller gauze. Do *not* place antibiotic or other ointments on the nonstick pad.

THIRD-DEGREE BURNS (FULL-THICKNESS BURNS)

The full thickness of tissue is affected, which includes all layers of skin and may include muscle and bones. The burned area is white, black, or leathery. There is often no pain at the deep site of the burn, due to nerve damage. Typically the tissue outside the third-degree burn goes to second and then first degree as you move out from the center. The first and second degree areas may be very painful.

Treatment Use local application of cold. But if a third-degree burn is large (over 5 to 10 percent of the body or the size of your stomach), and especially if the burn is on the trunk of the body, do not apply cold. At this point, the skin is burned away and the body cannot properly regulate temperature, so there is a risk of hypothermia. Burns to the face and neck should always be cooled to make sure the airway does not swell shut.

If blisters are present, they should be left intact. Clean the area gently and apply a sterile dressing. Nonstick Tefla pads covered with gauze are best for this. Once it is dressed, leave the burn alone unless you are out in the field for an extended period of time. In this case, you may want to immobilize the burned area so that further tissue damage does not occur through moving around.

Attempt to rehydrate the person, as volume loss does occur with burns. Do not force fluid down if the person is unable to swallow. Monitor closely for infection, and be extra careful of hypothermia—a severely burned person no longer has the ability to properly thermoregulate.

Evacuation Guidelines

Management of severe burns or burns to critical areas requires advanced medical care in a hospital setting. You need to evaluate the percentage of the body areas burned, the areas burned, and the depth of the burn (see illustration). You should evacuate any patient who has burns of the following types:

- Burns greater than 10 percent of the body surface.
- Burns to the lungs.
- Second- or third-degree burns to sensitive areas such as the face and neck, hands, feet, or genitals

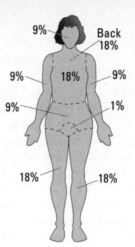

9% Back 18%

9% 18% 9%

9% 1%

18% 18%

IMPALED OBJECTS

Impaled objects can run the gamut from splinters in a finger to a tree limb protruding through the abdomen. You need to consider the forces that impaled the object and the effect the object is having on surrounding tissues. Severe bleeding, fractures, and major tissue damage can all occur with a deeply impaled object. The general rule is: Do *not* remove the object. The object may be acting as a cork. If you take the object out, the wound may start to bleed heavily. Furthermore, you may cause greater damage removing the object than when it first entered. You should *only* remove an impaled object if:

- Removing it is easy and safe for the patient
- The object prevents safe transport of the patient
- The impaled object may compromise the airway

Treatment The first priority is to control any bleeding that may be present. The second priority is to immobilize the object so that it will not move and cause more damage. Immobilize the object by building up pads around it or by using donuts made of bulky bandaging material, much as you would do for a blister. Be sure the object is secured in place. Prepare to evacuate your patient.

If a person has become impaled on a branch or fence post or similar object that is fairly immovable, immobilize the object in the person as best you can and then cut the object off about 6 inches (15.2 centimeters) from the person so you can bandage around it. Continue to immobilize the object.

MINOR IMPALED OBJECTS

These include splinters, rusty nails, slivers of glass, fishhooks, and rock shards impaled in superficial skin tissue. In most cases, you can remove the impaled object and treat the wound. If the object is easy to remove, try to have the patient do it herself.

If the object is in deep enough to cause bleeding, check to see if the patient has had a recent tetanus shot. It should be within at least 10 years or within 5 years if the wound is particularly dirty. If not, the patient should be evacuated to receive a tetanus booster. Ideally, the booster should be given within 24 hours.

Removing an Impaled Fishhook Fishhooks can easily be removed in the field. One method is to push the hook forward, following the curve of the hook until the barb protrudes through the skin. Cut the shank of the hook with wire cutters, and pull the hook out from the barb end.

RASHES

Rashes can be caused by a variety of things, including contact dermatitis (poison ivy), friction (butt rash or jock itch), or allergic reaction (see Anaphylaxis, page 312, and Animal and Insect Bites and Stings, page 306).

280

POISON IVY, POISON OAK, POISON SUMAC

Contact with these plants results in a rash caused by a sap component (urushiol), which is found on all parts of the plant at all times of the year. The sap can be carried on clothes or, on hot days, in a vapor around the plant. Scratching the rash will not spread it, but it should be discouraged because it can introduce infection or lead to scarring. The rash cannot be spread from person to person; however, it is possible to spread the oil (for example, if your boots get covered with the oil and then someone else picks up your boots). Inhaling smoke from the burning of these plants can cause the same rash on the lung surface, a serious injury that *cannot* be treated in the field. Treat lung exposure with PROP (see page 239) and prepare to evacuate your patient.

Treatment Wash the area thoroughly and use hydrocortisone cream (see Medications Profiles, page 328) to combat the itch. The rash is fairly harmless, just uncomfortable, and should disappear within four to seven days. Evacuation is generally not necessary. Be aware that some people are also allergic to these plants and can have a mild or a severe anaphylactic reaction.

FRICTION RASHES

Friction rashes are similar to hot spots (see Blisters, page 275). Repeated rubbing can cause a minor burn as well as wear away the top layer of skin. Friction rashes are especially common around the crotch and can be partially avoided by wearing loose underwear to minimize chafing and to help the area breathe. Try to avoid wearing nylon underwear, which holds in moisture and heat.

Treatment Have the patient apply petroleum jelly to the area of discomfort. If the itch persists, hydrocortisone cream can be used (see Medications Profiles, page 328).

EYE INJURIES

Immediate attention is required for eye injuries, since even a seemingly minor abrasion can cause significant damage. It is always prudent to be conservative and evacuate any eye injury to proper medical care. When treating an eye injury, the most important thing to remember is that when one eyeball moves, so does the other. So if you need to bandage an injured eye and keep it from moving, you must bandage them both. This obviously has an impact on the person's ability to hike out.

THERMAL BURNS

An eye burn should be treated as any other burn (see page 277). Cool the area with water. Cover both eyes with a sterile dressing. Prepare to evacuate your patient.

CHEMICAL BURNS

Any caustic chemicals in the eyes should be rinsed out using eye irrigation solution or clean water. Have the person turn her head to the side with the affected eye down and pour the irrigation fluid from the nasal side of the eye, to keep the chemical from flowing into the other eye. Prepare to evacuate your patient.

FOREIGN OBJECTS

Foreign objects in the eye are common, and can usually be removed with few complications. Pull the upper eyelid over the lashes of the lower eyelid. The lashes should be able to brush out any objects. If this does not work, try folding the upper eyelid outward over a matchstick and brushing the object out with a clean bandanna. You can also irrigate the eye as you would for a caustic burn. Irrigation is recommended for fire ash that may get into the eye.

IMPALED OBJECTS

If someone gets a branch or other object stuck in her eye, treat it as you would any other impaled object. If possible, leave the impaled object in place, stabilize it, and bandage both eyes to limit movement. Prepare to evacuate your patient.

CONTACT LENS PROBLEMS

Periodically a contact lens will get wedged back onto the rear surface of the eyelid. Contrary to popular belief, the contact lens cannot slide to the back of the eye. It typically floats off the cornea (the clear surface of the eye) and under the eyelids. Have the person look up, down, and side to side so that you can locate it. Then gently move it back in place. *Always* clean your hands before touching a contact lens.

Contact lenses should be removed from an unconscious person. With a soft lens, pinch the lens between two fingers and it will pop out. With a hard lens, place your finger on the outer corner of the eye and pull down. The lens will pop out. Store the lenses in the appropriate solution.

CONJUNCTIVITIS

Conjunctivitis (pinkeye) is an inflammation of the conjunctiva, the membrane that covers the white portion of the eye and the inside of the eyelids. It can be caused by foreign objects in the eye, chemical irritants, smoke, or infection. The surface of the eye is red and the blood vessels are enlarged. There also may be yellow or greenish pus. If infection is present, use antibiotic eyedrops. Make sure that your hands are clean before putting in or taking out contact lenses to prevent infection.

SNOWBLINDNESS

Snowblindness is a misnomer, because the injury can occur even off the snow. The major cause is overexposure (6 to 12 hours) to ultraviolet B radiation (UVB) from the sun causing sunburn (first-degree burn) to the cornea. UVB exposure is greater at high altitudes and on snowfields and glaciers, where the UVB radiation bounces off the white snow (this is where snowblindness gets its name). It also occurs on water with reflected glare. The best protection is good sunglasses or goggles that should filter out 99 percent of UVB light. On snowfields, side shields on the glasses are also essential. In an emergency, you can create sunglasses by cutting small slits for lenses in a piece of cardboard and wearing it like glasses.

The symptoms of snowblindness are pain in the eyes, redness, swollen eyelids, pain when looking at the light, and a feeling like "sand in the eyes." Snowblindness general resolves itself in 24 to 48 hours. Remove any contact lenses and place cool compresses on the eyes. The eyes should not be exposed to additional light, so patch both eyes for 24 hours.

NOSEBLEEDS

Nosebleeds are fairly common, and come in two types: anterior bleeds (from the front of the nose, the usual variety) and posterior bleeds (from the back of the nose inside the head, more unusual). Nosebleeds may occur spontaneously, without trauma, often after a large sneeze. They are especially common in cold weather, when the air dries out the nasal membranes. Sometimes the blood flow can be very heavy at first, but you should not be alarmed, as it is generally not dangerous.

Treatment Carefully monitor the airway, especially in patients with posterior bleeding, where there is a chance for the blood to run down the back of the throat. Have the person lean forward and ask if she tastes blood. If she does, encourage her to spit it out. In the meantime, apply direct pressure by pinching the nose, holding a piece of cloth or gauze, and the bleeding will eventually subside. There should be no need for evacuation unless the person has swallowed a great deal of blood or is having difficulty breathing. Do *not* have the person lean back or lie down, as she may aspirate blood into the lungs or swallow blood, which often provokes vomiting.

If the person experiences repeated, heavy nosebleeds, there may be cause for concern. You may want to evacuate in these cases, as some more serious condition may be involved.

DENTAL PROBLEMS

Any significant dental problem will require a dentist for proper treatment. These are often painful injuries that make it difficult to eat and potentially lead to infections. In the field, there are a number of temporary treatments you can perform to hold the patient over until she can be evacuated. For extended wilderness trips, it is advisable to carry a dental emergency kit, which contains a number of special materials useful for broken teeth, lost fillings, and so on. A patient with dental problems should eat only soft foods and cool liquids (avoid hot and cold foods) until proper dental care is available.

TOOTHACHES

Exposure of the tooth nerve, pulp, artery, or vein can cause severe pain. A toothache can also be caused by infection (see Infection, opposite).

Treatment Treatment is limited to pain medication and antibiotics. Avoid hot, cold, or spicy foods. Do *not* place aspirin on a tooth—aspirin is an acid and can cause a burn to the sensitive tissue.

BROKEN TOOTH

Tooth damage is most often associated with trauma. Thus, the possibility of associated head or neck injuries should be considered. Most importantly, the patient's airway should be checked and any debris that might impede breathing, including tooth fragments or blood, should be removed.

Treatment Position the patient on her side with the head down so that any further debris will drain out of the mouth as opposed to down the throat. If a cervical spine injury is suspected, maintain spine stability and log-roll the person onto her side (see Log Roll, page 248). Once the patient is alert and stable, rinse her mouth with clean, cool water to flush out the remaining debris, provide some degree of pain relief, and help stop bleeding. Bleeding can be controlled with direct pressure. Fold a piece of gauze and place it on the bleeding area. Have the person hold it or bite down on the gauze for 10 to 15 minutes until the bleeding stops. A moist tea bag also works well as a packing material.

FRACTURED TOOTH

A fractured tooth that is still in place with an exposed nerve will be extremely sensitive. This can be treated temporarily by applying topical oral pain relievers to the affected area and sealing the injury with dental wax or Cavit (a temporary filling material) until a dentist is available. Prepare to evacuate your patient.

KNOCKED-OUT TOOTH

A tooth that has been knocked out entirely may have a good chance of reattaching if it is replaced within an hour. Rinse the tooth with water to clean it. Avoid handling the root, which contains the delicate attachment fibers. Replace the tooth in its socket.

The replaced tooth—or any loose tooth—can be stabilized by splinting it to a neighboring tooth with dental floss or similar material. If it is not possible to replace the tooth, save the tooth and try to get the person evacuated as soon as possible. If the tooth is out and the tooth socket is bleeding, it can be packed to place direct pressure on the tissue to stop the bleeding. You can then seal the tooth area with dental wax. Prepare to evacuate your patient.

LOST FILLING

Fillings may pop out under an impact or spontaneously. If trauma is involved, follow the guidelines for a knocked-out tooth, above. If the filling has just popped out, seal the tooth area with dental wax. Prepare to evacuate your patient.

INFECTION

A cracked or broken tooth, a cavity, or a lost filling can all lead to a painful dental infection, often termed toothache. This occurs when bacterial infection grows either at the base of a tooth or inside the tooth itself. The symptoms are local inflammation and swelling, and a marked sensitivity of the tooth or neighboring teeth.

Infections require treatment by a dentist. These are painful problems, and there is a threat of the infection spreading into the bone and sinus cavity. The only treatments available in the field during evacuation are pain relievers such as aspirin and ibuprofen (see Medications Profiles, page 328). Prepare to evacuate your patient.

ENVIRONMENTAL INJURIES AND ILLNESSES

FLUID BALANCE

All the body's fluids make up one large body fluid pool. Fluid loss from any one source is reflected in the levels of all the body's other fluids. For example, profuse sweating will ultimately result in decreased blood volume. If a patient loses enough fluid through any manner—bleeding, sweating, vomiting, or diarrhea—the end result is the same: dehydration and, potentially, volume shock. Adequate fluid is also critically important in hot environments to help the body thermoregulate (see Heat Challenge, page 289, and Hypothermia, page 293). Remember, dehydration can kill!

If someone is chronically losing fluid (from diarrhea or vomiting), then you have a real emergency on your hands. Treat the cause of the fluid loss as best you can and rehydrate the patient. Be prepared to evacuate your patient.

Dehydration is always easier to prevent than it is to treat. So it is important to ensure that all members of your group replace their regular fluid losses by drinking adequate amounts of water (Basic Fluid Recommendations, page 59). Your body absorbs fluids best when you drink frequently and in small amounts, rather than drinking large amounts at one time. It also helps with fluid absorption if you drink while eating. A pinch of salt and sugar in the water will do if no food is available. Very dilute mixtures of sports drinks, like Gatorade (add just enough to taste), work well for this purpose.

Don't depend on feeling thirsty to tell you when to drink. Thirst is a late response of the body to fluid depletion. Once you feel thirsty, you are already low on fluids. The best indicator of proper fluid levels is urine output and color. You, and all the people in your group, should strive to be "clear and copious." Ample urine that is light colored to clear shows that the body has plenty of fluid. Dark urine means that the body is low on water and is trying to conserve its supply by hoarding fluid, which means that urine becomes more concentrated (thereby darker).

Fluid Electrolyte Replacement

A factor in overall fluid balance is the replacement of the body's electrolytes. In most cases the salts found in normal food consumption are adequate for salt replacement. In the event of severe dehydration, or in high exercise levels in hot environments, a solution of ½ teaspoon salt and ½ teaspoon baking soda per quart or liter of water can be used to replace lost fluid and salt. Use lukewarm fluids. Discontinue the fluids if the person becomes nauseated or vomits. Restart fluids as soon as the person can tolerate it. A solution containing 2 to 6 percent glucose and 30 milliequivalents/liter of sodium is recommended by the Wilderness Medical Society.

THERMOREGULATION

The body has a number of mechanisms to properly maintain its optimal core temperature of 98.6°F (37°C). Above 105°F (40°C), many body enzymes become denatured and chemical reactions cannot take place, leading to death. Below 98.6°F (37°C), chemical reactions slow down, with various complications that can lead to death. Understanding thermoregulation is important to understanding heat illnesses and cold injuries.

How Your Body Regulates Core Temperature

- Vasodilation increases surface blood flow, which increases heat loss (when ambient temperature is less than body temperature).
- Vasoconstriction decreases blood flow to the periphery (arms and legs), decreasing heat loss.
- Sweating cools the body through evaporative cooling.
- Shivering generates heat through increase in chemical reactions required for muscle activity. Visible shivering can maximally increase surface heat production by 500 percent. However, this is limited to a few hours because of depletion of muscle glucose and the onset of fatigue. Active exercise is much more efficient at heating than shivering.
- Increasing or decreasing activity will cause corresponding increases in heat production and decreases in heat production.
- Behavioral responses, such as putting on or taking off layers of clothing, will result in thermoregulation.

COLD CHALLENGE

Whenever you go into an environment that is colder than your body temperature, you are exposed to a cold challenge. As long as your levels of heat production and heat retention (positive factors) are greater than the cold challenge (negative factors), then you will be thermoregulating properly. If the cold challenge is greater than your combined heat production and heat retention, then you are susceptible to a cold illness such as hypothermia or frostbite.

Cold Challenge—Negative Factors

- Temperature
- Body wetness from rain, sweat, water
- Wind (see Windchill Index, page 288)

Heat Retention—Positive Factors

- Body size/shape—your surface-to-volume ratio affects how quickly you lose heat
- Insulation—type of clothing layers affects how well you retain heat
- Body fat—amount of body fat affects how quickly you lose heat
- Shell/core response—allows the body shell to act as a thermal barrier (see Shell/Core Response, page 241)

Heat Production—Positive Factors

- Exercise
- Shivering

Windchill

Windchill can have a major impact on heat loss through convection. As air heated by your body is replaced with cooler air pushed by the wind, the amount of heat you can lose in a given period of time increases. This increase is comparable to the amount of heat you would lose at a colder temperature with no wind. The windchill factor is a represented by a scale that shows the equivalent temperature given a particular wind speed (see Windchill Index, below).

Windchill Index

	Environmental Temperature °F									
Calm	40°	35°	30°	25°	20°	15°	10°	5°	0°	−5°
Wind Speed	Apparent Temperature °F									
5 MPH	35°	30°	25°	20°	15°	10°	5°	0°	−5°	−10
10 MPH	30°	20°	15°	10°	5°	0°	−10°	−15°	−20°	−25°
15 MPH	25°	15°	10°	0°	−5°	−10°	−20°	−25°	−30°	−40°
20 MPH	20°	10°	5°	0°	−10°	−15°	−25°	−30°	−35°	−45°
25 MPH	15°	10°	0°	−5°	−15°	−20°	−30°	−35°	−45°	−50°
30 MPH	10°	5°	0°	−10°	−20°	−25°	−30°	−40°	−50°	−55°
35 MPH	10°	5°	−5°	−10°	−20°	−30°	−35°	−40°	−50°	−60°
40 MPH	10°	0°	−5°	−15°	−20°	−30°	−35°	−45°	−55°	−60°

	Environmental Temperature °F										
	−10°	−15°	−20°	−25°	−30°	−35°	−40°	−45°	−50°	−55°	−60°
Wind Speed	Apparent Temperature °F										
5 MPH	−15°	−20°	−25°	−30°	−35°	−40°	−45°	−50°	−55°	−65°	−70°
10 MPH	−35°	−40°	−45°	−50°	−60°	−65°	−70°	−70°	−80°	−90°	−95°
15 MPH	−45°	−50°	−60°	−65°	−70°	−80°	−85°	−90°	−100°	−105°	−110°
20 MPH	−50°	−60°	−65°	−75°	−80°	−85°	−95°	−100°	−110°	−115°	−120°
25 MPH	−60°	−65°	−75°	−80°	−90°	−95°	−105°	−110°	−120°	−125°	−135°
30 MPH	−65°	−70°	−80°	−85°	−95°	−100°	−110°	−115°	−125°	−130°	−140°
35 MPH	−65°	−75°	−80°	−90°	−100°	−105°	−115°	−120°	−130°	−135°	−145°
40 MPH	−70°	−75°	−85°	−95°	−100°	−110°	−115°	−125°	−130°	−140°	−150°

HEAT CHALLENGE

In hot weather, especially with high humidity, you can lose a great deal of body fluid through exercise. This can lead to a variety of heat-related illnesses, including heat exhaustion and heatstroke. Heat challenge is a combination of a number of external heat factors. Balanced against this heat challenge is your body's methods of heat loss (passive and active). When the heat challenge is greater than heat loss (positive factors), you are at risk for a heat-related injury. In order to reduce the risk, you need to either decrease the heat challenge or increase your heat loss. Maintaining proper fluid balance is a central part of exercising in a heat challenge.

Heat Challenge—Negative Factors

- Temperature
- Exercise
- Humidity (see Heat Index, page 290)
- Body wetness from sweating, rain, or water
- Wind (see Windchill Index, opposite)

Passive Heat Loss—Positive Factors

- Body size/shape—your surface-to-volume ratio affects how quickly you lose heat
- Insulation—type of clothing affects how you lose heat
- Body fat—amount of body fat affects how quickly you lose heat
- Shell/Core Response—allows the body shell to act as a thermal barrier

Active Heat Loss—Positive Factors

- Radiant heat from the body
- Sweating—ability to sweat is limited by fluid levels and level of fitness
- Wind (see Windchill Index, opposite)

The Heat Index

Ambient temperature is not the only factor in creating the potential for heat injuries; humidity is also important. Since our bodies rely on the evaporation of sweat as a major method of cooling, high humidity reduces our ability to evaporate sweat and cool the body, increasing the risk of heat illnesses. The Heat Index, page 290, shows the relative effects of temperature and humidity.

Heat Index

	Environmental Temperature F° (C°)										
	70° (21)	75° (24)	80° (27)	85° (29)	90° (32)	95° (35)	100° (38)	105° (41)	110° (43)	115° (46)	120° (49)
Relative Humidity	Apparent Temperature F° (C°)										
0%	64° (18)	69° (20)	73° (23)	78° (26)	83° (28)	87° (31)	91° (33)	95° (35)	99° (37)	103° (39)	107° (42)
10%	65° (18)	70° (21)	75° (24)	80° (27)	85° (29)	90° (33)	95° (35)	100° (38)	105° (41)	111° (44)	116° (47)
20%	66° (19)	72° (22)	77° (25)	82° (28)	87° (30)	93° (33)	99° (37)	105° (41)	112° (44)	120° (49)	130° (54)
30%	67° (19)	73° (23)	78° (26)	84° (29)	90° (33)	96° (36)	104° (40)	113° (45)	123° (51)	135° (57)	148° (64)
40%	68° (20)	74° (23)	79° (26)	86° (30)	93° (34)	101° (38)	110° (43)	123° (56)	137° (58)	151° (66)	
50%	69° (20)	75° (24)	81° (27)	88° (31)	96° (36)	107° (42)	120° (49)	135° (57)	150° (66)		
60%	70° (21)	76° (24)	82° (28)	90° (33)	100° (38)	114° (46)	132° (56)	149° (65)			
70%	70° (21)	77° (25)	85° (29)	93° (34)	106° (41)	124° (51)	144° (62)				
80%	71° (22)	78° (26)	86° (30)	97° (36)	113° (45)	136° (58)					
90%	71° (22)	79° (26)	88° (31)	102° (39)	122° (50)						
100%	72° (22)	80° (27)	91° (33)	108° (42)							

Apparent temperature	Heat-stress risk with physical activity and/or prolonged exposure.
90°–104° (32–40)	Heat cramps or heat exhaustion possible
105°–129° (31–54)	Heat cramps or heat exhaustion likely. Heatstroke possible.
130° and up (54 and up)	Heatstroke very likely.

Caution: This chart provides guidelines for assessing the potential severity of heat stress. Individual reactions to heat will vary. Heat illnesses can occur at lower temperature than indicated on this chart. Exposure to full sunshine can increase values up to 15° F.

Heat illnesses are the result of elevated body temperatures due to an inability to dissipate the body's heat and/or a decreased fluid level. Always remember that mild heat illnesses have the potential of becoming life-threatening emergencies if not treated properly.

HEAT CRAMPS

Heat cramps are a form of muscle cramp brought on by exertion and insufficient salt.

Treatment Replace salt and fluid (see Fluid Balance, page 285) and stretch the muscle (see Stretches for Hiking, page 144). Kneading and pounding the muscle is less effective than stretching and probably contributes to residual soreness.

HEAT SYNCOPE

Heat syncope (fainting) is a mild form of heat illness that results from physical exertion in a hot environment. In an effort to increase heat loss, the blood vessels in the skin dilate to such an extent that blood flow to the brain is reduced, resulting in symptoms of faintness, dizziness, headache, increased pulse rate, restlessness, nausea, vomiting, and possibly even a brief loss of consciousness. Inadequate fluid replacement that leads to dehydration contributes significantly to this problem.

Treatment Heat syncope should be treated as fainting (see page 267). The person should lie or sit down, preferably in the shade or in a cool environment. Elevate the feet and give fluids, particularly those containing salt (commercial rehydration mix or ½ teaspoon salt and ½ teaspoon baking soda per quart or liter). The patient should not engage in vigorous activity at least for the rest of that day. Only after she has completely restored her body fluids and salt and has a normal urinary output should exercise in a hot environment be resumed, and then cautiously.

HEAT EXHAUSTION

This occurs when fluid losses from sweating and respiration are greater than internal fluid reserves (volume depletion). Heat exhaustion is really a form of volume shock. The lack of fluid causes the body to constrict blood vessels, especially in the arms and legs. To understand heat exhaustion, think of a car with a radiator leak pulling a trailer up a mountain pass. There is not enough fluid in the system to cool off the engine, so the car overheats. Adding fluid solves the problem.

The signs and symptoms of heat exhaustion are:

- Sweating
- Skin—pale, clammy (from peripheral vasoconstriction)
- Pulse rate increased
- Respiration rate increased
- Temperature normal or slightly elevated
- Urine output decreased
- Patient feels weak, dizzy, thirsty, "sick," anxious
- Nausea and vomiting (from decreased circulation in the stomach)

Treatment Victims of heat exhaustion must be properly rehydrated and must be very careful about resuming physical activity (it is best to see a physician before doing so). Treatment is as described for heat syncope, but the person should be *more* conservative about resuming physical activity to give the body a chance to recover. Have the person rest (lying down) in the shade. Replace fluid with a water-salt solution (commercial rehydration mix or ½ teaspoon salt and ½ teaspoon baking soda per quart or liter). Drink slowly; drinking too much, too fast very often causes nausea and vomiting.

Evacuation is not usually necessary. Heat exhaustion can become heatstroke if not properly treated. A victim of heat exhaustion should be closely monitored to make sure that her temperature does not go above 103°F (39°C). If it does, treat the person for heatstroke.

HEATSTROKE

Heatstroke is an immediate life-threatening medical emergency. A victim can die within minutes if not properly treated. Heatstroke is caused by an increase in the body's core temperature. Core temperatures over 105°F (41°C) can lead to death. The rate of onset of heatstroke depends on the individual's fluid status. To understand heatstroke, think of that same car pulling a trailer up a mountain pass on a hot day. This time the radiator has plenty of fluid, but the heat challenge of the engine combined with the external temperature is too much. The engine can't get rid of the heat fast enough and the engine overheats.

There are two types of heatstroke—fluid depleted (slow onset) and fluid intact (fast onset).

- **Fluid depleted** The person has heat exhaustion due to fluid loss from sweating and/or inadequate fluid replacement, but continues to function in a heat challenge situation. Ultimately, the lack of fluid minimizes the body's active heat-loss capabilities to such an extent that the internal core temperature begins to rise. *Example:* a cyclist on a hot day with limited water.
- **Fluid intact** The person is under an extreme heat challenge. The heat challenge overwhelms the body's active heat-loss mechanisms even though the fluid level is sufficient. This typically has a very fast onset. *Example:* a cyclist pushing hard on a 104°F day (40°C).

Signs and Symptoms of Heatstroke

The key to identifying heatstroke is *hot skin*. Some victims may have hot dry skin; others may have hot wet skin because they have just moved from heat exhaustion to heatstroke. Also look for:

- Peripheral vasoconstriction (skin gets pale)
- Increased pulse rate
- Increased respiratory rate
- Decreased urine output
- Increased temperature (may be over 105°F/41°C)—skin hot to the touch
- Skin that is wet or dry and flushed
- Severe changes in mental status and motor/sensory changes; the person may become comatose; possibility of seizures
- Pupils that are dilated and unresponsive to light

Treatment *Efforts to reduce body temperature must begin immediately!*
Move the patient (gently) to a cooler spot or shade the victim. Remove clothing. Pour water on the extremities and fan the person to increase air circulation and evaporation, or cover the extremities with cool wet cloths and fan the patient. Immersion in cool (*not cold*) water is also useful. Cooling extremities should be massaged vigorously to help propel the cooled blood back into the core.

After the temperature has been reduced to 102°F (39°C), active cooling should be reduced to avoid hypothermia (if shivering begins, it produces more heat). The patient must be monitored closely to make sure her temperature does not increase again. She will probably need fluids regardless of the type of onset. Apply basic life support (CPR) if needed. Afterward, there can be serious medical problems. Prepare to evacuate your patient.

HYPOTHERMIA

Hypothermia is a decrease in body core temperature to the point where normal body functions are impaired (see Shell/Core Response, page 241). The key to combating hypothermia is prevention. Although the risks are highest during cold winter conditions, hypothermia can happen at any time of the year.

The classic example of hypothermia is the summer hiker on Mount Washington in New Hampshire dressed in cotton shorts and a T-shirt. The weather changes rapidly. A sudden thunderstorm drops the temperature from 80°F (27°C) to 60°F (16°C) with strong wind and rain. In these conditions, hypothermia can start to occur almost immediately and become severe in less than an hour.

Prevention and Assessment Be aware of the causes of hypothermia, which are usually cool to cold temperatures combined with wetness and wind. Constantly evaluate the environmental conditions and the conditions of your group. Here are some guidelines to staying warm and avoiding hypothermia:

- Wear proper clothing. Choose materials that keep you warm even when wet.
- Wetness equals death. Have proper rain gear to keep you and your clothing dry.
- Eat small amounts of food at frequent intervals to maintain the body's energy reserves. Carry carbohydrates to snack on, because they provide quick energy, and protein and fat to eat before bed, because they burn slowly, providing energy overnight. Try not to push yourself to your physical limits in cold weather. Always leave your body with energy in reserve.
- Stay well hydrated. Dehydration quickens hypothermia, so force yourself to drink, even if you do not feel thirsty—up to 4 quarts (liters) a day in the winter or hot summer. Drink *hot* liquids. Try to avoid drinking excessive cold fluids, since body heat is used to warm them to body temperature.
- Avoid caffeine. It is a vasoconstrictor that increases the chances of peripheral frostbite.
- Avoid alcohol. It is a vasodilator and increases heat loss.
- Adjust your clothing frequently so that you are neither too hot nor too cold. If you are too hot and you begin to sweat, the wet clothing will rob you of heat 25 times faster than dry clothing. Be aware of the impact of windchill on increasing the rate of heat loss (see Windchill Index, page 288).
- Have pairs of people zip their sleeping bags together and sleep together as a preventative measure on cold nights.
- Be alert to sudden weather changes and be able to make a quick evaluation of your group's condition. Has the temperature dropped? Do people have their hats on? Has everyone been eating? Drinking? Is everyone wearing wind or rain gear? What is the condition of the weakest member of the group?

How to Assess if Someone Is Hypothermic

- Ask the person a question that requires higher reasoning in the brain (to count backward from 100 by nines). If the person is hypothermic, she won't be able to do it. (Note: there are other conditions, such as altitude sickness, that can also cause changes in reasoning ability.)
- If shivering can be stopped voluntarily, it is mild hypothermia. If shivering cannot be stopped voluntarily, it is moderate to severe hypothermia.
- If you can't get a radial pulse at the wrist, it indicates a core temperature below about 90°F (32°C). Check pulse and respirations *carefully*. Even after a full minute, you may not be able to detect a pulse or respi-

rations and yet the person may still be alive. The body may be using a massive shell/core response to maintain basic life functions.

- A severely hypothermic person may appear dead. The person may be rigid, blue, and curled up in a fetal position. Try to open her arm up from the fetal position; if it curls back up, the person is alive. Dead muscles won't contract—only live muscles.

Treatment The basic principles of rewarming a hypothermic patient are to conserve the heat she has and replace the body fuel she is burning up to generate that heat. If a person is shivering, she has the ability to rewarm herself at a rate of 4°F (2°C) per hour.

Stages of Hypothermia

Stage	Core Temperature	Signs and Symptoms
Mild	97–95°F (36–35°C)	Shivering begins—can be mild to severe Unable to perform complex tasks with hands Hands numb
Moderate	95–90°F (35–32°C)	Shivering becomes uncontrollable and violent Changes in mental status, mild confusion, higher reasoning becomes impaired; eventually becomes withdrawn, may show "paradoxical undressing"—person imagines they are warm and takes off clothing Muscle incoordination becomes apparent, movements slow and labored, stumbling pace
Severe	90–85°F (32–29°C)	Shivering stops Skin blue or puffy Unable to walk, confusion, muscles become rigid Incoherent/irrational behavior, becomes semiconscious Pulse rate decreases Respiration rate decreases
	85–80°F (29–27°C)	Unconscious Heartbeat and respiration erratic Pulse may not be palpable Cardiac and respiratory failure

Mild to Moderate Hypothermia

1. **Reduce Heat Loss** Remove patient from wind and cold if possible. Remove all wet clothing. Make sure the person is properly clothed (dry polypropylene, pile, and outer shell). Increase physical activity. Provide shelter.
2. **Add Fuel and Fluids** It is essential to keep a hypothermic person adequately hydrated and fueled. Food intake should include hot liquids, sugars, GORP. Avoid alcohol, caffeine, and tobacco or nicotine.
3. **Add Heat** Bring the patient near a fire or other external heat source. Provide body-to-body contact. Put her in a sleeping bag, in dry clothing, with a warm, dry person.

If the patient's condition improves, evacuation may not be necessary; but if condition worsens or does not improve, prepare to evacuate your patient when she is able, or send for help.

Moderate to Severe Hypothermia

1. Use all of the treatment methods above.
2. Reduce heat loss. Make *hypothermia wrap*. The idea is to provide a shell of total insulation for the patient. No matter how cold, patients can still internally rewarm themselves more efficiently than any external rewarming. Make sure the patient is dry and has a polypropylene layer next to the skin to minimize sweating. The person must be protected from any moisture in the environment. Use multiple sleeping bags, blankets, clothing, and foam pads to create a minimum of 4 inches (10 centimeters) of insulation all the way around the patient, especially between the patient and the ground. Include an aluminum space blanket to help prevent radiant heat loss, and wrap the entire ensemble in plastic to protect from wind and water. Use a plastic garbage bag as a diaper to prevent urine from soaking the insulation layers.
3. Add fuel and fluids. For people in severe hypothermia, the stomach has shut down and will not digest solid food but can absorb water and dilute sugars. Give a dilute mixture of warm water with sugar every 15 minutes. Dilute Jell-O works best, since it is part sugar and part protein. This will be absorbed directly into the bloodstream, providing the necessary calories to allow the person to rewarm herself (one box of Jell-O = 500 kilocalories of heat energy). Do *not* give full-strength Jell-O, even in liquid form—it is too concentrated and will not be absorbed.

Insulation

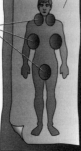

Apply Heat

Waterproof Barrier

4. Encourage urination. People often have to urinate due to cold diuresis. The body's vasoconstriction creates greater volume pressure in the bloodstream. The kidneys pull off excess fluid to reduce the pressure. A full bladder is a place for additional heat loss, so urinating will help conserve heat. You will need to help the person urinate. Open up the hypothermia wrap enough to do this and then cover the person back up. You will need to keep the individual hydrated with the dilute Jell-O solution.

5. Add heat. Heat can be applied to the skin where the major arteries are near the surface—at the neck for the carotid, at the armpits for the brachial, and at the groin for the femoral artery. Chemical heat packs such as the Heat Wave provide 110°F (43°C) for 6 to 10 hours. You can also use hot water bottles, warm rocks, towels, and compresses. For a severely hypothermic person, positive pressure ventilations (rescue breathing) can provide oxygen and heat.

You should not attempt to evacuate someone in this advanced state of hypothermia. Moving the person can cause the heart to stop. Send for advanced medical care or wait until the condition stabilizes.

Hypothermia and CPR

When a person is in severe hypothermia, she may *appear* to be dead: cold, blue skin; fixed and dilated pupils; no discernible pulse or breathing; comatose and unresponsive to any stimuli; rigid muscles. As a rescuer, you can't be sure, so your job is to rewarm the person and do CPR if indicated. If after rewarming the patient still doesn't respond, then she is dead. Treatment follows the saying "a hypothermic patient is never cold and dead, only warm and dead."

1. Make sure you do a complete assessment of heart rate before beginning CPR. Remember, the heart rate may be 2 to 3 per minute and the breathing rate one per thirty seconds. During severe hypothermia, the heart is hyperexcitable, and mechanical stimulation (including CPR, moving the patient, or after-drop, see page 299) may result in ventricular fibrillation, leading to death. As a result CPR itself may be contraindicated for some hypothermia situations. Also, instituting cardiac compressions while the heart is still beating on its own may lead to life-threatening arrhythmias. Check the carotid pulse for a longer time period (up to a full minute) to ascertain if there is some slow heartbeat. Even though the heart is beating very slowly, it is filling com-

pletely and distributing blood fairly effectively. External cardiac compressions are only 20 to 30 percent effective. Thus, the body may be able to satisfy its reduced circulatory needs with only 2 to 3 beats per minute. *Be sure the pulse is absent before beginning CPR.* Once you start doing CPR you will need to continue as you rewarm the person.

2. Ventilation may have stopped but respiration may continue. The oxygen demands for the body have been so diminished with hypothermia that the body may be able to survive for some time using only the oxygen that is already in the body. If ventilation has stopped, artificial ventilation (rescue breathing) may be started to increase available oxygen. In addition, blowing warm air into the person's lungs may assist in internal rewarming.

3. Perform CPR procedures (see Basic Life Support, page 245):
   - Check radial pulse; between 91° and 86°F (33° and 30°C) this pulse disappears.
   - Check for carotid pulse; wait at least a full minute to check for very slow heartbeat.
   - If there is a pulse but no breathing or slow breathing, give rescue breathing (also adds heat).
   - If there is no discernible heartbeat, begin CPR and be prepared to continue—persons with hypothermia have been given CPR for up to 3.5 hours and have recovered with *no* neurological damage.
   - Begin active rewarming.

IMMERSION HYPOTHERMIA

Cold water can kill. Since the body loses heat 25 times faster in water, immersion hypothermia occurs at a much faster rate. In 50°F (10°C) water, a person can be shivering uncontrollably in 15 minutes and can be unconscious in 30 minutes (see chart below). Be extremely vigilant in cold water, such as during stream crossings.

Expected Survival Time in Cold Water

Water Temperature	Exhaustion or Unconsciousness in	Expected Survival Time
70–80°F (21–27°C)	3–12 hours	3–indefinitely
60–70°F (16–21°C)	2–7 hours	2–40 hours
50–60°F (10–16°C)	1–2 hours	1–6 hours
40–50°F (4–10°C)	30–60 minutes	1–3 hours
32.5–40°F (0–44°C)	15–30 minutes	30–90 minutes
≤32°F (≤0°C)	Under 15 minutes	Under 15–45 minutes

Treatment Treatment for immersion hypothermia is the same as described above. In cold-water immersion hypothermia, the Shell/Core response may occur so rapidly that there is sufficient oxygen in the blood to maintain basic body functioning over an extended period of time. Contrary to the old "6-minute rule" for doing CPR, successful resuscitations have been made after over 40 minutes of submersion in cold water. Rewarm the patient with a hypothermia wrap and be prepared to give CPR. Remember, a person is never cold and dead, only warm and dead.

After-drop is a situation in which the core temperature actually decreases during rewarming, primarily an issue with sudden-onset hypothermia caused by cold water immersion. As the shell (the arms and legs) are rewarmed, the peripheral vessels in the arms and legs dilate. This dilation sends very cold blood from the shell to the core, further decreasing the core temperature, which can lead to death. If you are applying an external source of heat (chemical heat packs, hot water bottles, etc.), apply them *only* to the major arteries (see above). Avoid after-drop by applying heat to the core *only!* Do not expose a severely hypothermic victim to extremes of heat.

DROWNING AND NEAR DROWNING

Drowning occurs when liquid inhibits gas exchange in the lungs. There are two types of drowning. Wet drowning (85 to 90 percent of drownings) occurs when the person's lungs fill with water. Dry drownings (10 to 15 percent) take place when the person swallows water and then the larynx goes into spasm and closes off, preventing breathing. The most common cause of drowning is cold water immersion resulting in loss of muscle coordination and strength. The person becomes hypothermic (see page 293) and is no longer able to swim. He or she sinks below the surface and inhales water. The gasping reflex from sudden immersion in cold water can also trigger the person to swallow water and quickly lose consciousness.

Treatment The primary treatment is to administer CPR. In cases of dry drowning, you may not be able to force air through the spasming larynx. Massaging the muscles of the throat may relax them and allow you to ventilate the patient. If cold water is involved, treat for hypothermia. *Anyone who has been through a drowning or near drowning must be evacuated for advanced medical care.*

COLD-WEATHER INJURIES

In addition to hypothermia, cold weather can cause injuries to the periphery (skin and muscle tissue).

The following are factors in peripheral cold injuries:

- Low ambient temperature
- Wind chill
- Moisture
- Insulation
- Contact with metal or supercooled liquids
- Exposed skin
- Vasodilation
- Vasoconstriction
- Previous cold injuries
- Constricting garments
- Local pressure
- Cramped position
- Body type
- Dehydration
- Gender (men do worse in cold than women because they generally have less subcutaneous body fat)
- Caloric intake
- Diabetes, some medications
- Alcohol
- Caffeine, nicotine

FROSTBITE

Whenever the body is exposed to cold temperatures, it adapts. Everyone has experienced the "cold hands, cold feet" phenomenon known as a cold response. Peripheral circulation is reduced to the area to prevent heat loss. The area may be pale, cold, and numb. This may resolve itself spontaneously or quickly once heat or insulation is added.

The next, more serious stage is frostbite. Frostbite is a localized freezing of tissue caused by the shunting of blood away from cold areas of the body. As tissue begins to freeze, ice crystals are formed within the cells. As fluids inside the cells freeze, fluid from outside the cells enters. Cells may rupture from the increased water and/or from tearing by the ice crystals. *Do not rub frostbitten tissue;* it causes the ice crystals to tear the cells, creating additional tissue damage. As the ice melts, there is an influx of salts into the tissue, further damaging the cell membranes. Cell destruction results in tissue death and loss of tissue. Areas of the body and areas with a high surface-to-volume ratio—ears, nose, fingers, and toes—are the most susceptible.

FIRST-DEGREE FROSTBITE

First-degree frostbite involves freezing of only the top layers of skin tissue (similar to a first-degree burn). It is generally reversible. The skin will be pale and waxy. The tissue will feel numb. Most typically seen on cheeks, earlobes, fingers, and toes.

Treatment Superficial frostbite can be rewarmed in the field using skin-to-skin contact. *Never rub frostbitten areas.* Hands may be placed under the armpits, and cold feet can be placed on someone else's belly or in an armpit.

SECOND-DEGREE FROSTBITE

Second-degree frostbite involves freezing of partial layers of skin tissue (similar to a second-degree burn). The top layer feels hard and rubbery, but deeper tissue is still soft. The tissue may feel numb or there may be no sensation at all. Blisters may form after rewarming.

THIRD-DEGREE FROSTBITE

Third-degree frostbite involves deep tissue freezing of all the skin layers and can include freezing of muscle and/or bone. It is very difficult to rewarm the appendage without some damage occurring. The skin will be pale, and feel "wooden" all the way through. The tissue may feel numb or there may be no sensation at all. Blisters may form after rewarming.

Treatment of Second- and Third-Degree Frostbite Rewarming is accomplished by immersion of the affected part into a water bath of 100 to 108° F (37 to 42° C). *Use no hotter water or additional damage will result.* Monitor the temperature carefully with a thermometer. Remove constricting clothing. Place the appendage in the water and continue to monitor the water temperature. This temperature will drop, so additional warm water will need to be added to maintain the 100 to 108° F (37 to 42° C) temperature. *Do not* add this warm water directly to the injury. The water will need to be circulated fairly constantly to maintain even temperature. The affected appendage should be immersed for 25 to 40 minutes. Thawing is complete when the part is pliable and color and sensation have returned. Once the area is rewarmed, there can be significant pain. Discontinue the warm-water bath when thawing is complete.

- Do not use dry heat to rewarm. It cannot be effectively maintained at 100–108° F (37–42° C) and can cause burns, further damaging the tissues.

- Once rewarming is complete, the injured area should be wrapped in sterile gauze and protected from movement and further cold.
- Once a body part has been rewarmed, *it should not be used.* Also, it is essential that the part can be kept from refreezing. Refreezing *after* rewarming causes extensive tissue damage and may result in loss of tissue. If you cannot *guarantee* that the tissue will stay warm, *do not rewarm it.* Mountaineers have walked out on frozen feet and had them rewarmed with little or no tissue loss. Once the tissue is frozen, the major harm has been done. Keeping it frozen will not cause as much additional damage as rewarming and subsequent refreezing will.
- Blisters may form after rewarming. They should be protected from the cold because they are very likely to refreeze.

Prevention Prevention is the key. Even on three-season trips, superficial frostbite is possible. Keep an eye on each other, keep well fed, and stay well hydrated. Rewarm cold parts early. In cold weather, check for numbness as frequently as you check for blisters. People may be unaware or unwilling to let on that they are starting to get cold. Avoid caffeine (a vasoconstrictor—increases chances of frostbite) and alcohol (a vasodilator—increases heat loss and chance of hypothermia).

🍁 TRICKS OF THE TRAIL

Instant Frostbite In temperatures below freezing you need to be extremely careful.

- Liquids such as white gas can "supercool" in the winter (drop below their freezing point but not freeze). White gas also evaporates quickly into the air. Spilling supercooled white gas on exposed skin leads to instant frostbite from evaporative cooling. Always wear gloves when handling fuel.
- Touching metal with bare skin can cause the moisture on your skin to freeze to the metal. (In really cold conditions, even metal glasses frames can be a problem.) When you pull away, you may leave a layer of skin behind. Don't touch very cold metal with bare skin.

IMMERSION FOOT OR TRENCHFOOT

Immersion foot, or trenchfoot, is caused by prolonged exposure of the feet to cool, wet conditions. The body senses that it is losing heat rapidly and uses the Shell/Core response to reduce peripheral blood flow to that area and prevent further heat loss. The skin is initially reddened with numbness, tingling pain, and itching, then becomes pale and mottled and finally dark purple, gray, or blue. Later on, the affected tissue generally dies and sloughs off. In severe cases, immersion foot can involve the toes, heels, or entire foot. If circulation is impaired for more than 6 hours, there will be permanent damage to tissue. If circulation is impaired for more than 24 hours, the victim may lose the entire foot. Immersion foot causes permanent damage to the circulatory system, making the person more prone to cold-related injuries in that area. It can occur at temperatures as high as 60°F (16°C) if the feet are constantly wet.

Treatment Wash and dry the feet carefully. Rewarm gently and elevate slightly. Since the tissue is not frozen, as in frostbite, it is more susceptible to damage from walking on it. Patients should be evacuated by litter. Pain and itching are common complaints. Pain medications may help.

Prevention is the best approach to dealing with immersion foot. Keep feet dry by wearing appropriate footwear. Check your feet regularly to see if they are wet. If your feet get wet (through sweating or immersion), stop and dry your feet and put on dry socks. Periodic air-drying, elevation, and massage will also help. Change socks at least once a day (both liner and outer socks), and do not sleep with wet socks. Be careful of tight socks, which can further impair peripheral circulation. Canoeists and kayakers need to be especially careful.

TOXINS

The following sections are meant to be a general overview of how to treat toxins in the field. It is often difficult to identify specific toxins, so most of the treatments are for the symptoms of toxin exposure. You must carefully evaluate the type of reaction the patient is having to a toxin and determine whether evacuation to advanced medical care is required. When in doubt, transport. Toxins may cause long-term medical problems if not properly treated.

General Treatment for Toxin Exposure There are four basic types of toxins based on how the poison or toxin is introduced to the body: absorbed through the skin, ingested, injected, and inhaled. The basic principle for dealing with all toxins is to *remove* and *dilute*. For each type, the general treatment should be followed with the following specific treatments:

- **Absorbed Through the Skin** For dry toxin, brush off; for wet toxin, irrigate with water.
- **Injected** Support critical body systems; give medications where appropriate.
- **Inhaled** Clean, fresh air; PROP (see page 239).
- **Ingested** If possible, administer *activated charcoal* (25 to 50 grams)

mixed with water. Activated charcoal binds with whatever is in the stomach, allowing it to pass through the system without being absorbed by the body. Syrup of ipecac is used to induce vomiting to remove the toxin. For any unknown toxin, avoid having the patient vomit, since the toxin may do more damage if vomited up. Also, once vomiting begins, administering activated charcoal can be difficult.

ACIDS AND BASES

The major danger is burnt tissue when these products are swallowed. Be aware of the possibility of swelling of the esophagus and airway, which could compromise breathing.

Treatment *Do not induce vomiting,* as it could result in additional burns. Also, if any of the material is aspirated into the lungs, it could impair breathing. Carefully monitor airway, breathing, and circulation. Give activated charcoal if available. Prepare to evacuate your patient.

PETROLEUM PRODUCTS

The immediate danger in petroleum product poisoning is that the person may vomit and aspirate vapors and fluid into the lungs, which could seriously impair breathing. Carefully monitor airway, breathing, and circulation.

Treatment *Do not induce vomiting.* Give activated charcoal if available. Prepare to evacuate your patient.

MEDICINES OR PLANTS

If someone takes an overdose of medication or ingests a poisonous plant, induce vomiting by stimulating the gag reflex (carefully push a blunt utensil into the back of the person's throat) or by administering syrup of ipecac. If vomiting is unsuccessful, use water to dilute the poison. *Warning: Never* induce vomiting on a patient unless she is totally conscious to avoid possible aspiration. Prepare to evacuate your patient.

There are several toxic substances that you may bring with you on your trip. You should be aware of how to properly treat toxic exposure to these substances.

IODINE CRYSTALS

Iodine crystals may be used as a form of water purification. The iodine crystals are used to make a dilute iodine solution for purifying water; the crystals themselves are far too concentrated to ingest.

Treatment—Internal Ingestion of Iodine Crystals Drink starch in water (e.g., powdered milk). The starch will neutralize any remaining iodine in the stomach. Iodine is a strong intestinal irritant and most likely will cause immediate vomiting. If the patient vomits, carefully monitor airway, breathing, and circulation.

Treatment—External Burning by Iodine Crystals For contact with skin and/or eyes, flush with water for at least 15 minutes.

CARBON MONOXIDE

Carbon monoxide is a colorless, odorless gas that is a by-product of the combustion of stove fuel. In an enclosed or poorly ventilated space like a tent or a snow cave, the gas can accumulate. Symptoms include severe headache, nausea and vomiting, shortness of breath, and decreased hearing. If exposure continues, it leads to unconsciousness and death.

Treatment Prevention is the key. Don't use a stove or gas lantern in an enclosed space. If the patient is suffering from carbon monoxide poisoning, get her away from the source and into fresh air. Monitor the airway and give PROP (see page 239).

WHITE GAS

White gas, which is commonly used in backpacking stoves, is considered a toxic chemical. It is important to be aware of the hazards associated with the fuel and how to respond to a serious exposure.

- **Eyes** May cause irritation, discomfort, and excess redness and swelling of the eye. *Treatment:* Flush eyes with plenty of water for several minutes. Get medical attention if eye irritation persists.
- **Skin** Prolonged or widespread skin contact may result in the absorption of potentially harmful amounts of material. May cause irritation, local redness, and possible swelling. *Treatment:* Wash skin with plenty of soap and water until all traces of material are removed. Remove and clean contaminated clothing. Get medical attention if skin irritation persists or contact has been prolonged.
- **Inhalation** Vapors or mist may cause irritation of the nose and throat, headache, nausea, vomiting, dizziness, drowsiness, euphoria, loss of coordination, and disorientation. In poorly ventilated areas or confined spaces, unconsciousness and asphyxiation may result. *Treatment:* Remove to fresh air. If not breathing, give artificial respiration (see Basic Life Support, page 245).

- **Ingestion** If more than several mouthfuls are swallowed, abdominal discomfort, nausea, and diarrhea may occur. Aspiration may occur during swallowing or vomiting resulting in lung damage. *Treatment: Do not induce vomiting.* Give activated charcoal if available. Prepare to evacuate patient.

ANIMAL AND INSECT BITES AND STINGS

Animal bites and stings can transmit both toxins and infections. Bites from mammals may carry rabies and/or tetanus. Depending on where you go in the world, there are a variety of poisonous snakes. In North America there are only a few species that are poisonous. If someone is bitten by a mosquito, horsefly, chigger, or other insect, there is no great emergency. The bite will undoubtedly hurt and itch. The best treatment is a sting relief swab to control the initial pain and hydrocortisone cream to decrease itching (see Medications Profiles, page 328).

RABIES

Rabies is caused by a virus that attacks the central nervous system and is *always fatal* unless the victim has been protected by immunization or receives proper treatment. The virus is found in saliva, so infection is usually caused by bites. However, rabies can be contracted by saliva coming into contact with small cuts in the skin or mucous membranes. Currently, the mid-Atlantic states are experiencing the most intense wildlife outbreak of rabies seen in the United States in the last 25 years. Raccoons account for 75 percent of the cases reported, but rabies is also found in skunks, bats, foxes, and groundhogs, as well as in livestock and domestic animals. The incubation period, from infection with the virus to the onset of symptoms, is usually 2 to 12 weeks, but may be longer.

Rabid animals can appear either "furious" or "dumb." In the furious stage, the animal is aggressive and excited, snapping and biting at anything, often foaming at the mouth. In the dumb stage, the animal can seem docile, almost tame. It may be disoriented and lack coordination. These animals are especially dangerous because they are easily approached, but can still lunge and bite. Be cautious with your approach to wildlife, especially raccoons, and avoid touching any dead animals, because the virus can be transmitted to an open wound, even though the animal is dead.

Treatment First, treat the wound and stop any major bleeding (see Bleeding, page 241). The major concern with an animal bite is to clean the wound thoroughly with a povidone iodine solution and use an antibiotic ointment (see Wound Care, page 242). Anyone bitten by an animal should also be evacuated, especially if there is any suspicion that the animal was rabid. *Do not* try to capture a possibly rabid animal, because you only risk having another person bitten. Report the incident to the area rangers with a description of animal, behavior, and location.

PIT VIPERS

The pit viper family consists of copperheads, cottonmouths, and rattlesnakes. These snakes are found mainly in the southwestern and southeastern United States. Pit vipers are recognizable by their triangular-shaped head, pupils with vertical slits, and a heat-sensing pit behind the nostril. Pit vipers leave one or two fang marks. Envenomation only occurs in about 20 to 30 percent of bites. Envenomation is characterized by an immediate local reaction, marked by pain and swelling.

Treatment The most effective treatment is administraton of the specific antivenin for that snake, which usually requires that the patient be transported to a medical facility. Thus, the most important measure to be taken after a confirmed snakebite is evacuation. A suction extractor (such as the Sawyer Extractor) used immediately after the bite can remove up to 30 percent of the venom, but after the first few minutes, it is ineffective. This suction does not involve making any cuts in the skin. Do not use the "cut and suck" method; you only run the risk of damaging more tissue and will not remove much venom. The bite is a high-risk wound for infection, and should be treated accordingly (see Wound Care, page 242). After using the extractor, the area should be rinsed in a chlorine bleach solution (see page 245). Swelling will occur, so remove constricting items below the bite such as rings. Keep the affected area at or below the level of the heart to slow circulation of the venom. A healthy adult will become ill from pit viper venom, but is not likely to die. Children, infants, the elderly, and people in poor health are at greater risk. After any envenomation you should arrange for evacuation.

CORAL SNAKES

Coral snakes are found in the southern and southwestern United States. They are marked by alternating bands of red, yellow, and black. You can recognize the coral snake from the harmless scarlet king snake by remembering this rhyme: "red on yellow kill a fellow; red on black venom lack." They are not aggressive and bite only when provoked. The coral snake passes venom by chewing on the skin, as opposed to biting, so the snake must really grab on to you. If it has broken the skin, you must assume envenomation. The venom is a neurotoxin that causes nausea, rapid pulse, and rapid respiration, which can progress to respiratory failure and death. The effects of envenomation may be delayed for several hours.

Treatment Monitor respirations and treat with PROP as necessary (see PROP, page 239). Arrange for evacuation.

BLACK WIDOW SPIDER

The black widow delivers a low-pain bite, which can sometimes go undetected. Look for fever and chills, and severe cramps in the abdomen and extremities. The black widow is a small black spider. The female has a red hourglass on her abdomen.

Treatment These bites are rarely fatal. If the bite site can be localized, apply cold and evacuate.

BROWN RECLUSE SPIDER

The brown recluse is the most common culprit of serious spider bites in the United States. It tends to live under rocks and bark in relatively dry places. The spider has a dark fiddle-shaped mark on its back. Look for infection and necrosis—the liquefaction and breakdown of tissue. It can be mild at first, but grows more severe over time. Chills, fever, nausea, vomiting, joint ache, and rashes or hives may also appear as later signs.

Treatment Treat the wound and evacuate. If possible, save the spider for identification.

SCORPIONS

In North America, scorpions are found in the southwestern states and Mexico. There are numerous species, all of which inject a toxin from a stinger at the end of their tails. Scorpions feed at night and love crawling into things like boots and sleeping bags. In scorpion country, shake out items like your sleeping bag before going to bed, and shake out boots and clothes in the morning. During the day, scorpions hide from the sun in shaded places—under rocks, in woodpiles, and so on. Be cautious around these places. A scorpion sting is a pricking sensation followed by burning pain, swelling, numbness, tingling, and redness. Numbness may spread to the rest to the extremity. The toxin from most scorpions is nonlethal and is similar in severity to a bee sting.

The most dangerous is *Centruroides sculptuatus,* a small yellowish species about 3 inches (7.6 centimeters) long. It injects a neurotoxin that causes overstimulation of the nervous system, resulting in hyperactivity. Fatalities can occur in children and the elderly. Pain may become severe and the patient becomes very jittery.

Treatment Apply ice or cool water at the sting site and clean the wound. An antihistamine will help reduce swelling (see Medications Profiles, page 328). If the pain becomes severe or the patient shows nonlocalized symptoms, there is a more severe envenomation and the patient should be evacuated. In cases of *Centruroides* envenomation, an antivenin is available.

TICKS

Ticks can be found almost anywhere. The best defense against them is to wear hats, button up your shirt, tuck your long pant legs into your socks, or wear gaiters. Applying insect repellent to clothing and boots can also help. Also perform regular "tick checks." Adult ticks usually like to wander around the body for an hour or two before they attach, and they like to attach in a warm hairy place. Therefore, you should regularly run your fingers through your hair and closely examine your scalp. Ticks can also attach in the groin, under the arms, in or behind the ears, or occasionally underneath women's breasts.

Treatment To remove a tick with tweezers, grasp the tick's head as close to the skin as possible, paying careful attention to the head of the tick, which may still be under the skin. Pull it *straight* out. Do not grab the tick in the middle part of its body. Ticks may carry harmful bacteria, and squeezing their abdomen may inject the bacteria into the wound. There are also special "tick tweezers" designed to remove the tick completely. Do *not* burn or smother the tick with fluids. These methods are not effective in removing the tick and may also force infected fluid into the bloodstream. Evacuation is not necessary, but be sure to clean the area as you would any wound (see Wound Care, page 242).

If possible, save the tick for identification. Place it in a plastic bag with a small amount of vegetation. Live ticks can be tested to see if they are carrying a disease. Anyone who has an engorged tick removed should watch for signs of a tick-borne illness after the trip. Blood tests for some tick-borne diseases are available.

Lyme Disease

Lyme disease is an infection caused by a spiral-shaped bacterium called a spirochete. This bacterium is carried in the gut of the deer tick *Ixodes scapularis*. (Although other types of ticks have been shown to carry the spirochete, current research is not conclusive about whether other types of ticks, like dog ticks or wood ticks, can transmit the disease.) The tick becomes infected after feeding on the blood of an infected animal. Once infected, the tick can transmit the disease to its next host. Deer ticks are extremely small, with tick nymphs about the size of the period at the end of this sentence. This means that you may have been bitten without realizing it. The tick needs to feed for an extended period of time (usually 8 to 12 hours) before infection can occur. So just because you have found an attached tick does not mean that you have been infected. It is also possible that the tick was not carrying the disease. Most cases of infection occur between May and July, but Lyme disease has been found steadily through October, with cases reported all year long.

Detecting Lyme disease can be difficult, as the symptoms associated with the early stages–fever, headache, stiffness, lethargy, and myriad other mild complaints—are often dismissed as the flu. In some cases (about 25 percent), there is a red, ringlike rash that occurs at the site of the bite. The rash is often referred to as a "bull's-eye" rash because it has a red center surrounded by a red outer ring. Most typically, the rash expands and then fades within a few weeks after the bite. There is a blood test for Lyme disease, but it is not one hundred percent accurate. The test generally produces positive results in the later stages of the disease, but often turns up false-negative results in the early stages. Therefore, diagnosis in the early phase is frequently based on symptoms and the likelihood of a deer tick bite. Early detection means early treatment when the disease is most effectively controlled with antibiotics. Lyme disease can result in more serious symptoms, including arthritis, cardiac abnormalities, and meningitis (a potentially fatal central nervous system disorder) if left untreated. Since the symptoms of the disease do not appear until weeks or even months after a trip, it is *important that all group members understand the symptoms of Lyme disease* so they can seek proper medical help if they become symptomatic after the trip.

Rocky Mountain Spotted Fever

This disease is carried by a bacteria, and can be transmitted by the bites of dog or wood ticks. Watch for mild chills, appetite loss, and a general run-down feeling. These symptoms may worsen to severe chills, fever, headaches, muscle and bone pain, and sensitivity to light. Also, a spotty red rash (hence the name) may appear, usually starting at the wrists and ankles and spreading over the rest of the body. Normal onset of these symptoms is anywhere between 3 and 14 days after infection. Untreated, the mortality rate is 20 to 30%. Anyone who shows these signs should be evacuated. Since the symptoms of the disease may not appear until weeks after a trip, *it is important that all group members understand the symptoms* of Rocky Mountain Spotted Fever disease so they can seek proper medical help if they become symptomatic after the trip. Don't confuse the name of the disease with its location. Ticks carrying Rocky Mountain Spotted Fever are found all across the United States with the highest number of cases being found in the mid-Atlantic coastal states.

BEE STINGS

Bees, yellow jackets, hornets, wasps, and ants can be deadly for those who are allergic. In cases of a simple sting with no allergic reaction, treatment involves removing the stinger and treating the minor pain of the sting. Bees can sting only once and leave a stinger behind; yellow jackets, hornets, and wasps can sting repeatedly and do not leave a stinger.

Treatment If it is a bee sting, the stinger will be left behind with a venom sack. Be careful not to squeeze the venom sac, which would inject more venom into the wound. Use the edge of a knife blade to flick the stinger out. With any sting, a device called the Extractor can be used within the first few minutes to remove up to 30 percent of the venom. This can ease pain and swelling and reduce the severity of a reaction. As part of Universal Precautions (see page 244), after use, the Extractor should be rinsed with a bleach solution. Sting-eze will help relieve pain at the site. Ice packs

Stinger and Venom
Sac Left in Victim

Bee
Pulling
Away

Scrape out stinger using a knife blade

can help reduce mild swelling. Be alert for any systemic reaction (see Anaphylaxis, below).

ANAPHYLAXIS

Anaphylaxis is a dangerous systemic allergic reaction to a foreign substance that can be life threatening in many cases. Like other toxins, the foreign substance can enter the bloodstream through injection, inhalation, ingestion, or absorption into the skin. One of the most common causes of anaphylaxis, with one of the quickest periods of onset, is the common bee sting (injected toxin), with an onset of symptoms typically within the first 30 minutes of exposure. Allergic reactions to foods (ingested toxins) are slower, but equally dangerous. For an ingested toxin, the reaction can take up to several hours to develop.

In response to the toxin, the body releases histamine, which causes vasodilation and fluid leakage from blood vessels, resulting in swelling. In anaphylactic shock, this response is systemic in resulting in shock (see page 238). The greatest danger in anaphylaxis is to the patient's airway, which can swell shut, causing respiratory arrest and death.

In evaluating anaphylaxis, it is important to differentiate between a local reaction and a true systemic reaction. For a local reaction the patient's skin may be hot, with complaints of itchiness and hives appearing only at the site of the toxin. A systemic reaction is characterized by hives or swelling distant from the site or all over the body. In a systemic reaction, the airway may be constricted, causing labored respirations and wheezing. The patient's mental status will almost always be decreasing, and nausea, vomiting, and diarrhea may occur. *A systemic anaphylactic reaction can be a life-threatening emergency. The airway can swell shut and the person can die within minutes.*

Vitals in Anaphylaxis

- Pulse rate increased
- Respiration rate increased, labored, with possible wheezing
- Blood pressure possibly decreased
- AVPU—anxious, if severe anaphylaxis, possibly V, P, or U on the AVPU scale
- Skin hot, itchy, hives
- Temperature normal

Treatment In true anaphylaxis, the effects of the severe vasodilation must be countered. This can be most successfully done using the injectable drug epinephrine, a synthetic form of adrenalin. Epinephrine is a vasoconstrictor, so it counteracts the effects of the histamine. However, the histamine is still in the bloodstream and the effects of the epinephrine wear off in 15 to 20 minutes. The patient also needs to take an antihistamine, like Benadryl (see Medications Profiles, page 328). These bind with the histamine and prevent it from causing additional vasodilation. In severe cases, there may be a rebound of symptoms after the first dose of epinephrine wears off, requiring additional injections of epinephrine. The patient should continue to take antihistamines for 10 to 12 hours after the reaction. Any cases of anaphylaxis should be evacuated for medical followup. In addition to these medical treatments, be prepared for basic life support and PROP (see page 239).

Injectable epinephrine is found in the form of injectable pens and syringes. However, some of these forms, like the Epi-pen, contain only one dose. It is important to have at least two, if not three, doses with the patient because rebound of anaphylaxis is quite common. The patient should follow all instructions on the product for the proper method of injection. It is important to note *epinephrine is a prescription drug that requires a physician's approval for use.* There are individuals to whom giving epinephrine might be contraindicated.

GENERAL MEDICAL ISSUES

ABDOMINAL INJURIES AND GASTROINTESTINAL PROBLEMS

When a patient has "abdominal pain," it is exceptionally difficult to assess in the field just what the cause is. Rather than try to pin down an exact cause for abdominal pain, the goal should be simply to determine whether the problem is potentially serious and requires evacuation, or if it can be treated in the field and expected to improve. The following list of signs and symptoms, if associated with abdominal pain, warrant genuine concern and prompt evacuation:

- Presence of blood from mouth or rectum—indicates gastrointestinal bleeding
- Vomiting or diarrhea persisting for more than 24 hours; loss of fluid volume may be too great to replace in field
- Volume shock—indicates severe fluid loss from bleeding, vomiting, diarrhea, or dehydration
- Fever—indicates infection
- Tenderness/guarding—suggests internal injury
- Pain in the "pit of the stomach" not relieved by food or antacids—a classic symptom of a heart attack

Assessment of Abdominal Pain

Your approach to these problems is dictated by the mechanism of injury to the patient. If the abdominal pain is possibly the result of a recent injury, your assessment will focus on a physical exam. Otherwise, you will need to rely on a thorough medical history of the illness. Common sense is your greatest asset in assessing abdominal pain. Everyone has had stomachaches. Ask the patient to compare the present illness to past ones. Ask if the patient has any relevant existing illnesses or past injuries. The acronym OPQRST (see Patient Assessment, page 231) provides a useful framework for assessing the pain.

APPENDICITIS

Acute appendicitis is an infection and inflammation of a small pouch attached to the intestines. The typical pattern of signs and symptoms includes a low fever (101° F/38° C) with pain and tenderness located in the right lower quadrant of the patient's abdomen. Nausea and vomiting are common. The main concern is that the infected appendix will eventually rupture, spreading infected contents throughout the abdomen. If left untreated, a ruptured appendix can result in death.

Treatment Appendicitis requires surgery, and a ruptured appendix requires massive antibiotic treatment. If appendicitis is suspected, prepare your patient for evacuation. In the interim, monitor your patient closely.

CONSTIPATION

Constipation is the inability to have a bowel movement. Constipation occurs when too much water is absorbed from feces in the intestines. The feces becomes too hard to move along normally. This can be caused by a number of things, including diet, dehydration (the body needs to retain more fluid and absorbs it from stool), and lack of opportunity to take a bowel movement. It generally becomes a problem only when the situation causes discomfort.

Treatment The first form of treatment is prevention. Make sure that all members of your group have both time and privacy enough for their own comfort whenever nature calls, whether in camp or on the trail. Remind and encourage everyone in your group to eat high-fiber foods such as dried fruit or oatmeal on a regular basis. Most important, ensure that everyone drinks a minimum of 2 to 4 quarts (2 to 4 liters) of water per day. If someone does become constipated, the patient may consider taking a laxative. (See Medications Profiles, page 328.)

DIARRHEA OR VOMITING

There is a wide range of possible causes for diarrhea and vomiting, including viral or bacterial infection, contaminated food, food allergy, or soap in food. The major concern in the field is how quickly the body can lose large amounts of fluid. Diarrhea or vomiting for more than 24 hours can lead to dehydration and ultimately volume shock (see Shock, page 238). As with abdominal pain, it may be difficult in the field to determine the exact cause. It is more important to be able to recognize the signs of a serious condition that require advanced medical care.

Conditions with Diarrhea or Vomiting that Require Evacuation

- Fever
- Presence of blood
- Volume shock
- Diarrhea or vomiting lasting longer than 24 hours
- Pain lasting longer than 24 hours
- Any abdominal pain requiring evacuation (see Abdominal Injuries and Gastrointestinal Problems, page 313)

Treatment Generic treatments for less serious cases of diarrhea or vomiting are essentially the same.

1. Replace lost fluids orally with clear liquids—bouillon or other lear soups, weak Gatorade, or plain water with a pinch each of salt and sugar. Encourage the patient to drink slowly in small sips. If you are not able to replenish fluid losses this way, or if the patient is unable to keep the fluids down, the patient will become dangerously dehydrated. Treat for shock (see page 238) and prepare to evacuate the patient.
2. Once clear liquids are tolerated, move the patient to simple carbohydrates—bread, rice, tea, and toast. Continue giving fluids. Slowly move back to a normal diet as tolerated, and continue giving fluids.

Treatment for Vomiting In the case of vomiting, you need to carefully monitor your patient's airway to make sure that she does not aspirate vomit. Aspirated vomit in the lungs can lead to serious lung infections. If the patient is unconscious, you should place her on her side with the head down to let vomit drain from the mouth. Sweep the mouth after each bout of vomiting to clear it and make sure that the airway is still clear. If the airway is not clear, initiate basic life support (see page 245).

GASTROINTESTINAL INFECTIONS

There are a number of infectious diseases that are of particular concern to wilderness travelers. If you are traveling outside of the United States, there are other diseases that you may need to be prepared for, either with pretrip inoculations or by taking medication during your trip. You should check with your physician for specific information. See the Internet resources in the Bibliography. Many of these diseases may not present themselves until weeks or even months after the trip. I recommend that anyone traveling in remote areas of the world get a stool culture for ova and parasites upon return.

GIARDIA

Giardiasis refers to a syndrome of diarrhea, excess gas, and abdominal cramping caused by *Giardia lamblia,* a water-borne parasite that is world-wide in distribution. The symptoms usually occur one to two weeks after exposure to the parasite. *This one- to two-week time course is extremely important.* Since most trips are less than a week, people typically don't become symptomatic until after their trip. They may not associate their symptoms with being out on a wilderness trip. Also, not all people who have ingested the cysts become sick, so the few who do become sick may feel the cause is something other than water that all have been drinking. Travelers must be educated about the possibilities of giardia, so if they become symptomatic, they can seek out proper medical treatment. Failure to secure treatment can cause long-term gastrointestinal problems.

Giardia is a parasite that exists in two forms: a dormant cyst and the disease-causing form, a trophozite. The cysts are quite hardy and can survive even in extremely cold water. When the cyst is ingested, it metamorphoses into a trophozite that attaches to the intestinal wall, where it lives off its host. It is the trophozite that causes the symptoms of the disease. As feces move through the large intestine some of the trophozites are carried out and the trophozite changes back into the inactive cyst form. These excreted cysts often reinfect other water supplies. As backcountry travel use has increased, waste from both animals and people has spread to various rivers and streams, causing contamination. It is essential to remember that the spread of giardia is directly related to sanitation practices. Backcountry travelers usually contract giardia by drinking water from untreated or improperly treated sources. Boiling, chemical treatment of the water, and commercial water-filtration systems, used properly, eradicate the parasite (see Water Purification, page 83).

Symptoms of Giardia It usually takes 7 to 10 days for the giardia to begin functioning in the intestine. The cysts can also remain dormant in the body and suddenly begin to cause difficulty months later.

If you have any of the following symptoms for more than 24 hours, you should consult a physician. One or more of the following symptoms may continue for several weeks and their severity may very greatly. Mention your outdoor trip and specifically mention giardia. Unfortunately, some physicians are not familiar with this parasite and may misdiagnose your problem as something else.

- Diarrhea, often "explosive" and watery
- Bloating
- Gas, often described as "sulphurous"
- Violent vomiting
- Cramps
- Weight loss
- Loss of appetite

Treatment Giardia can be cured only with appropriate antibiotic treatment. Prior to seeing a physician, the one treatment is to maintain adequate fluid intake (see Fluid Balance, page 285). The diagnosis of giardiasis can be confirmed by inspecting a stool sample for the presence of the parasite. Because this test may not always identify the organism even if it is present, a physician may elect to treat you empirically for the infection. The use of antibiotics is usually highly effective in relieving symptoms and curing the disease. Failure to treat may result in long-term gastrointestinal problems.

CRYPTOSPORIDIUM AND CYCLOSPORA

Unfortunately, there are some new critters out there in the water. Both of these are *highly resistant* to iodine or chlorine but are large enough to be filtered out by a standard water filter.

Cryptosporidium is a protozoa that causes a diarrheal illness similar to *Giardia.* Symptoms include watery diarrhea, headache, abdominal cramps, nausea, vomiting, and low-grade fever that may appear 2 to 10 days after infection. Some infected people will be asymptomatic. It is most often spread by the feces to hands and then to the mouth. Careful handwashing is the best defense. *Cyclospora* is a recently discovered cause of diarrhea. It can cause a prolonged illness (average 6 weeks) with profound fatigue and loss of appetite and intermittent diarrhea.

Treatment Currently, there is no effective treatment for *Cryptosporidium*. Symptoms usually last 1 to 2 weeks, at which time the body's immune system is able to stop the infection. People with normal immune systems improve without taking antibiotics or antiparasitic medications. For people with compromised immune systems, this can be a dangerous disease. See your physician. In the backcountry your major concern is to maintain adequate fluid levels to prevent serious dehydration. Antidiarrheal medications may help with the symptoms.

In the backcountry, your major concern with *Cyclospora* is to maintain adequate fluid levels to prevent serious dehydration. *Cyclospora* can be treated with antibiotics.

OTHER INFECTIOUS DISEASES

TETANUS

Tetanus (lockjaw) is a bacterial disease that affects the nervous system. Tetanus bacteria are found in soil, especially in soil contaminated with animal feces. Tetanus may also be transmitted in animal bites. The tetanus bacteria are anaerobic—they grow in the absence of oxygen. The bacteria enter the wound (like a puncture wound from a rusty nail) and then the wound closes, creating an oxygen-free environment for the bacteria to grow in. Deep puncture wounds are most hazardous, but any anaerobic wound environment can be a breeding ground for tetanus, even minor scratches. The incubation period is typically 2 to 8 days, but may range up to several weeks. Common signs and symptoms include muscular stiffness in the jaw (lockjaw), followed by neck stiffness, difficulty in swallowing, abdominal muscle rigidity, spasms, sweating, and fever. Untreated, tetanus can lead to death.

Treatment Wounds should be thoroughly cleaned (see page 242). If the patient has not had a tetanus booster within the previous 10 years, she should receive a booster, preferably on the day of injury. A booster is also recommended if it is a severe wound and it has been more than 5 years since the last booster.

HANTAVIRUS PULMONARY SYNDROME

Hantavirus pulmonary syndrome (HPS) is a serious, potentially deadly respiratory disease that is carried by rodents. In recent years there have been cases of hantavirus among wilderness travelers. Currently, very few actual cases have been reported, mostly in rural areas of the western United States; however, according to the Centers for Disease Control, over half the people who have contracted the disease have died. The Centers for Disease Control reports, "Hantavirus pulmonary syndrome is a rare disease, and most tourists are not at increased risk for hantavirus infection. However, visitors to rural areas and nature resorts, campers, hikers, and others who take part in activities outdoors can become exposed to rodent urine, saliva, or droppings and become infected with hantavirus ... Travel to and within all areas where hantavirus infection has been reported is safe. Nevertheless, if you camp or hike in an area inhabited by rodents, you have a small risk of being exposed to infected rodents and becoming infected with hantavirus."

The most common rodent carriers are the deer mouse and the cotton rat. The deer mouse is found in most of the United States and Canada except for the southeastern United States. The cotton rat is found in the southeastern and southwestern United States.

The virus is found in rodent urine, saliva, and feces. In areas with high rodent concentrations such as nests, mist from urine or saliva or dust from feces can carry the virus. The most common way of becoming infected is by breathing in the virus through dust or mist. The disease can also be contracted from hand-to-mouth or hand-to-nose contact after handling contaminated materials, and can be spread by a rodent bite. The virus can be killed with common household disinfectants such as chlorine bleach.

Symptoms of hantavirus pulmonary syndrome appear anywhere from 3 days to 6 weeks after infection, but typically within 2 weeks. The early symptoms are similar to the flu—fever (101–$104°$F or 38–$40°$C), headache, nausea and vomiting, and abdominal, joint, and lower back pain. HPS patients develop fluid in the lungs, which quickly progresses to an inability to breathe. If you have been on an outdoor trip and have been exposed to conditions where rodent infestation could be a problem, and you begin to develop similar symptoms following your trip, contact your physician immediately and inform him or her that you have been in an environment where exposure to hantavirus was a possibility.

Preventing Hantavirus Infection According to the Centers for Disease Control, you can reduce the risk of infection by following these guidelines:

- Before occupying cabins or other enclosed shelters, open them up to air out. Inspect for rodents and do not use cabins if you find signs of rodent infestation.
- If you sleep outdoors, check potential campsites for rodent droppings and burrows.

- Do not pitch tents or place sleeping bags in areas in proximity to rodent feces or burrows or near possible rodent shelters (e.g., garbage dumps or woodpiles).
- Avoid coming into contact with rodents and rodent burrows or disturbing dens (such as packrat nests).
- Avoid sleeping near woodpiles or garbage areas that may be frequented by rodents.
- Try not to sleep on the bare ground. Use tents with floors. In cabins, use a cot with a sleeping surface at least 12 inches above the floor.
- Use only bottled water or water that has been disinfected by filtration, boiling, chlorination, or iodination for drinking, cooking, washing dishes, and brushing teeth.
- Store foods in rodent-proof containers and promptly discard, bury, or burn all garbage.

GENITOURINARY TRACT AND WOMEN'S HEALTH ISSUES

Infections of the genitourinary tract are most common in women. The most important way to prevent any health complications for the women on a trip is to stress the importance of attention to hygiene, proper hydration, and urination. These are the central factors in preventing urinary tract infections. Vaginitis, another common female health issue, is more directly related to stress and activity. Both conditions can be better avoided with open communication among group members.

URINARY TRACT DISORDERS

There are a number of conditions that can affect the sensitive tissue lining of the urinary tract and bladder. The most common is a urinary tract infection (UTI). It is common in women, since the urethra is shorter and it is relatively easy for bacteria to infect the bladder. Urinary tract infections are rare in men and should be cause for evacuation. Common causes for women include:

- **Inadequate Hygiene** Limited washing can increase bacteria levels on the skin, which can migrate to the urinary tract.
- **Dehydration** If you become dehydrated, the body attempts to compensate by retaining more water. This limits urination and allows bacteria more time to colonize before being flushed out of the bladder.

- **Infrequent Urination** This can be caused by dehydration or if the individual is not comfortable urinating outdoors and holds it in for a long time.
- **Trauma to the Urethra** Vigorous activity or bruising, such as from a bike seat or climbing harness, can cause infection.

Symptoms of a mild UTI include low pelvic pain, frequent urination in small amounts, cloudy or blood-tinged urine, and pain, tingling, or burning during urination. In some cases, the condition resolves itself in two or three days. However, if the condition persists for a longer time, or symptoms are more severe, then medical care will be required. If left untreated, the condition can become more serious, including kidney infection, which can be a life-threatening condition.

Treatment Urinary tract infections require antibiotics, so there is little you can do in the backcountry unless you are carrying prescription antibiotics. You should, therefore, return to medical care, but it does not require an emergency evacuation. In the interim, keep the external genitalia as clean as possible. Drink plenty of fluids to help flush the system. Vitamin C (1000 milligrams, four times a day) may also help. The excess vitamin C is absorbed from the blood into the bladder. It is acidic and lowers the pH of the bladder, making it more difficult for bacteria to grow. If the patient with symptoms of a UTI develops a fever and pain and tenderness in the lower back, suspect a kidney infection and prepare your patient for immediate evacuation.

VAGINITIS

Infection of the vagina occurs when something upsets the normal balance between the bacteria and yeast that inhabit the vagina. If one or the other grows out of control, vaginitis results. Changes in environment, tight clothing, strenuous or vigorous activity, stress, and hot, humid conditions, can all spur an infection. Symptoms of vaginitis include general itching or burning in the genital area and vaginal discharge that is white or "cheesy." Tingling or burning sensation on urination is also common and can be confused with a urinary tract infection.

Treatment Vaginitis requires medical treatment to cure but is not serious enough to require immediate evacuation. The symptoms can be temporarily relieved by douching daily with either 1 teaspoon of povidone iodine or 1 tablespoon of vinegar in 1 quart of water. A dry and cool environment with loose-fitting clothing will also increase comfort. Avoid nylon underpants, which hold moisture. Cotton underpants are preferable because cotton allows the air to circulate, minimizing the moist environment conducive to bacterial growth.

DIABETES

Diabetes is a chronic illness, so in most cases a person on your trip will be aware that she has the disease. The body produces the hormone insulin to metabolize glucose. Without the proper levels of insulin, the body's cells cannot process glucose and can be virtually starved. A person with diabetes has trouble maintaining the necessary balance of insulin for the glucose level in her body. Some diabetics are diet-controlled; they generally have enough insulin available but need to control the level of glucose in their blood by controlling what they eat. In more severe cases, the diabetic doesn't produce enough natural insulin and injects herself with insulin on a daily basis in order to metabolize glucose.

Most diabetics are very good at controlling their sugar-to-insulin balance. However, this regulation must also take into account the amount of exercise and food a diabetic gets each day. Those who are not used to the rigors of a backpacking trip may not be familiar with how to manage the insulin/sugar balance, which can lead to a diabetic emergency.

There are two basic types of diabetic emergencies: hypoglycemia (low blood sugar), which is the more common; and hyperglycemia (high blood sugar). In case of an emergency, it is essential that others on the trip be aware of this condition, another reason why all members of the group should fill out a health history form. Sugar levels in the brain are one of the causes of changes in the central nervous system that can lead to seizures, among other things.

General Treatment If you are unsure if a diabetic is hypoglycemic or hyperglycemic, go ahead and give sugar. It can't hurt. Keep in mind that anyone in your group (she doesn't have to be diabetic) can get a mild case of hypoglycemia if not eating properly. We all know how it feels at the end of a long day, when blood sugar levels are low and we feel tired and weak.

HYPOGLYCEMIA (LOW BLOOD SUGAR)

In hypoglycemia, the patient's glucose levels are too low. This can be caused by not getting enough glucose (change in diet, missed meal, more exercise than normal) or by taking too much insulin. Because of its rapid onset, if hypoglycemia is not recognized early and treated by providing simple sugars and fluids, it can progress to seizures, loss of consciousness, and eventually death. Such a situation warrants speedy evacuation if symptoms do not improve after giving sugar. Signs and symptoms include:

- Increased breathing rate
- Skin cool, clammy, very sweaty
- AVPU—decreased level of consciousness, irritability, confusion
- Restlessness, shakiness
- Faintness
- Unconsciousness

Treatment If the patient is conscious, give her fruit juice heavily laden with sugar. Make sure she eats regularly and takes medications properly. If unconscious, place sugar on lips and under tongue (honey works well). Monitor airway and breathing to make sure she does not aspirate. She may develop seizures (see Seizures, page 270). Prepare to evacuate. After a severe incident (coma, seizures) the patient should be evacuated to medical care.

HYPERGLYCEMIA (HIGH BLOOD SUGAR)

Hyperglycemia is a condition caused by a lack of insulin, which means that the blood sugar level is high, but not enough glucose is able to be metabolized. Signs and symptoms include:

- Gradual-onset, progressive malaise
- Flushed face
- Fruity breath odor
- Dehydration, patient is thirsty
- Drowsy
- Pulse rate rapid
- Headache, abdominal pain
- Weakness, shakiness
- Nausea, possible vomiting

Treatment Get the patient to take her insulin medication, and monitor her in the future. Rest; maintain body temperature and fluids. You may need to evacuate your patient.

ALTITUDE ILLNESSES

Reaching the summit of a high mountain peak can be one of the most exhilarating experiences of a backpacking trip. Understanding the physiological effects of altitude on the body is essential to a safe trip. First of all, what is high altitude? High altitude is defined on the following scale:

- High altitude—8,000–12,000 feet (2,400–3,700 meters)
- Very high altitude—12,000–18,000 feet (3,700–5,500 meters)
- Extremely high altitude—18,000+ feet (5,500+ meters)

ACCLIMATIZATION

The higher the altitude, the lower the available amount of oxygen to breathe. For example, at 18,000 feet (5,500 meters) the amount of available oxygen is 50 percent less than at sea level. Given time, the body can adapt to the decrease in oxygen molecules at a specific altitude. This process is known as acclimatization and generally takes 1 to 3 days at that altitude. For example, if you hike to 10,000 feet (3,000 meters) and spend several days there, your body acclimatizes to 10,000 feet. If you climb to 12,000 feet (3,700 meters), your body has to acclimatize again.

A number of changes take place in the body to allow you to operate with decreased levels of oxygen:

- The depth of respiration increases.
- Pressure in pulmonary arteries is increased, "forcing" blood into portions of the lung that are normally not used during sea level breathing.
- The body produces more red blood cells to carry oxygen.
- The body produces more of a particular enzyme that facilitates the release of oxygen from hemoglobin to the body tissues.

Here are a few basic guideline for proper acclimatization:

- Try not to fly or drive directly to high altitude. Start below 10,000 feet (3,000 meters) and walk up.
- If you go above 10,000 feet (3,000 meters), only increase your altitude by 1,000 feet (300 meters) per day and for every 3,000 feet (900 meters) of elevation gained, take a rest day.
- Climb high and sleep low—this is the maxim used by climbers. You can climb more than 1,000 feet (300 meters) in a day as long as you come back down and sleep at a lower altitude than you climbed to.
- If you begin to show symptoms of moderate altitude illness, *don't go any higher* until symptoms decrease. If symptoms remain, descend to a lower altitude.
- Different people will acclimatize at different rates. This means that you

may need to adjust your group's rate of ascent to accommodate the people who are acclimatizing more slowly.

- Stay properly hydrated. The body's fluid loss increases at high altitude (at least 3 quarts or 3 liters per day).
- Avoid tobacco and alcohol and other depressant drugs, including barbiturates, tranquilizers, and sleeping pills. These depressants further decrease the respiratory drive, especially during sleep, resulting in a worsening of the symptoms.
- Eat a high-carbohydrate diet (more than 70 percent of your calories from carbohydrates) while at altitude.

Since many people have not been to high altitudes, it is hard to know who may be affected by altitude illnesses. There are *no* specific factors such as age, sex, or physical condition that correlate with susceptibility to altitude sickness. Some people get it, some people don't. Most people can go up to 8,000 feet (2,400 meters) with minimal effects. If you haven't been to high altitude before, it is important to be cautious. If you have been at that altitude before with no problem, you can *probably* return to that altitude without problems as long as you are properly acclimatized. The major causes of altitude illnesses are going too high, too fast, and not giving the body proper time to acclimatize. This sometimes can be more of a problem for an athletically fit person than for someone who is out of shape. The fit person may be more used to pushing her body (breathing hard) and may not recognize that being winded is not as much from aerobic exercise as from lack of atmospheric oxygen.

ACUTE MOUNTAIN SICKNESS

Acute mountain sickness (AMS) is common at high altitudes. At elevations over 10,000 feet (3,048 meters), 75 percent of people will have mild symptoms. The occurrence of AMS is dependent upon the elevation, the rate of ascent, and individual susceptibility. Many people will experience mild AMS during the acclimatization process. Symptoms usually start 12 to 24 hours after arrival at altitude and begin to decrease in severity about the third day.

MILD AMS

Symptoms of AMS include headache, dizziness, fatigue, shortness of breath, loss of appetite, nausea, disturbed sleep, and a general feeling of malaise. Symptoms tend to be worse at night and when respiratory drive is decreased. Mild AMS does not interfere with normal activity and symptoms generally subside within 2 to 4 days as the body acclimatizes. As long as the symptoms are mild and only a nuisance, ascent can continue at a moderate rate. When hiking, it is essential that participants communicate any symptoms of illness immediately to others on the trip.

Treatment The only cure is either acclimatization or descent. Symptoms of mild AMS can be treated with pain medications for headache and acetazolamide (see Medications Profile, page 328). Both help to reduce the severity of the symptoms, but remember that reducing the symptoms is not curing the problem. Acetazolamide allows you to metabolize more oxygen, thereby minimizing the symptoms caused by poor oxygenation.

MODERATE AMS

Symptoms of moderate AMS include severe headache that is *not* relieved by medication, nausea and vomiting, increasing weakness and fatigue, shortness of breath, and decreased coordination (ataxia). Normal activity is difficult, although the person may still be able to walk on her own. The best test for moderate AMS is the sobriety test. Draw a straight line 6 feet long (2 meters) on the ground and ask the person to "walk a straight line" with the heel of the front foot touching the toe of the rear foot. A person with ataxia will be unable to walk a straight line. This is a clear indication that *immediate descent* is required. It is important to get the person to descend before the ataxia reaches the point where she cannot walk on her own (which would necessitate a litter evacuation).

Treatment At this stage, only advanced medications or descent can reverse the problem. Descending even a few hundred feet (70–100 meters) may help and definite improvement will be seen in descents of 1,000 to 2,000 feet (300 to 600 meters). Twenty-four hours at the lower altitude will result in significant improvements. The person should remain at lower altitude *until* symptoms have subsided (up to 3 days). At this point, if the person has become acclimatized to that altitude he or she can begin ascending again.

SEVERE AMS

The patient will display an increase in the severity of the aforementioned symptoms, including shortness of breath *at rest*, inability to walk, decreasing mental status, and fluid buildup in the lungs.

Treatment *Immediate descent to lower altitudes* (2,000–4,000 feet or 600–1,200 meters).

HIGH-ALTITUDE PULMONARY EDEMA

High-altitude pulmonary edema (HAPE) is less frequent than AMS and is more serious. HAPE results from fluid buildup in the lungs. The fluid in the lungs prevents effective oxygen exchange. As the condition becomes more severe, the level of oxygen in the bloodstream decreases. Symptoms include shortness of breath *even at rest,* tightness in the chest, marked fatigue, a feeling of impending suffocation at night, weakness, and a persistent productive cough that brings up white, watery, or frothy fluid. Confusion and irrational behavior are signs that insufficient oxygen is reaching the brain, eventually leading to impaired cerebral function and death.

One of the methods for testing for HAPE is to check recovery time after exertion. Check to see how long it takes your heart rate and breathing rate to slow down to their normal levels after exercise at your home altitude. This establishes a recovery baseline. As you go to altitude, see how long it takes you to recover. Initially, as you are acclimatizing, it will take longer, but then it should return to near your baseline. If at altitude you find that your recovery time continues to get longer, it may mean fluid is building up in the lungs, a sign of HAPE.

Treatment In cases of HAPE, *immediate descent is a necessary life-saving measure* (2,000–4,000 feet or 600–1,200 meters). Prepare to evacuate your patient. Anyone suffering from HAPE must be evacuated to a medical facility for proper followup treatment.

HIGH-ALTITUDE CEREBRAL EDEMA

High-altitude cerebral edema (HACE) is less frequent than AMS and is more serious. HACE is the result of swelling of brain tissue from fluid leakage. Symptoms include: headache, loss of coordination (ataxia), weakness, and decreasing levels of consciousness, including disorientation, loss of memory, hallucinations, psychotic behavior, and coma. It generally occurs after a week or more at high altitude. Severe cases can lead to death if not treated quickly.

Treatment *Immediate descent is a necessary life-saving measure* (2,000–4,000 feet or 600–1,200 meters). There are some prescription medications that may be prescribed for treatment in the field, but these require that you have proper training in their use. Prepare to evacuate your patient. Anyone suffering from HACE must be evacuated to a medical facility for proper followup treatment.

MEDICATIONS PROFILES

Following is basic information about some common medications that you might take on a trip. This information does *not* cover all of the specific aspects of each drug such as dosages, allergic reactions, precautions, or contraindications. Dosages and contraindications may vary with age or size of person. Dosages listed are for adults. It is your responsibility to carefully read all manufacturer's information before taking any drug. Remember also that research into the effects of various drugs or drug combinations on the human body is always going on. The information presented below may *not* be the most current.

Acetaminophen

Common Name: Tylenol
Use: Mild pain reliever, reduces fever. Good for headaches, muscle aches, and menstrual cramps. A good alternative to aspirin if person has an aspirin allergy. Will not upset the stomach. Does not reduce inflammation.
Adult Dose: 325 to 500 mg. every 3–4 hours, as needed. For short-term use the total daily dose should not exceed 4,000 mg.
Precautions: Do not drink alcoholic beverages if you are taking more than an occasional 1 to 2 doses. Individuals with liver disease should consult their physician before using this drug. Overdose can create permanent liver dam-age and lead to death. Treatment must be initiated within hours after over-dose to be effective.

Acetazolamide

Common Name: Diamox

Use: Acetazolamide allows you to breathe faster so that you metabolize more oxygen, thereby minimizing the symptoms caused by poor oxygenation. This is especially helpful at night when respiratory drive is decreased. This is a prescription drug.

Adult Dose: 125 mg. of acetazolamide taken at bedtime will improve sleep at altitude. For more moderate to severe AMS, 125 to 250 mg. twice a day is recommended. For many people 125 mg. provides the same effect with fewer side effects. Since it takes a while for acetazolamide to have an effect, it is advisable to start taking it 24 hours before you go to altitude and continue for at least five days at higher altitude.

Precautions: Acetazolamide results in frequent urination, so maintaining proper hydration is essential. Possible side effects include tingling of the lips and fingertips, blurring of vision, and alteration of taste. These side effects may be reduced with the 125 mg. dose. Side effects subside when the drug is stopped. Diabetics should consult their physician before using this drug.

Contraindications: Acetazolamide is a sulfonamide drug, so people who are allergic to sulfa drugs should not take it. Acetazolamide has also been known to cause severe allergic reactions to people with no previous history of acetazolamide or sulfa allergies. It is recommended to take a trial course of the drug before going to a remote location. The drug should not be given to women in the last months of pregnancy or to nursing mothers. People with liver or kidney disease should not take it without consulting with a physician.

Antacid

Common Name: Pepto-Bismol

Use: Antacid, for upset stomach, heartburn, indigestion, nausea, and diarrhea. Neutralizes excess stomach acid and protects stomach lining. If you are having diarrhea, taking a dose before eating may help.

Adult Dose: Two tablets chewed or dissolved in mouth every ½ to 1 hour, as needed, to a maximum of 8 doses in 24 hours. Best to take an hour after meals, and every 2 to 3 hours thereafter.

Note: A darkened coating of the tongue or darkening of the stool may occur with use. Both conditions are harmless and temporary.

Precautions: May prevent the absorption of other drugs, so avoid taking when on other medications. Do not take more than 16 tablets in 24 hours. Do not use maximum dosage for more than 2 weeks. Consult physician prior to giving Pepto-Bismol to teenagers during or after recovery from flu or chicken pox. If diarrhea is accompanied by high fever or continues more than 2 days, evacuate and contact physician.

Contraindications: Do *not* use this product if you are allergic to aspirin. Contact a physician prior to use if you are on anticoagulants (blood thinners), have diabetes, kidney disease, stomach ulcers, or gout.

Aspirin

Common Names: Bufferin, Bayer, Anacin
Use: Mild pain relief. Fever reduction. Anti-inflammatory.
Adult Dose: 650 mg. as needed with lots of water and food if possible.
Precautions: May irritate stomach, cause vomiting, abdominal pain or bleeding. Do not use if you have a history of peptic ulcers or related disorders. Can cause allergic reaction; watch for skin rashes and asthmalike symptoms. Overdose will cause dizziness and confusion. If ringing in the ears is present, discontinue immediately. Aspirin is also an anticoagulant, so it can lead to bleeding.
Drug Interactions: Aspirin may interact with Diabinase or other diabetes drugs to cause a dangerous fall in blood sugar for diabetics.
Contraindications: People with aspirin allergies, bleeding stomach ulcer, hemophilia, anemia, high blood pressure, kidney disease, liver disease, or gout. Diabetics and people who have allergic sinusitis or asthma should contact physician prior to taking.

Benzoin, Tincture of

Ingredients: Benzoin, alcohol 80%
Use: Use *only* as a topical solution on skin to provide a sticky surface for tape or moleskin to adhere to. Benzoin is not affected by wet or sweat. *Not* for internal use.
Directions for Use: Clean and dry the area. Apply a thin coating and let air dry until tacky, then apply tape or moleskin.
Precautions: Do *not* apply to open wounds. Do *not* take internally.

Diphenhydramine

Common Name: Benadryl
Use: Antihistamine, antiallergy medication. Inactivates histamine produced by allergic reactions. Provides temporary relief of sneezing, watery and itchy eyes, and running nose due to allergies and hay fever. Also helps relieve upper respiratory allergies.
Adult Dose: 25–50 mg ever 4–5 hours.

Precautions: May cause drowsiness. Avoid driving or hiking in dangerous terrain. Do not drink alcohol. Large doses may cause central nervous system depression or convulsions.

Contraindications: Antihistamines compound the effects of alcohol and other central nervous system depressants such as sedatives, tranquilizers, and sleeping pills. Consult your physician before taking an antihistamine with these other drugs. Consult your physician before taking if you have asthma, glaucoma, liver disease, or difficulty in urinating due to enlargement of the prostate gland.

Epinephrine

See the specific administration instructions in the kit. Also see Anaphylaxis, page 312.

Ingredient: Epinephrine 1:1,000 solution (a synthetic form of adrenaline)

Use: This drug is used for emergency treatment of severe allergic reactions that cause respiratory distress. It is a fast-acting bronchodilator that also reduces swelling in the throat to allow breathing. It also serves to constrict the capillary bed to restore the circulating blood volume. After injection, bronchodilation may occur within 5 to 10 minutes, with maximum effects within 20 minutes.

Adult Dose: 0.5 ml. of epinephrine solution from the syringe in the kit, injected into the muscle of the shoulder (deltoid) or thigh. Dose may be repeated in 10 to 15 minutes as needed. See the kit itself for attached administration instructions.

Adverse Effects: Increased heart rate, heart flutters, increased blood pressure, trembling, dizziness, anxiety, weakness, paleness, nausea, vomiting, and headache. Excessive doses cause very high blood pressure, and cardiac irregularities.

Precautions: Use according to directions attached to the kit. Epinephrine is light sensitive and should be stored in the box provided. Store at room temperature. Periodically check contents of the syringe. The solution should be clear and colorless. If it appears brown or cloudy or contains a precipitate, do not use. The effects of epinephrine may be potentiated by tricyclic antidepressants or by some antihistamines.

Contraindications: Must not be given intravenously. Administer into the muscle only. It should not be used on individuals in shock from blood loss. Epinephrine is a powerful cardiac stimulant. Use may be contraindicated in persons with high blood pressure, diabetes, thyroid disease, or heart disease.

Hydrocortisone Cream

Common Names: Cortaid, Lanacort
Use: Relieve redness, swelling, itching of skin. Use on skin rashes and irritations caused by eczema, insects, poison ivy/oak/sumac, soaps, detergents, cosmetics, and genital and anal itching.
Adult Dose: Apply cream to affected area not more than 3 to 4 times daily.
Precautions: External use only. Do not bandage or wrap the skin being treated unless directed to by a physician. Occlusive dressings increase the amount of medicine absorbed through the skin. Avoid contact in eyes. Do not use it for skin problems that are not listed on the package label without checking with a physician. Discontinue use after 7 days if itching is still present, and contact a physician. Do not use for external feminine itching if there is a vaginal discharge.

Ibuprofen

Common Names: Advil, Motrin
Use: Mild pain reliever, muscle relaxant, anti-inflammatory. Good for menstrual cramps.
Adult Dose: 200 to 400 mg. every 4 to 6 hours, as needed. Total daily nonprescription dose should not exceed 1,200 mg.

Precautions: Ibuprofen can irritate the stomach; take with food or milk. It should not be taken if there is a history of ulcers or severe indigestion. Ibuprofen can also produce gastrointestinal ulceration and bleeding. Ibuprofen also has a tendency to cause fluid retention, so care should be used in situations where fluid retention is a problem (example: acute mountain sickness or high-altitude pulmonary edema). Pregnant women should not take ibuprofen without consultation with a physician.
Contraindications: Do *not* take if you are allergic to aspirin or salicylates.

Laxatives

There are a variety of different medications used for constipation. Bulk-foming laxatives absorb liquid in the intestines and swell to form a soft, bulky stool. Hyperosmotic laxatives draw water into the bowel, causing increased bowl action and a soft stool mass. Lubricants coat the bowel with a waterproof film that keeps water in the stool, making it softer. Stimulant laxatives increase muscle contractions of the bowel to move the stool along. Consult your physician for a recommended laxative.

Povidone-Iodine Solution and Ointment

Common Name: Betadine

Use: Antiseptic (cleansing and sterilizing agent), topical antibiotic, water purification.

For cleaning and irrigation: Flush wound with povidone-iodine solution.

Mixing Solution: Mix about 1 to 1½ inches (2 to 4 centimeters) of povidone-iodine ointment with 1 liter of water (anywhere from 1:100 to 1:1000 concentration is acceptable). Allow to dissolve completely; wait 10 to 15 minutes. This solution can be safely stored in plastic bottles for extended periods, but may be slightly light sensitive.

For skin disinfection: Apply ointment directly to skin, or to sterile dressing to be placed over a wound.

Precautions: Individuals who are allergic to iodine. A chronic skin rash is the usual manifestation. Do not use directly in deep puncture wounds or on severe burns, and avoid contact with eyes.

Pseudoephedrine

Common Name: Sudafed

Use: Decongestant, for the common cold. Promotes sinus/nasal drainage. Relieves nasal congestion due to colds, hay fever, and upper respiratory allergies.

Adult Dose: 60 mg. tablets every 4 to 6 hours. Do not exceed 240 mg. in 24 hours.

Adverse Effects: Acts as a mild stimulant and makes some individuals restless or jumpy, inhibiting restful sleep. Reducing dose of drug usually relieves these side effects. Taking the last dose of the day several hours before bedtime will help prevent trouble sleeping.

Precautions: Do not exceed recommended dosage, because at higher doses nervousness, dizziness, or sleeplessness may occur. Do not take this product if you are presently taking a prescription anti-hypertensive or anti-depressant without consulting a physician first.

Contraindications: If you have high blood pressure, heart disease, diabetes, or thyroid disease consult your physician before taking this drug.

Sting Relief Swabs

Common Name: Sting-Eze

Use: Local immediate sting relief for nonallergic reactions.

Directions: Remove swab from packet, squeeze mini-vial between fingers, and apply using sponge end directly to sting site, spreading with your finger.

Precautions: Do not use in eyes or nose. Not for prolonged use, or use over large areas of the body. If swelling or pain persists, discontinue use.

Triple Antibiotic Ointment

Common Name: Neosporin ointment
Active Ingredient: Polymyxin B sulfate, Bacitracin Zinc, Neomycin, in a white petrolatum base
Use: To prevent skin infection in minor cuts, scrapes, and burns.
Adult Dose: Apply a small amount (an amount equal to the surface area of a fingertip) on the area 1 to 3 times daily. To clear up the infection completely, use the medication for the full time of treatment (even if symptoms have disappeared).
Precautions: For external use only. Do *not* use in the eyes or apply over large areas of the body. There is a separate product specifically designed for use in the eye. Stop use and consult a physician if the condition persists or gets worse, or if a rash or other allergic reaction develops. Do not use this product if you are allergic to any of the active ingredients. Do not use longer than 1 week unless directed by a physician. In case of ingestion, seek professional medical care or contact the nearest poison control center.

Zinc Oxide Ointment

Use: Skin protectant (total sunblock). Apply liberally to desired area (especially face).
Precautions: Do not take internally. Avoid eye contact. Do not apply to open wounds.

ORGANIZATIONS PROVIDING TRAINING IN WILDERNESS FIRST AID

Three of the most widely recognized organizations providing training and certification in Wilderness First Aid are listed below. Courses range from hours to weeks as well as specialized courses for groups with specific backgrounds and interests. Hosted by local organizations, all three schools teach courses throughout the country as well as the rest of the world. A basic wilderness first aid course is typically eight to sixteen hours. Advanced versions spanning around thirty-two hours leave one with an excellent background for most personal trips. The minimum standard for outdoor professionals is the Wilderness First Responder Course (WFR), which takes eight to ten days, or Wilderness EMT (WEMT), which takes a month.

- **S.O.L.O. Wilderness Medicine**
  RFD 1 Box 163, Tasker Hill
  Conway, NH 03818
  603-447-6711
  Web: www.stonehearth.com

- **Wilderness Medical Associates (WMA)**
  189 Dudley Road
  Bryant Pond, Maine 04219
  207-665-2707
  888-945-3633
  Web: wildmed.com

- **Wilderness Medicine Institute (WMI)**
  P.O. Box 9
  Pitkin, Colorado 81241
  970-641-3572
  Web: www.fcinet.com/wmi

Appendix

The Appendix section of this book provides you with forms and information for trip planning. Feel free to photocopy these as part of your trip-preparation process.

This manual was originally designed as an outdoor program field manual for the Outdoor Action Program at Princeton University. There is a great deal more material that applies to outdoor programs that would not fit within a book for general audiences. However, thanks to the World Wide Web, we are electronically publishing several additional chapters specially designed for outdoor programs. You can reach Adobe Acrobat versions of these chapters at the Outdoor Action Web site (www.princeton.edu/~oa/).

- Training College Wilderness Leaders
- The OA Leader Training Course
- Leadership and Group Dynamics
- Running a Wilderness Orientation Program
- Developing a Safety Management Program for an Outdoor Organization

HEALTH HISTORY

Gathering accurate information about the people going on your trip is important in planning a trip appropriate to the level of all participants. You need to be aware of everyone's physical condition and medical history. Here is a sample form that covers a range of such information. You can add to this form if you need more information.

HEALTH HISTORY FORM

(Please complete all sections and please print.)

FIRST NAME _____ LAST NAME _____

CLASS _____ HEIGHT (in inches) _____ WEIGHT (in pounds) _____

CURRENT PHYSICAL CONDITION: Please check the highest activity level in each category that you feel you can comfortably attain.

Walking (average 3 mph)	❑ 2 miles in 40 minutes	❑ 4 miles in 80 minutes
	❑ 6 miles in 120 minutes	❑ Unsure
Jogging (average 5 mph)	❑ 1 mile in 12 minutes	❑ 3 miles in 36 minutes
	❑ 5 miles in 60 minutes	❑ Unsure
Cycling (average 10 mph)	❑ 5 miles in 30 minutes	❑ 10 miles in 60 minutes
	❑ 20 miles in 120 minutes	❑ Unsure

CURRENT EXERCISE ACTIVITY: List any physical activities you engage in, their frequency, duration, and level of intensity.

Activity	Frequency	Approximate Time/Distance	Leisurely	Moderately	Intensely

SWIMMING ABILITY: ❑ Nonswimmer ❑ Poor ❑ Fair ❑ Good ❑ Very Good

IMMUNIZATION

Immunization	Required Interval	Last Immunization Date	Exemption
Tetanus	Within 10 years of time of trip. Recommended within 5 years.		Religious

CURRENT HEALTH STATUS: Please indicate if you have any physical disabilities or conditions that would interfere with or limit your participation in the trip. If you are unsure, explain the trip to your physician and ask for his/her advice. *(None of these will necessarily prohibit your participation, but for your own safety, we must be aware of such conditions.)* If you answer yes to any of these matters, please specify in detail below, indicating the item number.

1. Hearing or vision problems (do *not* include wearing glasses or contacts)	❏ Yes	❏ No
2. Respiratory problems	❏ Yes	❏ No
3. Back problems	❏ Yes	❏ No
4. Joint problems (knees, ankles, hips, etc.)	❏ Yes	❏ No
5. Any recent serious illness	❏ Yes	❏ No
6. Any recent hospitalizations	❏ Yes	❏ No
7. Serious reaction to high or low temperatures	❏ Yes	❏ No
8. Frequent muscle cramps	❏ Yes	❏ No
9. High or low blood sugar	❏ Yes	❏ No
10. Seizure disorders	❏ Yes	❏ No
11. Reactions to high altitude	❏ Yes	❏ No
12. Other	❏ Yes	❏ No

Item #	Detailed Description (include restrictions, if any)

ALLERGIES: Please indicate any allergies you have, your allergic reactions, and any medication required.

Allergy (check if applicable, write in others)	Reaction	Medication Required (if any)
Insect stings (bees, wasps, etc.) ❏ Yes		
Iodine or shellfish allergy ❏ Yes		

DIETARY RESTRICTIONS OR FOOD ALLERGIES (if vegetarian or Kosher, please indicate specific dietary restrictions):

MEDICATIONS: Please indicate any medications you are currently taking (other than allergy medications), for what condition, and whether you will need to take it during the trip. *If you need to take medication during the trip, be sure you have an ample supply.*

Medication	Condition	Do you need this during the trip?
		❑ Yes ❑ No
		❑ Yes ❑ No

TRIP LOGISTICS AND SAFETY PLAN

Whenever you go on a trip, make sure that you write up a complete trip plan and leave it with someone who is not going (your on-call person). Establish a time when you should be back, with a few hours leeway. Set a time after which the on call person should contact the appropriate authorities. Make sure that they have the appropriate emergency phone numbers to call in case you are overdue. Call the person when you return. Whenever you are out on the trail, sign in (and out if required) on any trail registers. This helps rangers locate you in a emergency and also helps establish usage patterns for the area.

TRIP ACTIVITIES _____ DATES _____

LOCATION _____ LEADERS _____

DRIVING ROUTE _____ DRIVING TIME _____

STARTING POINT _____

DAY 1 ROUTE _____

PLANNED CAMP _____

WATER LOCATIONS _____ MILEAGE _____

ELEVATION UP _____ ELEVATION DOWN _____ ESTIMATED TRAVEL TIME _____

EMERGENCY ACCESS _____

DAY 2 ROUTE _____

PLANNED CAMP _____

WATER LOCATIONS _____ MILEAGE _____

ELEVATION UP _____ ELEVATION DOWN _____ ESTIMATED TRAVEL TIME _____

EMERGENCY ACCESS _____

DAY 3 ROUTE _____

PLANNED CAMP _____

WATER LOCATIONS _____ MILEAGE _____

ELEVATION UP _____ ELEVATION DOWN _____ ESTIMATED TRAVEL TIME _____

EMERGENCY ACCESS _____

ESTIMATED DATE AND TIME OF RETURN _____

PERSON TO CALL IF OVERDUE _____

SAFETY ISSUES

ACTIVITIES _____

LIST ENVIRONMENTAL & ACTIVITY HAZARDS (Keep in mind static vs. dynamic environments):

_____

_____

_____

_____

SPECIFIC STEPS TO MINIMIZE ACCIDENT POTENTIALS LISTED ABOVE:

_____

_____

_____

_____

SUBMITTED BY _____ DATE _____

Emergency Telephone Numbers

_____

MENU PLAN

MEAL-BY-MEAL METHOD

BREAKFAST

Trip Day	Food Items	Quantity – 1 Person	Your Quantity
Day 1			
Day 2			
Day 3			

LUNCH

Trip Day	Food Items	Quantity – 1 Person	Your Quantity
Day 1			
Day 2			
Day 3			
Snacks			

DINNER

Trip Day	Food Items	Quantity – 1 Person	Your Quantity
Day 1			
Day 2			
Day 3			

RATION METHOD

BREAKFAST

Food Items	Quantity/Person/Day	Number of Days	Your Quantity

TRAIL FOODS

Food Items	Quantity/Person/Day	Number of Days	Your Quantity

LUNCH

Food Items	Quantity/Person/Day	Number of Days	Your Quantity

DINNER

Food Items	Quantity/Person/Day	Number of Days	Your Quantity

DESSERTS

Food Items	Quantity/Person/Day	Number of Days	Your Quantity

THREE-SEASON BACKPACKING TRIP TEACHING PLAN

The Teaching Plan serves as an overview of all the skills needed to successfully manage your trip. If you are teaching others, use this as your "cheat sheet" to make sure you cover everything. If you are doing other wilderness activities, in different seasons or ecosystems, you may need to create your own Teaching Plan.

EQUIPMENT
- What to bring/what not to bring
- Clothing
- Layering for temperature control
- Boots
- Backpacks
  - How to pack a pack
  - Putting on a pack
  - How to wear a pack
- Group Equipment

TRAVEL TECHNIQUES
- Pacing and rhythmic breathing
- Rest step
- Contouring
- Traversing an incline
- River crossings
- Rest stops
- Map reading
- Compass use

CAMP SETUP
- Location—minimal impact
- Tarp setup
- Stove use and cooking area setup
- Food and nutrition
- Cooking
- Fires—Leave No Trace
- Water purification
- Hygiene

LEAVE NO TRACE
- Backcountry travel
- Garbage and food waste disposal
- Human waste disposal
- Cleaning dishes and personal bathing
- Fires

FIRST AID
- First aid kit
- Foot and blister care
- Hypothermia and hyperthermia
- Adequate hydration and nutrition
- Fatigue prevention

SAFETY AND EMERGENCY
- Dynamics of Accident model
- Environmental briefing—based on location, activity, and season
- Preplanning
- Knowledge of general route/area
- Hazards from wildlife

WARM-WEATHER BACKPACKING EQUIPMENT LIST

This general equipment list is designed for basic multiday backpacking trips in temperate forest conditions (3-season). Typical temperature ranges would be 70's to 90°'s F (10 to 21° C) during the day with nighttime temperatures from 50's to 70°'s F (−1 to 10° C). For your own particular needs or for warmer weather or colder weather you will need to modify this basic list.

HEAD
- Wool/pile hat (optional)
- Brimmed hat (for sun protection)

UPPER BODY
- T-shirts as needed
- Cotton work shirt – long sleeve
- Lightweight synthetic long undershirt—polypropylene, or other hydrophobic, wicking fabric

- Lightweight fleece jacket/wool sweater—(e.g., Polartec 100)
- Wind jacket—nylon (can be same as rain jacket if waterproof/breathable—must fit over insulating layers)

LOWER BODY
- Underwear as needed
- 1 to 2 pairs of loose-fitting shorts
- Lightweight synthetic/wool long underwear bottoms—polypropylene, or other hydrophobic, wicking fabric
- 1 pair long pants, loose-fitting, light-colored cotton (no jeans)
- Swimsuit

FEET
- 1 pair of lightweight to midweight hiking boots: Boots should extend above the ankle and be leather/fabric or all leather with lug soles for traction. It is best if the boots can be waterproof, either by treating the leather with a waterproofing compound before the trip or if the boots have a Gore-Tex liner. Boots should fit comfortably with two pairs of socks, a light liner sock and a heavy wool sock.
- 1 pair of running shoes, sneakers, or sandals, for around-campsite wear and/or water activities
- 2 to 3 pairs of light synthetic/polypropylene liner sock
- 2 to 3 pairs of medium-weight wool or synthetic hiking socks
- Gaiters (optional)

SHELL LAYER
- Waterproof rain jacket—coated nylon or waterproof/breathable fabric
- Waterproof rain pants or rain chaps—coated nylon or waterproof/breathable fabric (optional)

TRAVEL GEAR
- External frame/internal frame pack with padded hipbelt
- Pack rain cover (optional, can use a garbage bag)

SLEEPING
- Sleeping bag—synthetic fill, rated to 40° F
- 1 closed cell foam sleeping pad (3/8 in.) or inflatable mattress. Pads provide insulation from the ground and padding for more comfortable sleeping (optional).

MISCELLANEOUS
- 2 1-quart water bottles or canteens
- 1 unbreakable cup with handle
- 1 unbreakable bowl
- 1 spoon
- 2 bandannas, multipurpose
- 1 flashlight with fresh, alkaline batteries (alkaline batteries last longer). Rechargable batteries are fun for short trips and are more environmentally friendly.
- 1 small towel
- 1 toilet kit: Just the essentials, biodegradable soap, toothbrush and toothpaste, comb, sunscreen, lip balm, insect repellent (no aerosols). Repellents with high concentrations of DEET may be hazardous (do not use products with more than 35% DEET, or use a non-DEET repellent).
- 1 pocket knife
- 3 heavy plastic garbage bags – one for sleeping bag, one for inside backpack, one as a rain cover
- 1 pair of sunglasses or clip-ons

- 2 pairs glasses or contact lenses (if needed); if you wear contact lenses and will have difficulty cleaning them in the field it is suggested that you bring glasses instead. Bring an eyeglass safety strap for your glasses.
- Any medications you will need to take during the trip (allergy medications, etc.)

OPTIONAL
- Small notebook and pencil or ballpoint pen
- Altimeter
- Camera and film
- Books and field guides
- Folding camp chair, such as Crazy Creek
- Musical instrument
- Drawing or painting supplies
- Handi-wipes or unscented Baby Wipes are great for basic face and hand washing. Also good for cleaning hands before cooking or when putting in contact lenses. Pack them out.

MODERATE-WEATHER BACKPACKING EQUIPMENT LIST

This is a general equipment list designed for basic multiday backpacking trips in temperate forest conditions (3-season). Typical temperature ranges are 50 to 70° F (10 to 21° C) during the day, with nighttime temperatures from 30 to 50° F (-1 to 10° C). For your own needs or for warmer or colder weather, you will need to modify this basic list. (See The Warm Weather Backpacking miscellaneous list for additional items.)

HEAD
- Wool/pile hat (must cover ears)
- Brimmed hat (for sun protection)

UPPER BODY LAYERS
- Lightweight synthetic long undershirt—polypropylene or other hydrophobic wicking fabric
- Medium-weight polypropylene top or wool shirt, long sleeve
- Medium-weight fleece jacket or wool sweater (e.g., Polartec 200)
- Wind jacket, nylon (can be same as rain jacket if waterproof and breathable; must fit over insulating layers)

HANDS
- Synthetic or wool glove liners

LOWER BODY LAYERS
- Underwear as needed
- Medium-weight synthetic or wool long underwear bottoms, polypropylene or other hydrophobic wicking fabric
- Lightweight wool or fleece pants (e.g. Polartec 100)

FEET
- 1 pair of midweight hiking boots. Boots should extend above the ankle and be leather and fabric or all leather with lug soles for traction. Boots should fit comfortably with two pairs of socks, a light liner sock and a heavy wool sock. Above all, make sure that your boots are well broken in. Non-broken-in boots invariably cause chafing and blisters.
- 1 pair of running shoes, sneakers, or sandals for around-campsite wear and/or water activities
- 2 to 3 pairs of light synthetic or polypropylene liner socks

- 2 to 3 pairs of medium-weight wool or synthetic hiking socks
- Gaiters (optional)

SHELL LAYER
- Waterproof rain jacket—coated nylon or waterproof/breathable fabric
- Waterproof rain pants or rain chaps—coated nylon or waterproof/ breathable fabric (optional)

TRAVEL GEAR
- External frame/internal frame pack with padded hipbelt and shoulder straps
- Pack rain cover (optional, can use a garbage bag)
- Trekking poles or hiking staff (optional)

SLEEPING
- Sleeping bag—synthetic fill, rated to 30° F (-1° C)
- 1 closed-cell foam sleeping pad ($\frac{3}{8}$ inch thick or 9 millimeters) or inflatable mattress; pads provide insulation from the ground and padding for more comfortable sleeping

COLD-WEATHER BACKPACKING EQUIPMENT LIST

This is a general equipment list designed for basic multiday backpacking trips in temperate forest conditions (3-season). Typical temperature ranges would be approximately 30 to 50° F (0 to 10° C) during the day with nighttime temperatures approximately 0 to 30° F (–17 to 0° C). For your own particular needs or for warmer weather or colder weather you will need to modify this basic list.

HEAD
- Wool/pile hat (must cover ears)
- Brimmed hat (for sun protection)

UPPER BODY
- Midweight synthetic long undershirt—polypropylene, or other hydrophobic, wicking fabric
- Expedition-weight synthetic long undershirt—polypropylene, or other hydrophobic, wicking fabric or wool

- Heavy-weight fleece jacket/wool sweater (e.g.. Polartec 300)
- Wind jacket—nylon (can be same as rain jacket if waterproof/breathable—must fit over insulating layers)
- Winter parka—synthetic or down filled

HANDS
- Synthetic/wool glove liners
- Synthetic/wool mittens

LOWER BODY
- Underwear as needed
- Midweight synthetic long underwear bottoms—polypropylene, or other hydrophobic, wicking fabric
- Expedition-weight synthetic long underwear bottoms—polypropylene, or other hydrophobic, wicking fabric
- Midweight fleece/wool pants (ex. Polartec 200)

FEET
- 1 pair of midweight hiking boots: Boots should extend above the ankle and be leather/fabric or all leather with lug soles for traction. It is best if the boots can be waterproof, either by treating the leather with a waterproofing compound before the trip or if the boots have a Gore-Tex liner. Boots should fit comfortably with two pairs of socks, a light liner sock and a heavy wool sock. In colder weather you may need insulated boots such as Sorels or army surplus "Mickey Mouse" boots or plastic shell mountaineering boots with insulated liners.
- 1 pair of running shoes, sneakers, or sandals, for around campsite wear and/or water activities.
- 2 to 3 pairs of light synthetic/polypropylene liner socks. Wearing liner socks underneath wool socks helps to prevent chafing since the friction is between the two pairs of socks, not between the boots and your feet.
- 2 to 3 pairs of medium-weight wool or synthetic hiking socks
- Gaiters (optional)

RAIN GEAR
- Waterproof rain jacket—coated nylon or waterproof/breathable fabric
- Waterproof rain pants or rain chaps—coated nylon or waterproof/breathable fabric (optional)

TRAVEL GEAR

- External frame/internal frame pack with padded hipbelt
- Pack rain cover (optional, can use a garbage bag)
- Sleeping bag—synthetic fill, rated to −10° F (−23° C)
- 1 closed cell foam sleeping pad (⅜ in.) or inflatable mattress. Pads provide insulation from the ground and padding for more comfortable sleeping.

GENERAL GROUP EQUIPMENT LIST

This is a basic group equipment list for a three-season backpacking trip for 10 to 12 people. You may need to modify it based on the size of your group, the length and remoteness of the trip, and specific trip activities.

SHELTER

- Tent or tarp and ground sheet
- 75-foot tarp line of ¼ inch braided nylon (22 meters of 6 millimeter)
- Small tarp to set up for cooking (optional)

COOKING

- Stove—one for 4 to 5 people. Two stoves give you more cooking options and are needed for groups from 6 to 15.
- Fuel bottles and fuel
- Funnel
- Strike-anywhere matches, waterproof matches, or lighter
- Nesting pots with lids—a 2-liter and 4-liter work well for groups up to 12
- Frying pan—8 to 12 inches depending on size of group
- Spatula
- Mixing spoon
- Pot gripper
- Biodegradable soap
- Plastic pot brush
- Plastic trash bags (plenty—double as emergency rain gear and for hypothermia wrap—see Hypothermia, page 293)
- Ziploc bags (plenty—double as map cases)

HYGIENE

- Water filter, iodine, or chlorine-based chemical treatment (have a backup method)
- Toilet paper

- Trowel
- 2 square feet aluminum foil (for tampons)
- Aspirin tablets (for tampons)
- Medical waste bag
- Chlorine bleach (for medical waste and dishwashing)

TRAVEL
- Compass
- Maps and guidebooks as needed
- Waterproof map case

MISCELLANEOUS
- 75 feet of bear bag line of $\frac{1}{4}$ inch braided nylon (22 meters of 6 millimeter)
- 2 carabiners for bear bagging
- 35 feet of parachute cord (11 meters)
- 1- or 1½-gallon collapsible water container (4–6 liter)

GENERAL REPAIR KIT
- Heavy-duty needles
- Stove repair parts and tools
- 30 feet of fishing line (9 meters)
- 5 safety pins
- 5 buttons
- 15 feet of duct tape on a golf pencil (5 meters)
- 3 clevis pins
- 3 split rings
- 15 feet of #20 wire (5 meters)
- 25 feet of braided nylon cord (7 meters)
- 2-inch Fastex pack buckle

FIRST-AID KIT

Here is a basic first-aid kit designed for a group of ten out for six days. Remember, this equipment won't do you any good unless you have been properly trained in how to use it. Take a wilderness first-aid course before going out into the backcountry. Modify the list as needed for the size of your group, length and remoteness of the trip, and specific trip activities.

Pack your first-aid kit into two separate kits: a basic kit for items that are used regularly, and an emergency kit for items that are used infrequently. The emergency kit, which might include specialty items and drugs with expiration dates, can be packed in a fanny pack and sealed by using zip ties on the two zipper pulls. Have the person who packed it date and initial the bag, including the expiration date of any medications.

BASIC KIT: PACKED IN A FIRST-AID POUCH

HARDWARE

1	sunscreen	10	2" x 2" gauze sponges
1	box mixed Band-Aids®	10	4" x 4" gauze sponges
1	8 oz. tincture of Benzoin	10	latex exam gloves
1	50 sq. in. moleskin	20	alcohol swabs
1	20 sq. in. Molefoam	1	trauma scissors
1	pkg. Spenco adhesive knit	1	tweezers
1	2" adhesive tape	1	cold pack
1	1" adhesive tape	5	maxi-pads

MEDICATION

20	Acetaminophen tablets	20	tube Betadine ointment
20	Ibuprofen tablets	1	tube petroleum jelly
20	antacid tablets	10	Sting-eze
12	triple antibiotic ointment packets		

REPORTING

3	Accident/Close Call Forms	2	SOAP Note Forms
3	Information Report Forms	2	Emergency Information Reports
6	quarters		

EMERGENCY KIT: PACKED IN A FANNY PACK

TISSUE INJURY

2	2" roller gauze	1	3" Ace bandage
5	2" x 3" Tefla pads	2	cold pack
2	triangular bandages	1	trauma dressing

HARDWARE

1	SAM splint	2	ammonia inhalants
1	thermometer	1	box waterproof matches
6	large blanket pins	1	reflective blanket
1	Microshield rescue mask	1	Extractor

MEDICATION

Benadryl tablets	laxative
Pseudoephedrine tablets	tube Hydrocortisone cream
Anakit* – epinephrine	bottle Polar Pure iodine

*(This is a prescription drug item. Any individuals on the trip with severe allergies to such things as bee stings should bring their own. Contact your physician for more information.)

THE BACKPACKER'S FIELD MANUAL

TRIP EXPENSES FORM

Keeping a good record of all your trip expenses is essential whether you are running an outdoor program or camping with friends who split up the costs at the end of a trip. Good record keeping will also show you where the bulk of the costs for the trip were and may help you reduce costs for future trips.

ACTIVITIES _____ **DATES** _____

LOCATION _____

LEADERS(S) _____

LEADER # _____ **PARTICIPANT #** _____ **TOTAL NUMBER #** _____

FOOD PURCHASES FOR _____ PEOPLE FOR _____ DAYS

_____ $ _____

_____ $ _____

_____ $ _____

_____ $ _____

TOTAL $ _____

EQUIPMENT PURCHASES

_____ $ _____

_____ $ _____

_____ $ _____

_____ $ _____

TOTAL $ _____

TRAVEL EXPENSES

VEHICLE _____ **MILEAGE START** _____ **MILEAGE END** _____ **TOTAL** _____

GAS AND OIL EXPENSES   **TOLLS**

$	$	$	$	$	$	$
$	$	$	$	$	$	$
$	$	$	$	$	$	$

CAMPING/LODGING EXPENSES

_____ $ _____

_____ $ _____

_____ $ _____

MISCELLANEOUS EXPENSES

_____ $ _____

_____ $ _____

_____ $ _____

TOTAL $ _____

TRIP LOG

Location

Activities

Dates

Leaders

Number of Participants

Drop Off/Put-In/Parking Lot: Driving Time

	Mileage/ Time	Route Traveled/ Trails Used	Water Availability	Terrain/Trail Conditions	Campsite
Day 1					
Day 2					
Day 3					
Day 4					
Day 5					

Permits Needed

Special Regulations

Ranger Station Location

Ranger Phone Number(s)

Maps Used

Special Equipment Needed

Alternate Route/Activities

Problems with Trip

Places to See/Avoid

EMERGENCY INFORMATION REPORT

This form should be filled out if medical or evacuation assistance needs to be obtained. One copy goes with those hiking out to arrange for help; one copy stays with the patient.

GENERAL					
DATE		TIME			
GROUP#					
LEADERS					
ACCIDENT					
ACTIVITY					
NUMBER INJURED/ILL					
VICTIM #1 NAME			SEX	AGE	WT.
LOCATION					
QUADRANGLE MAP				SECTION: NE NW SE SW	

EXACT LOCATION

TERRAIN:	○ TRAIL	○ FIELD
	○ WOODS	○ ROAD
	○ BRUSH	
SLOPE:	○ EASY	
	○ MODERATE	
	○ STEEP	

RESPONSE PLAN
○ WILL STAY OUT   ○ WILL SEND MESSENGERS OUT   ○ WILL EVACUATE TO ROAD
○ WILL EVACUATE SHORT DISTANCE TO SHELTER   ○ WILL EVACUATE TO TRAILHEAD

IF EVACUATING, GIVE DETAILS (EXACT EVACUATION POINT, ETA TO EVAC)

NAMES OF MESSENGERS

WHERE SHALL RESCUE TEAM MEET MESSENGERS?

SOAP NOTE

DATE	PATIENT NAME

RESCUER

SCENE

S   Symptoms

A   Allergies

M   Medications

P   Past History

L   Last Meal

E   Events

OBJECTIVE

Exam:

VITAL SIGNS

Time	Pulse	Resp.	B/P	Skin	Temp.	AVPU

ASSESSMENT AND TREATMENT PLAN

A = Assessment Plan	A' = Anticipated Problems	P = Treatment Plan

ADDITIONAL NOTES

Bibliography

If you want to learn more about the many topics covered in this book, here are some excellent resources.

Information in the age of the Internet is changing rapidly. In order to keep you up to date, I have included a list of Internet resources available through the World Wide Web. Please remember that Web sites change. The ones listed here were current at the time the book went to press. Be sure to check out the Outdoor Action Web site (www.princeton.edu/~oa). It is filled with information, including the OA Guide to Outdoor Resources on the Web with hundreds of links to outdoor-related sites.

GENERAL INTERNET RESOURCES

Backcountry Home Page: io.datasys.swri.edu/
Backpacker Magazine: www.bpbasecamp.com
Distilled Wisdom from the news group: rec.backcountry file://rtfm.mit.edu/pub/usenet/rec.back-country/
FTP Directory of Rec.Backcountry Newsgroup: file://rtfm.mit.edu/pub/usenet-by-group/rec.backcountry
GORP—Great Outdoor Recreation Pages: www.gorp.com/
Usenet Newsgroup: rec.backcountry news:rec.backcountry
Yahoo Backcountry Reference Page: www.yahoo.com/Recreation/Outdoors/Backcountry/
Yahoo Hiking Reference Page: www.yahoo.com/Recreation/Outdoors/Hiking/

PARKS AND PLACES TO GO INTERNET RESOURCES

American Discovery Trail: www.teleport.com:80/~walking/adt.htm
Appalachian Trail Home Page: www.fred.net/kathy/at.html
National Scenic Trails: www.yahoo.com/yahoo/Environment_and_Nature/National_Parks_and_Monuments/National_Scenic_Trails/
Pacific Crest Trail Association: www.gorp.com/pcta/default.htm
U.S. Forest Service Guide to America's Great Outdoors: www.fs.fed.us/recreation_homepage.html
Yahoo National Parks Reference Page: www.yahoo.com/Environment_and_Nature/Parks/US_National_Parks__Forests__and_Monuments/
Yahoo Parks Reference Page: www.yahoo.com/Environment_and_Nature/Parks/
Yahoo Trails Reference Page: www.yahoo.com/Recreation/Outdoors/Backcountry/Trails/

U.S. GOVERNMENT INTERNET RESOURCES

Army Corps of Engineers: white.nosc.mil/army.html
Bureau of Land Management: info.er.usgs.gov/doi/bureau-land-management.html
National Oceanic and Atmospheric Administration (NOAA): www.noaa.gov
National Park Service: www.nps.gov/nps

National Snow and Ice Data Center: eosims.colorado.edu:1733/
U.S. Department of the Interior: www.usgs.gov/doi/
U.S. Fish & Wildlife Service: www.fws.gov
U.S. Forest Service: www.fs.fed.us/
U.S. Geological Survey (USGS): info.er.usgs.gov

BOOKS AND INTERNET RESOURCES
Backpacker Magazine, Rodale Press, Emmaus, PA.

Chapter 1: Trip Planning
Berger, Karen. *Hiking & Backpacking.* New York: W. W. Norton & Company, 1993.
Logue, Victoria. *Backpacking in the 90's.* Birmingham, AL: Menasha Ridge Press, 1993.
Schad, Jerry, and David S. Moser. *Wilderness Basics.* Seattle, WA: The Mountaineers, 1993.
Simer, Peter, and John Sullivan. *The NOLS Wilderness Guide.* New York: Simon & Schuster, 1985.

Chapter 2: Equipment
Berger, Karen. *Hiking & Backpacking.* New York: W. W. Norton & Company, 1993.
Getchell, Annie. *The Essential Outdoor Gear Manual.* Camden, ME: Ragged Mountain Press, 1995.
Jeffrey, Kevin. *The Complete Buyers Guide to Outdoor Recreation & Equipment.* San Francisco: Foghorn Press, 1993.
MSR Whisperlite. Reprinted from MSR Whisperlite Maintenance Instructions, MSR Company, Seattle, WA.
Peak 1. Reprinted from Peak 1 Instruction and Repair pamphlet, The Coleman Company, Wichita, KS.
Schad, Jerry, and David S. Moser. *Wilderness Basics.* Seattle, WA: The Mountaineers, 1993.
Tilton, Buck. *The Wilderness Medicine Newsletter,* July/August 1994.
Internet Resources
The Outdoor Action Cold Weather Backpacking Equipment List: www.princeton.edu/~oa/bpcold.html
The Outdoor Action First Aid Equipment List: www.princeton.edu/~oa/firstaid.html
The Outdoor Action Group Equipment List: www.princeton.edu/~oa/groupeqp.html
The Outdoor Action Moderate Weather Backpacking Equipment List: www.princeton.edu/~oa/bpmod.html
The Outdoor Action Warm Weather Backpacking Equipment List: www.princeton.edu/~oa/bpwarm.html

Chapter 3: Cooking and Nutrition
Berger, Karen. *Hiking & Backpacking.* New York: W. W. Norton & Company, 1993.
Brunnell, Valerie, and Ralph Swain. *The Wilderness Ranger Cookbook.* Helena, MT: Falcon Press, 1990.
Bunnelle, Hasse. *The Backpackers Food Book.* New York: Simon & Schuster, 1981.
————. *Cooking for Camp and Trail.* San Francisco: Sierra Club Books, 1973.
Fleming, June. *The Well-fed Backpacker.* New York: Vintage Books, 1981.
Gray, Melissa, and Buck Tilton. *Cooking the One Burner Way.* Merrillville, IN: ICS Books, 1994.
Gunn, Carolyn. *The Expedition Cookbook.* Denver, CO: Chockstone Press, 1988.
Jacobson, Don. *The One Pan Gourmet.* Camden, ME: Ragged Mountain Press, 1993.
McHugh, Gretchen. *The Hungry Hiker's Book of Good Cooking.* New York: Alfred A, Knopf, 1987.
McMorris, Bill and Jo. *Camp Cooking.* New York: Lyons & Burford, 1988.
Prater, Yvonne, and Ruth Dyar Mendenhall. *Gorp, Glop & Glue Stew.* Seattle, WA: The Mountaineers, 1988.

Richard, Sukey, Donna Orr, and Claudia Lindholm. *NOLS Cookery.* Lander, WY: National Outdoor Leadership School, 1988.

Schad, Jerry, and David S. Moser. *Wilderness Basics.* Seattle, WA: The Mountaineers, 1993.

Simer, Peter, and John Sullivan. *The NOLS Wilderness Guide.* New York: Simon & Schuster, 1985.

Viehman, John. *Trailside's Trail Food.* Emmaus, PA: Rodale Press, 1993.

Chapter 4: Hygiene and Water Purification

Hampton, Bruce, and David Cole. *Soft Paths.* Harrisburg, PA: Stackpole Books, 1988.

Hostetter, Kristin. "The Water Filter Field Test," *Backpacker Magazine* (December 1996):56–70.

Jenkins, Mark. "What's in the Water," *Backpacker Magazine* (December 1996):56–60.

Simer, Peter, and John Sullivan. *The NOLS Wilderness Guide.* New York: Simon & Schuster, 1985.

Wilkerson, James A. *Medicine for Mountaineering and Other Wilderness Activities.* Seattle, WA: The Mountaineers, 1992.

Chapter 5: Leave No Trace Hiking and Camping

Hampton, Bruce, and David Cole. *Soft Paths.* Harrisburg, PA: Stackpole Books, 1988.

Hodgson, Michael. *The Basic Essentials of Minimizing Impact on the Wilderness.* Merrillville, IN: ICS Books, 1991.

Leave No Trace: Outdoor Skills and Ethics Series, National Outdoor Leadership School, Lander, WY, 1996.

Meyer, Kathleen. *How to Shit in the Woods.* Berkeley, CA: Ten Speed Press, 1989.

Simer, Peter, and John Sullivan. *The NOLS Wilderness Guide.* New York: Simon & Schuster, 1985.

Internet Resources

Cryptogamic Soil: www.nps.gov/care/crypto.htm

Leave No Trace Hotline: call 800-332-4100 for the latest Leave No Trace Information

Leave No Trace Web Site: www.lnt.org

Chapter 6: Wilderness Travel

Alter, Michael J. *Sport Stretch.* Champaign, IL: Leisure Press, 1990.

Anderson, Bob. *Stretching.* New York: Random House, 1980.

Berger, Karen. *Hiking & Backpacking.* New York: W. W. Norton & Company, 1993.

Brown, Gary. *Safe Travel in Bear Country.* New York: Lyons & Burford, 1996.

Fleming, June. *Staying Found: The Complete Map & Compass Handbook.* Seattle, WA: The Mountaineers, 1994.

Geary, Don. *Using a Map & Compass.* Mechanicsburg, PA: Stackpole Books, 1995.

Graydon, Don. *Mountaineering: The Freedom of the Hills.* Seattle, WA: The Mountaineers, 1992.

Herrero, Stephen. *Bear Attacks: Their Causes and Avoidance.* New York: Nick Lyons Books, 1985.

Kals, W. S. *The Land Navigation Handbook.* San Francisco: Sierra Club Books, 1983.

Owen, Peter. *The Book of Outdoor Knots.* New York: Lyons & Burford, 1993.

Randall, Glenn. *The Outward Bound Map and Compass Handbook.* New York: Lyons & Burford, 1989.

Schad, Jerry, and David S. Moser. *Wilderness Basics.* Seattle, WA: The Mountaineers, 1993.

Seidman, David. *The Essential Wilderness Navigator.* Camden, ME: Ragged Mountain Press, 1995.

Simer, Peter, and John Sullivan. *The NOLS Wilderness Guide.* New York: Simon & Schuster, 1985.

Viehman, John. *Trailside's Hints & Tips for Outdoor Adventure.* Emmaus, PA: Rodale Press, 1993.

Internet Resources

Intro to GPS (Global Positioning Systems) Applications: galaxy.einet.net/editors/john-beadles/introgps.htm

Orienteering & Rogaining Home Page: www2.aos.princeton.edu/rdslater/orienteering
Shaded Relief Maps of U.S. by State: fermi.jhuapl.edu/states/states.html
Usenet Newsgroup: news:rec.sport.orienteering
U.S. Geological Survey (USGS): info.er.usgs.gov
What Do Maps Show?: info.er.usgs.gov/education/teacher/what-do-maps-show/index.html

Chapter 7: Weather and Nature

Brown, Tom. *Tom Brown's Guide to Wild Edible and Medicinal Plants.* New York: Berkley Publishing, 1985.

Brown, Tom, and Brandt Morgan. *Tom Brown's Field Guide to Nature Observation and Tracking.* New York: Berkley Publishing, 1983.

Burt, William, and Richard Grossenheider. *Peterson Field Guides: Mammals.* Boston: Houghton Mifflin, 1976.

Chartrand, Mark. *The Audubon Society Field Guide to the Night Sky.* New York: Alfred A. Knopf, 1992.

Coombes, Allen J. *Eyewitness Handbooks: Trees.* New York: Dorling Kindersley, 1992.

Halfpenny, James. *A Field Guide to Mammal Tracking in North America.* Boulder, CO: Johnson Books, 1986.

Kricher, John, and Gordon Morrison. *Peterson Field Guides: Eastern Forests.* Boston: Houghton Mifflin, 1988.

———. *Peterson Field Guides: Ecology of Western Forests.* Boston: Houghton Mifflin, 1993.

Ludlum, David. *The Audubon Society Field Guide to North American Weather.* New York: Alfred A. Knopf, 1991.

Murie, Olaus. *Peterson Field Guide: Animal Tracks.* Boston: Houghton Mifflin, 1974.

Peterson, Lee Allen. *A Field Guide to Edible Wild Plants.* Boston: Houghton Mifflin, 1977.

Peterson, Roger Tory. *A Field Guide to the Birds East of the Rockies.* Boston: Houghton Mifflin, 1980.

———. *A Field Guide to Western Birds.* Boston: Houghton Mifflin, 1990.

Peterson, Roger Tory, and Margaret McKenny. *Field Guide to Wildflowers of Northeastern and North Central North America.* Boston: Houghton Mifflin, 1975.

Reifsnyder, William. *Weathering the Wilderness.* San Francisco: Sierra Club Books, 1980.

Rezendes, Paul. *Tracking and the Art of Seeing: How to Read Animal Tracks and Signs.* Charlotte, VT: Camden House, 1992.

Schad, Jerry, and David S. Moser. *Wilderness Basics.* Seattle, WA: The Mountaineers, 1993.

Steele, Frederic. *At Timberline: A Nature Guide to the Mountains of the Northeast.* Boston: Appalachian Mountain Club Books, 1982.

Stokes, Donald, and Lillian Stokes. *A Guide to Animal Tracking and Behavior.* Boston: Little Brown, 1986.

Sutton, Ann and Myron. *National Audubon Society Nature Guide to Eastern Forests.* New York: Alfred A. Knopf, 1985.

Watts, May Thielgaard. *Master Tree Finder.* Berkeley, CA: Nature Study Guild, 1963.

Williams, Jack. *The Weather Book.* New York: Random House, 1992.

Internet Resources

National Weather Service: www.nws.noaa.gov/
The Outdoor Action Guide to Animal Tracking: www.princeton.edu/~oa/tracking.html
The Outdoor Action Guide to Nature Observation: www.princeton.edu/~oa/naturobs.html
Yahoo Weather Reference Page: www.yahoo.com/Environment_and_Nature/Weather/

Chapter 8: Safety and Emergency Procedures

Brown, Tom, Jr., with Brandt Morgan. *Tom Brown's Guide to Wilderness Survival.* New York: Berkley Books, 1983.

Fuller, Margaret. *Forest Fires.* New York: John Wiley & Sons, 1991.

Hale, Alan. "Dynamics of Accidents Model," Bellefontaine, OH: International Safety Network, 1988.

Tilton, Buck. *The Basic Essentials of Rescue from the Backcountry.* Merrillville, IN: ICS Books, 1990.

Internet Resources

The Outdoor Action Guide to Developing a Safety Management Program for an Outdoor Organization: www.princeton.edu/~oa/safeprog.html

The Outdoor Action Guide to Outdoor Safety Management: www.princeton.edu/~oa/safeman.html

The Outdoor Action Guide to Running a Safe River Trip: www.princeton.edu/~oa/rivplan.html

Wilderness Risk Managers Committee: www.nols.edu/WRMC/WRMC.html

Chapter 9: First Aid and Emergency Care

Auerbach, Paul. *Medicine for the Outdoors.* Boston: Little, Brown, 1986.

Bezruchka, Stephen. *Altitude Illness: Prevention & Treatment.* Seattle, WA: The Mountaineers, 1994.

Bowman, William D., Jr., M.D. *The National Ski Patrol's Outdoor Emergency Care.* National Ski Patrol, 1988.

Consumer Reports Books. *Consumer Reports Books Complete Drug Reference,* Yonkers, NY, 1996.

Forgey, William, M.D. *Wilderness Medical Society Practice Guidelines for Wilderness Emergency Care.* Merrillville, IN: ICS Books, 1995.

————. *Wilderness Medicine.* Merrillville, IN: ICS Books, 1994.

Gill, Paul. *The Pocket Guide to Wilderness Medicine.* New York: Simon & Schuster, 1991.

Isaac, Jeff, and Peter Goth. *The Outward Bound Wilderness First-Aid Handbook.* New York: Lyons & Burford, 1991.

Ostfeld, Richard. "The Ecology of Lyme: Disease Risk," *American Scientist* (July–August 1997): 338–346.

Schimelpfenig, Todd, and Linda Lindsey. *The NOLS Wilderness First Aid Manual.* Harrisburg, PA: Stackpole Books, 1990.

Tilton, Buck, and Frank Hubbell. *Medicine for the Backcountry.* Merrillville, IN: ICS Books, 1990.

Wilkerson, James A. *Medicine for Mountaineering and other Wilderness Activities.* Seattle, WA: The Mountaineers, 1992.

Internet Resources

Altitude and Acute Mountain Sickness: www.aescon.com/ski/medicine/mtsick.html

Centers for Disease Control: www.cdc.gov/

Cryptosporidium—FDA document on foodborne pathogens: vm.cfsan.fda.gov/~mow/chap24.html

Giardia—FDA Hypertext document on foodborne pathogens: vm.cfsan.fda.gov/~mow/chap22.html

Giardia Information: ftp://d31rz0.Stanford.EDU/RJG/OEP/water

High Altitude and Its Effects on Performance: gopher://wilcox.umt.edu:70/00/UofM/hhp/altitude

LymeNet: www.lymenet.org/

The Outdoor Action Guide to High Altitude Illnesses: www.princeton.edu/~oa/altitude.html

The Outdoor Action Guide to Hypothermia & Cold Weather Injuries: www.princeton.edu/~oa/hypocold.html

Search & Rescue Resources on the Web: www.catt.citri.edu.au/emergency/es-www/es-www-sar.html

U.S. Public Health Service: phs.os.dhhs.gov/phs/phs.html

Yahoo Health Reference Page: www.yahoo.com/Health/

Yahoo Search & Rescue Reference Page: www.yahoo.com/Health/Emergency_Services/Search_and_Rescue

Index

chlorine:
    in first aid, 319–20
    in water purification, 85, 90–91
circulation, sensation, and motion (CSM),
        240–41, 255–56, 258–59, 261–62
circulatory system, first aid for, 250–51
cirrocumulus clouds, 168–69
cirrostratus clouds, 168–69
cirrus clouds, 168–69, 171
cleaning, *see* hygiene
clothing, 14–21, 344–49
    first aid and, 287, 293–96, 300–301, 308–9,
        322
    layering of, 16–21
    in Leave No Trace hiking and camping, 102
    and safety and emergency procedures,
        198–200, 204, 208
    washing of, 80–81
clouds, 197
    fronts and, 171–72
    in predicting weather, 175–76
    in thunderstorms, 172–75
    types of, 168–69
coastal winds, 166
cold challenge, 15, 287–88
cold fronts, 171–72
cold water immersion hypothermia, 298–99
Cold-Weather Backpacking Equipment Lists,
        348–50
cold-weather injuries, first aid for, 299–303
Coleman Peak 1 Feather 400 and 442, 42–46
compasses, 123–37, 139, 146
    declinations on, 125–29
    in fog, 130–31
    in heading to summits, 132–33
    north on, 123–26, 130–32
    in off-trail hiking, 146
    in retracing your steps to camp, 133–34
    for right areas, 125
    in safety and emergency procedures, 200, 203,
        205, 207
    shadow, 179
    with swamps in your way, 136–37
    taking bearings with, 125–27, 130–37
    telling time with, 180
    using maps with, 125–31, 137
    when you are lost, 137
    in wilderness navigation, 129–30
compound leaves, 181–83
compressed gas stoves, 40, 46–53
concussions, first aid for, 269–70
conductive heat loss, 15
conifers, 180–82, 185–87
conjunctivitis (pinkeye), first aid for, 282
consciousness level, 236, 239, 246, 265, 267–71,
        282, 291, 293, 299, 304, 323, 327
constipation, first aid for, 314, 332

contact lens problems, first aid for, 282–83
convective heat loss, 15
cooking, 350
    in advance of trips, 64
    at altitude, 68
    backpacking stoves for, 40–52
    in bear country, 156, 160
    Coleman Peak 1 Feathers for, 42–46
    equipment for, 13, 38–53
    general guidelines, ingredients, and recipes
        for, 67–76
    in Leave No Trace hiking and camping, 105,
        112–13
    measurement equivalents for, 76
    MSR Whisperlites for, 46–53
    outdoor baking and, 39–40, 75–76
    in setting up campsites, 153–55
    typical menu items in, 68–70
coral snake bites, first aid for, 307–8
corn, rice, and beans, recipe for, 75
cotton, avoiding use of, 21
counterbalance method, 158–59
CPR:
    in BLS, 245–47
    in first aid, 229–30, 245–47, 266, 293,
        297–99
    hypothermia and, 297–99
    in safety and emergency procedures, 211,
        213–14
crickets, 177
crown fires, 215
Cryptosporidium:
    first aid for, 317–18
    water purification and, 86, 88, 95
cumulonimbus clouds, 168–69, 172, 197
cumulus clouds, 168–69, 172, 197
Cyclospora, 317–18

dairy, 56–58, 63–64
day packs, 25
debris huts, 219–21
declinations:
    on compasses, 125–29
    in heading to summits, 133
    on maps, 126–28
    in wilderness navigation, 129
definitive care, 238
dehydrated foods, 62
dehydration, 285–86, 300, 313–15, 320, 323
dental problems, first aid for, 283–85
depth water filters, 86, 91–98
dessert, typical menu items for, 69
dew, 177
diabetes, first aid for, 322–23
diapers, 111
diarrhea, 285, 306, 313, 315, 317, 329–30
digit dislocations, first aid for, 264

instant rice, preparation of, 70
internal frame packs, 23–30
intracranial pressure (ICP), 268–71
iodine:
    first aid and, 242, 304–5, 307, 321, 333
    in water purification, 85–88, 97
Isaac, Jeff, 14–15, 237, 239, 243
ischemia, first aid for, 240

jewelweed, 188–89
joint fractures, first aid for, 258
junipers, 185–86

kilometers per hour, calculation of, 10
kneecap dislocations, first aid for, 264
knocked-out teeth, first aid for, 284–85
knots, 160–64
Kosher meal planning, 66–67

lacerations, first aid for, 274–75
lakes, drinking water from, 222
land breezes, 166
lateral drift, 133–34
latitude, 119
latrines, 107–8
laxatives, 314, 332
Leave No Trace hiking and camping, x, 99–116,
    194, 344
    in backcountry travel, 103–6, 140
    in bear country, 112, 156
    campfires in, 101, 112–16
    campsites in, 102, 104–6
    dealing with human waste in, 106–11
    at end of trips, 116
    garbage in, 111–12
    general principles of, 100–102
    and hygiene, 79, 105
    leaving what you find in, 101
    medical waste in, 111, 116
    in menu planning, 62–63
    off-trail, 146
    packing in and out in, 101
    in temperate forest trips, 102–3, 107
    in trip planning, 4, 8, 100
    water in, 105–7, 112
    in wilderness travel, 146, 153, 156
    and wildlife, 102–3, 105, 107, 189
leaves, 177, 181–85
legumes, 57–59
lightning, 173–75
    dangers of, 175
    direct strikes of, 211
    distances from, 210
    ground currents from, 211–13
    physics of, 173–74
    physiological effects of, 211
    return strikes of, 173–74, 211–12

safety and emergency procedures for, 209–14
    warning signs of, 210
line abreast method, 152
line astern method, 152
line of sight, 133
line searches, 208–9
liquid fuel stoves, 40–46
lobed leaves, 181–85
location, 3–4
log rolls, 248–49, 266
longitude, 119
lost fillings, first aid for, 285
lost groups and group participants, 130–31,
    137–38, 202–9
low clouds, 168–69
lower leg fractures, first aid for, 255, 258
lower torso, 234
low-use areas, 100–101, 104
lunch, typical menu items for, 68–69
Lyme disease, first aid for, 310

macaroni and cheese, recipe for, 73
magnetic bearings, 126–28
magnetic north, 123–25, 130–31
maples, 182–83
maps and map reading:
    colors in, 120
    contour lines in, 121–22
    declinations on, 126–28
    in fog, 130–31
    latitude and longitude in, 119
    legends in, 120–22
    measuring distances with, 123
    north on, 126
    in off-trail hiking, 146
    orienting of, 129, 137
    in safety and emergency procedures, 200, 203,
        205, 207
    scales of, 119–20
    taking bearings with, 126–28, 130–32
    using compasses with, 125–31, 137
    when you are lost, 137–38
    in wilderness travel, 119–32, 137, 139–40,
        146
Marrison haul system, 159–60
measurement equivalents, 76
meats, 59, 64
medical waste, disposal of, 111, 116, 245
medications, 339
    in first aid, 253–54, 272, 280–82, 284, 303–4,
        306–7, 312, 314, 318, 323–38, 352–53
    in patient assessments, 236
    profiles of, 328–38
membrane water filters, 85–91
men:
    backpacks for, 26
    Leave No Trace hiking and camping for, 106

pots, 38–39, 67, 81–82
povidone-iodine solution and ointment, 242, 333
precipitation:
   accidents and, 195, 197–98
   first aid and, 287, 289, 293–94
   fronts and, 170, 172
   in predicting weather, 176–77
   and safety and emergency procedures, 210,
      213, 219, 225
   in thunderstorms, 172
pressure points, 242
pretrip checklist, 5–6
preventable accidents, 194
pristine areas, 100, 103–5, 114
proteins, 56–57
pseudoephedrine, 333
pulse:
   in first aid, 239, 245–47, 268–69, 291, 293–95,
      297–98, 308, 312, 323, 327
   in patient assessments, 236
PUR Hiker Microfilter, 85–91

quadriceps stretches, 145
quaking aspens, 182–83
quesadillas, recipe for, 73

rabies, first aid for, 306–7
radiant heat loss, 15
radios, 207
rainbows, 177
rashes:
   first aid for, 280–81, 308, 310, 332
   from poisonous plants, 188
recipes, 70–75
rectangular sleeping bags, 31
recycling, 63
red morning sky, 176–77
Reifsnyder, William, 175
remote locations, accidents in, 195
repairs, equipment for, 13
repetitive stress injuries (RSIs), 144, 147
respiration, see breathing
respiratory system, first aid for, 250
rest, 142–43
   first aid and, 323–24
   in safety and emergency procedures, 199,
      225
rest, ice, compression, elevation (RICE),
      253–54
rhododendrons, 177
rice, instant, 70
rinsing, 80–81
river birches, 183
rivers:
   crossing of, 149–52
   drinking water from, 222
road crossings, 152–53

rockfall exposure:
   in accidents, 197
   in off-trail hiking, 147–48
rocks and banks, undercut, 149
Rocky Mountain Spotted Fever, 310–11
rocky slopes and trails, hiking on, 147
ropes:
   river crossings with, 151
   for knots, 160–64
routes, planning of, 8–11

safety and emergency procedures, 191–225, 344
   and accidents, 193–99, 203, 225–26
   basic approach to, 193
   evacuations in, 199, 201–2, 216–17
   in forest fires, 214–18
   information gathering in, 200–201, 206–7
   for lightning, 209–14
   for lost group members, 202–9
   with outside aid, 200
   sending for help in, 199–200, 202, 205, 208,
      218
   trip leaders in, 192–93, 195–97, 201
   weather in, 202–4, 209–14, 216–21, 224–25
   in wilderness travel, 192–93, 197, 199, 218–24
   see also first aid
safety shadows, 212–13
salt and salts:
   in first aid, 286, 290–92, 300, 315
   in hygiene, 80, 82
   water purification and, 98
SAM Splint, 256–57, 265, 267
sanitary waste disposal units, 109, 154
sassafras, 182, 184
scorpion bites, first aid for, 308–9
scouring brushes, 81–82
sea breezes, 166
searches, 203–4, 206–9
   halting of, 209
   hasty, 207
   line, 208–9
   secondary, 207–8
seasons:
   accidents and, 195–96
   in first aid, 293
   in Leave No Trace hiking and camping, 102,
      106
   and safety and emergency procedures, 221
second-degree burns, first aid for, 277
second-degree frostbite, first aid for, 301–2
seeds, 57
Seidman, David, 204
seizures, first aid and, 270–71, 323
serving sizes, 58–59, 76
shadow compasses, 179
shagbark hickories, 184
sheet bends, 163